The Colonizing Trick

Critical American Studies Series

George Lipsitz, University of California–San Diego, series editor

The Colonizing Trick

NATIONAL CULTURE AND IMPERIAL CITIZENSHIP
IN EARLY AMERICA

David Kazanjian

CRITICAL AMERICAN STUDIES

University of Minnesota Press
Minneapolis || London

Parts of the introduction and chapter 1 were originally published in "Race, Nation, Equality: Olaudah Equiano's *Interesting Narrative* and a Genealogy of U.S. Mercantilism," in *Post-Nationalist American Studies*, ed. John Carlos Rowe (Berkeley: University of California Press, 2000), 129–65. Parts of chapter 1 were originally published in "'To ship as cook': Notes on the Gendering of Black Atlantic Maritime Labor," *Radical Philosophy Review* 5, no. 1–2 (2002–3) and in "Mercantile Exchanges, Mercantilist Enclosures: Racial Capitalism in the Black Mariner Narratives of Venture Smith and John Jea," special issue on "PanAmericanisms" in *CR: The New Centennial Review* 3, no. 1 (Spring 2003), published by Michigan State University Press. Part of chapter 2 was originally published in "Racial Governmentality: Thomas Jefferson and the African Colonization Movement in the United States," *Alternation: Journal of the Centre for the Study of Southern African Literature and Languages* 5, no. 1 (1998): 39–84. Part of chapter 3 was originally published in "Charles Brockden Brown's Biloquial Nation: National Culture and White Settler Colonialism in *Memoirs of Carwin, The Biloquist*," *American Literature* 73, no. 3 (September 2001): 459–96. Part of the epilogue was published in "'Yankee Universality': H. C. Carey's Racial Mercantilism," special issue on "Race and/or Nation" in *New Formations* 47 (2002): 87–110.

Published by the University of Minnesota Press
111 Third Avenue South, Suite 290
Minneapolis, MN 55401-2520
http://www.upress.umn.edu

Library of Congress Cataloging-in-Publication Data

Kazanjian, David, 1967–
    The colonizing trick : national culture and imperial citizenship in early America / David Kazanjian.
        p.   cm. — (Critical American Studies series)
    Includes bibliographical references and index.
    ISBN 0-8166-4237-0 (HC : alk. paper) — ISBN 0-8166-4238-9 (PB : alk. paper)
    1.United States—Race relations—Sources.   2. United States—Foreign relations—Sources.   3. Citizenship—United States—History—Sources.   4. Acculturation—United States—History—Sources.   5. Nationalism—United States—History—Sources.   6. Political culture—United States—History—Sources.   7. Imperialism—History—Sources.   8. Universalism.   9. Particularism (Theology).   10. Criticism, Textual.   I. Title.   II. Series.
    E184.A1 K33 2003
    305.8'00973'09034—dc22

                                                                                    2003013601

Printed in the United States of America on acid-free paper

The University of Minnesota is an equal-opportunity educator and employer.

12 11 10 09 08 07 06 05 04 03   10 9 8 7 6 5 4 3 2 1

But to return to the colonizing trick. It will be well for me to notice here at once, that I do not mean indiscriminately to condemn all the members and advocates of this scheme, for I believe that there are some friends to the sons of Africa, who are laboring for our salvation, not in words only but in truth and in deed, who have been drawn into this plan—Some, more by persuasion than any thing else; while others, with humane feelings and lively zeal for our good, seeing how much we suffer from the afflictions poured upon us by unmerciful tyrants, are willing to enroll their names in any thing which they think has for its ultimate end our redemption from wretchedness and miseries; such men, with a heart truly overflowing with gratitude for their past services and zeal in our cause, I humbly beg to examine this plot minutely, and see if the end which they have in view will be completely consummated by such a course of procedure. Our friends who have been imperceptibly drawn into this plot I view with tenderness, and would not for the world injure their feelings, and I have only to hope for the future, that they will withdraw themselves from it;—for I declare to them, that the plot is not for the glory of God, but on the contrary the perpetuation of slavery in this country, which will ruin them and the country forever, unless something is immediately done . . . Hear your language, proclaimed to the world, July 4th, 1776—☞ "We hold these truths to be self evident—that ALL MEN ARE CREATED EQUAL!!"

—*David Walker's Appeal*

Contents

Preface and Acknowledgments

*T*he striking cover image the University of Minnesota Press has chosen for *The Colonizing Trick*, "An Available Candidate. The One Qualification for a Whig President," is from an 1848 cartoon depicting either Zachary Taylor or Winfield Scott dressed in full military regalia, holding a bloodstained sword and sitting on a pyramid of skulls. Taylor and Scott were generals who led U.S. troops in the U.S.–Mexico War and were, by the time of the cartoon, seeking the Whig party's nomination for president. The cartoon mocks them for the bloody qualifications they would bring to the presidency, and so makes a dramatic statement against the war. However, the sensational anonymity of the skulls carefully conceals important elements of the history to which the cartoon bears witness. Are these Mexican or U.S. victims? The question remains open, for many in the United States who expressed antiwar sentiments, regardless of party affiliation, did so in the name of, rather than in opposition to, racial nationalism. U.S. victory in the war opened the possibility that thousands of Mexicans would be incorporated into the United States as citizens, and, as I argue in chapter 4, U.S. politicians and citizens alike were anxiously unsure about Mexican racial identity. Thus, it is not so much violent territorial acquisition that antiwar sentiment opposed—indeed, many of those opposed to the war thirsted for more territory—as the potential threat to white citizenship. As the reader will see, the cartoon's criticism may itself express a racially particularized vision of the very imperial U.S. citizenship *The Colonizing Trick* seeks to trace.

The following provided much needed institutional support for my research in its early stages: while I was at the University of California, Berkeley, the Rhetoric Department, repeatedly and generously; the Doreen B. Townsend Center; the Graduate Division; the Mangasar Mangasarian Fellowship Fund; the Armenian General Benevolent Union; and the Gulbenkian Foundation. I thank the University of California's Humanities Research Institute and its entire staff for a most productive and enjoyable residential fellowship. In the past few years, the John Carter Brown Library, the National Endowment for the Humanities, Queens College, the Queens College English Department, the PSC–CUNY Research Foundation, the Africana Studies Department at Brown University, and the Center for Place, Culture, and Politics at the Graduate Center, City University of New York, all enabled the research that went into this book. I also thank librarians at Queens College, the Graduate Center, the New York Public Library, the Schomberg Center, Brown University, the John Carter Brown Library (especially director Norman Fiering, Susan Danforth, and Richard Ring), the University of Texas, Austin (especially at the Benson Latin American Collection), the Bancroft Library, the Library of Congress, the National Archives, and the Public Record Office in London.

Many people have contributed to this research in so many ways, I quite simply could not have written *The Colonizing Trick* without them. Let me begin where this project began. At Stanford and Sussex, Regenia Gagnier, Gayatri Chakravorty Spivak, and Laura Chrisman laid the foundations for this thinking, and Laura and Gayatri have continued to challenge my work for years. At Berkeley, I was guided by a wonderful dissertation committee: I thank Carolyn Porter and Katherine Clay Bassard for their encouragement, as well as David Lloyd and Marianne Constable for their enduring and sympathetic criticism. Kaja Silverman was informally very much a part of this group too, and what I have learned from her still drives me to be a better scholar and teacher. And I could not have dreamed up a more outstanding dissertation director than Judith Butler.

I am most fortunate to have worked collectively with groups of scholars who have directly and indirectly stimulated my research, and who have reminded me again and again of the richness of collaborative work. The members of the Humanities Research Institute's Residential Research Group on "Post-Nationalist American Studies"—John Carlos Rowe, George Sánchez, Katherine Kinney, Barbara Brinson Curiel, Henry Yu, Jay Mechling, Steven Mailloux, and Shelley Streeby—brought their diverse talents to bear. In one dissertation group, Donna Jones, Dina Al-Kassim, David Eng, Emma Bianchi, Vikki Bell, and Florence Dore offered just the right blend of careful, close, critical, and sympathetic reading. In another, I worked with a group of outstanding readers and friends; Carolina Gonzales, Colleen Lye, Donna Jones, Donna Hunter, and Michelle Wolfson were so helpful and fun as to almost make one not want to finish the dissertation and leave the group. Rakesh Bhandari gave much thought to my ideas on Marx, generously sharing his own ideas as well as a seemingly endless list of citations. Since then, colleagues at the John Carter Brown Library at Brown University's Africana Studies Department and at the Center for Place, Culture, and Politics at the CUNY Graduate Center also pushed and encouraged my research, especially Robert Aguirre, Karen Racine, Lewis Gordon, Tony Bogues, Nada Elia, and Neil Smith. I am most grateful to the participants in the John Carter Brown Library Fellows Luncheon (October 1999), the "Between History and Literature: Rethinking the Slave Narratives" conference at Brown University (March 2000), the Haverford College "Food for Thought" colloquium (April 2000) graciously organized by Theresa Tensuan, and to numerous participants at the annual American Studies Association conference.

I thank my students at Queens College and the Graduate Center, CUNY, who never cease to make me think new ways about my work. In particular, I am grateful to Seleena Baijnauth, Shirley Carrie, Rachel Fox, Kenneth Lobban, Fotini Marcopulos, Ronald Milland, Mi Sun Nam, Joanne Noel, and Arti Tripathi for researching and reading with me many of the texts I write about, and again to Shirley for doing important follow-up research at the Public Record Office. Naomi C. Reed has helped me immensely with the final work on the manuscript, and I thank her for her insights.

Jamie Skye Bianco, Jim Groom, Mischa Edwards, and Jill Toliver have been wonderful interlocutors at the Graduate Center. I have been unfailingly supported by my colleague Tony O'Brien, whose commitments enliven me to no end. Jyotsna Uppal not only made it possible to live through the often hectic life of a CUNY junior faculty member, but also gave astute comments on struggling drafts. Carrie Hintz has been a remarkably fun ally. Hugh English responded generously to my introduction. Steve Kruger, Barbara Bowen, Patricia Clough, John Weir, and Nancy Comley have been exceedingly generous in their support; I am lucky to have them as colleagues and mentors.

For their encouragement and intellectual engagement, I am most grateful to Chris Castiglia, Nikhil Pal Singh, and Alicia Schmidt-Camacho, who engaged my work from literary, historical, and theoretical angles. Priscilla Wald and Dana Nelson have long been uncommonly generous. Chris Newfield encouraged my work on Brown and Carey. Chris Conway read my U.S.–Mexico War/Caste War chapter with care. Daniel Rosenberg gave helpful responses to my work on black mariners. Francis Kerr did a deft copyedit for the *American Literature* version of my chapter on Brown. Marcus Rediker has been an intellectual and political spark: a "shipmate." Peter Onuf shared his challenging comments on an early draft of my work on Jefferson, and I hope I responded adequately. Shane Moran also encouraged that work. Seth Moglen, Brent Edwards, and Gus Stadler gave wonderful close readings of sections of the book when they were mere talks or essays. Marc Nichanian's intellectual care is a model for me. John Mowitt made helpful suggestions on my reader's reports. I am very grateful to Richard Morrison for enthusiastically encouraging this project from the start, to George Lipsitz for thoughtfully supporting it, and to others at the University of Minnesota Press for shepherding it through the production process, including Pieter Martin, Laura Westlund, Douglas Armato, and Julia DuSablon.

A Evelina, por tu casa preciosa donde leí y escribí tan feliz, y a Rebeca, quien me dio su casa y su amistad incomparable en Tejas durante mis investigaciones sobre las novelas de la guerra entre los Estados Unidos y México; con tristeza, digo gracias y adiós.

I also thank my entire family for their support. In particular, Rosanna Kazanjian, my mom, who always lends an open ear while animating me with new ways of living. Ernest and Hélène Sargeant's generosity and intellectual curiosity are unsurpassable.

Judith Butler's persistent, meticulous efforts to theorize the conjuncture of subjugation and subjectification as a crucial element of any political or social theory have inspired my efforts to an incalculable degree. She has my profound appreciation, admiration, and friendship. David Eng enriched this project immensely not only by commenting on sections of it but also by becoming engulfed with me in another fascinating project, *Loss*, that was the epitome of collaborative research. Anahid Kassabian first taught me the power of such research, and continues to learn and struggle with me, gleefully; Leo and Maral add no small part to that glee. Fred Moten has always pushed my theoretical-political concerns to the edge; this book would be much impoverished without his generosity. As comrades and friends, Laura Harris and David Johnson keep giving me hope for the work that we do. Miranda Joseph brought me countless insights, especially about Marx, and opened her house (and library) to me most generously. Alys Weinbaum has worked "alongside" me for so long, sometimes literally but always in spirit—I can hardly thank her enough for her persistent acumen. I also send incalculable love and thanks to Emma Bianchi, Rob Miotke, and Shay Brawn for friendships that recast the meaning of family, and for offering brilliant comments on the project when I needed them—and again to Emma, my brilliant buddy, for widening my eyes with every encounter. I double thank many of these people, as well as Neon Weiss, for keeping my nose blissfully *out* of this project just when I needed it.

Finally, to María Josefina Saldaña, Fina, Josie, words fall so short. I thank her for teaching me more than anyone else, for putting up with my often all-consuming work, and for inspiring me to continue learning about and struggling for social justice. For surprising me around every corner. And for making life a joy. A mi compañera, todo.

Articulation, Graft, Flashpoint

In 1829, a free black used-clothes dealer and tailor named David Walker published *David Walker's Appeal, In Four Articles, Together With A Preamble, To The Coloured Citizens Of The World, But In Particular, And Very Expressly, To Those Of The United States Of America.* The fourth "article" of the *Appeal* offers a sharp critique of one of the most extensively debated policy proposals of the colonial and antebellum periods, a proposal commonly known as "colonization": the deportation and resettlement of black Americans outside the territorial boundaries of the United States. Walker takes particular pains to address a peculiar aspect of the colonization movement: that many black and white colonizationists understood the movement as emancipatory. As my epigraph indicates, rather than simply rejecting "the colonizing trick" as a cynical or duplicitous ploy, Walker insists that his readers reckon with colonization's attempt to make deportation consistent with the lofty ideals of "salvation," "truth," "humane feelings," "good," "redemption," and "the glory of God"; the "trick" is precisely the production of this consistency.[1] With the force of Walker's famous irony ("I . . . would not for the world injure their feelings"), this passage alerts readers to the serious problem that even "friends to the sons of Africa" consider colonization a "deed," "plan," or "procedure"—a utilitarian rendering of such ideals. Although these "friends" offer this "plan" as a realization of the equality promised by the Declaration of Independence, Walker challenges their interpretation of what makes "ALL . . . EQUAL." Walker thus calls for the difficult task of interpreting the articulation—"imperceptibly," "by persuasion"— of a racially and nationally codified policy with an emerging, Enlightenment conception of equality. I take up just this task in *The Colonizing Trick*.

Walker's call still speaks to scholars of colonial America and the antebellum United States, who have long been vexed by the paradoxically simultaneous emergence, toward the end of the eighteenth century, of apparently contradictory discursive practices: universal egalitarianism, on the one hand, and the particularistic hierarchies of race and nation, on the other hand. Embodied in the institution of modern liberal citizenship, universal egalitarianism presumes to ignore all the myriad, particularistic differences among subjects—trade, heritage, wealth, race, gender, religion, the list is supposedly infinite—in order to apprehend each subject equally. The state, which plays the role of presumer, agrees not to value or hierarchically codify such differences in order to see only the citizen, a subject formally abstracted from its particularisms and hence formally and abstractly equal to all its fellow citizens. Ideally, then, all such citizen-subjects can exercise the rights offered by the state regardless of their particularisms. For example, when this citizen-subject enters the voting booth, it supposedly leaves its particularisms behind, exercises its right to vote and therefore be represented alongside every other citizen, and then picks those particularisms back up again as it leaves the booth. Even more ideally, subjects in civil society learn to act like little states themselves, agreeing not to place hierarchical values on each other's particularisms. For example, when such a subject enters the marketplace to exchange goods with another subject, each supposedly leaves its particularisms behind and encounters the other as a formally and abstractly equal being exchanging formally and abstractly equal goods.[2]

Of course, these presumptions do not have a particularly salutary history. In fact, the rise of universal egalitarianism was coincident with the rise of numerous, hierarchically codified, particularistic differences—perhaps most spectacularly in the Americas the vigorously materialized ideas of race, on one hand, and nation, on the other. In the face of this "problem," it has often been assumed or even claimed that universal egalitarianism is more modern, and that racism and nationalism, if not the very ideas of race and nation, would eventually dissipate as egalitarianism grew stronger and more pervasive. From this perspective, the "problem" of what Americanists used to call "the peculiar institution," slavery, was rectified with the Thirteenth Amendment to the U.S. Constitution, as was the exclusion of women from citizenship by the Nineteenth Amendment. In each case, the principle of universal egalitarianism supposedly won out in practice, as previously excluded subjects were included in the formal and abstract equality of citizenship. Racial and gender inequalities that continue to exist after these amendments could then be understood as temporary, practical failures of the principle of universal egalitarianism; once all subjects in all contexts have been incorporated into this principle, then inequality will have been overcome. Universal equality has thus been represented as necessarily contradicted by, or antagonistic with, the hierarchical codification of particularistic identities.

Take, for instance, Bernard Bailyn's important 1986 study, *Voyagers to the West: A Passage in the Peopling of America on the Eve of the Revolution*:

> While Americans of the Revolutionary generation struggled for freedom and equality in public life, they remained remarkably insensitive to the human consequences of deprivation. In such a world—where the blatant humiliation of inferiors by social superiors was a matter of common experience and where degrading physical punishment for civil and criminal offences was routine—the utter debasement of chattel slavery needed little justification, and lesser forms of servitude were regarded as normal.
>
> None of this was unique to America. These were common characteristics of the *ancien régime*, pre-modern in its social concerns and conditions. But while America shared these characteristics of eighteenth-century society, its way of life was unique. The colonists lived in exceptional circumstances and shared a peculiar outlook.[3]

Though initially attentive to the normalization of inequality in early America, this passage restricts that inequality to a private, underdeveloped realm of irrational affect by distinguishing "freedom and equality in public life" from "pre-modern," "insensitive" practices of "humiliation." These presumptive distinctions between public and private, modern and premodern, reason and affect, in turn enable the familiar, exceptionalist rhetoric of the second paragraph. Though old, eighteenth-century America had "common" problems such as slavery, the passage suggests that they were destined to be left behind with the rest of the *"ancien régime"* as modern America's "unique," "exceptional," and "peculiar" qualities came to the fore. By implication, the passage suggests that any lingering traces of these "common" problems, such as racism, are fundamentally "pre-modern."

Bailyn's passage is a classic instance of ideology: a prescription posing as a description. It presumes that chattel slavery was *of* the *ancien régime*, so naturally it would be replaced by the modern, just as the eighteenth century leads naturally to the nineteenth, twentieth, and twenty-first centuries. However, simply calling chattel slavery a "common characteristic of the *ancien régime*" does not make it or the racial formations it inaugurated "pre-modern" "concerns and conditions," destined to be left behind by the inexorably meliorist march of history. As scholars of race and slavery have increasingly shown, though it certainly had historical conditions of possibility, chattel slavery in the Americas was a distinctly modern institution characterized by the lifelong and heritable quality of its servitude, as well as by the quite new ideas of race it materialized.[4]

In addition, the colonists to whom Bailyn refers can now be said to have "shared a peculiar outlook" as American colonists only as an effect of the often bloody and violent instantiation of another distinctly modern particularism: nationalism. Universal egalitarianism throughout Europe and the Americas eventually took the form not simply of citizenship but rather of national citizenship. Consequently, as scholars of nationalism have shown, the formal and abstract equality of citizen-subjects was paradoxically qualified by the modern, "invented tradition" of systematically enforced national identity, such that the putatively universal equality of national citizen-subjects depended upon the systematic exclusion of various nonnational subjects from equality altogether. Though one nation's citizens as a whole were meant to be formally and abstractly equal to another nation's citizens, the exceptionalism that characterizes nationalism—on display in Bailyn's passage—constructs national hierarchies that belie such equality.[5] Furthermore, and as we will see throughout *The Colonizing Trick*, when we consider that the modern nation form is always also a racial formation, it becomes entirely difficult to call universal egalitarianism more historically modern than particularisms such as race and nation.[6]

This historical problematic of the relationships among race, nation, and equality is at once a *philosophical* problematic of the relationship between universalism and particularism, urging a further revision of the presumptions of universal egalitarianism. For a particular racial or national identity to be systematically applicable to an entire population and to be hierarchically valued above all other racial or national identities, it must also have universal pretensions. In other words, the normative homogeneity of racial and national particularities entails a certain universality. As Étienne Balibar has written, "Nationalism admittedly is *particularistic*, inasmuch as it claims that national entities have different roots, that they must keep control over their *own* members who 'belong' to them in some strong sense, and that they must remain isolated from one another in order to preserve their identity. . . . But nationalism as an ideology is *also universalistic*, and this in at least two senses": first, nationalism "supported the idea of formal equality . . . thus removing notions of castes and status groups and local privileges," and second, in order to think of itself as exceptional the nation "has to think of itself . . . as immediately universal in its singularity."[7] Indeed, Balibar is just one of a number of contemporary political theorists and philosophers who have begun to theorize this distinctly modern, epistemological *interdependence* of universalism and particularism.[8]

It is just this historical and philosophical problematic that David Walker, in 1829, urged his readers to "examine . . . minutely." That a massive deportation project meant to purge the United States of all its black subjects could be widely understood as a form of emancipation, as a realization of the declaration that "ALL MEN ARE CREATED EQUAL," calls for a reexamination of the modern conjunction of equality, race, and nation. Inspired by Walker's call, *The Colonizing Trick* addresses a historical, philosophical, and epistemological question: how might we characterize the dynamic relationships, forged during the colonial and antebellum periods within global economic and political systems, between universal egalitarianism and the particularistic discursive practices of race and nation? Specifically, I conduct historical and literary critical examinations of four sets of texts that correspond to four crucial, historical flashpoints: the narratives of black merchant mariners confronting the mercantilist development of the Atlantic economy between the 1720s and the 1850s; Thomas Jefferson's published texts and private correspondence advocating the colonization of black Americans, as well as early nineteenth-century black American critiques of colonization; Charles Brockden Brown's contribution to the emergence of a self-conscious, national literature amid the U.S. government's aggressive policy to assimilate Iroquois communities between the 1790s and 1810s; and, finally, the treaties, government documents, and ubiquitous popular novelettes that gave meaning to the U.S.–Mexico War and the Yucatán's Caste War during the 1840s and 1850s. These particular flashpoints effectively define or congeal racial and national formations that had previously been relatively indefinite or fluid. What is more, these emergent racial and national formations do not contradict universal egalitarianism; rather, they articulate with it, giving equality a restricted, formal, and abstract meaning. Taken together, these flashpoints enable a comparative study of multiple (rather than binary) racial formations and the global (rather than simply national or domestic) systems in which they emerged.

On one hand, each set of texts is characterized by emerging efforts to realize equality. For instance, black mariners engaging in the mercantile trade can be seen to seek not only the accumulation of capital, but also social recognition as subjects who, in the act of laboring and exchanging, could be equal to their fellow laborers and exchangers. Jefferson and many of his fellow advocates of colonization before the 1820s explicitly seek the emancipation of black Americans from slavery. Brown envisioned a national literature that was free from the hierarchies and antagonisms common in Europe. Finally, the U.S.–Mexico War concludes with the Treaty of Guadalupe Hidalgo's promise of "all the rights of citizens" to Mexicans incorporated into the United States, a promise echoed by the novelettes.

On the other hand, each set of texts simultaneously represents the vigorous and exploitative codification of race and nation during each historical flashpoint. Black merchants are increasingly frozen out of the merchant marine trade by mercantilist regulations as well as the quotidian racism and nationalism of white merchants and sailors in North Atlantic ports and ships. Colonizationists explicitly seek both to colonize Africa with Western economic, political, and religious systems, and to create a white nation-state by purging North America of African Americans. Brown's work—echoing U.S. Indian policy as well as the emerging fields of ethnography and archeology—represents Native Americans as idealized, disembodied forms whose assimilation is the always incomplete precondition for the transformation of white settler colonials into national citizen-subjects. Finally, the novelettes and government documents on the U.S.–Mexico War and the Caste War transform Manifest Destiny from a westward, white settler colonial discursive practice to a southward, neocolonial discursive practice.

My examination of these flashpoints suggests that racial and national codification forged a constitutive, if unstable, relationship with universal egalitarianism. That is, the systematic production and maintenance of hierarchically codified, racial and national forms actually enabled equality to be understood as formally and abstractly universal. The subjection of U.S. citizens as formally and abstractly equal to one another and to citizens of other nations depended upon the vigorous and substantial subjection of North Americans to racial and national codification. As such, *The Colonizing Trick* delves into the dense historicity of a mode of power Judith Butler has described as the paradoxically simultaneous "process of becoming subordinated by power as well as the process of becoming a subject." Argues Butler in *The Psychic Life of Power*:

> As a form of power, subjection is paradoxical. To be dominated by a power external to oneself is a familiar and agonizing form power takes. To find, however, that what "one" is, one's very formation as a subject, is dependent upon that very power is quite another. . . . If, following Foucault, we understand power as *forming* the subject as well, as providing the very condition of its existence and the trajectory of its desire, then power is not simply what we oppose but also, in a strong sense, what we depend upon for our existence and what we harbor and preserve in the beings that we are. The customary model for understanding this process goes as follows: power imposes itself on us, and, weakened by its force, we come to internalize or accept its terms. What such an account fails to note, however, is that "we" who accept such terms are fundamentally dependent on those terms for "our" existence.[9]

In *Scenes of Subjection*, Saidiya V. Hartman engages the difficult work—already begun, of course, by the Foucault to whom Butler refers—of assembling a historical genealogy of such a process of subjection. For Hartman, the quotidian archives of racial servitude in North America bear material and discursive traces of just this paradoxical mode of power:

> The scenes of subjection examined here focus on the enactment of subjugation and the constitution of the subject . . . I argue that the barbarism of slavery did not express itself singularly in the constitution of the slave as object but also in the forms of subjectivity and circumscribed humanity imputed to the enslaved; by the same token, the failures of Reconstruction cannot be recounted solely as a series of legal reversals or troop withdrawals; they also need to be located in the very language of person, rights, and liberties. For these reasons the book examines the forms of violence and domination enabled by the recognition of humanity, licensed by the invocation of rights, and justified on the grounds of liberty and freedom.[10]

Hartman's attention to "the forms of subjectivity and circumscribed humanity imputed to the enslaved" is so important because it offers a historically and theoretically rich account of a mode of subjection that did not simply disappear with the Thirteenth Amendment. By locating scenes of subjection in "the mundane and quotidian" world of slavery rather than only in "the shocking spectacle" of slavery's brutal violence, Hartman urges us to see the systematic reiteration of quite specific modes of unfreedom in the midst of discourses and practices apparently devoted to freedom. She also urges us to assemble much more nuanced accounts of the intimate relationships, increasingly common in North America after the seventeenth century, between modes of unfreedom and modes of freedom.

The Colonizing Trick contributes to this historical genealogy of subjection by excavating and interpreting a series of eighteenth- and early nineteenth-century archives that bear witness to the diverse and diffuse ways modern, codified conceptions of equality were articulated with modern, codified conceptions of race and nation. I also trace the ways these conceptions themselves reformulated and were reformulated by modern conceptions of gender. As this articulation emerged, I argue, capacious practices of freedom were increasingly restricted to a formal equality fleshed out by precise—if unstable—racial, national, and gendered materialities. Though much of *The Colonizing Trick* is devoted to limning this articulation, I also heed Fred Moten's concern that accounts of subjection risk becoming "an obsessive recording of mastery" if they do not also attend to the scenes in which subjection is "cut and augmented" by or "appositional" to persistently capacious modes of freedom.[11] In the midst of my account of this powerful articulation, then, the reader will find practices, or perhaps just fleeting instances, of its undoing. Power, understood as subjection, is reiterative and systematic, but it also repeats itself differently or even fails to repeat, allowing the very systematicity of its system to be exposed and troubled. Reiteration, it should be remembered, necessarily exceeds its normative effects and, consequently, the historicity of the norm.

The texts and contexts that follow thus archive the vigor with which liberal notions of freedom and equality articulated with disciplinary embodiments of social hierarchy in the face of the remarkably diverse revolutionary potentials of the eighteenth and early nineteenth-centuries.[12]

Articulation

One term emerged repeatedly from the colonial and antebellum archives I researched for this project, leading me to read it as a capacious figure for the dynamic, discursive, and material relationships among race, nation, and equality, and giving *The Colonizing Trick* a certain historical and theoretical arc: "articulation," along with its related verbal and substantive forms "articulate" and "article." A look at the lexical history of this term orients the frequent explicit and implicit encounters we will have with it. "Articulation" found its way into the Romance languages from the Greek word for "joint," *arthron*, which was translated into Latin as *artus*, "joint," and *articulus*, "little joint." In both Greek and Latin, however, these words had linguistic significance too. The Stoic grammarians used them to refer to what we today call pronouns and articles, and for the Roman rhetorician Quintilian *articulus* referred to what we call the definite article "the." Classically, *articulus* was also a rhetorical figure in which a series of single words separated by commas, and thus silent pauses, were strung together without coordinating conjunctions, achieving a dramatic, staccato effect.[13]

Though it might be assumed that the linguistic meanings of these terms were metaphors, transferred from an original, literal meaning of a bodily joint, this etymological progression is by no means certain. What we find, rather, is a set of terms in which bodily and linguistic meanings co-mingle. We also find the trace of a paradox that will intensify in the Romance languages, and take on special significance in my study. In both their bodily and their linguistic meanings, these terms signify acts or states both of connection and separation. "Articulate," in the bodily sense of a joint, refers both to a point or act of connection or juncture and to a discrete segment or segmentation (to the discrete limbs that meet at a juncture); grammatically, an "article" at once connects words to other words and stipulates or distinguishes the word to which it refers. As a classical figure, *articulus* at once connects and separates a series of words with commas and silences.

Between the thirteenth and the fifteenth centuries, these terms continued to refer to bodily joints as points or acts of connection and separation, while their linguistic significance proliferated in English. During this period, "article" could refer to the separate portions, clauses, statutes, or acts of a written document, particularly a legal or religious document such as the Apostles' Creed. Military regulations were referred to as articles of war, and each element of a contract or treaty could be called an article, as could each count or charge of a religious or legal indictment. Indeed, the transitive verb "to article" meant "to indict," as well as "to bind to particular stipulations," as in the phrase "to article with the enemy." By the early eighteenth century, secular and nonlegal meanings of "article" multiplied, as the term was used to mean a discrete literary composition in a newspaper or journal, and even more generally a specific or especially important matter or moment, with the phrase "of great article" meaning "of great moment." The paradoxical co-mingling of connection and separation continued to resonate, with the verb "articulate" meaning both "to joint" or "to join" and "to separate" or "to divide into distinct parts." In the seventeenth century, a certain normative meaning of the term emerged with "articulate" signifying clear, distinct, or even proper speech. In addition, the noun "articulation" came to signify an especially clear or distinct utterance. It is in this normative sense that the term becomes an important statement in the discursive formations of colonialism, with "civilized man" increasingly described as being able to articulate language clearly, and "uncivilized man" marked as inarticulate.[14]

Noah Webster's dictionaries exemplify this semantic constellation. For example, in his 1828 *American Dictionary of the English Language*, half a page is taken up by definitions of "article" and its various forms, definitions that shift back and forth between the bodily and the linguistic, the connective and the disconnective. Webster's text catalogues the rich ambiguity of this figure, beginning with the terms' root in the Latin and Greek for "a joint" and proceeding through definitions such as "A single clause in a contract, account, system of regulations, treaty, or other writings; a particular separate charge or item, in an account," "In *botany*, that part of a stalk or stem, which is between two joints," "In *grammar*, an adjective used before nouns, to limit or define their application," "To draw up in distinct particulars," and "To bind by articles of covenant or stipulation."

The 1828 *American Dictionary* even extends this ambiguity to the early American context of merchant capitalism, remarking that "article" can mean "A particular commodity, or substance; as, an *article* of merchandize; salt is a necessary *article*." At once "particular" and subject to the logic of formal equivalence that animates the exchange of commodities under capitalism (a logic I will examine in detail below), this economic meaning resonates especially vividly with the paradoxical conjunction of particularity and universality. Remarkably, this economic definition is immediately followed by a quotation attributed to "Darwin," apparently Erasmus Darwin: "The *articles* which comprise the blood."[15] The dictionary's own articulation of an economic definition with a biological definition, indeed its representation of the Darwin sentence as an example of the economic definition, implicitly invokes the commodification of bodies under the racialized figure of blood. Enslaved bodies thus haunt even this most mundane of texts, precisely at the conjunctures of particularity and universality, discourse and body. Amplifying this implicitly racialized sense of articulation, the figure's colonial import comes into view a few definitions later, with the adjective "articulate" defined as "sounds distinct, separate, and modified by articulation or jointing. This articulation constitutes the prominent difference between the human voice and that of brutes. Brutes open the mouth and make vocal sounds, but have, either not at all, or very imperfectly, the power of articulation."[16]

These terms thus signify ambivalent relationships among material and discursive elements that are connected in integrated, constitutive, and differential ways. Drawing on this constellation's expression in colonial and antebellum texts, I read "articulation" as a theoretical figure: a term that is implicated in the social formations it seems simply to be describing. Articulation figures the mode of connection among discursive practices of race, nation, and equality and offers a way of understanding how relationships between discourses and bodies came to be lived in North America in the eighteenth and early nineteenth centuries. In *The Colonizing Trick*, then, I will use the figure of "articulation," in its late eighteenth- and early nineteenth-century senses, to open up the study of race, nation, and equality in North America to a flexible and comparativist, historical and textual specificity.

David Walker's Appeal, In Four Articles, Together With A Preamble, To The Coloured Citizens Of The World, But In Particular, And Very Expressly, To Those Of The United States Of America again offers us a case in point. In this text, indeed in its very title, the figure of articulation names *both* the increasingly self-evident co-mingling of universal equality with particularized racial and national identities *and* Walker's effort to trouble that self-evidence. By organizing his own text into "Four Articles," Walker mimics the very legal and governmental speech acts—such as the Declaration of Independence and the Constitution—that expressed such co-mingling, the very speech acts that made such an articulation articulate, or clear and self-evident. The particular articles of the U.S. Constitution, for instance, combine to produce "we the people of the United States" who are both nationally particularized ("we the people *of the United States*") and racially particularized (the "whole number of free persons" referred to in Article 1, section 2). Yet Walker's mimicry is also an appropriation and a rewriting, a critique of U.S. white supremacy from within the terms of its own discursive practices. By addressing the "Coloured" as "Citizens" both "Of The World" and "Of The United States Of America," and by quoting and revising the Declaration of Independence in the final pages of the *Appeal*, Walker rewrites America's racially and nationally particularized claims to universal equality. Against the racialist articulation of whiteness with citizenship and the imperial articulation of the United States with the world, Walker offers a counterarticulation: "coloured" particularity with the "citizen's" global equality.

This is a practice Walker follows throughout the *Appeal*, both formally and argumentatively. For instance, a footnote in article 4 declares:

> And still [the white] holds us up with indignity as being incapable of acquiring knowledge!!! See the inconsistency of the assertions of those wretches—they beat us inhumanely, sometimes almost to death, for attempting to inform ourselves, by reading the *Word* of our Maker, and at the same time tell us, that we are beings *void of intellect!!!!* How admirably their practices agree with their professions in this case. Let me cry shame upon you Americans, for such outrages upon human nature!!! If it were possible for the whites always to keep us ignorant and miserable, and make us work to enrich them and their children, and insult our feelings by representing us as *talking Apes*, what would they do? But glory, honour and praise to Heaven's King, that the sons and daughters of Africa, will, in spite of all the opposition of their enemies, stand forth in all the dignity and glory that is granted by the Lord to his creature man.[17]

In this passage, articulation functions at once as a figure for the white nationalist conception of equality and as a figure for Walker's efforts to counter that conception. On the one hand, whites distinguish their own humanity from the inhumanity of blacks with "assertions" of physical force—"they beat us inhumanely, sometimes almost to death, for attempting to inform ourselves"—and "assertions" of discursive force—they "insult our feelings by representing us as *talking Apes*." Black bodies are broken, disarticulated in a bodily sense. Yet this bodily disarticulation is also discursive, since the breaking of bodies is also a breaking of information, of "intellect," of "the *Word*," so that black speech is shattered, rendered inarticulate in a discursive sense. Yet this discursive disarticulation is also embodied, as it is uttered by inhuman black bodies, the bodies of apes. Embodied speech emerges as an inarticulate, particularized, black speech "void of intellect" so that white speech may emerge as the disembodied, articulate, universal sign of the intellect as such.

On the other hand and in response, Walker articulates an embodied speech that claims humanity: "Let me cry shame upon you Americans, for such outrages upon human nature!!!" Turning an inarticulate utterance, the "cry," into an articulation of human nature, and presenting that utterance as part of the fourth article of his *Appeal to Coloured Citizens*, Walker engages the tropological movement of the figure of articulation. He names the articulation of race, nation, and equality to which blacks are subjected, and yet also turns that naming into the condition of possibility for another subjectification, another articulation of another humanity. In this way, the *Appeal* seizes on the condensed ambivalence of the "article's" material and discursive elements in order to disarticulate modern, racial nationalism and rearticulate a global, egalitarian citizenship irreducible to racial and national codification.

To take another example, consider Thomas Jefferson's account of digging through Indian graves in "Query XI—Aborigines" of the *Notes on the State of Virginia*. Faced with published European claims that there was no such thing as American Indian culture or history, and in particular with a debate over whether Indian gravesites, or "barrows," could be considered cultural monuments, Jefferson writes:

> I know of no such thing existing as an Indian monument: for I would not honour with that name arrow points, stone hatchets, stone pipes, and half-shapen images. Of labour on the large scale, I think there is no remain as respectable as would be a common ditch for the draining of lands: unless indeed it be the Barrows, of which many are to be found all over this country. . . . There being one of these in my neighbourhood, I wished to satisfy myself whether any, and which of these opinions [on why barrows were constructed] were just. For this purpose I determined to open and examine it thoroughly.[18]

Jefferson's equivocation over the status of Indian culture—"I know of no such thing existing as an Indian monument . . . unless indeed it be the Barrows"—figures at once the white settler demand for uncivilized aborigines who must be removed from the land they are wasting, and the demand of America's emerging national culture for a history that could compete with that of Europe. To resolve this equivocation, he performs his own reasoned civility by conducting an empirical examination.

Jefferson proceeds to give a detailed description of the graves, and we soon find him apparently covered in dirt and bones, smashing and pulling apart skeletons: "The sculls were so tender, that they generally fell to pieces on being touched. The other bones were stronger. . . . I was particular in my attention to . . . part of the right-half of the under-jaw [of a child]. The processes, by which it was articulated to the temporal bones, were entire; and the bone itself firm to where it had been broken off . . . I conjecture that in this barrow might have been a thousand skeletons."[19] Is Jefferson combing through a gravesite with skeletons fresh enough to have bones still "articulated" to one another by ligaments? This is unclear, since the ethical sphere of graverobbing is subordinated to the pragmatic sphere of "opinions" on barrow construction, itself instrumental to the polemical sphere of debates over America's historicity. Self-evidently clear to Jefferson, however, is that the Indian's inability to construct a proper, civilized "monument" authorizes the treatment of Indian remains as objects of study whose purpose is to satisfy the accumulation of knowledge. The barrows are, to Jefferson, evidence not of the Indians' civil life but rather of their dead, protocivility. They can thus be considered an assimilable, archeological sign of white settler America's own, exceptional ancient history.[20]

Remarkably, Jefferson immediately equates this embodied evidence with discursive evidence; following his account of the barrows, he suggests that "the aboriginal inhabitants of America" originally migrated from Europe:

> It is to be lamented then, very much to be lamented, that we have suffered so many of the Indian tribes already to extinguish, without our having previously collected and deposited in the records of literature, the general rudiments at least of the languages they spoke. Were vocabularies formed of all the languages spoken in North and South America, preserving their appellations of the most common objects in nature, of those which must be present to every nation barbarous or civilised, with the inflections of their

nouns and verbs, their principles of regimen and concord, and these deposited in all the
public libraries, it would furnish opportunities to those skilled in the languages of the old
world to compare them with these, now, or at any future time, and hence to construct the
best evidence of the derivation of this part of the human race.[21]

Again, this passage at once presumes the passing of Indian life and clings to an ob-
jectified record of its presence. Committed to clearing the land for white settlers and
yet desperate to give those settlers a culture with historical depth, Jefferson imagines
American public libraries as spaces within which that presence could be contained and
mastered. Civilized white settlers can thus subject the remains of uncivilized Indians to
an archeology and a philology that signify both America's natural history and its cultured, scientific present. Yet Jefferson must disarticulate the embodied and discursive
remains of Indian presence ("they generally fell to pieces," "collected . . . the general
rudiments at least") in order to articulate this sign in his *Notes*—itself one of America's
foundational discursive articulations. This material and discursive disarticulation and
rearticulation performs the assimilation of Indians as dead objects of knowledge for a
white settler culture itself on the road to white national civility.

The figure of articulation will also appear in chapter 4 of *The Colonizing Trick*
when I consider the Treaty of Guadalupe Hidalgo, which formally concluded the
U.S.–Mexico War in 1848. Article 9 of the treaty has become well known for promising equality to Mexicans incorporated into the United States after the war. It reads in
part: "The Mexicans who, in the territories aforesaid, shall not preserve the character
of citizens of the Mexican Republic . . . shall be incorporated into the Union of the
United States and be admitted . . . to the enjoyment of all the rights of the citizens of
the United States." The postwar legacy of discrimination against Mexican-Americans/
Chicanos made this seem like a broken promise, but in chapter 4 I argue that the ironic effect of this discrimination was the fulfillment of that very promise. As we will see,
the condition article 9 places upon the "enjoyment" of equality as a U.S. citizen—a
negation of "the character of citizens of the Mexican Republic"—implies full assimilation to white civility.

What is more, the recognition offered to Mexico and its citizens by the treaty did
not simply make Mexico and the United States equal nation-states. The discursive
formation of which the treaty was a part at once granted Mexico formal equality and
inaugurated a new, corporate, neocolonial treatment of Mexico, one that did not depend on direct military or white settler occupation. Thus, the formal and abstract
equality offered by article 9's "all the rights of citizens" was articulated with racial and
national distinctions between Mexicans and Americans produced by war. By reading
the treaty in the context of U.S. government documents and popular literature about
the U.S.–Mexico War, and the related Caste War in Yucatán, we can trace this articulation, and understand article 9 as one element in a larger set of practices that discursively and materially embodied citizenship in racial and national particularity.

At other times in this study, the figure of articulation looms implicitly, as, for
instance, in Charles Brockden Brown's uncompleted novel, *Memoirs of Carwin, the*

Biloquist, published in serial form in *The Literary Magazine* between 1803 and 1805, a text I will consider at length in chapter 3. In the novel's opening scenes, Carwin, the narrator and protagonist, describes an event that, as he puts it, "ascertained my future destiny."[22] Rushing home one afternoon with the news that he has allowed his father's cows to escape their pen, and certain that his father will punish him, Carwin seeks a shortcut through a dangerous and frightening rocky pass:

> These terrors are always lessened by calling the attention away to some indifferent object. I now made use of this expedient, and began to amuse myself by hallowing as loud as organs of unusual compass and vigour would enable me. I uttered the words which chanced to occur to me, and repeated in the shrill tones of a Mohock savage . . . "Cow! cow! come home! home!" . . . These notes were of course reverberated from the rocks which on either side towered aloft, but the echo was confused and indistinct. [Brown's ellipses][23]

Carwin stays in the rocky pass to examine this echo, risking further punishment from his father. Indeed, day after day he returns to the pass, obsessed with mastering the echo: "Could I not so dispose my organs as to make my voice appear at a distance?" he asks himself.[24] His success makes him a biloquist, or ventriloquist, but it also comes at a cost. The very inquisitiveness that led him to master this echo pushes him to leave his family's rural home and set out into the early nineteenth-century Atlantic world, where he cannot resist using his biloquial skills for questionable moral purposes.

Certainly a familiar Brownian allegory of modernity's dangers—Carwin's "thirst of knowledge," his disdain for rural tradition, his amoral tendencies—this passage also allows Carwin's "future destiny" to emerge from a curious, colonial scene of embodied articulation. Through "speculation" and "experiment," Carwin assimilates the inarticulate "shrill tones of a Mohock savage"—a striking instance of Webster's "brutes"—and modernizes them first into "notes," and later into a "powerful" voice "instrument."[25] The condition of possibility for Brown's cautionary tale about modernization is itself an allegory of colonial assimilation. Crucially, neither *Memoirs of Carwin* nor its more well-known sequel *Wieland* ever again mentions the "Mohock savage"; indeed, both texts work diligently to suppress the colonial origins of their critiques of modernity. However, by attending to this inaugural scene we can read Carwin's tale as an allegory for late eighteenth- and early nineteenth-century efforts by the U.S. government to "civilize" or assimilate Iroquois communities through land expropriation and forced education. That such an allegory should take the form of a colonial distinction between inarticulate, savage tones and an articulate, civilized voice shows how the figure of articulation indexes the emergence of imperial citizenship in early America.

Thus, throughout *The Colonizing Trick* the tropological movement of articulation will guide my analyses of the interactions among discursive practices of race, nation, and equality. Let me emphasize that this tropological movement is not simply a historically specific instance of semantic change. It is not caused simply by the political and social transformations I will discuss, nor were those transformations merely effects of this movement. Rather, I am making a hermeneutic claim: attention to the multiple, shifting meanings of articulation in the colonial and antebellum periods allows us to trace and interpret the constitutive relationships among emerging conceptions of race, nation, and equality.

"Articulation" has also had a more recent history as a Marxian theoretical category that informs my project. Stuart Hall's 1980 essay "Race, Articulation, and Societies Structured in Dominance" brilliantly relates this category, which was for him at the time a "new theoretical paradigm," to the study of race.[26] Hall begins by showing how André Gunder Frank's critique of the 1950s dependency theory of the United Nations Economic Commission for Latin America (ECLA) sparked theoretical reflection on and debate over how to characterize the relationships among apparently different elements of social formations. For instance, Frank and Ernesto Laclau famously debated the relationships between what seemed, from the perspective of then-classical Marxism, to be different modes of production: European capitalism and plantation slavery in the Americas.[27] Hall gleans from this debate that slavery and capitalism can be articulated together:

> Slave plantation owners thus participated in a general movement of the world capitalist system: but on the basis of an internal mode of production—slavery in its modern, plantation form—not itself "capitalist" in character. This is a revolutionary proposition in the theoretical sense, since it departs from that very teleological reading of Marx which produced, in Frank, the indefensible thesis that Latin America has been "capitalist" since the Conquest. What we have now, in opposition to the thesis of "inevitable transformation" of pre-capitalist modes and their dissolution by capitalist relations, is the emergent theoretical problem of an articulation between different modes of production, structured in some relation of dominance. This leads on to the definition of a social formation which, at its economic level, may be composed of several modes of production, "structured in dominance."[28]

In the structuralist Marxism of Louis Althusser and Étienne Balibar's *Reading Capital*, Hall continues, articulation helps "to construct a non-reductionist theory of the superstructural or extra-economic aspects of social formations."[29] Furthermore, articulation helps us to understand the historically specific connections of those super-structures to the economic relations Frank and Laclau discussed:

> The unity which [economic and extra-economic elements] form is thus not that of an identity, where one structure perfectly recapitulates or reproduces or even "expresses" another; or where each is reducible to the other; or where each is defined by the same determinations or have exactly the same conditions of existence; or even where each develops according to the effectivity of the same conditions of existence; or even where each develops according to the effectivity of the same contradiction . . . The unity formed by this combination or articulation, is always, necessarily, a "complex structure": a structure in which things are related, as much through their differences as through their similarities. This requires that the mechanisms which connect dissimilar features must be

shown—since no "necessary correspondence" or expressive homology can be assumed as given. It also means—since the combination is a structure (an articulated combination) and not a random association—that there will be structured relations between its parts, i.e., relations of dominance and subordination. Hence, in Althusser's cryptic phrase, a "complex unity, structured in dominance."[30]

As a way of thinking the mode of connection among elements of social formations, this structuralist understanding of articulation offers a crucial challenge to economistic, culturalistic, developmentalist, and mechanistic theories of race.

As Hall notes, it also challenges

all those explanations which ascribe racism-in-general to some universal functioning of individual psychology—the "racial itch," the "race instinct"—or explain its appearance in terms of a general psychology of prejudice. The question is not whether men-in-general make perceptual distinctions between groups with different racial or ethnic characteristics, but rather, what are the specific conditions which make this form of distinction socially pertinent, historically active. What gives this abstract human potentiality its effectivity, as a concrete material force? . . . The histories of these different racisms cannot be written as a "general history" (Hall: 1978; Hall, et al.: 1978). Appeals to "human nature" are not explanations, they are an alibi.[31]

This challenge has renewed import to the study of race and nation in the United States today, a study all too often characterized by generalized "models" of racism and nationalism that would have been familiar to Hall in 1980. In particular, as we saw in Bailyn's *Voyagers to the West*, racial and national formations are still explained by developmentalist theories, in which racial and national particularisms are represented as fundamentally atavistic, while egalitarianism is represented as a fundamentally more modern, and thus more dominant, ideal. Alternately, existential or psychological theories of projection uninformed by psychoanalysis continue to use the model of a subject projecting onto the other that which it does not like about itself, without explaining the conditions of possibility for a subject who projects or likes or dislikes, or the historically specific conditions under which this general, projecting, liking, and disliking subject is active or inactive.[32]

Finally, classical Marxian theories of contradiction also tend to represent racial and national particularisms as necessarily contradicted by or antagonistic with universalisms such as equality, rather than considering how the latter might depend upon, or even intensify the former.[33] As will become clear in the next section of this chapter, I view Marx's critique of citizenship as central to an account of the interactions among racism, nationalism, and egalitarianism. However, my research suggests that in eighteenth- and nineteenth-century North America, historically specific articulations of racial and national codification are more likely supplementary to—and thus often constitutive of—historically specific articulations of formal and abstract equality. Consequently, efforts to turn such a supplement toward a contradiction or an antagonism are as precarious as they are urgent.

Like the structuralist Marxism to which it primarily refers, even Hall's account of articulation offers a certain generalized model of racialization. He tends to represent elements of social formations as relatively discrete "levels" or "parts" articulated to one another through "connections" or "mechanisms."[34] As such, in his 1980 article he remains wary of the messy co-mingling of articulation's discursive and bodily meanings that I have emphasized. Writes Hall,

> The term [articulation] itself is by no means unproblematic . . . [It] has an ambiguous meaning, for, in English, it can mean both "joining up" (as in the limbs of the body, or an anatomical structure) and "giving expression to" (cf: Foster-Carter: 1978). In Althusserian usage, it is primarily the first sense which is intended. There are, in any case, theoretical objections to the notion that one structure "gives expression to" another: since this would be tantamount to seeing the second structure as an epiphenomenon of the first (i.e., a reductionist conception), and would involve treating a social formation as an "expressive totality"—precisely the object of Althusser's initial critique of Hegelianism. . . . Nevertheless, we would continue to insist on the potentially generative value of the term and its cognate concepts, which give us a start in thinking the complex unity and *differentiae specificae* of social formations, without falling back on a naïve or "vulgar materialist" reductionism, on the one hand, or a form of sociological pluralism on the other.[35]

I would like to suggest that the "generative value of the term" to which Hall refers in the second part of this passage stems precisely from the "ambiguous meaning" of which he is wary in the first part. This wariness leads Hall to reduce the term's discursive significance to Foster-Carter's "giving expression to." Yet, as we have seen, the bodily and discursive meanings of articulation are deeply intertwined with one another. Even taken alone, articulation's discursive significance is not reducible to the unidirectional and mechanistic sense of "giving expression to," and thus Hall's concern about the "reductionist conception" of the term itself reduces articulation's capaciousness.

Attention to this capaciousness in the eighteenth and nineteenth centuries exposes articulation's work as a figure, calling on us to read and interpret it each time it emerges, explicitly (as with the Treaty of Guadalupe Hidalgo) or implicitly (as with Brown), in texts from this period. Articulation is neither a model to be applied to texts nor a technique by which discrete social structures can be located and related, for it is not separable from the linguistic and social formations to which it might be applied. Rather, it is a hermeneutic, a critical lens that not only opens up readings of these formations (as with Jefferson), but also is read by them (as with Walker) so that its own meaning shifts and shades into other meanings. As Hall writes presciently, articulation indicates "a certain approach, rather than providing in itself a theoretical resolution to the problems it indexes."[36]

For instance, the term's normative meaning—"clear or proper speech"—at times allows it to fix its referents, to construct hierarchical distinctions between good speech and bad speech and even to make claims about the humanity of various speakers. In a passage I considered above, Walker foregrounds this normative, fixed meaning when he shows how embodied speech is represented as inarticulate black speech, or the inhuman speech of apes, so that disembodied speech can be represented as articulate white speech, or human intellect as such. In response, Walker cuts articulation loose from its normative moorings by reiterating its bodily and discursive meanings: "Let me cry shame upon you Americans, for such outrages upon human nature!!!"[37] He counters a fixed, hierarchical articulation of speech and bodies that sought to naturalize "human nature" with an embodied articulation, a "cry" that makes "human nature" a sign of a future justice, a freedom to come. Similarly, *Memoirs of Carwin* fixes a distinction between the inarticulate savage and the articulate citizen-subject in order to launch a debate between white settler traditionalism and white settler modernism. A reading of *Memoirs of Carwin* that attends to the echoes of the "shrill tones of a Mohock savage" can trouble that distinction and reconsider such foundational debates.

At each of these moments in the recent genealogy of articulation—Frank's critique of ECLA, Laclau's critique of Frank, Althusser and Balibar's structuralism, and Hall's re-reading of that structuralism—Marx represents a crucial touchstone. To continue culling the bodily and discursive significance of articulation, and to nudge Hall's structuralist interpretation toward an interpretation of articulation as a theoretical figure, I too will revisit Marx, attending to the always underelaborated but rich traces in his texts of bodies and discourses intersected by race, nation, and equality. In particular, I want to examine Marx's suggestion that, under capitalism, substantial, human relations are not simply transformed into abstract relations of formal equivalence. Rather, those abstract relations of formal equivalence are always articulated with—or, to use another of Marx's terms, grafted onto—material, particularized identities.

Graft

When capitalism first emerged as an economic and political force, Marx argues in the first volume of *Capital*, it worked to break down current ways of making sense of and giving value to social relations, while simultaneously instituting new ways of making sense of or giving value to social relations. Marx describes the process of breaking down in part 8 of *Capital* in economic terms as "a process which divorces the worker from the ownership of the conditions of his own labour" through expropriation, so-called "bloody legislation" against the expropriated, the agricultural and industrial revolutions, and colonization.[38] In turn, in the first chapter of *Capital* Marx calls the new, capitalist way of making sense of social relations, or the form in which social relations are valued under capitalism, the "value form."[39]

How, then, does this devaluing and revaluing process function? That is, how is the value form established? In the first chapter of *Capital*, Marx describes this process by using the production and exchange of the commodity, or "the product of labour," as an exemplary instance of social relations "manufactured" under capitalism.[40] He explains that two materially different objects, such as a coat and linen, are equated with each other on the basis of a third commodity shared by the coat and the linen. That third commodity is abstract labor, or labor that has been abstracted from its particular qualities:

> By equating, for example, the coat as a thing of value to the linen, we equate the labour
> embedded in the coat with the labour embedded in the linen. Now it is true that the
> tailoring which makes the coat is concrete labour of a different sort from the weaving
> which makes the linen. But . . . weaving too, in so far as it weaves value, has nothing to
> distinguish it from tailoring, and, consequently, is abstract human labor . . . [or] human
> labour in general.[41]

Under the value form, then, one does not simply weave linen and tailor a coat; one weaves and tailors value, a mode of equivalence that allows two materially different objects and actions to become the same. In effect, the value form transforms the particularistic aspects of social relations into the universal and abstract form of "human labour in general."

In addition, as Marx explains in "The Chapter on Capital" from the *Grundrisse*, under capitalism abstract labor is represented not only as the basis for the economic *equality* of commodities, but also as the basis for the economic *freedom* of the laborer. The valuing of abstract labor over particular labor allows each laborer to sell his or her labor on the market and to receive wages for it. The wage-laborer, or the laborer who sells his or her abstract labor, is the *free* economic subject of capitalism because he or she is said to be formally and abstractly *equal* to all other laborers. The laborer's freedom is his or her abstraction from particularity, from the social qualities that differentiate one laborer from another; he or she is freed from particularity. "Freedom" thus acquires a precise meaning through the logic of abstract equivalence. The very substance of sociality—that which "stipulates" subjects "not only in an equal, but also in a social relation" to one another, as Marx writes—is the active valuation of "freedom" as formal and abstract equivalence.[42]

Crucially, Marx is not claiming that commodity production and exchange are the only social relations transformed by the value form. Rather, it seems as if he makes the commodity the exemplary instance of the value form in action to help his readers: he thought they encountered commodities so persistently in everyday life that they would understand the value form argument most readily if its role in commodity exchange were foregrounded.[43] In fact, he suggests, all social relations are subject to the value form: "The exchange of exchange values is the productive, real basis of all *equality* and *freedom*. As pure ideas they are merely the idealized expressions of this basis; as developed in juridical, political, social relations, they are merely this basis to a higher power."[44]

Another significant "juridical, political, and social relation" animated by the value form under capitalism is the institution of modern citizenship. In *Capital* and in the *Grundrisse*, Marx illustrates this by comparing the value of the commodity to the value of the citizen. For instance, "The linen, by virtue of the form of value, no longer stands in a social relation with merely one other kind of commodity, but with the whole world of commodities as well. As a commodity it is a citizen of that world."[45] To be representable as a citizen, then, a subject must be abstracted from its particularities just as a coat and tailoring or linen and weaving are abstracted from their particularities. This formally abstract citizen-subject is thus brought into a relationship of formal and abstract equality with its fellow citizen-subjects, and this relationship is represented as freedom. That is, subjects in capitalist civil society become citizens to the extent that they understand themselves as formally and abstractly equivalent to other subjects.

The value form thus represents subjects as rational abstractions, formally equivalent and legally free, in order to be representable as constituent members of civil society.[46] The theory of value functions as a critique not only of commodity exchange, but also of the logic of freedom and equality in civil society "as developed in juridical, political, social relations." What is more, the logic of abstract equivalence does not simply reflect the ideals of freedom and equality. Rather, the embodiment of the value form in complex social and cultural relations actually generates those very ideals.[47]

Embodiment is actually a crucial element of the value form, for universal and abstract equivalence does not simply eliminate all material particularity. Rather, that equivalence re-forms particularity:

> However, it is not enough to express the specific character of the labour which goes to make up the value of the linen. Human labour-power in its fluid state [im flüssigen Zustand], or human labour, creates value, but is not itself value. It becomes value in its coagulated state [in geronnenem Zustand], in objective form. The value of the linen as a congealed mass [Gallerte] of human labour can be expressed only as an "objectivity" [Gegenständlichkeit], a thing which is materially different from the linen itself and yet common to the linen and all other commodities.[48]

The exchange of the coat and the linen gives a formal, abstract, and universal meaning to what were the "fluid," particular human actions of weaving or tailoring. Yet this formal, abstract, and universal meaning has a substantiality here—it is "coagulated," "congealed," and "objective." The value form produces a universal abstraction with a form that has jelled or solidified anew. In other words, the value form effectively departicularizes the particularisms of precapitalist social relations and then reparticularizes those social relations. Though this passage does not explain exactly how this substantiality is different from the substantial particularity of the coat and the linen before they were capitalist commodities, it does suggest that capitalist production and exchange creates a universal abstraction with a newly solidified, particularized body. This odd articulation of universal abstraction with particularized substantiality is succinctly represented by what Marx, in the *Grundrisse*, calls the "double existence" of the commodity: "As a value, the commodity is general; as a real commodity it is particular."[49]

Traces of this materialization of equality can also be glimpsed in one of the most familiar (though shortest) sections of *Capital*, "The Fetishism of the Commodity and Its Secret *[Der Fetischcharakter der Ware und sein Geheimnis]*." Here, the commodity-form has a "mysterious character" in the sense that products of labor appear to have an innate, "wonderful" value in their own right.[50] That is, "the commodity reflects the social characteristics of men's own labour as objective characteristics of the products of labour themselves, as the socio-natural properties of these things."[51] In effect, the materiality and sociality of labor—"the expenditure of human brain, nerves, muscles and sense organs," of "men [who] . . . work for each other"—is transferred to the commodity and animates the thingliness of that object. This leads to one of the most well-known sentences of *Capital*:

> The commodity-form, and the value-relation of the products of labour within which it appears, have absolutely no connection with the physical nature of the commodity and the material *[dinglich]* relations arising out of this. It is nothing but the definite social relation between men themselves which assumes here, for them, the phantasmagoric form *[die phantasmagorische Form]* of a relation between things.[52]

Literally "the place of assembly for phantasms," the word "phantasmagoria" was coined in English in 1802 as a name for an exhibition of optical illusions produced by a trick lantern.[53] This passage thus indicates that a "definite social relation between men themselves" takes a hallucinatory form, as if the new relation appeared in the form of an optical illusion. This form is spectral, unclear—not simply abstract, but rather bearing an odd, haunted materiality. The section on the fetish character of the commodity suggests not that the value form progressively obliterates particularity, but that it re-forms particularity into a haunted or, to use Althusser's term, overdetermined substantiality.[54] If the commodity represents a fetishized universal abstraction, and if the commodity is one example of capitalist social relations, then other examples of social relations under capitalism—such as the citizen—presumably also represent fetishized universal abstraction. As a fetishized universal abstraction, then, the citizen can be said to embody a relationship between universal abstraction and substantialized particularity.

Marx does not pay much attention to the question of what happens to the specific social particularities abstracted by the value form, particularities such as the differences among a coat, linen, corn, and gold, or the differences among subjects before they are transformed into citizens. Are those particularities abstracted away completely, or are they re-formed? If abstraction has a substantiality, if it remakes and revalues substance from a "fluid" state to a "coagulated," "congealed," or "fetish" state, what happens to the particularities that marked labor power in its "fluid state"? Do they reemerge, revalued and in some new relation to universal equality and freedom? Since new "particularities," such as race and nation, vigorously emerge at the precise historical moment at which the value form abstracts subjects and commodities from their particularities, and at which capitalism represents this abstraction as "freedom," we would seem to need an account of "particularity" under the value form. Marx's failure to consider carefully this question has resonated throughout the Marxian tradition, leaving many critics to argue that the value form progressively destroys or erases all particularities.[55] Yet Marx's emphasis on the substantiality and materiality of universal abstraction—its "coagulated" and "congealed" character—suggests that, far from being destroyed or erased, substantialized particularity enters into a dynamic relationship with universal abstraction.

In fact, Marx's rarely read letters and passages on slavery in the Americas do furtively consider what happens to social particularities such as race and nation when formal, abstract equality becomes the reigning way of rendering economic and political freedom.[56] Although always critical of slavery as an unjust practice, Marx was unable to account fully for what he occasionally considered a feudal form of labor in the midst of the United States, a country he called "the most modern form of existence of bourgeois society."[57] At times he claims that universal free wage labor is the *sine qua non* of capitalism; as he writes in the *Grundrisse*, "Capital ceases to be capital without wage-labor."[58] This allows him to suggest, and generations of Marxists after him to argue explicitly, that slavery in the Americas is an anomaly or even an atavism because it is not wage labor. Slavery and race emerge from such arguments as mere residues of premodern, precapitalist modes of production that will simply dissipate in the face of the bourgeois revolution, after which the "real" struggles for freedom from wage labor would begin.[59] Here we see a Marxian version of the argument we saw in Bailyn at the beginning of this chapter, a version, as we also saw above, that Hall challenges.

However, Marx is also at times uncomfortable with this dogmatic position. In notebook 4 of the *Grundrisse*, for example, he writes cryptically in parentheses: "(The fact that slavery is possible at individual points within the bourgeois system of production does not contradict [my argument about the exchange relation]. However, slavery is then possible there only because it . . . appears as an anomaly opposite the bourgeois system itself)."[60] This passage does not claim that racial slavery *is* anomalous. To say that slavery "*appears* as an anomaly" is to suggest that, from the perspective of classical liberalism itself, slavery is anomalous; that is, liberalism makes itself make sense by anomalizing slavery. Thus a *critique* of liberalism would need to offer another *interpretation* of "the anomalous"—another interpretation, that is, of the relationship between the value form and the particularistic logic of racial slavery.

Marx does occasionally hint at an interpretation of this "anomalous" status in the U.S. context. For example, in *Theories of Surplus Value*, he writes that on southern U.S. plantations:

> Where commercial speculations figure from the start and production is intended for the world market, the capitalist mode of production exists, although only in a formal sense, since the slavery of Negroes [*der Negersklaverei*] precludes free wage labor, which is the basis of capitalist production. But the business in which slaves are used is conducted by *capitalists*. The mode of production which they introduce has not arisen out of slavery but is grafted on to it. [*Die Produktionsweise, die sie einführen, ist nicht aus der Sklaverei entsprungen, sondern wird auf sie gepfropft.*][61]

This passage wavers between two perspectives and ultimately offers a hybrid of both perspectives with the figure of the graft. From the perspective of production, it insists on a mode-of-production narrative that makes "the slavery of Negroes" an atavistic vestige of the past. Slavery "precludes free wage labor," and thus production on southern U.S. plantations could only be capitalist "in a formal sense." Yet even this grudging acceptance of U.S. plantation slavery as "formal" capitalism belies another, less explicit perspective: that of *trade* ("production . . . *intended for* the world market"). From this perspective, capitalism looks more like a world system. Whereas the production perspective tends to take the nation-state as a given unit of analysis and to posit a linear and uniform narrative of development through which each nation-state must pass, the perspective of trade considers multiform and uneven development among nation-states dependent upon one another in a capitalist world economy.[62] It is this shift, I want to suggest, that leads the passage to consider slavery's role within capitalism. That is, from the perspective of trade and the world system, slavery can be understood as "grafted onto," rather than necessarily anterior to, outside of, or contradictory to capitalism. This suggests that when "nation" is taken as a self-evident category, slavery and racialization are occluded or dismissed as incidental, whereas when the question of the nation form is raised, slavery and, implicitly, "race" become social relations whose precise relationship to capitalism needs to be articulated.

Marx's figuration of this relationship as one of "grafting" is rich indeed here. The passage opposes a necessary or even natural development (*entspringen* as "to arise from," "to derive from") to an actively forced articulation (*pfropfen* means "to graft" in an agricultural sense as well as "to cork" or "to plug," even colloquially "to stuff" something into something else). *Entspringen* would indicate that the mode of production of the plantation capitalists is derived from slavery and, while originally enabled by slavery, will eventually advance beyond slavery or leave slavery behind. To the contrary, by suggesting, with *pfropfen*, that plantation capitalism is "stuffed with" slavery or "grafted onto" it, the passage insists both on a more forced and on a more imbricated relationship between capitalism and racial slavery (*die Negersklaverei*), deemphasizing any sense of capitalism leaving racial slavery behind. The verb *pfropfen* urges us, I would suggest, to read this forced imbrication carefully.[63]

We find a similar point in "The Working Day" chapter of *Capital*, vol. 1. After admitting that "Capital did not invent surplus labor," Marx distinguishes forced labor systems of antiquity from modern forced labor:

> It is however clear that in any economic formation of society where the use-value rather than the exchange-value of the product predominates, surplus labour will be restricted by a more or less confined set of needs, and that no boundless thirst for surplus labour will arise from [*entspringt*] the character of production itself. . . . But as soon as peoples whose production still moves within the lower forms of slave-labour, the *corvée*, etc. are drawn into [*hineingezogen werden*] a world market dominated by the capitalist mode of production, whereby the sale of their products for export develops into their principal interest, the civilized horrors of over-work are grafted onto the barbaric horrors of slavery, serfdom etc. [*wird den barbarischen Greueln der Sklaverei, Leibeigenschaft usw. der zivilisierte Greuel der Überarbeit aufgepfropft.*] Hence the Negro labour in the southern states of the American Union [*die Negerarbeit in den südlichen Staaten der amerikanischen Union*] preserved a moderately patriarchal character as long as production was chiefly directed to the satisfaction of immediate local requirements. But in proportion as the export of cotton became of vital interest to those states, the over-working of the Negro, and sometimes the consumption of his life in seven years of labour, became a factor in a

calculated and calculating system. It was no longer a question of obtaining from him a certain quantity of useful products, but rather of the production of surplus-value itself. The same is true of the *corvée*, in the Danubian Principalities for instance.[64]

When we read that in antiquity "no boundless thirst for surplus labour will arise *[entspringt]* from the character of production itself," it seems that under capitalism such a boundless thirst *will arise* from the character of production itself, thereby changing the character of forced labor, perhaps from slavery to wage labor. Yet when the passage turns to the capitalist mode of production, it posits neither such a natural connection between production and surplus labor, nor a necessary derivation of that boundless thirst from production. Neither does it make the familiar claim that free wage labor becomes the exclusive form of coercion, nor does it suggest that slavery becomes atavistic.

Rather, as in the *Grundrisse* passage, it shifts to the perspective of world trade and continues to examine forced labor, characterizing its place within global capitalism: "As soon as [forced laborers] are drawn into *[hineingezogen werden]* a world market dominated by the capitalist mode of production, whereby the sale of their products for export develops into their principal interest, the civilized horrors of over-work are grafted onto *[aufgepfropft]* the barbaric horrors of slavery." The verb *hineinziehen* has more force than "to draw into" might suggest, and could be translated "to drag into" or "to pull into." Indeed, the root *ziehen* can mean "to extract" or "to pull," as in extracting the root of a number, extracting a plant from the ground, or pulling a person's hair. *Ziehen* can also mean "to build" or "to erect," and even "to cultivate," "to grow," or "to breed." This ensemble of meanings suggests a forced union of slavery and capitalism, even a constructed union with a natural appearance. The sense of cultivation or breeding in particular is even more resonant when the same sentence repeats the *Grundrisse*'s figure of the graft: *"aufgepfropft."* Furthermore, by distinguishing *"Sklaverei"* (slavery) from *"Leibeigenschaft"* (serfdom) and in the next sentence explicitly invoking *"die Negerarbeit"* (Negro labor), this passage leaves no doubt about racial slavery's deep connections to capitalism. Finally, by quite specifically locating racial slavery *"in den südlichen Staaten der amerikanischen Union,"* it implicitly invokes racial slavery's deep connection to the nation form, thereby linking race, nation, and capitalism. While racial slavery in the United States may seem to be a barbaric horror when compared with the civilized horror of wage labor, the very distinction between barbarism and civility loses its significance by the end of this passage. Instead of a familiar opposition, slavery and wage labor here become common elements subject to calculation and codification.

Let us remain with *pfropfen* in the sense of "to graft" for a moment, then. The graft, or that which is grafted onto a host, is neither strictly natural nor strictly artificial. It is at once secondary or foreign to the host, and, after some time and if successful, legibly one with that host in such a way that the violent act of grafting itself becomes illegible. If, as the passages above suggest, grafting figures the relationship between national forms of racial slavery and capitalism, or racial and national codification and the abstract equality of the value form, then we need to consider how racial and national particularities are not erased under or developed away by the value form, but vigorously and actively produced at or conjoined with—indeed articulated with—the moment of abstraction.

We can thus say that Marx's ambivalence about the anomalous status of racial slavery under capitalism signals both the limit and the possibility of the Marxian critique of the value form and of classical liberal citizenship. By seizing on the generative ambivalence between the perspectives of production and of trade, we can understand this moment of abstraction as the moment in which abstract equality and racial and national codification are actively produced and grafted or conjoined. The calculation of subjects as citizens could be said to depend upon the codification of racial and national particularity, and vice versa, such that the very categories of sameness and difference, or the universal and the particular, articulate together.

Indeed, this figure of the graft echoes Marx's use of another term: *Gliederung*. For instance, the introduction to the *Grundrisse* pays great attention to the relationships among different elements, factors, or instances in social formations:

> It would therefore be unfeasible and wrong to let the economic categories follow one another in the same sequence as that in which they were historically decisive. Their sequence is determined, rather, by their relation to one another in modern bourgeois society, which is precisely the opposite of that which seems to be their natural order or which corresponds to historical development. The point is not the historic position of the economic relations in the succession of different forms of society. Even less is it their sequence "in the idea" (Proudhon) (a muddy notion of historic movement). Rather, their order [*Gliederung*] within modern bourgeois society.[65]

At stake in this passage is the distinction between a historical narrative that describes a sequence of events—say, feudal serfdom is followed by capitalist wage labor—and an analysis that explains the relationships among different elements of contemporary society—say, the relationships between plantation slavery and wage labor. If we try to explain contemporary society from the perspective of a historical narrative—as many political economists did in Marx's day, and as we saw Bernard Bailyn do at the beginning of this chapter—we are tempted to say that slavery, like serfdom, is an atavistic, premodern social relation whose continuing existence in the capitalist era of wage labor is either anomalous or irrelevant, destined to be overcome. On the other hand, from the perspective of the order or structure *(Gliederung)* of these relations within modern bourgeois society, though we might still say that wage labor is a central element, we must also account for the modern relationship of wage labor to slavery. While this passage draws on the former historical narrative, it also emphasizes that the latter form of analysis addresses modern social relations in all their complexity. The historical perspective is reductivist in the sense that it ignores or downplays any elements of contemporary society that belong more properly, according to its narrative, in an earlier historical moment.

However, *Gliederung* does not simply mean "order" or "structure." The root *Glied* can mean "limb," as well as a military "rank" and a mathematical "term," and *gliedern* can mean "to articulate," with all the shades of bodily and discursive meanings carried by the English word I have discussed in this chapter. In fact, *Gliederung* is the very term that Althusser and Balibar, in *Reading Capital*, translate as "articulation," as well as "articulated combination," "arrangement," "structure," "division," "formation," or "order."[66] It is also the term Hall's work appropriates. *Gliederung* thus carries with it the sense of potentially hierarchical relationships among elements that are connected in integrated, constitutive, differential, and material or substantive ways—mutually constitutive, embodied elements. What is more, as a figure of discursive and bodily articulation that also names the articulation of discourses and bodies, *Gliederung* is not entirely separable from the textual and historical contexts to which it might be applied. Thus, it cannot simply be applied to social formations; its role *in* those textual and historical contexts, in their ambiguous connections among language and bodies, must also be interpreted.

The 1828 edition of Noah Webster's *American Dictionary*, which I discussed above, pulls this set of Marxian figures back into early America. The first four definitions of the noun "articulation" read:

ARTICULATION, *n*. In *anatomy*, the joining or juncture of the bones. This is of three kinds: 1st, *diarthrosis*, or a movable connection, including enarthrosis, or the ball and socket joint; arthrodia, which is the same, but more superficial; ginglymus, or hinge-like joint; and trochoid, or the wheel and axle: 2d, *synarthrosis*, immovable connection, as by suture, or junction by serrated margins; harmony, or union by straight margins; and gompho-sis, like a nail driven in a board, as the teeth in their sockets: 3d, *symphysis*, or union by means of another substance; as synchondrosis, union by a cartilage; syssarcosis, union by muscular fibres; synneurosis, union by a tendon; syndesmosis, union by ligaments; and synostosis, union by a bony substance. . . .

2. In *botany*, the connection of the parts of a plant by joints; also the nodes or joints, as in cane and maize. . . .

3. The forming of words; a distinct utterance of syllables and words by the human voice, by means of closing and opening the organs.

4. A consonant; a letter noting a jointing or closing of the organs.[67]

From the ligaments of Jefferson's buried Indian skeletons and the words of his archived Indian languages, to the distinct utterance of Carwin's too-human biloquism and the indistinct tones of the less-than-human Mohock savage, we read a textual and material struggle over the very embodiment of U.S. citizenship. Marx's figure of the graft indexes this struggle, urging us to locate the nodes or joints that connect words and bodies, to be aware of the precise kinds of connection and their tendency to appear natural or organic, to see in apparent harmony the violence of teeth driven into their sockets as nails into a board.

Working in his clothing shop on Beacon Hill, David Walker was regularly responsible for repairing the coats of sailors whose ships had docked in Boston Harbor. As he set out to circulate his *Appeal* in the South, he mailed copies to potentially sympathetic preachers and newspaper editors and arranged for those very sailors to act as clandestine carriers. It has even been suggested that he sewed copies of his *Appeal* into the linings of those coats, hoping to spread his word in a maritime world teaming with radicals and dissidents, misfits and outcasts. Perhaps he hoped that a few copies sewn into the coats of white sea captains would find their way into the hands of house slaves or other black tailors in Providence, Savannah, Liverpool, or Kingston, slaves and tailors who would surely be the first to clean and repair those coats once the captains returned home.[68] In fact, enough copies of his *Appeal* found their way out of Boston to cause a national crisis of sorts. Writes Sean Wilentz,

> Within weeks of being printed, copies of the first edition were discovered circulating among the blacks of Savannah, Georgia. At about the same time, and over succeeding months, authorities seized additional copies in ports of call from Virginia to Louisiana. Legislators in Georgia and Louisiana became so alarmed that they enacted harsh new laws restricting black literacy, including a ban on the distribution of antislavery literature. (Similar legislation narrowly passed the Virginia House of Delegates but expired in the state senate; North Carolina enacted its own versions of the restrictions in the autumn of 1830).[69]

Walker was also denounced by northern journalists for the pamphlet's tone, a tone questioned even by abolitionists Benjamin Lundy and William Lloyd Garrison. The mayor of Savannah and the Governor of Virginia wrote to Boston's mayor, Harrison Gray Otis, requesting Walker's arrest, and rumors reached Boston that a bounty had been offered for Walker. Otis acknowledged his "abhorrence" of Walker's pamphlet, but refused to take legal action against the author.[70] Though Walker produced two more editions of the *Appeal*, his life and work were cut short when he was found dead outside his tailoring shop on June 28, 1830.[71]

As a tailor who labored for wages, Walker's repair work "tailored value," as Marx might have said. As a free black man, however, Walker's race was grafted onto that wage labor. He seems to have acknowledged as much when he addressed his *Appeal* "To The Coloured Citizens Of The World, But In Particular, And Very Expressly, To Those Of The United States Of America." Against the articulation of racial and national particularity with abstract universality, Walker articulates a "coloured" universality, at once taking it for granted—he addresses "Coloured" people as if they were already "Citizens Of The World" and "The United States Of America," though of course strictly speaking they were not—and prophetically uttering it into existence.

Literally sewing his articulations into the value he tailored, Walker's work is more than just a figure for Marx's graft—for the graft is also "just a figure." Walker's work is figurative work in the strongest sense of the term, work that seizes on the discursive and material ambiguity of words and bodies to disarticulate and rearticulate relationships among race, nation, and equality. Walker wrote an appeal—itself overflowing with the cadences of black orality—to transform bodies. The antebellum responses to his utterance—legal prohibitions against embodied speech, extralegal prohibitions against embodied life—offer an echo of the articulatory power that utterance surely had.

Just as the English word articulation ambiguously invokes bodily and discursive figures for linkage and separation, so too are Marx's names for the complex linkages and distinctions among race, nation, and capitalism embodied names: *geronnenem Zustand, Gallerte, Fetischcharakter, phantasmagorische Form, pfropfen, Gliederung*. This tropological movement prompts us to look closely at specific instances of such linkages and distinctions, at textual and historical moments—such as Walker's *Appeal* against the colonization movement—when the formal equality of citizenship is actively articulated with or grafted onto codified racial and national forms. It is to those instances that *The Colonizing Trick* turns.

Flashpoint

"The true picture of the past flits by," writes Walter Benjamin in the fifth of his *Theses on the Philosophy of History*. "The past can be seized only as an image which flashes up *[aufblitzt]* at the instant when it can be recognized and is never seen again." In thesis six, Benjamin continues, "To articulate the past historically *[vergangenes historisch artikulieren]* does not mean to recognize it 'the way it really was.'[72] It means to seize hold of a memory as it flashes up *[aufblitzt]* at a moment of danger."[73] Benjamin pries the figure of articulation loose from its normative meaning here, offering a counterintuitive image of clear or precise historical speech: the flash, literally of lightning *(der Blitz)*. The dangerous, fleeting, elusive, even blinding elements of memory are precisely the qualities of articulate history. Writing this history does not mean passively recognizing a smooth and fixed sequence of events; rather, it means catching glimpses of those flashes, as if they were individual frames of a film running too slowly to be sutured into a moving image.

While *The Colonizing Trick* traces articulations of race, nation, and equality, it is also divided into four chapters that correspond, as I have mentioned, to four historical and textual flashpoints. This figure of the flashpoint has, for me, strong affinities with Benjamin's work of *aufblitzen*. While the English term "flashpoint" is often used to signify the breaking out of chaos, particularly "riots" or "disturbances" by "mobs" or "rogue states" that need to be "extinguished" or "contained" by police or military action, in its strictest sense the term refers to the process of igniting a liquid, of turning a liquid into flame. Here, I interpret such a process less as a breaking out of chaos than as a material transformation with powerful effects. "Flashpoint" in this sense refers to the process by which someone or something emerges or bursts into action or being, not out of nothing but transformed from one form to another; *and*, it refers to the powerful effects of that emergence or transformation. Each chapter of *The Colonizing Trick* focuses on just such a moment of emergence and transformation. Take, for instance, the transformation of the Atlantic, during the eighteenth and early nineteenth centuries, into a racially and nationally codified space in which a restricted notion of equality took on new importance—the subject of chapter 1. Race, nation, and equality are emergent during this period in the sense that they are transformed from relatively fluid concepts in the first two-thirds of the eighteenth century to relatively congealed, coherent, and yet volatile concepts by the middle of the nineteenth century.

Additionally, each of the flashes I have seized upon has been obscured by accepted or fixed narratives of eighteenth- and nineteenth-century America. Consequently, each troubles those accepted narratives. While there is nothing exclusive about these particular flashpoints—there are of course many others—they stand out for a number of reasons. First, they address a constellation of racial formations, offering a comparative picture that resists generalized or binary models of race. Also, each was important in its time but has subsequently suffered scholarly neglect. For instance, historical events such as the rise and fall of black maritime labor or the Caste War in Yucatán have been virtually ignored in Americanist scholarship, as have texts such as Venture Smith's *A Narrative of the Life and Adventures of Venture, a Native of Africa*, William Butterworth's *Three Years Adventures, of a Minor, in England, Africa, The West Indies, South-Carolina and Georgia*, George Henry's *The Life of George Henry*, the anonymously authored *Claims of the Africans*, and U.S.–Mexico War novelettes. Events that have as of late begun to receive some attention, such as the African colonization movement or the U.S.–Mexico War, I put in new contexts, considering colonization's early period before 1830 and the U.S.–Mexico War's intimate connection to the Caste War. Similarly, I consider uncanonical texts written by canonical authors, such as Thomas Jefferson's correspondence and Charles Brockden Brown's unfinished *Memoirs of Carwin, the Biloquist*. Finally, from texts that have drawn the interest of critics, I seek to cull neglected discursive strands, such as mercantilism from Equiano's *Interesting Narrative* or African colonization and, as we saw above, amateur archeology from Thomas Jefferson's *Notes on the State of Virginia*. Indeed, I want to suggest that well-known, early American historical moments and textual archives look quite different from the perspective of these underexamined events, texts, and contexts.

For instance, the U.S.–Mexico War (the subject of chapter 4) has not been as extensively examined as the Civil War in U.S. literary and historical studies, and it is often represented as a trial run or prequel to the Civil War, itself often represented as the most important turning point of the nineteenth century for the United States (hence the pervasive term "antebellum"). Additionally, both wars are all too often exclusively cast as conflicts over slavery and black/white racial formations. To the contrary, the U.S.–Mexico War, as Chicano Studies scholars have long emphasized, was an extremely multifaceted conflict, involving multiple, shifting racial and national formations— Indian, white, black, Mexican, Anglo, Tejano, Californio—and cutting across multiple, emergent national boundaries—the United States, Texas, Mexico, Yucatán, and even Cuba, Spain, France, and England. Attention to these elements of the U.S.–Mexico War repositions both wars in a global context and allows us to consider how they helped to transform multiple, rather than binary, racial formations. What is more, when we represent the U.S.–Mexico War as a run-up to the Civil War, and the Civil War as a victory for emancipation, we lose track of the ways the U.S.–Mexico War actually entrenched U.S. racial formations and enhanced U.S. imperialism, particularly as the U.S.–Mexico War fed into one of the most successful Indian uprisings of the postconquest Americas: the 1847 Caste War. By asking how the entrenchment of racial formations depends upon the enhancement of U.S. imperialism, we can disrupt the nationalist narrative of progress that makes the U.S.–Mexico War and the Civil War one long story of justice won.

Consider another example, one that also hinges on representations of the Civil War. A stark distinction between slavery and freedom tends to divide the nineteenth century into discrete, proslavery and antislavery periods and forces. However, for black sailors on the Atlantic—whom I discuss in chapter 1—the distinction between enslavement and freedom is consistently subordinated to the distinction between land and sea. While of course expressing a desire for freedom, black sailors often downplay the differences between formal emancipation and slavery, and explicitly describe the life of seafaring black slaves as more free than the life of free blacks on land. Similarly, the multifaceted arguments for colonization to which David Walker refers in his *Appeal*—discussed above and again in chapter 2—trouble the slavery/emancipation binary. When forced deportation and resettlement of tens of thousands of blacks looks emancipatory to many early Americans, we have to reconsider the very meaning of "emancipation" by examining the competing kinds of freedom that are being condensed into that capacious concept.

By bringing apparently disparate archives and methods into contact with one another, I also hope to move beyond the all-too-pervasive impasse between the historicist rejection of contemporary continental philosophy or critical theory and the ahistorical application of contemporary theoretical "models" to the colonial and antebellum periods. In this interest, throughout *The Colonizing Trick* I work to read contemporary theoretical texts from the perspective of eighteenth- and nineteenth-century primary material as much as I read the primary material in light of contemporary theoretical texts. It is this practice—exemplified in this chapter by my effort to read articulation as a theoretical figure—that, I hope, works in the spirit of Benjamin's call "to seize hold of memory as it flashes up at a moment of danger."

In fact, Benjamin's call is itself not entirely foreign to early America. During the late eighteenth century, scientific communities on both sides of the North Atlantic found themselves embroiled in a series of debates over the nature and meaning of electricity, debates that reached a flashpoint of sorts in a dispute between Benjamin Franklin and Benjamin Wilson, ultimately arbitrated by King George III, over the proper shape of the lightning rod. As Trent A. Mitchell has shown so well, this dispute involved more than the scientific validity of Franklin's pointed rods and Wilson's blunt rods: "These debates were resolved not when it was recognized that one theory or method was inherently superior to the others, but when one of the opposing factions persuaded a larger or more politically influential audience to support its agenda . . . the entire debate was shaped as much, if not more by a contest over control of the social and physical spaces where the issue should be resolved, as by the purely scientific issues at hand."[74] The debate epitomized the political stakes of Enlightenment knowledge, for both Franklin and Wilson shared the claim that lightning was a form of electricity, and thus threatened to overturn the prevailing understanding of lightning as an instrument of Divine Providence. But it also set Franklin, the American colonial, against the ultimately victorious Wilson, who had connections with King George's court, at the very moment Anglo-American tensions were reaching a boiling point.

The political import of this seemingly objective debate, though easily cropped out by the positivistic framework of much of today's scientific and historical discourse, was clear to late eighteenth-century observers. Wrote one: "Thus with many, the opinions of a philosopher as to the *blunts*, and the *points*, were regarded as the index of his opinions as to the American war." Snickered another: "While you Great George, for knowledge hunt,/ And sharp conductors change for blunt,/ The nation's out of joint:/ Franklin a wiser course pursues,/ And all your thunder useless views,/ By keeping to the point."[75] Thus the lightning rod debate became part of a struggle over the proper articulation of a "nation out of joint." To read this debate as a flashpoint for struggles over power and politics, as most people seem to have done in the eighteenth century, I want to suggest, is to articulate the past historically by seizing hold of memory as it flashes up *[aufblitzt]* at a moment of danger.

The Colonizing Trick begins, then, on the eighteenth-century Atlantic, in ships and ports that have only recently become objects of careful study. In chapter 1, I show how early U.S. mercantilism was not simply an economic policy designed to increase the productive efficiency of the national economy. Rather, mercantilist policies were part of a more extensive discursive practice that articulated the formal equality of capitalist exchange with racial and national codification. Eventually, this mercantilist discursive practice also reformulated black masculinity and femininity by pushing black men into feminized seaside labor. I make this case through historically contextualized readings of the personal narratives of such North Atlantic sailors as Olaudah Equiano, Venture Smith, John Jea, William Butterworth, and John Willock. These texts tie the historical rise and decline of black sailors between 1720 and 1850 to what can be called, drawing on Marx, the steady, mercantilist *enclosure* of the North Atlantic.

The most important avenue of employment for North American black men during the eighteenth century, the merchant marine trade became increasingly inhospitable to black mariners during the nineteenth century. The texts I examine represent the desires and efforts of black mariners to become financially independent from and socially equal to white mariners. However, they also indicate that such desires and efforts were persistently dashed, as white mariners and merchants increasingly robbed and cheated black mariners, justifying this unequal treatment by appealing to the very codified, racial, and national forms found in the political-economic discourse of the period. I thus show how mercantilism—understood as a discursive practice that took both governmental and quotidian forms—transformed the late eighteenth- and early nineteenth-century North Atlantic by simultaneously consolidating national economies, entrenching the codification of racial and national identity among North Atlantic subjects, and facilitating the emergence of formal and abstract equality among white U.S. citizens.

Finally, I trace the rise of a discourse of providership among black sailors to the nineteenth-century feminization of black sea labor that accompanied the decline in black seamanship. The eighteenth-century rise of black sailors had enabled and been aided by the labor of black women in coastal regions and ports, as extensive, cross-gender economic alliances were forged in black communities. As mercantilist discursive practices equated economic productivity with fixed nationality and whiteness, noncitizen black sailors were increasingly restricted to the few, feminized shipboard berths, primarily stewards and cooks. By the mid-nineteenth century, this transformation emerges in the personal narratives of some black sailors as an anxious attachment to gender hierarchy within black family units. That is, some black sailors countered the feminization of their labor by hyperbolizing its masculinity and, consequently, de-emphasizing the socioeconomic role of black women. Thus the enclosure of North Atlantic maritime labor within a racially and nationally codified, formal equality also restructured black masculinity and femininity in the Atlantic zone.

In chapter 2, I consider how late eighteenth- and early nineteenth-century proposals to colonize black Americans paradoxically came to be valued as the completion of the American Revolution's emancipatory promise of universal equality. I examine the published writings and private correspondence of Thomas Jefferson on colonization, as well as black American critiques of colonization by Phillis Wheatley, David Walker, and Maria Stewart.

As I suggested earlier, black critics of colonization such as Walker argue that colonization proposals are particularly dangerous when they produce a precise and rhetorically powerful vision of equality articulated with racial and national hierarchies. Drawing on these critics, I trace this emancipationist strand of colonization discourse to Jefferson, who, faced with the incomplete arrival of freedom in the United States due to the persistence of slavery, renders a distinctly American freedom by means of a technical, governmental logic. That is, Jefferson argues that a successfully executed policy of calculating the number of black Americans in the United States, paying for the emancipation of those held in slavery, and funding the exportation and resettlement of all black Americans outside the territorial boundaries of the United States would emancipate all Americans from slavery and realize equality in its most universal sense. In Jefferson, I argue, colonization paradoxically both creates and responds to the racial and national calculability of populations subject to governance. Paying particular attention to Jefferson's interest in a continuing, neocolonial relationship between the United States and the new, black American state in Africa, I stress colonization's dual, interrelated roles: the racial purification of a domestic space and the exercise of imperial power over a foreign space. By reading Michel Foucault's work on the Enlightenment problematic of government with Jeffersonian colonization discourse, I locate a racial governmentality that animates Jeffersonian liberalism. This chapter's turn to Foucault shows how Marx and Foucault are less dissonant than is often assumed shows, in particular, how governmentality illuminates crucial aspects of the value-form's racial graft.

In turn, I consider how black American critiques of colonization work to articulate alternative relationships among equality, race, and nation. Prophesied by Phillis Wheatley in the 1770s, these critiques in the 1820s and 1830s not only acknowledged the power of Jefferson's precise vision of equality articulated with racial and national hierarchies. They also produce a black enlightenment or appositional discourse at once in response to and at odds with Jeffersonian colonization.[76] By interrogating the articulation of race, nation, and equality, this black enlightenment discourse works to disrupt Jeffersonian colonization with what might be called (to borrow a phrase from Alys Weinbaum and Brent Edwards) a critical, black globality.

In chapter 3, I reevaluate Brown's role as a founder of American literature by placing his prose writings and *Memoirs of Carwin, the Biloquist* within the emergence of a self-conscious movement for a national culture between the 1790s and 1810s. I show how the central figures of *Memoirs of Carwin*—the echo of a "Mohock savage" and Carwin's imitation, incorporation, and mastery of that echo as "biloquism" or ventriloquism—allegorize the emergence of national citizenship from the ritualistic assimilation of the "Mohock savage." It is this allegory, I suggest, that formulates the terms of the two-century-long debate among literary critics over whether Brown was a critic or a defender of modernization. I develop this reading of an emerging American aesthetic by locating an intertextual relationship between *Memoirs of Carwin* and Immanuel Kant's *Critique of Judgement*. Both Brown and Kant allegorize the emergence of a subject capable of modern, aesthetic judgment from an ambivalently assimilated autochthon—in both cases, the figure of the Iroquois. I thereby place Brown within a wider, Enlightenment discourse on colonialism and aesthetics.

In turn, I place Brown's work within a wider set of U.S. discursive practices that aestheticized and assimilated Iroquoian cultures and communities. As an answer to the call of U.S. cultural elites to produce American cultural forms not derived from Europe, Brown's aesthetic incorporation of the "Mohock savage" was buttressed by contemporaneous movements in the developing spheres of ethnography, archeology, and government policy. Ethnographic theories of "redness" as a racial form that could "become white," as opposed to unchangeable and inassimilable "blackness," proliferated at the end of the eighteenth century, as did archeological interest in Native American cultures in general and Iroquois cultures in particular. In addition, during this period the U.S. government was pursuing a policy of "civilization," directed in particular at the Iroquois Confederation, involving education policy, land policy, and the Trade and Intercourse Acts.

In *Memoirs of Carwin*, the volatile energies of modernization eventually take the form of an array of fears—about immigration, Catholicism, Jacobinism, Illuminatism, Masonry, mass political action, and fraternal desire—all of which allegorically derive from white settler colonialism's "unfinished business": the incomplete assimilation and mastery of the Indian. That is, the incomplete task of Indian assimilation haunts Brown's America, manifesting itself as a series of threats from inassimilable others. By situating Brown's literary work within these aesthetic, anthropological, and governmental discursive practices, I trace the emergence of a self-conscious national culture to a Brownian refiguring of America's white settler colonial foundations.

In chapter 4, I examine the discursive and material linkages between two mid-nineteenth-century wars. With the U.S.–Mexico War winding down, and the U.S.

military occupying Mexico City, Yucatecan Creoles called on U.S. President Polk to rescue them from a massive Maya uprising and, possibly, to annex the entire Yucatán peninsula. Though the U.S. Congress hesitated to authorize annexation, it nonetheless acquiesced to informal aid for the Creoles. At war with central Mexico, the United States thus found itself in an ambivalent alliance with southern Mexican Creoles in their war against an oppressed indigenous majority—an alliance that provoked much debate and anxiety in the United States over the racial and national form of U.S. citizenship. It is this ambivalent alliance, and its subsequent effects on pan-American racial and national formations, that I consider in chapter 4.

I begin with a governmental archive that includes congressional debates over the "Bill for the Relief of Yucatán," letters between U.S. and Yucatecan military and political officials, and President Polk's efforts to make Yucatán a U.S. protectorate. Though the Creoles represent themselves as white citizens, they are represented in the United States as Indians embracing civilization while the Maya and the central Mexican authorities are represented as barbarous Indians waging war on civilization. This indianization of the Mexican differs markedly from the racial formations circulating in nineteenth-century Mexico as *mestizaje*. However, at the historical moment when the U.S.–Mexico War feeds into the Caste War, these two very different, national traditions of racial formation briefly articulate, allowing Yucatecan elites to pursue a race war against the Maya and the United States to extend Manifest Destiny to the south.

As one of the first wars to be mass mediated while it was happening, the U.S.–Mexico War was avidly and popularly consumed in the United States. In particular, the proliferation of novelettes about the war by such authors as Harry Halyard, Harry Hazel, and Charles Averill gave most Americans, including soldiers, their first, comprehensive "interaction" with Mexicans, Texans, Tejanos, and Californios. By iterating and reiterating a remarkably consistent codification of identities, this early culture industry forged racial, national, and gendered borders that effectively reinvented "Mexico" and "America" for a mass readership in the United States. Most strikingly, the novelettes, like the government documents, give Mexicans a distinctly Indian racial form by ritually distinguishing between inassimilable black Americans, on one hand, and Indians or Mexicans who "choose" between barbarity and civility, on the other hand. The novelettes thus leave open the possibility of Mexicans becoming American through assimilation to whiteness. I argue that this popular fiction cannot be considered simply an artifact of U.S. popular culture and domestic racial ideology, nor can the U.S.–Mexico War it thematizes be considered simply a border war. Rather, these novelettes allegorize pan-American transformations in racial, national, and class formations, transformations that stretch deep into the Yucatán.

In the final section of the chapter, by setting the Treaty of Guadalupe Hidalgo's promise of "all the rights of citizens" to Mexican Americans within this historical and discursive context, I show how that promise entails specific, racial and national obligations. The treaty effectively conditions those rights on the assimilation of Mexican Americans, the production of a comprador class in Mexico, and the eradication of

Indians throughout North America. This is most vividly dramatized by the fact that, at the moment the ink was drying on the treaty, U.S. citizens were obliged to participate with Mexican elites in a race war against Mayans who themselves were fighting for other, more capacious forms of equality. I thus locate the constitutive, historical, and textual limitations of the treaty's promise of equality. My epilogue extends this neocolonial resolution of the U.S.–Mexico War into the future of U.S. imperialism by examining U.S. political economist Henry Charles Carey's 1847 text *The Past, The Present, and The Future*. A text that at once invokes all the flashpoints I consider in *The Colonizing Trick* and theorizes their implications for the future of the United States, *The Past, The Present, and The Future*, as well as Marx's own inability to generate a critical interpretation of Carey, show how U.S. power would flow out of eighteenth- and early nineteenth-century national culture and imperial citizenship.

Taken together, the four flashpoints I examine depict early America as a white settler colony whose domestic scene is constitutively related to the global because of its deep integration in geopolitical systems such as trans-Atlantic labor flows, Euro-American political economy, imperial ventures in North America and Africa, pan-American racial formations, and North American transnational capital. Understood in this sense, early America no longer makes sense within the exceptionalist paradigms that have so persistently plagued U.S. literary and historical studies. For instance, we will see that the United States did not emerge on the world scene as an imperial power at the end of the nineteenth century, as is often claimed. Rather, even before its formal foundation as a nation-state, the imperial form of "America" was explicitly taking shape. It is in this sense, I suggest, that the United States can be thought within colonial discourse studies and postcolonial theory and not, as has been proposed in U.S. literary studies, by simply equating the postrevolutionary United States with the decolonized Latin American states of the nineteenth century or the decolonized "third world" of the twentieth century.[77]

Finally, I offer *The Colonizing Trick* not so much as a truer narrative of the way America really was, to paraphrase the Benjamin passage with which I began this section. Indeed, Benjamin suggests that such a process is relentlessly sad, a process doomed to failure: "The nature of this sadness stands out more clearly if one asks with whom the adherents of historicism actually empathize. The answer is inevitable: with the victor. And all rulers are the heirs of those who conquered before them. Hence, empathy with the victor invariably benefits the rulers."[78] Rather, I hope to seize upon flashpoints that shed light, or at least some sparks, on images of today, images of race, nation, and equality whose place in the narrative of "America" might seem to be fixed eternally, but are in a state of flux, transformation, and struggle to which the following pages bear witness.

CHAPTER 1

Racial Capitalism: Mercantile Exchanges and Mercantilist Enclosures

> After I had been sailing for some time with [Capt. Thomas Farmer], I at length endeavoured to try my luck and commence merchant. . . . Thus was I going all about the islands upwards of four years, and ever trading as I went, during which I experienced many instances of ill usage, and have seen many injuries done to other negroes in our dealings with whites.
>
> *The Interesting Narrative of the Life of Olaudah Equiano,*
> *or Gustavus Vassa, the African*

> I take the liberty, Mr. Chairman, at this early stage of the business, to introduce to the committee a subject . . . that requires our first attention, and our united exertions. No Gentleman here can be unacquainted with . . . the impotency which prevented the late Congress of the United States from carrying into effect the dictates of gratitude and policy. The union, by the establishment of a more effective government, having recovered from the state of imbecility that heretofore prevented a performance of its duty, ought, in its first act, to revive those principles of honor and honesty that have too long lain dormant. The deficiency in our Treasury has been too notorious to make it necessary for me to animadvert upon that subject. Let us content ourselves with endeavouring to remedy the evil. To do this a national revenue must be obtained; but the system must be such a one, that, while it secures the object of revenue, it shall not be oppressive to our constituents. Happy is it for us that such a system is within our power; for I apprehend that both these objects may be obtained from an impost on articles imported into the United States.
>
> James Madison, Annals of Congress, *106–7*[1]

*O*n July 4, 1789, four months into its first session, the newly established U.S. Congress celebrated thirteen years of formal independence by passing its first tariff bill. The bill placed duties of 5 to 15 percent on approximately thirty different goods, ranging from nails to carriages, with the highest rates reserved for "articles of luxury."[2] When James Madison proposed this "endeavour" with the first nonprocedural words uttered in the new Congress, quoted above, he called the representatives' "first attention" and "united exertions" to a national economic policy, offering the tariff as a way "to remedy the evil" of a nearly bankrupt treasury.[3] Concurring with Madison on the floor of the House, Massachusetts Representative Fisher Ames took up the call: "Good policy and sound wisdom demonstrate the propriety of an interchange between the different States of the Union: to procure this political good, some force was necessary. Laying a small duty upon foreign manufactures must induce . . . one fellow citizen to barter with, or buy of another, what he had long been accustomed to take from strangers."[4] Just two years later, in his *Report on Manufactures*, Alexander Hamilton developed this argument for a tariff even further by calling for a comprehensive mercantilist system of state-sponsored, national economic development to include not only tariffs, but also other import restraints, export subsidies, substantial investment in the national infrastructure, and legal and monetary support for key domestic industries.

Yet the congressional tariff debate and Hamilton's *Report* suggest that such mercantilist policies promised to do more than fill the treasury. Madison, Ames, and Hamilton offer a formula for the creation of a precise logic of equality that would take the political form of citizenship—the very logic and form that Marx, as we saw in the previous chapter, calls the value form. They suggest that policies such as the Tariff of 1789 will help to transform the diverse and famously antagonistic "constituents" of the early United States into "fellow citizens" because these "constituents" will be forced to exchange commodities with one another. Just as the differences between commodities are suspended when they enter the market and are exchanged, so too will the "constituents" enter the market, leave their differences and antagonisms behind, encounter each other equally as fellow exchangers, and be united. These subjects will recognize their full fellowship as citizens once they have been recognized in state policy and by each other as exchangers rationally abstracted from their differences and antagonisms and represented as formally equivalent units of a population engaging in lively economic exchange. In the words of Ames and Madison, the tariff will help "force" that rational abstraction and "induce" that equivalence, thereby "reviving" the very "potency" and "union" of the nation.[5]

However, the citizenship Madison, Ames, and Hamilton envision is not just a formal and abstract equality. In the congressional debate and Hamilton's *Report*, this formal and abstract equality is rhetorically supplemented by a series of precisely articulated particularities. For instance, by differentiating U.S. economic subjects from what Ames calls "foreign" or "strange" economic subjects, the tariff will not only "force" the "constituents" to leave their particularities behind and gain abstract equality; paradoxically, it will also give that equality a particular, national form. That is, since the "constituents'" encounters with "fellow" American exchangers will increase as their encounters with "foreign" or "strange" exchangers decrease, this equality will become "American."

What is more, the national equality these statesmen have in mind is not just a domestic affair. As Pennsylvania Representative Thomas Fitzsimons, another Madison ally, argued to Congress during the tariff debate:

> The merchants of this country have . . . succeeded in discovering one [channel] that bids
> fair to increase our national importance and prosperity, while at the same time it is lucra-
> tive to the persons engaged in its prosecution. I mean, sir, the trade to China and the East
> Indies. I have no doubt but what it will receive the encouragement of the general gov-
> ernment for some time to come. There is scarcely any direct intercourse of this nature,
> but what requires some assistance in the beginning: it is peculiarly necessary in our case,
> from the jealousy subsisting in Europe of this infant branch of our commerce.[6]

According to Fitzsimons, the tariff will provide funds to subsidize U.S. merchants in their newly enjoined battle with European merchants over the profits generated by access to colonial markets. Eventually, it will put the United States on par with, and thus make it at least formally equal to, the European imperial powers, realizing the full potency of the nation. Thus, the national union of fellow citizens depends not simply on the domestic economy; nationality and fellowship themselves depend upon the development of U.S. imperial power.

Madison also registers the gendered form of the equality his fellow legislators have in mind by saturating his call for a national tariff in a discourse of masculine power, authority, and rationality: the "impotency," "deficiency," and "imbecility" of the nation must be addressed by the "power" of male legislators elected by restricted male suffrage. The citizens they sought to "force" out of the tariff were not only men by law; women, of course, had not yet gained full citizenship rights. These citizens were also forged in Anglo-American discursive practices that figured rationality and national potency as masculinity.[7]

In addition, as Hamilton's *Report* makes clear, the mercantilist equalization of American citizens need not disrupt racial slavery: "Ideas of a contrariety of interests between the northern and southern regions of the Union are in the main as unfounded as they are mischievous. . . . Mutual wants constitute one of the strongest links of political connection; and the extent of these bears a natural proportion to the diversity in the means of mutual supply. Suggestions of an opposite complexion are ever to be deplored as unfriendly to the steady pursuit of one great common cause and to the perfect harmony of all parts."[8] Arguing against those who would "mischievously" criticize the southern plantation system as inconsistent with the wage-labor system of the north, Hamilton offers a way to unite both systems in a perfectly harmonious common cause—indeed, in a singular "complexion." His economic system implicitly promises to realize this common cause by producing citizens whose unity depends upon racial slavery.

As a systematic elaboration of the mercantilist positions of political leaders such as Madison, Fitzsimons, and Ames, Hamilton's *Report* figures the emerging nation as an articulated combination, a "perfect harmony of parts" each joined by "the strongest links of political connection." A state program that would turn "diversity in the means of mutual supply" into "mutual wants," the *Report's* mercantilism envisions a grafting of differences, a fusing of diverse constituents, economies, and interests that, though initially forced, would eventually and paradoxically become naturally harmonious. As we have seen, that harmonious equality is decidedly not just universal or abstract, however. Articulated on the floor of the House in 1789 and again in Hamilton's 1791 *Report*, it is deeply material, fleshed out by particular racial, national, and gender forms.

On August 1, 1789, less than one month after the passage of the Tariff of 1789, Olaudah Equiano published *The Interesting Narrative of the Life of Olaudah Equiano, or Gustavus Vassa, the African* in London. An account of his life from his birth in West Africa in 1745 to his experiences of capture, middle passage, slave labor, manumission, "free" labor, and antislavery agitation, the *Narrative* traces Equiano's attempts to tie fragments of his African past to the Euro–U.S. present forced upon him, and thereby to constitute a new identity. Yet each of those attempts proves fleeting, for each persistently threatens to collapse, to recoil on him and recode him as slave, as raced property. Persistently transgressing fixed institutional identities, Equiano just as persistently finds the space of transgression an unfixed and unstable one, a space occupiable for only a brief moment, if at all. Of these attempts one of the most important, given the tenacity with which Equiano pursues it, is his engagement in the trans-atlantic merchant marine trade. As he puts it in the passage in the opening epigraph, "I at length endeavoured to try my luck and commence merchant."[9]

Equiano's "endeavour" is not unique. During the eighteenth century, black men from North America took to the mobile and ambiguously national space of the North Atlantic in striking numbers, finding seafaring industries much less saturated by the legal and extralegal racism that was becoming increasingly prevalent on shore. Whether free or enslaved, these black mariners supplemented their strenuous maritime labor and paltry wages with "perquisites" and "ventures"—modest, for-profit trades of what goods they could accumulate on their own with other traders in ports and ships throughout the Atlantic. Though black women rarely shipped out, they did find shore work more readily available in coastal cities, and so formed extensive social, political, and economic units with black men in the orbit of sea ports.[10] This eighteenth-century rise of black men employed in seafaring industries is not only expressed in maritime records of the period.[11] It is also insistently expressed by black Atlantic literature, as nearly every black narrative written during this period plots labor on the deep sea or coastal waters.[12]

However, like many other black men who entered or were forced to enter the merchant marine trade in the late eighteenth and early nineteenth centuries, Equiano encountered an increasingly hostile terrain, signified by the "many instances of ill usage" and "injuries done to other negroes in our dealings with whites" he mentions in the epigraph. By the turn of the nineteenth century, such "instances" and "injuries" become central features of black mariner narratives, suggesting that racial codification and exploitation had begun to spill into the North Atlantic, making black mariners increasingly disillusioned with the sea. Indeed, even more quickly than their numbers had risen in the eighteenth century, black mariners abandon the North Atlantic and seafaring industries in the nineteenth century.[13]

The 1789 conjuncture of these two "endeavours"—the first U.S. tariff and Equiano's mercantile labor—opens a window to a critical genealogy of the rise and decline of black mariners during a period when modern discursive practices of race, nation, equality, and gender were just beginning to congeal. Indeed, as I will argue in this chapter, the racially particularized, gendered, imperial nationalism glimpsed in the 1789 tariff debate and Hamilton's *Report* is constitutively related both to the mercantile ventures of black mariners and to the "instances of ill usage" and "injuries" in their "dealings with whites" mentioned by Equiano. The very particularized tendencies of terrestrial capitalism that pushed black men to the sea in the eighteenth century eventually enclosed the North Atlantic itself, pushing black men off the sea in the nineteenth century.

In the increasingly frequent "instances of ill usage" and "injuries" of black mariners on the North Atlantic, we can locate quotidian traces of the constitutive relationship between racial, national, and gender codification and formal, abstract equality glimpsed in the 1789 tariff debate and Hamilton's *Report*. Rather than simply being excluded from this capitalist calculation of "freedom," black merchant mariners came to be ritually invoked as the limit of that logic, giving equality a racial-national coherence that would, by the mid-nineteenth century, take a precisely gendered form. Neither an aberration from, nor a contradiction of, the formal and abstract equality that animates modern citizenship under capitalism, hierarchically codified identities actually sustained that very equality. Consequently, we need to understand mercantilism not simply as an economic policy, but rather as a set of discursive practices that articulated formal and abstract equality with the codification of race, nation, and gender in the North Atlantic during the late eighteenth and early nineteenth centuries. Certainly, as we will see in this chapter, black mariners do sometimes deploy the practices of mercantile capitalism sufficiently to buy or to maintain their freedom from slavery and to become relatively socially and financially secure. Yet we will also see that black mariners are increasingly, systematically, and ritually barred from the formal and abstract equality of mercantile capitalism by mercantilist discursive practices.

I begin with an account of mercantilism's role in the formation of racial nations in the eighteenth- and early nineteenth-century North Atlantic zone. I then consider how mercantilist discursive practices transformed the quotidian world of Atlantic ships and ports by examining the personal narratives of sailors from the period. Finally, I offer an interpretation of this quotidian, mercantilist transformation by culling from Marx's critique of "so-called primitive accumulation," and in particular his account of the English enclosure movement, a rich morphology of formal equality's articulation with modern, particularistic discursive practices.

On Mercantilism and Racial Nations

Tariffs had been an important part of the economic policy of many of the states united under the Articles of Confederation, and before that they had been part of the economic policy of the British American colonies.[14] As such, they were just one manifestation of an extensive system of economic nationalism known as "mercantilism." But what was mercantilism in eighteenth- and nineteenth-century North America? Let us start with a somewhat traditional economic and historical answer to this question. Beginning in the sixteenth century, in order to unify and increase political power and monetary wealth within their dominions, the European powers forged varying degrees of centralized governmental regulation of territorially specific economies. This regulation was achieved through policies designed to accumulate bullion, to effect a favorable balance of trade, to develop a diversified and more or less self-sufficient balance of agriculture and manufacture, or simply to manage a range of economic crises. Examples of such policies include protectionist measures such as tariffs, other import restraints, preferential treaties, and monopolies for joint-stock or chartered companies, as well as encouragement measures, including export subsidies such as bounties, drawbacks, and state-funded infrastructural development. These policies make up the extensive systems of economic nationalism now widely called "mercantilism."[15]

As the white settler colonization of the Americas accelerated in the eighteenth century, merchant capital flooded into North America along channels of commerce carved by a complex British mercantilist structure. Writes Richard B. Sheridan, summarizing the vast historical research on British American colonial economies:

> One stereotypical view of early American history is that the colonists revolted against political and economic tyranny imposed by the British government with the goals of establishing a small property-owning democracy and a system of competitive enterprise free from intervention by government. Countering this laissez-faire myth is the view that within their restricted sphere of influence, colonial governments sought to control, regulate, restrain, and stimulate activity and thus to guide economic and social development. Colonial governments responded to popular demand by establishing public markets and regulating the price of country produce entering towns and cities. They enacted laws to fix wages in certain occupations; to license such quasi-public functionaries as porters, draymen, millers, smiths, and gravediggers; to fix wharfage and storage rates and fares on ferries; to set prices on bread and other basic commodities. . . . [C]olonial authorities laid down standards of quality and measure for commodities and certain manufactured goods. Moreover, able-bodied males were required to work a certain number of days in the year on . . . public-works projects. . . . By means of compulsory or statute labor and tax revenues, Indian trails and bridle paths were upgraded to wagon roads that served as arteries of migration and trade . . . In sum, political establishments sought to foster development.[16]

After U.S. independence, and despite the complaints of U.S. revolutionaries in the Declaration of Independence about Britain's oppressive mercantile system, merchant capital expanded in North America as an effect of U.S. mercantilism.[17] The *Annals* of the first U.S. Congress and Hamilton's 1791 *Report* testify to the initially moderate U.S. mercantilist policies that began with the Tariff of 1789 and then steadily expanded, especially after the end of the War of 1812.[18] Marshaled first to hold the North American colonies in the economic orbit of Britain, the very same mercantilist policies, with minor alterations, were by the late eighteenth century marshaled to structure a North American orbit of its own. Global economic expansions, upturns, and downturns thus took the particular "shapes" of imperial nation (Britain), white settler colony (British North America), and emerging imperial nation (United States), in part through remarkably similar mercantilist policies instituted and controlled by changing political centers. The United States was not simply founded by a community of enterprising merchants; U.S. "enterprise" was founded and sustained by a concerted, state-sponsored, mercantilist management of merchant capital.[19]

This mercantilist production of U.S. "enterprise" can also be set within the more global context of the emergence of historical capitalism. There is a strong case to be made that mercantilist policies have been a necessary (though not sufficient) historical condition for the rapid development of capitalist productive efficiency. As Giovanni Arrighi, Fernand Braudel, and Immanuel Wallerstein have shown, the seventeenth and eighteenth centuries saw the European powers begin to prioritize the development of their own territorially specific economies through a range of policies—including protectionism and encouragement—that enabled the emergence of the national bourgeoisie and the nation-states. As Arrighi explains:

> The central aspect of this tendency was the strengthening of "forward and backward linkages," in Albert Hirschman's (1958) sense, between the consumers and the producers of a given territorial domain—a strengthening which involved not just the establishment of intermediate (mainly "manufacturing") activities linking domestic primary production to domestic final consumption, but also the forcible "delinking" of producers and consumers from relationships of dependence on foreign (primarily Dutch) purchases and sales.[20]

Indeed, Arrighi continues, such mercantilist policies were crucial steps on the road to global hegemony: "In order to catch up with and overtake the early comers, the late-comers had radically to restructure the political geography of world commerce. This is precisely what was achieved by the new synthesis of capitalism and territorialism brought into being by French and British mercantilism in the eighteenth century." A set of policies can be called "mercantilist," on these accounts, because it nationalizes an economy by strengthening the state so that it can enforce a temporary delinking from sparsely regulated international trade and a concomitant expansion and diversification of agriculture and manufacture within a territorially discrete space.[21]

According to Wallerstein, since the seventeenth-century economic slowdown and consolidation of the European world-economy, every core state that has unilaterally embraced "freedom of trade" (either more or less in fact or merely in name) had first consolidated its hegemony by means of "state policies of economic nationalism . . . [which] revolved around a concern with the circulation of commodities, whether in terms of the movement of bullion or in the creation of balances of trade (bilateral or multilateral)."[22] First the Dutch and then the British successfully pursued policies whose "*middle*-run objective . . . was the increase of overall efficiency in the sphere of production."[23] These policies sought "market superiority in agro-industrial productive efficiency lead[ing] to dominance of the spheres of commercial distribution of world trade, with correlative profits accruing both from being the entrepot of much of world trade and from controlling the 'invisibles'—transport, communications, and insurance. Commercial primacy [led] in turn to control of the financial sectors of banking (exchange, deposit, and credit) and of investment (direct and portfolio)."[24]

The United States followed suit by pursuing the very same, imperial-nationalist policies after its independence, as William Earl Weeks suggests in his study of colonial America and the nineteenth-century United States.[25] Weeks shows how governmental "neo-mercantilist policy" from the 1790s to at least 1861, particularly in the maritime sector, helped to forge discursive and material links among colonial and national union, collective security, and economic expansion.[26] He thus insists that "the home market cannot be understood apart from its international context . . . the development of the nation cannot be understood apart from the development of the empire."[27] Mercantilist policies, though they may have been advocated for different and contradictory reasons, have thus facilitated the successive rise of the United Provinces, Britain, and the United States to hegemonic status in the capitalist world system.[28]

However, in "The Nation Form: History and Ideology" Étienne Balibar helps us to think of mercantilism as more than just a technical set of state policies. Noting that "*non-national* state apparatuses aiming at quite other (for example, dynastic) objectives have progressively produced the elements of the nation-state or, if one prefers, they have been involuntarily 'nationalized' and have begun to nationalize society." Balibar argues that "it is quite impossible to 'deduce' the nation form from capitalist relations of production," for "in the history of capitalism, state forms other than the national have emerged and have for a time competed with it before finally being repressed or instrumentalized." It is only the immense power of nineteenth-century, Euro–U.S. nationalist historiographies that has taught us to perform such a deduction by rote, to see in every nonnational social formation a "pre-national formation." Rather, Balibar continues, there was not "a single inherently 'bourgeois' political form, but several"— the seventeenth-century Dutch United Provinces being one crucial example. "The nascent capitalist bourgeoisie seems to have 'hesitated,'" Balibar writes, "between several forms of hegemony. Or let us rather say that there existed different bourgeoisies, each connected to different sectors of exploitation of the resources of the world-economy. If the 'national bourgeoisie' finally won out, even before the industrial revolution," we need to examine more closely the discursive practices that worked to transform "social formations into national formations." Indeed, Balibar lists mercantilism as one such discursive practice.[29] For Balibar, then, capitalism emerged and even thrived under a variety of political forms. To understand how the nation form became the dominant political form for capitalism, we must investigate the discursive practices—such as mercantilism—that articulated capitalism with nationalism.[30]

In this sense, mercantilism can be thought of as discursive practice that gave a *national* shape to merchant capital at the beginnings of historical capitalism. As merchant capital flowed into the Atlantic theater after the sixteenth century, European mercantilist measures emerged almost immediately to regulate and direct that flow. The U.S. Tariff of 1789 was simply the first such measure enacted by the Congress of this new territorial dominion known as the United States in response to the more recent flow of merchant capital into the North American theater in the late eighteenth century.

As I argue in the introduction, the modern nation form is also supplemented by racial formations. Indeed, as we saw at the beginning of this chapter, Hamilton's *Report on Manufactures* linked national economic development to the amelioration of North-South tensions without challenging racial slavery. We thus should not be surprised that as mercantilist regulations began to enclose the North Atlantic within nationally particularized zones, the institutionalization of race within U.S. seafaring industries proceeded apace. The protectionist strains of U.S. mercantilism placed tight restrictions on trade by noncitizens, and since blacks were denied full citizenship, protectionism systematically nationalized and racialized economic activity.[31] For instance, in 1796, the U.S. government began requiring that mariners carry Seaman's Protection Certificates attesting to their national citizenship. Black sailors, however, were often either denied these papers altogether or denied whatever meager protections they provided. Relatedly, the U.S. Navy stopped enlisting blacks in 1799. Perhaps most devastatingly, the Negro Seamen Acts, which began in South Carolina in 1822 and quickly spread to all the other southern states, required that black sailors be imprisoned while their ships docked in southern ports.[32] One historian has estimated that at least 10,000 black sailors were incarcerated under these acts.[33] In addition, agents in ports who hired seamen became powerful middlemen in the 1820s and 1830s and institutionalized "white first" hiring in the U.S. maritime industry.[34] Also after the 1820s, legal restrictions on black ownership of and command over maritime vessels intensified, ending the rare success stories of merchant mariner families such as the Cuffes, the Fortens, and the Wainers and precluding future black upward mobility within this sector.[35] Finally, as the maritime job sector tightened for black men in the early nineteenth century, feminized, service-oriented positions such as stewards and cooks became increasingly necessary to black sailors, and the relative increase in wages for those berths between 1820 and 1850 even made them increasingly desirable.[36] As we will see later in this chapter, black mariners responded by masculinizing their role on shore as providers.

The personal narratives of sailors who labored and traded in ships and ports throughout the North Atlantic, to which I will now turn, offer a quotidian and often critical lens on this interdependent, historical articulation of formal equality with race, nation, and gender. The narratives I will discuss in the rest of this chapter are not the most overtly radical texts of the period, such as Quobna Ottobah Cugoano's *Thoughts and Sentiments on the Evil of Slavery* or Robert Wedderburn's political treatises.[37] Rather, they are texts of subjection, texts that vividly perform the paradoxical simultaneity of the subordination by power and the creation of subjectivity.[38] Taken up in the crosscurrents of emerging, particularistic discursive practices and capitalist egalitarianism, these texts are ambivalent, agonistic and rarely simply "resistive" or "accomodationist."

Uncommon Sufferings, Common Sufferings

W. Jeffrey Bolster's important 1997 study *Black Jacks: African American Seamen in the Age of Sail* documents both the rise and the decline of black sailors during the eighteenth and nineteenth centuries, linking this transformation to the emergence and eventual erosion of cross-racial solidarity among common seamen. Yet a close reading of his characterization of this linkage raises some difficult questions. Writes Bolster at the beginning of his text, "Moral complacency and the desire for privilege led whites to *incorporate* race into the social structure of the early modern Atlantic world. White colonial culture *superimposed* racial meanings on a form of labor organization that need not have been racial" (my italics).[39] White sailors and merchants, he reiterates later in the text, "unconsciously developed new assumptions about blacks," since "The widespread conviction of equality among white men in antebellum America *rested in part on* a sense of superiority to blacks" (my italics).[40] In his 1996 article "'Every Inch a Man,'" Bolster makes a similar point: "Black sailors remained painfully aware of the very real limitations to equality in the maritime workplace. But overtly racist actions by other sailors were often subordinated to the requirements of shipboard order," until the nineteenth century saw a "*growing assumption* among white sailors that" more subordinate, lower skilled shipboard positions "naturally belonged to men of color. No such *assumptions* had characterized the late-eighteenth-century maritime world" (my italics).[41]

The figurative terms "incorporate," "superimposed," "rested in part on," and "growing assumption" do a lot of work for Bolster in these passages. As tropological presuppositions, they hold the place of an account of the precise relationship between racism and egalitarianism in the North Atlantic zone, offering instead an implicit set of conjectures about the form of that relationship. By representing race as a secondary (if powerful) add-on, these tropes suggest that race is fundamentally distinct from egalitarianism. In addition, race and equality are so generally construed that, though they exist in different proportions to one another, their meanings apparently remain consistent over the course of some two centuries. In Bolster's account, "equality" has a uniform, positive value throughout these centuries, and access to it is simply limited by the increasing awareness of "race," which has a uniform, negative value. Consequently, Bolster's tropological presuppositions position racism as, ultimately, a problem of individualized moralities, desires, and psyches: "unconsciously developed assumptions," "widespread convictions," and "a sense of superiority."

To a certain extent Bolster himself acknowledges this problem in his discussion of the role port agents who hired seamen, so-called crimps, played in the decline of black mariners:

> But the crimps themselves were no *deus ex machina*: no single group ever is. Crimps mediated social and cultural changes in American seaports at mid-century and, in the process, affected seaport society and culture. Crimps emerge not as the cause of black Americans' circumscribed opportunities at sea, but as the exemplar of social changes that reworked the meanings of waged work and race in the Atlantic maritime world. As black sailors' story so clearly shows, the invigorated white supremacy fundamental to the market revolution made the hard times of free blacks even harder.[42]

Here, Bolster neither naturalizes equality nor psychologizes race, and he also resists the mechanistic stance in which particular historical events, such as the rise of the crimps, directly cause the decline of black sailors. Instead, he suggests that such events are mediate or exemplary of some wider but as yet indeterminate invigoration of racism, some more complex reworking of "waged work and race in the Atlantic maritime world." The complex indeterminacy of the "invigorated" and "reworked" "meanings" to which Bolster refers at the end of *Black Jacks* reopens a set of questions he seemingly closes elsewhere in his text: How were the relationships between race and work re-formed in the late eighteenth and early nineteenth centuries? How might we more precisely characterize this "invigorated" or "reworked" moment that drove black men off the sea in the nineteenth century?

The first sentence of the first known slave narrative written by a black North American sets the scene for this moment. Briton Hammon's *A Narrative of the Uncommon Sufferings and Surprizing Deliverance of Briton Hammon, A Negro Man, Servant to General Winslow, of Marshfield, in New-England* (1760) begins by plotting a movement from the shore to the sea: "On Monday, 25th Day of *December,* 1747, with the leave of my Master, I went from *Marshfield,* with an Intention to go a Voyage to Sea, and the next Day, the 26th, got to *Plymouth,* where I immediately ship'd myself on board of a Sloop, Capt. *John Howland,* Master, bound to *Jamaica* and the *Bay*" (3).[43] This Christmas Day departure reverses the Puritans' migratory errand narrated by William Bradford's *Of Plymouth Plantation,* as it leaves Plymouth behind for the very sea Bradford represents as an obstacle. Hammon's text is often classified as a captivity narrative, rather than as a slave narrative, because immediately after this first sentence he recounts his arrival in the Americas, his shipwreck "on *Cape-Florida,*" and his capture by "barbarous and inhuman Savages" (6). Yet Hammon's confinement extends beyond the traditional lineaments of the captivity genre.

Soon after his initial captivity among Indians, he is rescued by a Spanish Captain, whom Hammon knew from a previous incident when the captain was himself a captive of the English: "The Way I came to know this Gentleman was, by his being taken last War by an *English* Privateer, and brought into *Jamaica,* while I was there" (7). In turn, this formerly captive captain turns Hammon over to the governor of Cuba, who agrees to pay the Indians ten dollars for Hammon. After living in the governor's castle in Havana for a year, Hammon is seized in the street by a press-gang, and put in prison for refusing to serve on a Spanish ship of war; merchant ships were much preferred to military ships by mariners of the day, due to the significantly harsher conditions of the latter. Finally released to the governor and put back to work in the governor's castle, Hammon "endeavour'd three Times to make my Escape" from the castle to ships about to set sail. Only on the third escape does Hammon succeed—thanks to yet another captain "who was a true *Englishman*" for refusing to turn Hammon back to the Spanish governor—and ship off to Jamaica, then London, and then Boston. On the final leg of his journey, Hammon serendipitously encounters a familiar passenger: his original master, with whom he returns to New England, again a slave.

In the midst of all these captivities on shore, however, we find perhaps the most remarkable element of this narrative: despite his repeated and urgent efforts to escape the shore for the sea, Hammon is almost entirely silent about what happens to him while he is on board ship or at sea. He seems to resist including under the titular "Uncommon Sufferings" any details about seafaring life. In effect, the narrative plots a drive toward silence, a continual struggle to return to a maritime world about which we are hardly told anything. It would seem that for Hammon, the only "common" element of life, the only realm of no recordable "sufferings," exists in the sea's "wooden world."[44]

In fact, the narrative recounts just two incidents from the many shipboard months of Hammon's life. First, Hammon tells of a "very smart Engagement" one of his ships had with a "French 84 Gun Ship," in which he was "disabled in the Arm, and render'd incapable of Service, after being honourably paid the Wages due to me" (11–12). Yet this incident seems worthy of inclusion as an "uncommon suffering" precisely because it disables Hammon, driving him off the sea: "I was put into the *Greenwich* Hospital where I stay'd and soon recovered.—I then ship'd myself a Cook on board Captain *Martyn*, an arm'd Ship in the King's service" (12).

Second, Hammon recounts what the title announces as his "surprizing deliverance," or the chance encounter with his master on a ship bound for Boston:

> I work'd on board Captain *Watt's* Ship almost Three Months, before she sail'd, and one Day being at Work in the Hold, I overheard some Persons on board mention the Name of *Winslow*, at the Name of which I was very inquisitive, and having ask'd what *Winslow* they were talking about? They told me it was *General Winslow*; and that he was one of the Passengers, I ask'd them what *General Winslow*? For I never knew *my good Master*, by that Title before; but after enquiring more particularly I found it must be *Master*; and in a few Days Time the Truth was joyfully verify'd by a happy Sight of his Person, which so overcome me, that I could not speak to him for some Time—*My good Master* was exceeding glad to see me, telling me that I was like one arose from the Dead, for he thought I had been Dead a great many Years, having heard nothing of me for almost Thirteen Years. (13)

The narrative concludes with Hammon apparently echoing his master's sentiment: "*And now, That in the Providence of that GOD, who delivered his servant* David out of the Paw of the Lion and out of the Paw of the Bear, *I am freed from a* long *and* dreadful Captivity, among worse Savages than they; *And am return'd to my* own Native Land, to Shew how Great Things the Lord hoth done for Me . . ." (14). Read within the context of a narrative that is persistently silent about seafaring life, that refuses to include seafaring life under the category of "uncommon sufferings," this ringing endorsement of Hammon's return with General Winslow to terrestrial slavery in New England echoes with a certain irony. Could Hammon's repeated question—"what *General Winslow*?"—his inability to speak to his master, and his initial refusal to believe an admittedly astonishing encounter be read not as joyful surprise but as exasperated incredulity, and thus as a struggle to come to terms with the end of his common seafaring life and the harsh reality of his return to New England slavery? Though we cannot be sure, in part because of the ever-present role of white amanuenses and editors in early black literature, it is possible that Hammon saw in Winslow's image of Lazarus rather a Job surprisingly delivered to new "Uncommon Sufferings." For this narrative to be published in 1760, Hammon certainly had to endorse the man who owned him and the life to which he was bound. Consequently, the very inclusion of his "deliverance" within this narrative of "Uncommon Sufferings"—the suggestion that the "deliverance" might itself be an "Uncommon Suffering," that the "surprise" of the "deliverance" might be viewed with some ambivalence—further amplifies Hammon's rigorous silence about life on the sea.

Hammon's early eighteenth-century seafaring life emerges from this narrative as so desirable, so opposed to his life on shore, that he spares no effort to return to the sea and refuses to speak of the sea as "uncommon sufferings." As a figure for the sharp rise in black sailors during the eighteenth century, this silence marks the sea's relative freedom from racialized exploitation.[45] Since Hammon is silent about that freedom, we need to look to other mariner narratives to understand its meaning. As we will see, black mariner narratives increasingly fill Hammon's silence over the course of the eighteenth and nineteenth centuries with accounts of sea life. What is more, these accounts are characterized by increasingly common sufferings, as well as by incessantly—indeed ritually and systematically—dashed hopes.

Endeavoring to Be a Citizen of the World

In *Blues, Ideology, and Afro-American Literature*, Houston A. Baker Jr. inaugurates his epochal call for a "new American literary history" with an astute reading of the political economics of Olaudah Equiano's *Narrative*. Baker eschews the "traditional" guiding perspectives or, in Foucauldian terms, "governing statements" of U.S. literary study—statements such as "religious man," "wilderness," "migratory errand," "increase in store," and "New Jerusalem"— as well as the traditional canon of U.S. literary history.[46] Reading under a set of "new governing statements" such as the "economics of slavery" and "commercial deportation," Baker performs the work of both critiquing the "traditional" perspective by exposing its veneer of self-evidence, and displacing that perspective by pursuing another.[47] He summarizes his reading as follows:

> [The *Narrative*'s] middle section represents an active, inversive, ironically mercantile ascent by the propertied self from the hell of "commercial deportation" [i.e., the slave trade]. It offers a graphic "re-invention" of the social grounding of the Afro-American symbolic act par excellence. It vividly delineates the true character of Afro-America's historical origins in a slave economics and implicitly acknowledges that such economics *must be mastered* before liberation can be achieved.[48]

Baker allows us to see the *Narrative* not simply as a narrative of religious or existential self-discovery and personal development, but rather as a text about the dynamic and historically specific relationship between race and capital.[49]

Yet Baker's untroubled representation of the *Narrative* as an "Afro-American" text imposes some crucial limits on his perspectival shift. William L. Andrews has called the *Narrative* an "Afro-English" text on the grounds that Equiano spent much more time in England than he did in the United States, and other critics, too, have stressed the national ambivalencies of the text.[50] As Chinosole argues, "As a man who is marginal to many countries and cultures, including West African, West Indian, American, and British, but as a man, most accurately, of the high seas, Equiano assumes a variety of voices for a variety of audiences. . . . Critics trying to decide which national literary canon owns Equiano's work miss his international importance."[51] Baker's challenge to the traditional canon of American literary history does not address the "Afro-English" aspects of the *Narrative* or the "international importance" to which Chinosole refers, and thus leaves the "American" in "American literary history" at least partially in its traditional place.

Paul Gilroy's "black Atlantic" framework has encouraged the study of such national ambivalencies. In the spirit of Baker's call, Gilroy proposes his own set of new governing statements or, in his words, "intermediate concepts, lodged between the local and the global, which have a wider applicability in cultural history and politics precisely because they offer an alternative to the nationalist focus which dominates cultural criticism."[52] Of particular importance to Equiano's text is Gilroy's emphasis—drawn from the historical research of Peter Linebaugh and Marcus Rediker—on the underexamined role of "sailors, moving to and fro between nations, crossing borders in modern machines that were themselves micro-systems of linguistic and political hybridity."[53] Read in the context of Gilroy's project and the research of Linebaugh and Rediker, Baker's representation of the *Narrative* as an exclusively "Afro-American" text would thus seem to be determined by the national framework of his project to refigure "*American* literary history."

In fact, on closer consideration even Baker's salutary reframing of the *Narrative* in political-economic terms is limited by his subtly nationalist perspective.[54] Throughout his reading, Baker uses the terms *mercantile* and *mercantilism* interchangeably. For instance, expanding on Equiano's "ironically mercantile ascent," Baker writes (using Equiano's European name, Gustavus Vassa): "It is, ultimately, Vassa's adept mercantilism that produces the conflation of a 'theory' of trade, an abolitionist appeal, and a report of African conjugal union that conclude *The Life of Olaudah Equiano.*"[55] Baker seems to mean that Equiano's *mercantile*—that is, *commercial* in a general sense—endeavors can be read as complex, more-than-economic blendings of racial, sexual, and political statements. However, Baker's use of the word *mercantilism* as if it meant mercantile trade in general obscures mercantil*ism*'s historically specific role in nation formation and, in turn, occludes much of the economic and historical specificity of the *Narrative*. Baker's failure to consider how Equiano narrates his mercantile encounters with mercantil*ism*—a political-economic system that helped to form nation-states—thus mirrors his failure to consider the *Narrative* not only as part of an African American literary canon, but also as a text about the interdependent emergence of nation and race.[56]

Alerted by Baker to the *Narrative*'s political-economic import, reminded by critics such as Chinosole of the text's "international importance," and pushed to consider a transatlantic framework by Gilroy, Linebaugh, and Rediker, we can begin to see that Equiano's mercantile endeavors are striking and precarious precisely because they confront capitalism at the moment of the emergence of modern racial and national formations—an emergence made possible in part by the discursive practices of mercantilism.[57] Let us turn, then, to Equiano's narrative.

Olaudah Equiano begins to learn the terms of the merchant marine trade and its productive potential over the course of the first five chapters of the *Narrative*, particularly when, after the horrors of the Middle Passage (55–61; 32–37) and a brief but brutal period in Virginia slavery (62–64; 38–40), he is sold to Michael Henry Pascal, a Royal Navy lieutenant and captain of a merchant ship called the *Industrious Bee* (63; 40). Equiano represents his sale to Pascal as a blessing after the misery of the Middle Passage and Virginia, signaling that "industriousness" and mercantile capitalism accrue meaning in relative opposition to his past misery. From this point on he tries to gain access to mercantile capitalism, again and again attempting to make his way by forging equivalencies with traders. Trading eventually becomes one of Equiano's most persistent responses to both his violent entrance into the European world-economy of the late eighteenth century, and his relentless subjection to the regimes of capitalist exchange, production, accumulation, and circulation.

In fact, Equiano repeatedly and carefully marks this integration into the European world-economy. For example, in the somewhat controversial first two chapters of the *Narrative*, he represents his homeland as based on subsistence economies.[58] As Joseph Fichtelberg notes, this representation is historically suspect, since "Benin had a thriving commerce, extensive markets, and widely circulating currency" at the time.[59] Yet the account of his homeland can be read as an allegory of the different degrees of West Africa's integration into the European world-economy, told from the perspective of a man whose memories of his childhood have no doubt faded, and who set out in part to write a tactical, antislave trade text for European consumption. Whereas "the Kingdom of Benin" is "a country where nature is prodigal of her favours, our wants are few and easily supplied" (36; 16), the coast is replete with European economic and cultural objects and is marked by Christian customs (53; 31). Followed in the next paragraph by Equiano's first sight of a slave ship, this differentiation between inland and coastal regions dramatizes Equiano's socioeconomic transformation.

We know from chapters 4 and 5 that Equiano had long engaged in "trifling perquisites and little ventures" in the interest of scraping together some form of sustenance, as most slaves did (94; 65). For instance, he tells us that plantation slaves often traded to supplement their restricted rations: "The wretched field slaves, after toiling all the day for an unfeeling owner, who gives them but little victuals, steal sometimes a few moments from rest or refreshment to gather some small portion of grass, according as their time will admit. This they commonly tie up in a parcel; either a bit's worth (six-pence) or half a bit's worth; and bring it to town, or to the market, to sell" (108; 77–78). However, with his formal declaration of "commenc[ing] merchant" in chapter 6 following his sale to Mr. Robert King, a Quaker merchant from Philadelphia who hires Equiano out to the English merchant mariner Captain Thomas Farmer, Equiano's trading is no longer a "trifling" or "little" pursuit of sustenance within local economies. Rather, his declaration in chapter 6 marks his active engagement with merchant capital and the world-economy's sphere of circulation. That is, chapter 6 marks the beginning of his attempt to "realize" commodity capital on the market by transforming it into money capital, which could in turn be reinvested in commodity capital and transformed once again into money capital, with profit." "To try my luck and commence merchant" thus carries more weight than "trifling perquisites and little ventures."

Most immediately, Equiano acts in the interest of saving enough money to buy his freedom, and thereby to extricate himself from the life cycle of capital as a laboring object of exchange. Yet we can also hear in Equiano's use of the infinitive "to commence" an interest that is manifested in the scenes of trading he subsequently recounts. Just as the infinitive is a verb form that exposes itself to an open-ended futurity, a potentiality not fully figured but nonetheless anticipated, Equiano's declaration "to commence merchant" inaugurates an attempt to realize not just his material sustenance, not even just his economic independence, but also his freedom as an active social subject in this new world that has forced itself upon him. In other words, he is hoping to have free subjectivity conferred to him by actively engaging in the logic of capitalist accumulation and exchange.

This is not just any free subjectivity, however, but precisely subjectivity as it "means" in this new capitalist world: formal and abstract equality, of the kind Madison invokes in the tariff debate, and Marx critiques in his account of the value-form, which I discuss in the introduction. That is, the subjectivity of the economic and political actor in civil society under capitalism is supposed to be "freed" (i.e., abstracted) from material particularities, a freedom that renders all subjects in civil society formally interchangeable and thus formally and abstractly equal. The hope embedded in this phrase "to commence merchant," then, is that by mastering the mechanics of mercantile exchange, Equiano will accede to the ontological status he figures repeatedly in the *Narrative* by signifying on the Christian humanist terms of the golden rule: "Do unto all men as you would men should do unto you" (61; 38). Equiano hopes to accede to the ontological status, that is, of a subject formally and abstractly equal to all the subjects around him, and therefore "free." "To commence merchant" signifies Equiano's attempt to use capitalist mercantile exchange as a weapon against capitalist slavery, as a tool that would solder freedom to formal and abstract equivalence, and as a lever or mochlos,[60] that would propel him into that freedom.

Equiano's mercantile strategy is, on its own terms, a certain success. While many of Equiano's trading ventures end up with whites robbing or swindling him out of his capital, he nonetheless does eventually buy his freedom (135–38; 101), get married (235; 178), and become a transatlantic advocate of British missionary and capitalist development in Africa—development he represents as a means to abolish the slave trade and deliver Africa (he writes of the continent as such) to European modernity (chapter 12). However, he never accedes to the radical freedom beyond racial oppression that he had envisioned. In other words, he attains particular financial, imperial, and gendered freedoms, but he fails to access the formal and abstract equality he had associated with freedom as such. How, then, do we make sense of Equiano's failures and his successes?

Let us consider in detail Equiano's first attempt to "try [his] luck and commence merchant." Upon landing at "Santa Cruz Island," or St. Croix, in a British ship of his new master, a Quaker merchant from Philadelphia, he and a friend who is also a slave are robbed by "two white men" of three bags of fruit they had intended to trade (117; 85). As these men run "to a house . . . adjoining the [island's] fort," Equiano and his friend plead for the return of their bags of fruit. As Equiano explains, these whites "not only refused to return them, but they swore at us, and threatened if we did not immediately depart, they would flog us as well" (117; 85). When Equiano and his partner proceed to explain that "those three bags were our all, that we brought them with us to sell, and that we came from Montserrat, and shewed them the vessel," they get in even worse trouble:

> But this was rather against us, as they now saw we were strangers as well as slaves. They still therefore swore, and desired us to be gone; and even took sticks to beat us; . . . We went to the commanding officer of the forts, and told him how we had been served by some of his people; but we obtained not the least redress: he answered our complaints only by a volley of imprecations against us, and immediately took a horse-whip, in order to chastise us, so that we were obliged to turn out much faster than we came in. (117–18; 85)

The crucial phrases here are "they now saw we were strangers as well as slaves" and "how we had been served by some of his people," for they tell us that Equiano and his partner have stumbled into a nationalist conflict as well as a racial conflict in this scene. Initially, it seems as if "the two white men" express only a sense of racial superiority by so boldly robbing Equiano and his partner: Equiano names their whiteness and notes that the robbers declare their right to flog the two black men. However, when the robbers see Equiano's and his partner's ship and hear their defense of themselves as merchants, these white men realize Equiano and his partner are not only Africans but also are trading under the British flag. Equiano marks this by distinguishing the term *strangers*, most often invoked to signify national difference in the period, from the term *slaves* in the phrase "they *now* saw we were strangers *as well as* slaves." While the commanding officer's assault on Equiano and his partner with "imprecations" and "a horse-whip" also seems to figure only his understanding of them as slaves, the text again tells us that this officer grasps both the racial and national difference between the two parties when Equiano and his partner present their case as a conflict between themselves and "some of [the commander's] people."

What does this emphasis on national difference as well as racial difference tell us? At the time of this incident, in the mid- to late 1760s, St. Croix was part of the Danish West Indies, together with St. Thomas and St. John. The Spanish, English, Dutch, French, and Danish had fought over these islands since the Spanish exterminated or enslaved the "Carib Indians" Columbus first encountered in 1493 during his second voyage. After Denmark took control of all three islands in 1733 (initially under the auspices of the Danish West Indies Company and then directly under the Danish Crown), it fought for decades against slave uprisings and British attempts to seize the islands. In fact, Britain took control of St. Thomas for ten months in 1801 and 1802, and held all three islands between 1807 and 1815.[61]

The islands emerged as a cauldron of colonial rivalry while Denmark struggled to assert its economic control, in part because of the islands' small size and the relative weakness of the Danish military. In addition, since the Danes left the islands open to settlement by any European subjects, the Danish West Indies Company and the crown found themselves in constant competition and confrontation with foreign residents and creditors. Indeed, most Danish profits seem to have come from the smuggling trade in slaves and sugar when periods of war interrupted the trade of the British and French. The 1760s in particular found the Danes imposing mercantilist measures on St. Croix while opening St. Thomas to relatively free trade in a desperate if contradictory effort to assert economic control over the islands.[62]

Thus, in the everyday world of the St. Croix port where Equiano and his partner attempt to trade their "whole stock" (117; 85), the Danish commanding officer and the two white men—perhaps themselves Danish or perhaps simply nationally allied with the Danes against the British—are actors in, and are immediately aware of, a complex set of racial and national antagonisms characteristic of the region's mercantilist conjuncture. The two white men are incited to violence by, and the commanding officer invokes his authority from, a racism articulated with nationalism. In turn, Equiano and his partner are violently barred from the formal and abstract equality of mercantile exchange by this articulation. It is because Equiano frames this mercantile "endeavour" as a quest for freedom, and then traces the material manner in which that freedom is bound to emerging, racially and nationally codified equality, that we can glimpse mercantilist discursive practices at work on St. Croix.

A few years after Equiano's incident on St. Croix, a white English boy from Yorkshire named Henry Schroeder incurred some injuries of his own after sailing into the very same St. Croix harbor as a seaman on an American ship called the *Neptune*. Decades later, writing under the pseudonym William Butterworth, Schroeder recounted his time on St. Croix in the midst of his own narrative, *Three Years Adventures, of a Minor, in England, Africa, The West Indies, South-Carolina and Georgia*.[63] This remarkable text narrates the emerging articulation of race, nation, and equality encountered by Equiano from the perspective of a white sailor who also longs for cross-racial solidarity and the end of slavery. The moments when Equiano's narrative and Schroeder's narrative intersect—as they do on St. Croix—paradoxically dramatize the emerging racialized and nationalized gap between white and black sailors.

Three Years Adventures positions itself from its first pages as an abolitionist text that links "the cause of degraded Africans" with that of "the wretched crews" of white sailors on slave ships, "whose half-famished bodies bore marks of ill treatment, often resorted to in the paroxysms of passion, or the wantonness of caprice" (iv). What is more, the text links racism to nationalism by declaring its opposition to both. For instance, after telling an African acquaintance he encounters on the shore of Benin that he imagined evil spirits to be black, Butterworth tells us that his acquaintance's "wife showed a beautiful set of teeth, as she good humoredly laughed at my ignorance, in imagining the evil spirit to be black; when all the world (she said) knew that he was white. So much, thought I, for the prejudices of education, habit, superstition, and other weaknesses" (70). Butterworth's self-critical recognition of this woman's ironic retort leads him to expand his commentary on racial prejudice: "As the interposition of an opaque body causes an eclipse of the sun and moon, so prejudice causes a mental eclipse, often total, with continuance; unless some favourable circumstance, equivalent to the motion of the revolving spheres, produces an alteration in the relative condition of the objects eclipsing and eclipsed" (70–71). The very words of this extended metaphor seem to contort in a concerted effort to avoid the traditional figuration of prejudice as blackness, offering instead a contrast between the static opacity of prejudice and the mobile, differential interrelatedness of its passing. Butterworth immediately illustrates this metaphor by telling of a boxing duel between two crewmates that was interrupted by a French captain who tells them they should not "'ill treat one another'" since they "'have ill treatment enough to bear from your officers'" and "enemies now to contend with on board" (71). After bringing all the crew back to his ship for "brandy and sea biscuits" and conversation "in the most affable and agreeable manner," the French captain's "gentlemanly deportment and suavity of manners won the hearts of all" (71). This encounter helps Butterworth expand his critique of racism to a critique of nationalism by convincing him "of the erroneousness of national antipathies. I had been prejudiced against a Frenchman from cradled infancy, so had all our crew; I knew not wherefore, nor did any one of them. The trammels of prejudice now gave way; reason irradiated my mind; and, from that moment, I became a young citizen of the world, and looked on all mankind as my brethren. I weighed actions; merit preponderated in the French captain's favour; and prejudice was no more" (72).

This personal enlightenment, reiterated throughout the text, nonetheless leads Butterworth to overlook hierarchies that transcend his good will. Indeed, it is precisely as a confidently enlightened "young citizen of the world" that Butterworth differs from black sailors such as Equiano. Nowhere is this difference more clear than in Butterworth's account of his time on St. Croix. At the very beginning of this account, Butterworth notes the severity of Danish mercantilist restrictions on foreign sailors, and in turn explains how and why he and his English shipmates set out to thwart those restrictions by, for instance, going out after curfew to "a rum store" owned by "an aged Spanish lady": "As the Danish soldiers took every opportunity to annoy the sailors of all nations, we, in return, prided ourselves in tricking the Danish soldiers" (375). When the Danes take countermeasures, Butterworth indignantly writes that they "thus frustrat[ed] another of our plans for defeating their wishes to make us conform to laws, repugnant to our feelings as Englishmen, who, in the land of freedom, know no such restrictions" (377). Though early in the narrative he declared himself free from national prejudice, on St. Croix he rushes into a national conflict on the grounds that his nation is superior. Of course, Butterworth's comparison between St. Croix and England is faulty, and it obscures the mercantilist conjuncture in which he is caught up. Though England had fewer restrictions on Englishmen than the Danish colony of St. Croix did, English colonies at the time often had more restrictions on Danes than Denmark did. These mercantilist restrictions sought to link economic practices with national identity, and thus to nationalize capitalist productive efficiency: They sought to produce "citizens of the world" whose consolidated national identities would give them an edge in global competition, not citizens whose national identities would give way to the universal equality of "world" citizenship.

Butterworth inadvertently reveals this mercantilist meaning of "citizen of the world" a few pages later. One evening, while trying to get involved in smuggling operations that seek to thwart mercantilist restrictions for personal profit—known as "the False Trade" (401)—Butterworth is picked up by Danish soldiers for violating curfew and is marched toward the island's fort. He escapes, however, by running to the beach and into the sea, and swimming to the *Neptune*—along the way filling his feet with "the large sharp prickles of the sea-egg, or urchin" (407). Foiled in his effort to thwart non-English mercantilist restrictions, Butterworth then resorts to the very nationalist claims supported by English mercantilism when he tells his yarn to his shipmates: "The pain was acute, and increased till it became almost past bearing; so that, had it not been for the love of liberty, inherent in the breast of an Englishman, I should have been better in the fort, with whole feet, than where I then was, having them full set with these sharp quill-like points" (407). By naturalizing the superiority of the English, Butterworth obscures the fact that his nationalized, terrestrial freedom is a condition of possibility for his participation as a "young citizen of the world" in a world-economy under British hegemony. That is, Butterworth can so confidently proclaim his global enlightenment precisely because it is underwritten by his citizenship within an imperial nation such as Britain. Indeed, in the midst of his account of these St. Croix incidents, Butterworth again reveals the nationally specific conditions for his world citizenship when he criticizes the "impetuous spirits of the Irish" on the island when compared with the "arguments of the cooler English" (379).

Butterworth's chiasmatic representation of nationally specific, terrestrial privilege—"Englishmen . . . in the land of freedom," "the love of liberty inherent in the breast of an Englishman"—is also deeply racialized, and so differs markedly from the maritime freedom to which Equiano aspires. Despite his declaration of support for world citizenship beyond racial and national prejudices, Butterworth decries his captain's refusal to let the ship's slaves help unload goods from their boat, as the other American ships do (381). Butterworth further reveals this racialization when he states that "At St. Croix, negroes who have committed any offence, are generally sent to the fort to be punished, which is done privately and cruelly, by flogging"—a type of punishment he proceeds to describe in brutal detail (382). As we saw above, Equiano's incident at this very fort confirms Butterworth's account. Even more significantly, however, the difference between the two men's escapes from detention highlights the racially and nationally particular conditions of Butterworth's faith in world citizenship. While Butterworth is sustained by "the love of liberty, inherent in the breast of an Englishman," Equiano flees to his ship beaten, robbed, and disillusioned, and then returns to the island to beg for some redress. Writes Equiano, just after he has been rebuked by the commanding officer of the fort in the passage I discussed above: "I now, in the agony of distress and indignation, wished that the ire of God, in his forked lightning, might transfix these cruel oppressors among the dead. Still, however, we persevered; went back again to the house, and begged and besought them again and again for our fruits" (118, 85). Though he does get some of his stolen goods back, and later sells them for a profit, as we will see Equiano finds even this partial redress to be short-lived.

Equiano's "injury" on St. Croix is neither incidental nor unique. The *Narrative* recounts a series of incidents in which he is excluded from formal and abstract equality on the basis of its articulation with the codification of race and nation. Immediately after the St. Croix incident, for example, Equiano rejects an offer of freedom from French merchantmen, choosing instead to remain a slave on a transatlantic merchant ship. As he explains,

> Had I wished to run away, I did not want opportunities . . . and particularly at one time, soon after this. When we were at the island of Guadaloupe there was a large fleet of merchantmen bound for Old France; and, seamen then being very scarce, they gave from fifteen to twenty pounds a man for the run. Our mate, and all the white sailors, left our vessel on this account, and went on board of the French ships. They would have had me also gone with them, for they regarded me, and swore to protect me, if I would go; and, as the fleet was to sail the next day, I really believe I could have got safe to Europe at that time. However, as my master was kind, I would not attempt to leave him; still remembering the old maxim, that "honesty is the best policy," I suffered them to go without me. Indeed my captain was much afraid of my leaving him and the vessel at that time, as I had so fair an opportunity: but I thank God, this fidelity of mine turned out much to my advantage hereafter, when I did not in the least think of it; and made me so much in favour with the captain, that he used now and then to teach me some parts of navigation himself. But some of our passengers, and others, seeing this, found much fault with him for it, saying, it was a very dangerous thing to let a negro know navigation; thus I was hindered again in my pursuits. (123; 90)

Though Equiano says "I really believe I could have got safe to Europe at that time" and thus become free under French auspices, his deep distrust of such nationally bound, terrestrial freedom keeps him from fleeing. By saying "However, as my master was kind," he makes clear that he is not choosing Britain over France, but rather transatlantic, mercantile slavery with his relatively trustworthy master over formal freedom in Europe. His decision positions him against both racism and nationalism, and holds out the hope of a radical equality beyond both. This hope found a certain realization in his relations with his white shipmates while they too sailed the seas.[64] Though Equiano makes clear that these seamen "regarded" him and "swore to protect" him in France, his decision to stay behind suggests that he believed such fidelity would carry little weight on land. He thus decides that sea-bound "honesty" is more valuable than terrestrial freedom in France since his servitude allows him to remain a transatlantic merchant laborer.

As the passage above suggests, this decision to stay aboard ship initially seems wise, for Equiano learns more about the merchant marine trade. The reactions of the "passengers, and others," however, indicate that "navigation" knowledge was increasingly restricted by discursive practices of racism and nationalism. To them, Equiano tells us, "it was a very dangerous thing to let a negro know navigation" precisely because such knowledge carved out a certain space of freedom, albeit a precarious one. The immediacy of the passengers' perception of the danger of navigation knowledge in Equiano's hands suggests that these racial and national restrictions were obvious or self-evident: "But some of our passengers, and others, *seeing this*, found much fault with him for it." In turn, the passengers' relatively successful invocation of a prohibition against Equiano—"and thus I was hindered again in my pursuits"—indicates the pervasive, disciplinary power of this articulation.

A few pages later, in an account of a trip he made, just after the repeal of the Stamp Act, as a slave on a British American ship to Charleston, South Carolina, in 1766,[65] Equiano elaborates on this articulation of race, nation, and equality. The Stamp Act repeal has long been represented as one of the key victories of the colonial American desire for freedom from British tyranny, and thus as part of the struggle for equality culminating in U.S. independence. However, Equiano's account shows us that the most significant common thread between the Stamp Act repeal and the emergence of an independent United States was not a glorious desire for freedom and equality, but rather an emerging understanding of equality as entirely consistent with the codification of racial and national identities. What is more, his account suggests that mercantilism played a role in articulating this consistency.

The Stamp Act was one of the many mercantilist policies the British Parliament conducted in North America. Colonial American anger over the act precipitated the 1765 Stamp Act Congress, held at New York City Hall. On October 19, the congress published a Declaration of Rights and Grievances, which decried taxation without representation, and called for "boycotts" of British goods until the act was repealed.[66] Though the declaration certainly disturbed British authorities, it was the many petitions from English merchants, in which they complained about the impact of colonial boycotts on their businesses and themselves called for the repeal of the Stamp Act, that caused the greatest stir in Parliament. The combined force of the New York Declaration and the English merchants' petitions led Parliament to repeal the act.[67]

Equiano offers an alternative history, however. He suggests that, in North America in 1766, this transatlantic aspect of the Stamp Act repeal was hardly noticed, as burgeoning American nationalism represented the repeal as simply an effect of colonial resistance:

> We arrived at Georgia, and, having landed part of our cargo, proceeded to Charlestown with the remainder. While we were there I saw the town illuminated; the guns were fired, and bonfires and other demonstrations of joy shewn, on account of the repeal of the stamp-act. Here I disposed of some goods on my own account; the white men buying

them with smooth promises and fair words, giving me, however, but very indifferent payment. There was one gentlemen particularly who bought a puncheon of rum of me, which gave me a great deal of trouble; and although I used the interest of my friendly [British] captain, I could not obtain anything for it; for, being a negro man, I could not oblige him to pay me. This vexed me much, not knowing how to act; and I lost some time in seeking after this Christian; and though, when the sabbath came (which the negroes usually make their holiday) I was inclined to go to public worship, but, instead of that, I was obliged to hire some black men to help me to pull a boat across the water to go in quest of this gentleman. When I found him, after much entreaty, both from myself and my worthy captain, he at last paid me in dollars, some of them, however, were copper, and of consequence of no value; but he took advantage of my being a negro man, and obliged me to put up with those or none, although I objected to them. Immediately after, as I was trying to pass them in the market amongst other white men, I was abused for offering to pass bad coin; and though I shewed them the man I had got them from, I was within one minute of being tied up and flogged without either judge or jury; however, by the help of a good pair of heels, I ran off and so escaped the bastinadoes I should have received. I got on board as fast as I could, but still continued in fear of them until we sailed, which, I thank God, we did, not long after; and I have never been amongst them since. (128–129; 94–95)

By juxtaposing the celebrations over the Stamp Act repeal on the streets of Charleston with an account of being swindled by white American colonials, Equiano tells us that he has been barred from the formal and abstract equality of mercantile exchange that the repeal supposedly recognized. The market into which Equiano enters fails to confer equality upon him not just because he is passing "bad coin" of "copper"— there was, in fact, a lively copper coin trade in the colonies at the time.[68] Rather, the market fails because Equiano is understood both as black ("for, being a negro man, I could not oblige him to pay me," "he took advantage of my being a negro man") and as British ("although I used the interest of my friendly [British] captain, I could obtain nothing for it"). Equiano's text suggests that these American colonials are celebrating an equality irreducibly bound to, and consistent with, racial and national codification. They are joyously recognizing their mutual identity by hierarchically differentiating it from Britishness and blackness.

Paradoxically, when the Tariff of 1789 went into effect in the United States twenty-three years later, the duties it imposed were not unlike the British Stamp Act duties. The common "American" thread between the Stamp Act repeal celebrations and the first U.S. Congress was thus not universal "free trade" among equal citizens of the world. The 1766 repeal, as a move away from protectionism, and the 1789 tariff, as a move toward protectionism, are entirely contradictory on that score. Rather, as Equiano's account makes clear, the common thread between these two events is formal and abstract equality—embodied by the Charleston market and the "fellow citizens" Representative Ames invoked on the House floor—articulated *with* racial and national codification—encountered by Equiano when he is swindled, and scripted by the tariff debate. We see this articulation both in Equiano's 1766 and in Madison's, Ames's, and Fitzsimons's 1789.

Even after Equiano buys his freedom, he encounters this articulation. In fact, Equiano acknowledges "that my first free voyage would be the worst I had ever made" (142; 105). As he explains,

> During our stay at this place [Savannah, Georgia], one evening a slave belonging to Mr. Read, a merchant of Savannah, came near to our vessel, and began to use me very ill. I entreated him, with all the patience I was master of, to desist, as I knew there was little or no law for a free negro here; but the fellow, instead of taking my advise, persevered in his insults, and even struck me. At this I lost all temper, and fell on him and beat him soundly. The next morning his master came to our vessel as we lay alongside the wharf, and desired me to come ashore that he might have me flogged all round the town, for beating his negro slave. (139; 102)

Though Equiano informs his captain of his fight with Mr. Read's slave, and the captain promises to take care of the matter, the conflict escalates: "The captain being on board when Mr. Read came and applied to him to deliver me up, he said he knew nothing of the matter, I was a free man. I was astonished and frightened at this, and thought I had better keep where I was, than go ashore and be flogged round the town, without judge or jury" (139; 103). Equiano knows that his freedom will not be recognized in a slave state, but he is "astonished" to discover that his Captain will not assist him on the ship. He is "astonished," in other words, to discover that he does not fully understand the meaning of his newly obtained freedom even on his ship.

His initial response to this situation is an affective and principled one; he decides to insist on his freedom: "At that instant a rage seized my soul, and for a while I determined to resist the first man that should attempt to lay violent hands on me, or basely use me without a trial; for I would sooner die like a free man, than suffer myself to be scourged by the hands of ruffians, and my blood drawn like a slave" (140; 103). But his captain and shipmates preach caution, and finally agree to hide Equiano until they leave port. To hide, however, Equiano must leave the ship and go ashore, lest Mr. Read search for him on board. Paradoxically, then, Equiano's formal freedom as an emancipated sailor leads him into a conflict that makes it necessary for him to leave the ship for a place where his freedom has no meaning. By emphasizing that Mr. Read "knew nothing of the matter" because Equiano "was a free man," the text implies that, had Equiano still been an enslaved sailor, his behavior would have been his *master's* responsibility, and thus the captain would have acted in his own interest and protected his property, Equiano, from Mr. Read. Instead, Equiano's freedom is rootless, at home neither on ship nor in Savannah.

The loss of Equiano's newly formalized freedom on his ship at the hands of a slave owner "protecting" his slave dramatizes the loss of maritime spaces where black merchants could realize a freedom relatively detached from racial and national codification. Consequently, Equiano is persistently pulled toward a bounded, nationally defined space. His formal freedom actually increases the strength of that pull, such that the only way he can protect himself is to renounce his formal freedom and become a technically unfree subject by hiding in the nationally defined space of Savannah. His ploy works, but, as if to mark the impossibility of a freedom detached from racial-national codification, Equiano concludes with a difficult recognition of what awaits him back on board ship, despite his recent emancipation: "So I consented to slave on as before" (141; 105).

The very repetitive nature of the "incidents" and "injuries" I have examined under-scores a crucial aspect of Equiano's text: his mercantile failures are neither incidental nor unique, but systematic and constitutive of the logic of formal and abstract equality. That is, Equiano does not encounter simply an exclusion from such equality, but a *constitutive* exclusion ritually iterated and reiterated in the Atlantic zone at least in part by a mercantilist system. Eventually, he abandons his efforts, offering a sharp condemnation of the merchant marine trade in the last chapter of his narrative: "I had suffered so many impositions in my commercial transactions in different parts of the world, that I became heartily disgusted with the seafaring life, and was determined not to return to it, at least for some time." (220; 167).

Strikingly, Equiano's concluding renunciation of the sea is echoed at the end of Henry Schroeder's narrative: seafaring, declares the narrator Butterworth, "is as irk-some as precarious, and, hitherto, has proved as unprofitable as unpleasant!" (482). Again, however, this convergence marks a divergence. Having taken to the sea due to what he describes as youthful passion and a lack of reason, rather than enslave-ment as with Equiano, Butterworth repeatedly tells us how he longed to return to the "freedom" of his life on the shores of England. By the time he returns to his family after three years at sea, Butterworth has his image of England confirmed. Though he "knew not how to face home, after an absence of three years, spent in obscurity and unprofitableness," he nonetheless returns at the end of the narrative to "the arms of an indulgent mother, encircled by other branches of the family, all overjoyed at beholding the returned prodigal, for whom the fatted calf was soon killed" (486–87). Quickly learning the trade of "copperplate-printing" and "engraving," Butterworth became moderately successful as he lived out his life in England. His persistent long-ing for the shore, confirmed by the glowing account of his return, contrasts marked-ly with the longing for the sea and the disappointed return to the shore depicted by Equiano's narrative.

Thus, when Butterworth candidly remarks at the end of his narrative on "the prin-ciple of equality, which was a term just coming into vogue; much talked about, little understood; in theory captivating, in practice disappointing" (313), he speaks to an articulation allegorized throughout *Three Years Adventures* and Equiano's *Interesting Narrative*. Equality came "into vogue" on the North Atlantic precisely through its systematic, quotidian iteration and reiteration with the codification of racial and na-tional identities in ports like St. Croix and Charleston, and on ships like the *Neptune* and the *Industrious Bee*. The discursive practices of mercantilism systematized degrees of "disappointment" by "captivating" all sailors within the hierarchical articulation of race, nation, and equality.

Defenseless Strangers and Strange Mixtures

In 1798, *A Narrative of the Life and Adventures of Venture, a Native of Africa* was published by Charles Holt.[69] Over three chapters, this narrative tells the story of Venture Smith's life, from his birth around 1729 in Dukandarra, Guinea, to his capture by slave traders, his march to the sea and his Middle Passage, his struggles with a series of masters in Rhode Island, Connecticut, and Long Island, and his efforts as a free black entrepreneur.[70] Often regarded as either a problematic text of accommodation or a heroic text of early black capitalism, Smith's narrative can, to the contrary, be seen to dramatize the conjoining of racial and national particularity with capitalist forms of equality that we saw in Equiano's narrative and, thus, to offer a quite detailed account of the historical articulation that black mariners eventually found so untenable. However, unlike Hammon and Equiano, who were deep sea mariners, Smith spends most of his life engaged in the coastal trade along the shores of New England. He doggedly maintains his connections with the land even as he persistently takes to coastal trade routes to make a living. By depicting a liminal space between sea and shore, Smith's narrative initially figures the coastal maritime world as a necessary supplement to black economic achievement on land. Yet by the end of the narrative Smith's achievements have come at a cost so great that this liminal space seems to disappear altogether, becoming enclosed by the racial and national codification of equality.

The first chapter, which tells of Smith's childhood in West Africa, begins with an ambivalent recollection of his past: "By [my father's] first wife he had three children. The eldest of them was myself, named by my father, Broteer" (3). With the objective "three children," the detached "of them," and the subordinate clause "named by my father" separating "myself" from "Broteer," this passage marks Smith's forced detachment from his African name. Indeed, the narrative never again invokes the name "Broteer." Yet the ambivalent "myself" echoes throughout the first chapter's carefully constructed account of eighteenth-century West Africa. Implicitly countering Western ethnocentrisms about Africa and differentiating West African servitude from racial slavery in the Americas, this first chapter, like the first chapters of Equiano's *Narrative*, carves out a space of opposition to racial slavery's injustices. Though the autobiographical "myself" emerges out of that space, it can never simply return to the African "Broteer." For by the end of the first chapter Smith has been taken by slave traders to the coastal town of Anamaboe to be sold and renamed:

> On a certain time I and other prisoners were put on board a canoe, under our master, and rowed away in a vessel belonging to Rhode Island, commanded by Captain Collingwood, and the mate Thomas Mumford. While we were going to the vessel, our master told us all to appear to the best possible advantage for sale. I was bought on board by one Robertson Mumford, steward of said vessel, for four gallons of rum, and a piece of calico, and called Venture, on account of his having purchased me with his own private venture. Thus I came by my name. All the slaves that were bought for that vessel's cargo, were two hundred and sixty. (9)

This monetary and linguistic transaction, occurring around 1737 on the cusp of the Middle Passage, aims to transform Smith into a generic sign of commercial speculation and capitalist exchange, to abstract his very being into the formal logic of value.

The second chapter of the narrative begins with an eight-year-old Smith having arrived in Rhode Island via Barbados "after an ordinary passage, except great mortality by the small pox" (9). Taken to his master's Narragansett residence, Smith initially accedes to his transformation by asserting his loyalty to his master and receiving lavish, patronistic praise in return. Soon, however, Smith begins to resist his masters with physical struggle, an escape scheme, and bitingly sarcastic wit. Once Smith is given the opportunity by a new master to purchase his own freedom, however, he ceases these overt acts of resistance and adopts a different strategy, one he will pursue vigorously to his final days: he claims his own name and the subjugation it figures. That is, he begins to accumulate capital of his own by engaging in his own ventures, selling his own labor and goods on the side to whites he encounters while being hired out by his masters, in the interest of saving enough money to buy his freedom. As we saw earlier in this chapter, the terms "perquisites" and "ventures" were commonly used in the Atlantic zone during this period to name sailors' efforts to trade and earn for themselves. In Smith's efforts to claim the very term that also marked his own enslavement, to articulate freedom with a word that always means slavery—venture—we see the paradox within which Smith writes his life. It is precisely this paradox that fills the silence left by Hammon's narrative.

Smith ends chapter 2 with his purchase of his own freedom, and begins chapter 3 with an account of his move to Long Island and his immediate prowess as a free laborer:

> In the space of six months I cut and corded upwards of four hundred cords of wood. Many other singular and wonderful labors I performed in cutting wood there, which would not be inferior to the one just recited, but for brevity sake I must omit them. . . . This money I laid up carefully by me. Perhaps some may enquire what maintained me all the time I was laying up money. I would inform them that I bought nothing which I did not absolutely want. . . . as for superfluous finery I never thought it to be compared with a decent homespun dress, a good supply of money and prudence. Expensive gatherings of my mates I commonly shunned, and all kinds of luxuries I was perfectly a stranger to; and during the time I was employed in cutting the aforementioned quantity of wood, I never was at the expense of six-pence worth of spirits. (18–19)

Throughout chapters 2 and 3, the narrative works to convert the "myself" of the narrative's first paragraph into this thrifty, hard-working subject who incessantly chronicles his labors and their monetary worth. Smith even calculates the value of the life and death tragedies he suffers. After telling of his futile efforts to stop his son from shipping out on a whaling voyage, he explains: "My son died of scurvy in this voyage, and Church [his son's master] has never yet paid me the least of his wages. In my son, besides the loss of his life, I lost equal to seventy five pounds" (19). He writes in a similar vein of his oldest child's death: "I procured her all the aid mortals could afford, but notwithstanding this she fell a prey to her disease, after a lingering and painful endurance of it. The physician's bill for attending her during her illness amounted to forty pounds" (21). Once again, after working for years to purchase his wife's freedom, Smith calculates his prudent timing: "I purchased my wife Meg, and thereby prevented having another child to buy, as she was then pregnant" (19). Repeatedly slipping from serious concern for his family's well-being to serious concern for his savings, equating the value of his family with the value of his labors by incessantly calculating the cost of both, Smith does not just coldly calculate the cost of death in these passages. He also implicitly gives his calculable labors the incalculable value of life.

This oscillation between calculable and incalculable values suggests that Smith wants something more than just capital from his ventures. Or rather, to Smith capital means more than just wealth. As with Equiano, capital, it seems, means an expansive, social, substantial freedom. Smith's ventures throughout chapter 2 are consistently tied to his efforts to purchase his own freedom, and, throughout chapter 3, the freedom of his enslaved family, friends, and even casual acquaintances. Smith thus not only seeks to gain access to and control over the formal and abstract equality of capitalist exchange—in which subjects enter the market, momentarily suspend the differences between their commodities and between their own identities, and encounter each other as formally and abstractly equal exchangers of formally and abstractly equal commodities—but he also seeks to convert that formal and abstract equality into a much more substantial freedom.[71] Rather than simply seeking inclusion in formal and abstract equality, Smith strives to practice equality as a weapon against the racism by which he and other Africans were named on the cusp of the Middle Passage.

Actively claiming the very terms of his own subjugation, Smith, like Equiano, succeeds in a certain way. After he purchases his own freedom and that of many others, he buys a large plot of land, a small fleet of ships, and a few houses. Yet he places at least as much emphasis on the repeated injustices he suffers in his mercantile endeavors as on his successes. After purchasing his own freedom around 1765, for instance, Smith refuses to celebrate: "Being thirty-six years old, I left Col. Smith once for all. I had already been sold three different times, made considerable money with seemingly nothing to derive it from, had been cheated out of a large sum of money, lost much by misfortunes, and paid an enormous sum for my freedom" (18). This misfit between the formal equality of capitalist exchange and the substantive freedom Smith seeks steadily takes on greater import as the narrative progresses.

For instance, early in chapter 3 Smith highlights both the marine trade's relative freedom from land-based racism and the increasing power of that racism:

> In the night time I fished with sernets and pots for eels and lobsters, and shortly after went a whaling voyage in the service of Col. Smith. After being out seven months, the vessel returned laden with four hundred barrels of oil. About this time I became possessed of another dwelling house, and my temporal affairs were in a pretty prosperous condition. This and my industry was what alone saved me from being expelled that part of the island [i.e., eastern Long Island] in which I resided, as an act was passed by the select-men of the place, that all negroes residing there should be expelled. (20)

Perhaps it is Smith's wealth that protects him from expulsion, but by writing "This *and* my industry" he seems to suggest that his hard earned "prosperous condition" was not his only safeguard. "This" may refer to the maritime labor that took him off the island for seven months, or, relatedly, to his connections to Col. Smith. Free and prosperous, but also well connected and out of the sight of local whites for much of the year, Smith seems here to acknowledge that "industry" is not sufficient to forge freedom, that the maritime world is a necessary supplement to his hard work, a counterforce to increasing, terrestrial racism.

According to the 1771 census, eastern Long Island, or Suffolk County, had the largest population of any county on Long Island, with a total population of 13,128, 11 percent of which was black. With an ample labor pool, the white political structure might have turned against poor and enslaved blacks in order to relieve white competition over labor and/or land. Such expulsions were increasingly common during the Revolutionary era and were at times coupled with land expropriation, to which Smith might have become vulnerable. Indeed, three paragraphs later Smith tells us that a few years after this act, "I disposed of all my property at Long Island, and came from thence into East Haddam," Connecticut (20). I will return to this racialized form of enclosure in the last section of this chapter, but for now I want to note that, by linking his apparently narrow escape from expulsion to his sudden move, he shows us how economic activity on land was being increasingly racialized during the Revolutionary period.

Smith proceeds to show how tenuous even maritime industry was becoming for black mariners at the end of the eighteenth century by paying particular attention to the repeated instances in which he is bilked and swindled in the coastal trade: "During my residence at Long Island, I raised one year with another, ten cart loads of water melons, and lost a great many besides by the thievishness of the sailors" (20). Then, he immediately expands on this "thievishness": "Since my residence at Haddam neck, I have owned of boats, canoes and sail vessels, not less than twenty. These I mostly employed in the fishing and trafficking business, and in these occupations I have been cheated out of considerable money by people whom I traded with taking advantage of my ignorance of numbers" (21). In the very next paragraph, the narrative suggests that Smith's misfortunes might be due to something other than his mathematical skills:

> About twelve years ago, I hired a whale-boat and four black men, and proceeded to Long Island after a load of round clams. Having arrived there, I first purchased of James Webb, son of Orange Webb, six hundred and sixty clams, and afterwards with the help of my men, finished loading my boat. The same evening, however, this Webb stole my boat, and went in her to Connecticut river, and sold her cargo for his own benefit. I thereupon pursued him, and at length, after an additional expense of nine crowns, recovered the boat; for the proceed of her cargo I never could obtain any compensation. (21–22)

By cheating Smith, these sailors do not simply deprive Smith of money; they also refuse to recognize him as an equal in exchange, effectively enacting a quotidian version of the Long Island expulsion act. This theft from an all-black crew and, in particular,

Smith's failure to "obtain any compensation" suggest that white traders on the northeastern U.S. coast increasingly respected little cross-racial solidarity with black mariners. Once again, the relative freedom blacks experienced on the sea in the eighteenth century seems to become quite tenuous toward century's end.

Despite his relative prosperity, such instances lead Smith effectively to repudiate mercantile capitalism by the end of his life. Crucially, he concludes the narrative with the following incident from around 1781, filled with bitterness and despair at the final outcome of his mercantile strategy to claim the very terms of his own subjugation:

> Being going to New-London with a grand-child, I took passage in an Indian's boat, and went there with him. On our return, the Indian took on board two hogshead of molasses, one of which belonged to Capt Elisha Hart, of Saybrook, to be delivered on his wharf. When we arrived there, and while I was gone, at the request of the Indian, to inform Captain Hart of his arrival, and receive the freight for him, one hogshead of the molasses had been lost overboard by the people in attempting to land it on the wharf. Although I was absent at the time, and had no concern whatever in the business, as I was known to a number of respectable witnesses, I was nevertheless prosecuted by this conscientious gentleman, (the Indian not being able to pay for it) and obliged to pay upwards of ten pounds lawful money, with all the costs of court. I applied to several gentlemen for counsel in this affair, and they advised me, as my adversary was rich, and threatened to carry the matter from court to court till it would cost me more than the first damages would be, to pay the sum and submit to the injury, which I accordingly did, and he has often since insultingly taunted me with my unmerited misfortune. Such a proceeding as this committed on a defenceless stranger, almost worn out in the hard service of the world, without any foundation in reason or justice, whatever it may be called in a christian land, would in my native country have been branded as a crime equal to highway robbery. But Captain Hart was a *white gentleman*, and I a *poor black African*, therefore it was *all right, and good enough for the black dog*. (22)

At first glance, this seems to be a simple instance of a white captain swindling an elderly black sailor. However, the language Smith uses to describe this incident tells us more than a first glance might suggest. Why, first of all, is Smith held responsible for this business in which he "had no concern whatever"? It would seem that he is known to this Captain Hart, just as he says he "was known to a number of respectable witnesses," as someone with resources. His parenthetical "the Indian not being able to pay for it" suggests as much. Presumably, though Smith is not venturing anything on this day, Captain Hart goes after him precisely because Smith's previous ventures have allowed him, despite many similarly unjust swindles, to participate successfully in mercantile capitalism. Hart's unjust suit thus punishes Smith for his efforts to claim the terms of his own subjugation. That is, the suit attempts to resubjugate Smith for his efforts to participate in the very system of capitalist exchange that sought to reduce him to a mere venture.

On what grounds does Hart punish Smith? Smith would seem to know a good deal about Hart's rationale since he tells us that Hart "often since insultingly taunted me with my unmerited misfortune." From these taunts, it seems that Smith gleaned his punishment on racial grounds. When he gives his own interpretation of the incident in the final two sentences of the paragraph, he emphasizes that Hart's effort relies on the racial distinction between "a *white gentleman*" and "a *poor black African,*" "*the black dog.*" Yet Smith also emphasizes another distinction Hart seems to invoke. He suggests that Hart understood him also as a "stranger," a term more often used at the time to mark national differences, as we saw in Equiano's narrative. In effect, Hart seems to remind Smith that they also do not share an emerging, U.S. national identity. With the fervor of the Revolution still bubbling throughout the colonies, Hart may be at the forefront of quotidian racial and national imaginings in his insistence that Smith cannot participate in economic activity. Hence, Hart turns to the courts, within which Smith's lack of citizenship would have made his legal standing tenuous. The language of this passage thus urges us to see not just the racial distinction with which Hart rejects Smith's effort to produce substantial freedom through engagement in the formal and abstract equality of capitalist exchange. It also suggests that Hart articulates such formal and abstract equality with emergent, particularized, national identity.

Finally, Hart's need to reiterate incessantly the terms of his bilking of Smith—"he has often since insultingly taunted me with my unmerited misfortune"—specifies the character of this articulation. As with Equiano, it is not simply that Smith is excluded from equality. Rather, Hart apparently must ritually reinvoke his exclusion of Smith, turning that exclusion into a kind of perpetual performance—indeed, a discursive practice—that enables Hart to venture on. If economic historians have found diverse, mercantilist efforts on the part of emerging nation-states to nationalize economic activity during the eighteenth and early nineteenth centuries, then perhaps we can see in Smith's increasingly furtive mercantile exchanges a fertile, racialized, quotidian ground for such efforts.

The "strangeness" attributed to Smith in this final scene is repeatedly invoked by another mariner narrative also set partially on the eastern U.S. seaboard: *The Voyages and Adventures of John Willock, Mariner.*[72] Like Smith's narrative, Willock's *Voyages* was first published in the United States in 1798. Indeed, Willock goes to sea on May 10, 1781, the apparent year of Smith's encounter with Elisha Hart. Yet a close reading of the figure of the "stranger" in *Voyages* suggests that Willock's "strangeness" has markedly different implications for his everyday life as well as for the everyday life of late eighteenth-century North America.

A tale of a young white Scottish boy who, Crusoe-like, takes to the sea out of a headstrong and naive disdain for his family, *Voyages* quickly foregrounds emerging North Atlantic nationalisms. Early in the narrative, Willock gives his impression of Cadiz, where his ship has docked in 1783: "The inhabitants of Cadiz are a strange mixture of French, Portuguese, Italians and Moors, Irish adventurers and English smugglers. Pride, laziness, and filth, are their characteristicks. They have much external sanctity, and on some occasions are very devout" (90). This national menagerie is also registered by the Spanish authorities, yet in a more systematic fashion: "Upon

entering [the town], officers appointed for the purpose strictly search them, if strangers, for prohibited goods; and as no one is allowed to take Spanish money out of the
kingdom, people disposing of their goods here, must either take goods in return, or
bills of exchange" (89–90). Invoking one of the tactics Spanish mercantilism deployed
to nationalize wealth within its dominions, Willock reveals how governmental discursive practices of the period transformed the meanings of national identities. The "inhabitants" to which Willock refers are systematically transformed by Spanish colonial
policy from a general "strange mixture" into a codified population of "strangers" and
Spaniards, just as the "Spanish money" circulating among these diverse inhabitants
is nationally codified by export restrictions. In the process of being subjected to and
subjectified within these national policies, the searched strangers and the exempt Spaniards learn to understand "a strange mixture" as a systematic hierarchy of nationally
codifiable subjects.

Even in those moments when Willock resists such national subjectification, the
narrative exposes the difficulty of such resistance in the face of the burgeoning nationalism of the European world-economy. After being captured off an American ship by
a Turkish ship and marched through Morocco, Willock arrives in the town of Mogodore with a large group of captive French, Spanish, and English mariners: "Though
we were of different countries and religions," Willock declares, "both national and
religious differences were lost, in the consideration that we were all Europeans and
Christians" (156). However, when they appeal to "the first European vessel which had
arrived during our stay in the place," they are met "with a Dutch indifference" by the
ship's Dutch ambassador: "He promised, courtier-like, to do every thing in his power
for us: and courtier-like, I suppose, thought no more about us, for we never heard another word of the business" (159). "Soon after this," they have "the like success" with
a Portuguese ship's ambassador (159). Willock invokes the feudal term "courtier" to
describe the Dutch ambassador's obsequiousness, but the suffix "-like" marks the term
as an analogy, thereby also highlighting the difference between feudal governmental
forms and this scene of emergent, mercantilist competition. Depicting at once the
vigorous diversity of the Atlantic zone and the competitive struggle among national
powers, Willock reveals an emergent tension between burgeoning nationalisms and
the traditional alliances among workers on ships.

Though Willock and his fellow mariners hold out hope for "the arrival of ambas-
sadors from Britain and America; from either of which we made ourselves certain of
obtaining every thing we wished," those hopes are also dashed in the face of Atlantic
nationalism (164). When the British ambassador arrives, they approach him with the
utmost respect and a vivid account of their sufferings, but meet only this dismissal:
"'You sailed in an American bottom, you say? Why do you not apply to the great
Mr. Washington? he is the most proper person to procure your liberty . . . Had your
country remained under the British government, you might then have had some claim
upon my friendship, but as matters now stand, if one word from me would procure
you liberty, you should not have it'" (164). When Willock replies "that other two
young men and myself were natives of the British dominions, and were willing to

enter on board of a man of war, if he would procure liberty for us," the ambassador turns a deaf ear: "Without deigning to answer us, he turned round, and with a stately air walked into another apartment" (164). Willock's "European and Christian" solidarity among captive sailors is suddenly tenuous in the face of the imperial nationalism of this British official, wounded by U.S. independence. As the battleground between the British and the United States shifted to the Atlantic after the War of Independence, such British resentment of the American merchant marine came to the fore, in this case making Willock a stranger to Britain.

In two crucial scenes in eastern U.S. ports, however, Willock's "strangeness" is transformed in a way Smith's could never be. Early in the narrative, Willock is cruelly beaten by his captain for failing to find the ship's "candle-snuffers"—devices used to adjust the wick of a candle or a lamp. Willock is then sent into New York City, where their ship is docked, to purchase "a pair of snuffers":

> Glad to be relieved on any terms from his barbarity, I made every exertion my little remaining strength would admit of, and got ashore, resolving to see him no more: but alas! I was a stranger, without money or friends, and at so late an hour, no house would admit me, so that I had no alternative but to return to the ship. A man in the street directed me to a brazier's, and having purchased a pair of snuffers, I once more went on board, firmly determined to make my escape in the morning. (35)

Willock represents the shore as a welcome escape from the brutality of his shipboard superior, thereby reversing the sea and shore relationship found in the black mariner narratives I have been considering. In addition, he is helped with his transaction by "a man in the street" despite being a thirteen-year-old "stranger" wandering an unfamiliar city at a late hour. This apparently minor incident reflects a quotidian acceptance of white "strangers" on the shores of the United States that contrasts with Smith's many incidents of bilking and swindling in general and his encounter with Hart in particular.

Much later, after Willock and his fellow captives are freed from the North African captivity mentioned above, they return to Alexandria, Virginia. Again he rejoices upon arriving on U.S. shores, and with apparent good cause, for the narrative depicts a scene in which Alexandrians flock to welcome him. Because the sailors had formed a bond by sharing what resources they could garner under captivity, and because some of the captives are from the United States, all are treated with equanimity by the Alexandrians: "We . . . were met and welcomed by every one in the town, who knew, or had ever heard of us. Every one was anxious to hear the story of our captivity, to relieve our wants, and make us forget our long and painful bondage" (217). Willock proceeds to depict this welcome in most dramatic terms:

> An American has very little of the Frenchman about him. His invitations are not ceremonious, but they are from the heart. Many invitations we were obliged to refuse, for this day at least, as we had agreed among ourselves, before we cast anchor, to make our first visit to a house where we were all acquainted, in order to spend the day all together.

Thither we went, and were immediately surrounded by almost every person in the town, who had the slightest acquaintance with any of us.

We had the most pleasant day I ever experienced. I had yet neither got myself rigged out with cloaths, nor any birth to enable me to make money to purchase them; but I was in the land of liberty, plenty and peace, I never bestowed a thought on to-morrow, and ragged as I was, like the first pair in paradise, I knew not that I was naked. We told our sufferings to a multitude of both sexes, and many of our female friends, like Desdimonia, "loved us for the dangers we had passed:" and "we loved them that they did pity us." After spending a very jovial afternoon, we sallied forth into the streets, and in walking down to the river, I was met by an old acquaintance, one Farria, mate of a brig which traded to Philadelphia. (218)

Invited back to Farria's house for the evening, Willock comments: "For my own part, I enjoyed that evening a happiness to which I had long been a stranger, and often blessed the memory of Columbus, for having discovered a country, where so much peace, harmony liberty and plenty, may be attained without any violent exertions to come at them" (219).

Willock's "strangeness"—already represented as unproblematic in his late night encounter on the streets of New York—is dramatically transformed in Alexandria into familiarity. The Alexandria scene enacts the civilizing myth of "New World" colonization and the national myths of immigrant success and melting pot diversity all at once. Yet the paradoxical nationalism with which Willock introduces the scene of radical democracy in Alexandria—"An American has very little of the Frenchman about him"—suggests that these myths of universality are supplemented by particularity. The discursive practices of national and racial identity circulating in the North Atlantic in the 1780s seem to subjectify Willock as one of Butterworth's "young citizens of the world," a subject abstracted into formal equality with other Americans, a formal equality supplemented by emergent national identities. Willock is thus able to maintain his confidence about the sea to the final pages of *Voyages*: "As I am not to be deterred by the misfortunes of my past life from prosecuting my favourite employment, but mean immediately to visit some other part of the globe, I beg leave for the present to bid my reader adieu: if my after life should be productive of any thing deserving his notice, we may perhaps renew our acquaintance upon some future occasion" (283).

The narrative even hints at the racial form of Willock's emergent sense of belonging. Twice Willock identifies not as a British subject, but rather as a white colonial: first, as we saw above, when he declares to the British ambassador in Mogodore that he is a native of "British dominions" (164); and second, when he represents himself to a "Moorish" governor in North Africa as "from America," even though he is actually from Scotland and has only been sailing on a U.S. ship (99). These two moments suggest that Willock's narrative transforms his Scottish origins into a transatlantic, white colonial identity that makes his "strangeness" in the United States not so very strange.

By following Willock along his circuitous path to Alexandria, we see emergent nationalisms in the Atlantic zone pushing him toward the United States and steadily subjectifying him as no stranger to America. His abject poverty does not prevent him from initially partaking in "liberty, plenty and peace"; his lack of any future employment does not prevent his initial abstraction into what he represents as a perpetual, Edenic present. In turn, by following Venture Smith along his path to disillusionment we can see how Willock's national familiarity depends upon a racialized equality. The egalitarianism of mutual recognition in the late eighteenth-century United States—represented in economic and social exchanges of money, goods, and stories in the ports and markets of Connecticut and Virginia—expresses an abstract equality articulated with increasingly codified racial and national particularities. Read together and against Smith's narrative, *Voyages* suggests that, in the United States of the 1780s, a "strangeness" articulated with whiteness actually enables the emergence of a paradoxically universal particularity of formally equal Americans.

A Preacher of the Gospel

In *The Life, History, and Unparalleled Sufferings of John Jea, the African Preacher,* published around 1815, John Jea offers a spiritual autobiography for which maritime labor is also a crucial touchstone.[73] As Jea tells us in the first sentences of his narrative, he was born in 1773 in Old Callabar, Southern Nigeria, and in 1775 he and his family were "stolen, and conveyed to North America, and sold for slaves" in New York to Oliver and Angelika Triehuen. Working as a field slave in rural New York under the "very cruel" Triehuens, Jea initially rejects the proslavery preachings of his masters' Dutch Reformed Church: "My rage and malice against every person that was religious was so very great that I would have destroyed them all, had it been in my power" (94). Yet Jea soon learns to use religion against slavery. When he is brutally punished by his master for his initial efforts to "know God" for himself, he redoubles his efforts, perhaps sensing his proximity to a powerful discourse. When he gains his freedom around 1788, he begins to travel throughout the Atlantic zone as a strident and unorthodox itinerant preacher who never fully affiliates with any institutional church. As Graham Russell Hodges has shown, Jea blends traces of his childhood Efik cosmology with the Dutch Reformed theology of his first masters and with many of the varieties of Methodism that circulated among blacks and the poor in the late eighteenth- and early nineteenth-century Atlantic world.[74]

Unlike Equiano or Smith, however, Jea never places much stock in mercantile capitalism, declaring at one point that he took to the sea

> not to seek mine own interest, but the interest of my Lord and Master Jesus Christ; not for the honour and riches of this world, but the riches and honours of that which is to come: I say, not for the riches of this world, which fadeth away; neither for the glory of man; not for golden treasure; but my motive and great concern was for the sake of my Lord and Master, who went about doing good, in order to save poor wicked and sinful creatures. (145)

For Jea, ships and ports function primarily as sites for spiritual articulations. Though Jea eschews the lure of freedom through mercantile capitalism, he certainly makes a living from the sea for a good part of his life, often as a cook on deep sea vessels. By representing labor as a means to his evangelical ends, Jea works to pry black subjectivity loose from racial capitalism, and to render a spiritual identity beyond commodification.

This effort is strikingly figured when he addresses his "dear reader . . . born in Britain" early in the narrative:

> Recollect that as you possess much, much will be required; and, unless you improve your advantages, you had better be a slave in any dark part of the world, than a neglecter of of [sic] the gospel in this highly favoured land; recollect also that even here you might be a slave of the most awful description:—a slave to your passions—a slave to the world—a slave to sin—a slave to satan—a slave of hell—and, unless you are made free by Christ, through the means of the gospel, you will remain in captivity, tied and bound in the chains of your sin, till at last you will be bound hand and foot, and cast into outer darkness, there shall be weeping and gnashing of teeth for ever. (93)

By setting chattel slavery within the larger context of human slavery to sin, this passage works against the dichotomy between positively valued whiteness, material wealth, and freedom on the one hand, and negatively valued blackness, poverty, and slavery on the other. Positing a realm of disadvantage, darkness, and enslavement to which white slaveowners are particularly susceptible, Jea renders an alternative realm of advantage, light, and freedom available to enslaved Africans. In turn, he represents slavemasters as keeping blacks from this realm of spiritual freedom—"our master would make us work, and neglect the concerns of our souls" (94)—rather than as keeping blacks from participating fully in mercantile capitalism, as Smith does.[75] The sea thus emerges from Jea's text as a potential zone of spiritual freedom, both in his lifelong commitment to evangelizing on ships and ports—"it pleased God to put it into my mind to cross the Atlantic main" (123)—and in his persistent invocation of water as a figure for baptism and freedom (99).

Yet the sea is not simply the site of Jea's theology of antislavery and antiracism. As a medium on which he can travel more readily than the shore, it offers a mobility that figures freedom itself: "you must think that I suffered very much by travelling to and fro; but I counted it all joy that I was worthy to suffer for the glory of God" (136). Consequently, the injustices he suffers at the hands of white masters and fellow sailors do not function as obstacles to an ideal mobility defined by freedom through economic opportunity; rather, mobility as evangelical itinerancy makes spiritual freedom possible.

Because he is not concerned with mercantile capitalism, Jea does not chronicle repeated incidents of swindling and bilking as exemplary instances of oppression under racial capitalism. Rather, he recounts his encounters with the injustices of slavery, with the "sinfulness" of those around him—particularly slave masters and sailors who prohibit or mock his religious fervor—as well as with the orthodox theologies of religious officials whom he debates in England. Toward the end of his narrative, however, Jea does recount an incident that brings him into contact with the historical articulation of race, nation, and equality I have examined throughout this chapter.

Sailing in the British brig *Iscet of Liverpool* out of Portsmouth in 1810, Jea and his shipmates are captured off the coast of Brittany by a French privateer. After being marched to prisons in Cambria and then in Brest, Jea and his shipmates are "sent on board of a French corvette, under American colours, to go and fight against the English" (155). However, Jea and some twenty other sailors refuse to "enlist under the banner of the tyrants of this world; for far be it from *me* ever to fight against Old England, unless it be with the sword of the gospel" (155). Consequently, all are imprisoned again by the French. Jea's anti-American, pro-English stance was common among Atlantic blacks of the period, since British tactics during and after the American Revolution had included suppression of the slave trade and offers of freedom to black Americans who fought against the Americans.[76] In addition, the most active abolitionist movement of the day was solidly based in Britain, and blacks had for some time seen England as a place they could live more freely. However, we must also notice that Jea's pro-English sentiment is not unqualified; he expresses a willingness to suspend that sentiment if his religious convictions were to direct him so, "unless it be with the sword of the gospel." This tactical national allegiance indicates that for Jea, freedom is not yoked to national identity; rather, the freedom he seeks is tied to a "gospel" that could readily abandon any such identity.[77]

After receiving harsh treatment in prison, all the sailors except Jea consent to fight the British, so the French authorities bring him before "the council and head minister of the Americans" (155). This time Jea suppresses his anti-Americanism, instead taking a pacifist position: "I told them I was determined not to fight against any one and that I would rather suffer any thing than do it. . . . I was determined not to do any work, for I would rather suffer any thing than fight or kill any one" (155). The American officials nonetheless force Jea to express his views on nationality:

> The head minister then asked me what I was at, that I would not fight for my country. I told him that I was not an American, but that I was a poor black African, *a preacher of the gospel*. He said, "Cannot you go on board, and preach the gospel there?"—"No, Sir," said I, "it is a floating hell, and therefore I cannot preach there." The *[sic]* said the council, "We will cool your Negro temper, and will not suffer any of your insolence in our office." So they turned me out of their office; and said that I had liberty to go any where in the town, but not out of the town; that they would not give me any work, provisions, or lodgings, but that I should provide it myself. (155)

Tying a critique of working conditions on ships of war to his anti-Americanism, Jea asserts a syncretic identity: poor, black, African, and a preacher of the gospel. By again subordinating his pro-English sentiment to these other identities—he does not even mention England here—Jea's syncretism carves out a heterodox Christian identity irreducible to nationality. Against this, the American minister, a Mr. Veal, furiously works to subject Jea to a racially and nationally codified identity, first by seeking Jea's service in the military, then by representing Jea's refusal as irrational, and finally by punishing Jea with forced vagabondage.

Ironically, apparently because he cannot apprehend Jea's syncretic identity, Veal deprives Jea of material goods but gives him the freedom he values most: mobility. Jea immediately begins preaching about the town, and within a few days he gains the favor of the French officials as well as "the nobility and gentry," who give him food and shelter in exchange for his sermons (156). This infuriates the American officials, who in vain press the French inhabitants to turn Jea away. After over a year, a peace is declared, and Jea applies to the "American counsellor," a Mr. Dyeott, for a passport to England, which is predictably refused: "He denied me, and said that he would keep me in France until he could send me to America, for he said that I was an American, that I lied in saying I was married in England, and that I was no African. I told him with a broken heart, and crying, that I was an African, and that I was married in England" (157). Jea persists in his efforts to leave for England, and describes in detail his many trips back and forth between the American officials and the more sympathetic French officials. Eventually, the latter obtain his passport to England, where Jea arrives to find his family well. After thanking God and appealing to the reader's own religious sentiments, Jea ends the narrative.

From this climactic sequence, "America" emerges as a racial and national figure that Jea counters with a mobile, syncretic identity. Dyeott ignores Jea's religious identity, and insists that Jea is neither English nor African, but American and black; whereas the former constellation would give Jea an unorthodox freedom, the latter would reduce him to chattel slavery. By recounting this exchange in such detail, Jea emphasizes that the war in which Veal and Dyeott seek to impress him is one for the freedom and equality of a racially particularized "America."

This war is, of course, the War of 1812 between the British and the United States, a war that Immanuel Wallerstein has called "more or less the last act of the settler decolonization of the United States."[78] Despite its formal independence, by 1812 the United States had not significantly eroded British maritime power, in particular British control over Atlantic trading. Consequently, the United States saw an opportunity to increase both its Atlantic and its continental power when the British and the French renewed fighting on the continent. By the end of the war with the Treaty of Ghent in 1814, Britain still had neither surrendered Canada nor ceded the main pillar of its maritime power: the navigation code's monopoly of carriage. The United States did, however, take crucial steps toward securing western and southern North America with the grudging blessing of the British. At stake in the international struggle that ensnares Jea, then, is the solidification of territorially specific economies with an eye to hegemony in the world system. The War of 1812 was fought through mercantilist principles and practices, and consequently increased the demand on North Atlantic subjects to declare national allegiance.

In effect, Jea offers us a history-from-below of this war and its mercantilist conjuncture, showing how it subjectified even its most minor players within quotidian national and racial discursive practices. The vigor with which Veal and Dyeott attempt to impress Jea into service against the British as an irrational, inarticulate "Negro" American with no freedom of will, and their utter inability to comprehend the syncretic subjectivity with which Jea counters their efforts, show how world system conflicts materialize in the local worlds of ships and ports. These U.S. bureaucrats assume a self-evident articulation of race, nation, and equality to the point of bafflement at anyone who would deny or refuse such an articulation.

"To Ship as Cook"

When Jea offers his marriage in England as proof that he is not American, he does not simply claim the British abolitionist mantel. He also invokes a crucial, gendered element of black maritime labor. During the eighteenth century, black women increasingly took shoreside service work in Atlantic ports as black men shipped out, and marriages that bridged the sea and shore divide gave each the confidence that they had another source of income, not to mention affective support, to survive volatile times. However, the rise of mercantilism placed extreme stress on this arrangement, such that by the middle of the nineteenth century the gendered form of black maritime labor had been transformed. By invoking his wife, then, Jea reminds us that, though black mariners were nearly all men, their labor was by no means uncomplicatedly or uniformly gendered. Since Jea tells us nothing more about his wife, we have to turn to other narratives for a more precise account of the gendered form of black maritime labor at this mercantilist conjuncture. In this section, drawing on two neglected but exemplary narratives separated by nearly a century—*Memoirs of the Life of Boston King, a Black Preacher* (1798) and *The Life of George Henry* (1894)—I suggest that the rise and decline of black Atlantic mariners is indexed by a transformation in the historical articulation of race, gender, and labor. Whereas during the eighteenth century black mariners formed extensive, relatively egalitarian social and economic bonds with black women who worked in the ports of the maritime sector, with their nineteenth-century decline black mariners saw their shipboard labor deskilled and feminized, to which some responded with a new, masculinist conception of their maritime work.

Born a slave in South Carolina in the late 1750s or early 1760s, Boston King spent much of his early life being hired out in the coastal or deep sea trades, until he eventually fled slavery to the British navy. Between March and June of 1798 *The Methodist Magazine* serialized his narrative, and a passage from the first installment reveals the gendered aspects of eighteenth-century black maritime labor. Writing about his first voyage on a British warship after escaping slavery, King recounts his efforts to disembark in New York and give land labor a try:

> Here I endeavoured to follow my trade, but for want of tools was obliged to relinquish it, and enter into service. But the wages were so low that I was not able to keep myself in clothes, so that I was under the necessity of leaving my master and going to another. I stayed with him four months, but he never paid me, and I was obliged to leave him also, and work about the town until I was married. A year after I was taken very ill, but the

Lord raised me up again in about five weeks. I then went out in a pilot-boat. We were at sea eight days, and had only provisions for five, so that we were in danger of starving. On the 9th day we were taken by an American whale-boat. I went on board them with a chearful countenance, and asked for bread and water, and made very free with them. They carried me to Brunswick, and used me well. Notwithstanding which, my mind was sorely disstressed at the thought of being again reduced to slavery, and separated from my wife and family.[79]

As a nominally free and independent individual at the start of this passage, King nevertheless struggles to survive under both the extremely harsh conditions of a common British naval seaman (for conditions on military vessels were significantly worse than on merchant vessels) and the exploitable circumstances of a black wage laborer in North America. In effect, he finds that the freedom he obtained upon escaping slavery also cut his terrestrial social bonds to a black community.

In turn, the phrase "until I got married" marks a significant transformation in his working as well as his personal life: the formation of a new, economic, and affective bond with a woman herself likely working in sectors of the economy tied to New York's maritime industries. King can now afford to ship out as a merchant mariner (first on "a pilot-boat" and then on "an American whale-boat") under decidedly better conditions than he encountered on the British man-of-war, knowing that he and his wife, and perhaps the wider black community in New York to which he is now likely tied through his marriage, can help each other through difficult straits, such as downturns in the mercantile economy and the ever-present threat of racial exploitation. King's marriage gives his nominal freedom some material substance, transforming his itinerant poverty into "a chearful countenance." The separation "from my wife and family" that makes him "sorely disstressed" is thus not simply the distance between them when he is at sea and she is in port; in fact, at such moments they are rather tightly bound to one another in a maritime social and economic web. Rather, he is "disstressed" at the ever-present possibility that capture or shipwreck might deprive him of his job as a mariner, cut his affective and material bond to his new community, and eventually drive him back into the lonely poverty of a single, isolated, landlocked black wage laborer or even slave.[80]

Singular research by Gary Nash has confirmed this gendered form of black Atlantic maritime labor, showing that diverse communities of eighteenth- and nineteenth-century blacks in northern U.S. seaports were sustained by extensive links between male seafaring labor and female shoreside labor, with women holding a range of jobs in the economies of ports that ringed the Atlantic. The high ratio of black women to men in seaports from which many black mariners shipped out after 1820, when federal census takers began to enumerate blacks by gender, is just one illustration of the social and economic links between black men at sea and black women on the shore.[81] As Laura Tabili puts it in her work on the British maritime sector, although women rarely worked as mariners in the Anglo-American world, maritime labor was nonetheless deeply gendered: "The division of labor between men and women occurred before a ship set sail, but the work of both sustained the industry, and maritime wages conferred benefits in shore communities."[82] This kind of linkage was not as common among white sailors who, as W. Jeffrey Bolster has shown, tended to be "geographically mobile, unmarried, and unlikely to stick with the sea unless promoted. Black sailors were older than their white shipmates; more rooted in their homeports; more likely to be married; more likely to persist in going to sea; and more likely to define themselves with dignity as respectable men because seafaring enabled at least some of them to provide for their families."[83]

Bolster's final reference to a discourse of providership requires much more careful consideration, however. That we see little trace of such a discourse in King's narrative is instructive. In fact, I contend that we do not begin to see such a discourse in black mariner literature until well into the nineteenth century. Even more important, I want to argue that this discourse is less an individualized, personal mode of male self-definition, as Bolster suggests, than a historical articulation, a structural phenomenon that indexes the gendered dynamics of the decline of black mariners. During this decline we see a transformation in social and economic relations between black men and women, with a masculinist conception of labor supplanting what had been, in the maritime sector at least, a more egalitarian social web.

Toward the end of the eighteenth century antagonisms began to emerge in this racialized sector of the Atlantic economy that would develop in markedly gendered terms. Again, Bolster's work is suggestive: "Right up to the Civil War, many black men paradoxically assumed the most 'feminine' roles aboard white-dominated ships to maintain their masculine roles as respectable providers in the black community."[84] The claim that the labor of black sailors was simultaneously feminized in the world economy and masculinized within black socioeconomic and familial networks seems strong, though we need to add some historical specificity. From the end of the eighteenth century, black men were increasingly restricted to service-oriented berths such as stewards and cooks. Simultaneously on land, this kind of service work was being vigorously feminized: work that was traditionally done by women was devalued as "unskilled" and poorly remunerated, while at the same time women were actively excluded from much "skilled" labor and were pushed into newly emerging service sectors.[85] In fact, this gendered division of labor seems to have been particularly strong among African Americans in northern seaports, as service-oriented work was one of the only avenues of employment available to urban black women.[86]

In addition, we must remember with Tabili, who sees this tendency continuing in the twentieth-century British maritime sector, that "Black men's assignment to shipboard women's work and their relegation to unskilled work were not parallel processes but part of the same process. The gendering of work and the gendering of skill mutually reinforced and were built into the racializing of work and the racializing of skill."[87] Tabili begs precisely the question we must consider here, if we are to evaluate Bolster's claim about a discourse of providership. Exactly how were gendered work and skill "built into" the racialization of work and skill on the North Atlantic?

To begin with, if the systematic rise of racial nationalism throughout the Atlantic in discursive practices such as mercantilism drove black men off the sea, then surely the gendered form of this nationalism gave that driving-off a particular shape. Since economic and political citizenship in North America was increasingly codified as a masculine identity and was concentrated in the hands of men, any mariner who accrued an ambivalent national identity—as did all black mariners, excluded as they were from national citizenship—was ambivalently gendered too.

Consider the 1789 debate over the first U.S. tariff with which I began this chapter. As the epigraph shows, James Madison figures the lack of a national tariff as a lack of national masculinity: the "impotency," "deficiency," and "imbecility" of the nation must be addressed by the "power" of male legislators elected by restricted male suffrage. Yet as we saw, Madison and his allies did not only seek to raise money for the national treasury and masculinist power for the nation with taxes on imports; they also sought to shore up national citizenship by discouraging imports and encouraging domestic production, exchange, and circulation. When Massachusetts Representative Fisher Ames declared that "Laying a small duty upon foreign manufactures must induce . . . one fellow citizen to barter with, or buy of another, what he had long been accustomed to take from strangers," he and Madison took for granted that these citizens were white men by law.[88] In addition, these citizens were forged in Anglo-American discursive practices that figured economic rationality and national potency as masculinity. The tariff debate is thus an archive of the emergence of what Dana D. Nelson has called "national manhood."[89]

Adam Smith vigorously exemplifies these discursive practices in *The Wealth of Nations*. For Smith, the economic actor is only a full individual if he is "naturally" a national subject:

> Every individual is continually exerting himself to find out the most advantageous employment for whatever capital he can command. It is his own advantage, indeed, and not that of the society which he has in view. But the study of his own advantage naturally, or rather necessarily leads him to prefer that employment which is most advantageous to the society. . . . every individual endeavours to employ his capital as near home as he can.[90]

By contrast, the subject whose "own advantage" is not "necessarily" "advantageous to [a] society" that is his "home" society is not a proper individual. He is, rather, a merchant:

> A merchant, it has been said very properly, is not necessarily the citizen of any particular country. It is in a great measure indifferent to him from what place he carries on his trade; and a very trifling disgust will make him remove his capital, and together with it all the industry which it supports, from one country to another. . . . The merchants knew perfectly in what manner [foreign trade] enriched themselves. It was their business to know it. But to know in what manner it enriched the country, was no part of their business.[91]

Smith complains in markedly gendered terms throughout *The Wealth of Nations* about these nonnational, deficient individuals known as merchants, decrying not only their flightiness but also their irrational "clamour and sophistry," as well as their selfish and deceitful, greedy, and wasteful ways.[92] The nonnational merchant as a feminized figure for nonnational economic activity functions as the very negation of, or threat to, the wealth of nations.[93]

Smith's characterization of the nonnational merchant draws discursively from eighteenth-century, Anglo-American debates over the gendered form of capital and labor, as well as the tenuous political and economic subjectivity of women. For instance, the very characteristics with which Smith depicts the nonnational merchant also emerge in eighteenth-century economic debates over the worthiness of credit. As Terry Mulcaire has argued, the imaginative, flighty, unstable, feminine form of Credit, invariably depicted as a woman, gave the capitalist marketplace a fantasmatic substance of passionate virtuousness with which to identify. However, that substance was rigorously supplemented by "political, social, and economic 'mechanisms' of positive power to manage those contradictions and conflicts" represented by Credit's unstable femininity. Consequently, in this discourse on Credit, "The state is no night watchman over an intrinsically rational and self-regulating marketplace; on the contrary, applying what Cato calls the 'proper regulations' to passions unleashed by the rise of commercial society requires the active engagement of state power in the market." Thus, a supplementary relationship emerges between feminized credit and masculinized regulatory mechanisms.[94]

Because, as we have seen, black sailors were ritually barred from citizenship and were likely to evade or to resist national identities, while simultaneously earning a living by supplementing their meager sea wages with their own mercantile "perquisites" and "ventures," their participation in mercantile capitalism was precariously gendered. To the extent that they tried to become economic "citizens of the world" by, as Olaudah Equiano writes, "commenc[ing] merchant" without being subjectified within national economies, the masculinity of their *nonnational* labor was suspect.[95] This offers one way of accounting for the simultaneous gendering and racializing of work and skill among North Atlantic black mariners.[96]

Did this transformation take the form of what Bolster calls a discourse of manly providership among black men? He suggests that throughout the eighteenth and nineteenth centuries the black mariner's pursuit of "manly equality" or "potent male identities" as "respectable masculine providers" expressed an inevitable "wish" for or interest in a generally strong subjectivity.[97] By contrast, I want to argue that such a pursuit—the form of which we will need to specify much more carefully, allowing for historical ambiguities and agonisms—emerged in the late eighteenth century as black men were increasingly restricted to feminized shipboard labor. The pursuit to which Bolster refers thus functioned not as a personalized character trait but rather as a defense against the increasingly raced and gendered form of mercantile capitalism during this mercantilist conjuncture. That is, we can trace a shift from a relatively egalitarian labor relationship between black men and women in the maritime sector during the eighteenth century—exemplified by Boston King's narrative—to a masculinist discourse of maritime labor among black men whose labor was being deskilled and feminized by racial capitalism.

The Life of George Henry, first published in 1894, exemplifies this shift, showing how the male preserve of sea labor had been transformed by the end of the nineteenth century into a defense against service work figured as women's work.[98] Born in 1819 in Virginia to enslaved parents, Henry, like Olaudah Equiano and Venture Smith, spends his adult life pursuing mercantile capitalist success. Sustained by relatively stable, free black economic networks in the North, Henry becomes what he calls "a respectable colored man," a member of the black bourgeoisie. Yet he also struggles against entrenched racism, and uses his narrative to expose and to decry pervasive racial exploitation.

As this struggle unfolds, the narrative performs an ever-more individuated masculinity that works to differentiate itself from "women's work." For instance, at the very beginning of his narrative Henry makes clear his hatred of household service work:

> I remember, when a boy, a man by the name of George Thompson, of my own name, provided that at his death mother and her family were to be free, but another man named Camm Griffith, being educated and skilled, still held her in bondage. But I caught the sound of freedom and was determined not to be fettered by any man. He tried his best to make me a dining room servant and wait on table, but having a dislike for that profession he did not succeed. I always had a mind above anything like that. So I studied how to get out of it. When one day he had a table full of company, I blew my nose in an offensive way, and something sticking to the plate that I handed to a guest, he became exasperated, and he highly delighted me by ordering me out; so he had no further use for me in that dining room. (6–7)

Sounding out "freedom" for the first time, Henry enters into a classed and raced conflict with his master. To counter Griffith's demand that he embody a polite dinner servant, Henry carefully stages a parody ("I studied how to get out of it"), offering a hyperembodiment that literally overflows the limits to which he has been assigned. "Sticking to the plate" that figures the promise of freedom Griffith broke, then, is "something" and some sound, "an offensive way" that echoes with all the domestic labor Henry's mother likely performed, all the clattering plates she handled in hope of some day getting her family to freedom. Expecting that Griffith will fail to understand the parody and rather be simply "exasperated" at a slave's natural incivility, as in fact happens, Henry delights in his ability to outstudy his "educated and skilled" master.

At the same time, the text makes clear that there is something about the labor of "waiting on table" that Henry especially "dislikes," above and beyond or perhaps in and through his mother's own domestic laboring. Indeed, he claims that he "always had a mind above anything like that" "profession" in particular, as if his body were weighed down not only by unfree labor in general, but precisely by "use . . . in that dining room." Henry's delight here is also a gendered one, a delight in thwarting his master's effort to bring him down to women's work.

This gendered delight is amplified in the next few paragraphs. First, Henry expresses a sartorial masculinity: "In those days they made the boys, when quite large, wear what they called 'Bandauns,' a sort of loose frock, and one day the boys all put theirs on and went off, but I determined to wear no such thing as that, so I bundled mine up, carried it down the hill, made a fire and burned it up . . ." (8). This individuated rejection of a feminine "frock" and of all "the boys" who compliantly wore one leads, in turn, to the next paragraph's rejection of childrearing. The "old folks" of his community

> tried to get me to nurse the children while the women were out to work, another occupation I always hated. So I studied how I should get out of that. I got a pin and tormented the child so bad they drove me out of that, and declared I should never mind any more children of theirs. I was determined to do none of their mean, low, occupations around houses. I aspired to something higher. (8)

Explicitly rejecting the "mean, low, occupations around houses" that women perform—when they are not "out to work" in the fields alongside men—Henry again performs a solitary act of "studied" resistance. Here, however, he does not raise himself above his master, but rather above the "old folks" of his own community just as he had risen above the other "boys" in their "Bandauns." The "sound of freedom" Henry "caught" working under Griffith thus works an ever more consistent beat as *The Life of George Henry* unfolds, articulating a determinate, individuated masculinity that simultaneously challenges and genders raced work.

This call for a more manly sound of freedom prefaces Henry's turn to sea labor in chapter 4, entitled "Efforts Toward Fame and Glory":

> Seeing vessels often coming into the harbor, and talking with the sailors, brightened my hopes of a better future than the dark and benighted ages in which I then lived, and in the words of Hon. Charles Sumner: "No honest, earnest effort in a good cause can fail." So I determined to make that effort, and thought best to go by water and widen my ideas of civilization. So the "boss" under whom I was working built a vessel on purpose to satisfy me, knowing that he would never be able to subdue me to the occupation I was then working at. This vessel was built on Strother's Point and was called Llewyllen. . . . I enlisted as cook, under Henry Weaver, her commander, the first captain I ever sailed with, also a crew of four others. I was just getting in my glory. I could see something of the outside world, without being shut up in one place altogether. (12)

As if to counter his subordination as a service worker under a new master, Henry retrospectively situates his first maritime job not only as the condition of possibility for freedom from slavery—"a better future than the dark and benighted ages in which I then lived"—but also as the first step in a progressive narrative of individual achievement: "I was just getting in my glory." Indeed, when he recounts his dockside conversations with sailors, Henry invokes the tradition of black sea labor passed on orally throughout the Atlantic, a tradition of stories that perhaps harkened back to the better times of the eighteenth century. The power of sea labor emerges from this passage in opposition to the "mean, low, occupations around houses" conducted by women, even though—indeed, I want to suggest, precisely because—he will be working in the ship's galley. Since he will indeed be shut up in the kitchen, Henry individuates his sea labor, cutting short any comparisons with his fellow shipmates and highlighting the distances he, as a glorious individual seaman, will travel from women's work.

The narrative continues to intensify the individuated masculinity of Henry's feminized sea labor, charting his emergence as a fearless and daring self-made man fighting against the injustices of slavery and racism. For instance, the narrative strikingly converts feminized sea labor into hierarchical, masculine providership in its first representation of Henry's wife, Annie Gordon:

> Just before I quit the Lewellyn, I came home from Alexandria one afternoon late, and I went to Dr. Murphy's where I supposed I had married a woman who would have been some use to me, named Annie Gordon, daughter of Betsey Parker. I did'nt eat any dinner aboard, and it was so late when we got in I would'nt commence loading that afternoon. I supposed I had a wife and a home. I sent for her to get me some supper. It was getting late and I was quite hungry. Just as she got my supper pretty well under way, her mistress sent for her, and said she must wait upon her first. I had to do the best I could, but it was the first time I found out I had neither wife nor home. I made up my mind then and there. I had two children by her, a girl and a boy. I said to myself, madam you may have your woman and her children. I will never work myself to death to raise children for your use. I never revealed the secret to any living being on earth, what I intended doing. I made out that I was delighted with my new schooner and new situation. The owners thought I was perfectly contented and there would be no more talk about quitting. I kept on making regular trips as usual, trip after trip. (33–34)

Unlike King, who narrates his way into his marriage, Henry introduces his wife suddenly and in the past tense—"I had married"—without any account of their history together. As a necessary assumption, an unspoken precondition for the very narration of his life, Annie Gordon's existence emerges as a normative ideal always already lost to slavery under her mistress—"I supposed I had married a woman who would have been some use to me," "I supposed I had a wife and a home," "it was the first time I found out I had neither wife nor home." By contrast, King's marriage is represented as a condition of possibility for his "chearful" emergence from poverty and social isolation, and a crucial element in his continuing good fortune.

Indeed, this scene condenses the losses of slavery—"her mistress sent for her, and said she must wait upon her first"—with Henry's loss of masculinity as a cook on the *Llewyllen/Lewellyn*. The moment he steps ashore, his feminized service work at sea is displaced onto his own hunger, and this hunger is in turn displaced onto the compensatory ideal of a useful wife cooking his meal. Annie Gordon's mistress thus disturbs the gendered order to which service work had been restored on land, undermining Henry's already precarious masculinity as well as her servant's freedom. Though Henry produces a critique of the injustice of his wife's mistress out of this scene—"I said to myself, madam, you may have your woman and her children. I will never work myself to death to raise children for your use"—he also genders that injustice as a challenge to his masculinity by engaging in another individualized, indeed completely isolated, act of resistance: "I never revealed the secret to any living being on earth, what I intended doing." Separating himself from his wife as he had separated himself from "the boys" who compliantly wore "Banduans" and the "old folks" who tried to make him take care of children, Henry leaves Annie Gordon in the doubly feminized position of domestic, racial servitude and single motherhood.

In the next four paragraphs, Henry's "secret" resistance to slavery takes an increasingly gendered form. First, he explains that he was so adept at getting timber, he would finish his work early and go hunting:

> I was also considered a great gunner. . . . In those days it was against the law for a colored man to carry a gun, but I carried one regularly every winter, and sometimes killed so much game that I could'nt bring it home, had to leave it on the shore. The biggest shot I ever made was eighteen ducks at one fire. I used to go off, two miles from home, and stay a night and a day gunning. I gave out my proclamation, that if any man love that gun better than his life, he could take it away from me. I would have shot him quicker than I would a duck. And there never was a man that attempted to molest me with a gun. But any other colored man in that neighborhood, caught with a gun, would have had the life chased out of him. (34–35)

Coming immediately after his account of his wife, this passage displaces Henry's "secret" resistance to her mistress onto his struggle against racist restrictions on "gunning," a consummate figure for the power of masculinity. His prowess again takes an individuated form, the "secret" becoming a "proclamation" against "any man," both the white men who would deny him his right to bear arms and "any other colored man" who was too weak to exercise that right.

Henry then tells of a frightening encounter he had while walking alone through the dark woods one night:

> When arriving about midway in the woods I saw something look white, like a sheet, so I had my dirk open in my hand and started boldly towards it. It wavered and wavered, as though it was most up to me, and I got so scared that my hands fell paralized and powerless. . . . But when I got up to it I found it to be a large whiteoak tree that had been cut down and stripped off for tan bark, and become dry, and it being damp that night everything else looked dark around, except that which had a white look, so I got up on it, sat up on it, and rolled on it, for a quarter of an hour. After that nothing could scare me. I was "boss" after that. (35–36)

This victory over his fear of the "whiteoak tree" allegorizes Henry's struggle against the ideology of whiteness. He discovers the mundane, "dry," "cut down and stripped" impotency of an image that had seemed to hold supernatural power. Yet again, this victory takes the form of an individualized masculinity when he ritually demonstrates his potency as "'boss'" by trouncing "that which had a white look."

In the following paragraph, Henry turns his victory over whiteness into a joke directed toward a group of women while he is on shore leave:

Another time I came home from Alexandria, no one knew I was in the river. I heard of the girls being at a dance and I went there, stationed myself outside till the dance broke up, so as to have some fun with the girls, as they were going home. As soon as the girls came out, I ran ahead of them and got to a place said to be haunted. I got one side of the road, pulled my coat up over my head, and streached myself on my hands and feet, and made two groans as the girls passed by. They started and outran a horse. . . . One was bedridden for two weeks and the others liked never to have got over it. I went aboard again and staied all night. Did'nt dare to let it be known that I was ashore, or they would have declared I was the ghost, as I was up to all such tricks. (36)

In this scene, Henry has moved from trouncing "that which had a white look" to inhabiting the power of that very whiteness, turning his own fear of whiteness against these women with an elaborate plan carried out the minute he steps foot on shore. An individuated masculinity again seems to compensate for his feminized labor on the sea by turning against shoreside femininity. His subjectification as a powerful man resisting racism here slips precipitously into his subjection within racialized masculinity, as he embodies the very power he had sought to oppose. Unsettled by his own inability to control the masculinity over which he had so recently become "boss," Henry expresses a profound, self-critical regret which he immediately displaces onto a renewed masculinity: "I was the sorriest man around there, and abused the young men for letting the girls go home alone. If I had been there I should have seen them home" (36). With this passage, in which he both separates himself from his role in the joke by blaming "the young men" and imagines himself as another, better man by claiming that he might have walked the women home, Henry critiques and disavows his own subjection. Yet his unsettled regret persists: "I made up my mind I never would do such a thing again, though it was 'all in fun'" (36).

Despite this persistent regret, the very next passage, which begins chapter 10, continues to articulate an individuated masculinity:

I will here give you a sketch of my history with Sally Griffin, to let you know that I was a man. She lived in Alexandria, on King street. She and her nephew owned the schooner Lewellyn, that I was master of for ten years. She was built on Strother's Point. After I wore her out, had another one built, the Susan Ellen, and I was making money for her, just the same as if you were shaking it off a tree. I went up one day in a hurry to pay her the money and she knocked my hat off, and I declared by all the Gods in creation that she should never take another cent out of my hands. (37)

By now master of the vessel on which he had begun working as a cook, Henry renews the conflict with white, female power he had begun with his wife's mistress. Out of this conflict, he produces an economic subjectivity supplemented by individualized masculinity. However, though Henry is no longer a cook, he is still a racialized, nonnational merchant whose labor is ambiguously gendered. The shifting signifier "she" exposes this ambiguity, as it refers first to Griffin, then to the *Llewyllen*, then to the *Susan Ellen*, and again to Griffin. The one ambiguous referent—"and I was making money for her"—ties "her" both to the *Susan Ellen*, the ship on which he was making money, and to Sally Griffin, the owner to whom he was giving most of the profits. Femininity emerges as a figure for the subjection with which he is struggling, as a figure for both the power of his female boss over him and the power of the ship that houses his ambiguously gendered labor. Henry stakes his freedom on attaining independence from both forms of power, and so devotes his narrative to "letting us know that he is a man" by figuring sharp differentiations between femininity and masculinity. *The Life of George Henry* maintains this form to its end, consistently coupling Henry's maritime drive toward independence and against pervasive racism with defensive assertions of the masculinity of his labor.

Later in the narrative, Henry attains his freedom by arriving on free soil in Philadelphia. Seeking shelter in the house of a black Baptist deacon, Henry explains that "I made known my desire, and stated that I was a member of the Baptist Church, and did not want to go among strangers" (46). Henry emphasizes his lack of national identity as a tenuously free noncitizen by representing white Philadephians as "strangers"—confidently reversing the identity Equiano and Smith were subjected to, and Willock was able to shed. The deacon turns him away, but Henry stays thanks to the intervention of the deacon's wife. After praising "all the female sex of the world" because of this woman's kindness, Henry explains that for his next job he was obliged to ship out as a sea cook:

> After leaving the good woman I went down upon the wharf, seeking for the first time my own living. Onward, onward, my mind flowed heavy to commence my career for freedom. Freedom! . . . Coming down from my lofty position as captain, I was obliged to ship as cook. For as I came North I found prejudice here greater than in the Southern States. I had to content myself with nine dollars a month as steward. But with all this I felt the proud dignity of manhood about me, and was determined to take up with anything that had money in it. (48)

With echoes of Harriet Wilson's *Our Nig*, Henry challenges the abolitionist discourse that pitted Northern modernity against Southern backwardness by foregrounding the modernity of racism in the North. However, *The Life of George Henry* places this challenge in the specific context of feminized black sea labor. Though he has just celebrated "the good woman" who asserted her domestic power by giving him shelter in her home, Henry nonetheless defends himself against domestic femininity by supplementing his own return to service work with an assertion of his masculinity: "I felt the proud dignity of manhood about me." This assertion seems necessary to continue the narrative of his rise to "freedom," since to this narrative "freedom" means access to the very formal and abstract equality of mercantile capitalism that we have seen throughout this chapter.

Let me conclude this section by pausing over the phrase "to ship as cook," for it carries all the implicit agonism and outright antagonism that characterized such labor across two centuries. An active decision to break from burgeoning racial nationalism on land, "to ship" long held an open-ended promise of a freedom to come for black men and women, an infinite possibility figured in this phrase by the infinitive. Yet by the time George Henry took to the sea, that possibility had been decidedly circumscribed, enclosed as it was in racially restricted labor that had been at once deskilled and feminized. For mariners like George Henry, this antagonism initiated a compensatory, individuated masculinity that sought to keep "the sound of freedom" ringing. "As cook" thus figures the circumscription of the promise of "to cook." Reading King's and Henry's narratives today, we can trace the rise of a mutually reinforced relationship among race, gender, and labor that ritually and systematically subjectified black men and women who sought freedom in the treacherous waters of racial capitalism's mercantilist conjuncture.

Enclosing the Open Sea

I have suggested that the intimate relationships among race, nation, and equality represented by the mariner narratives coincide with a period of intense, mercantilist regulation of North Atlantic economies, a regulation that took the form of racial nationalism. We see this intensification in Equiano's increasingly frequent "ill usage" throughout the Atlantic: at the hands of Danish officials in St. Croix and Stamp Act repeal celebrants in Charleston, South Carolina, as well as white passengers wary of his navigation knowledge; in Smith's quotidian encounters with the racial enclosures of the Long Island expulsion act as well as the "thievishness" of sailors and coastal traders; and in Jea's struggles with U.S. officials in France during the War of 1812, and particularly his efforts to wrest a mobile, spiritual freedom from imprisonment and forced vagabondage. King's reliance on his shoreside wife to survive the volatility of this conjuncture on the sea, and Henry's individuated claim to masculinity in the face of the seaside enclosure of his labor within the feminized service sector, show how this intensification also racialized gender in the Atlantic zone.

Disparate in their engagements with and against racial capitalism, these narratives nonetheless bear witness to a formative moment in which race, nation, gender, and equality are paradoxically constitutive of one another, forming what Étienne Balibar has called a "historical articulation":

> The connection between nationalism and racism is neither a matter of perversion (for there is no "pure" essence of nationalism) nor a question of formal similarity, but a question of historical articulation. . . . This is to say, by the very same token, that the articulation of nationalism and racism cannot be disentangled by applying classical schemas of causality, whether mechanistic (the one as the cause of the other, "producing" the other according to the rule of the proportionality of the effects to the cause) or spiritualistic (the one "expressing" the other, or giving it its meaning or revealing its hidden essence). . . . We must add one remark in conclusion on this hypothesis. Articulation—even complementarity—does not mean harmony.[99]

This historical articulation emerges not as the mechanistic or spiritualistic "superimposition" of a general and regressive notion of race upon a general and progressive notion of equality, as Bolster suggests, but rather in the paradoxical form, at once anticipatory and constitutive, figured by Cedric J. Robinson in his epochal study *Black Marxism: The Making of the Black Radical Tradition*:

> The historical development of world capitalism was influenced in a most fundamental way by the particularistic forces of racism and nationalism. This could only be true if the social, psychological and cultural origins of racism and nationalism both anticipated capitalism in time and formed a piece with those events which contributed directly to its organization of production and exchange.[100]

To say that world capitalism was influenced "in a most fundamental way" by racism and nationalism is to say that the very "worldliness" of world capitalism, its global economic development and the universalism of its political and ideological forms (such as citizenship, individualism, aesthetic culture), depends upon the vigorous production and maintenance of particularistic social identities. Indeed, the very modernity of capitalism consists in the paradoxical, agonistic, and at times antagonistic articulation of universalisms and particularisms. If Robinson and Balibar help us to reread this mercantilist conjuncture, they also urge a rereading of Marx's own account of mercantilism from the quotidian perspective of the mariner narratives. I would like to conclude this chapter with such a reading.

As I argue in the introduction, Marx's account of the emergence of the value-form—or the material form taken by economic, juridical, political, and social relations among people under capitalism—does not simply show how substantial, human relations are transformed into abstract relations of formal equivalence. Marx repeatedly suggests that those abstract relations of formal equivalence are always supplemented by material, particularized identities. Whether he writes of the transformation of "human labor-power in its fluid state" to "value in its coagulated state . . . as a congealed mass of human labor," or of "the definite social relation between men themselves which assumes, for them, the phantasmagoric form of a relation between things," Marx figures formal, abstract equality as having a complex, material, substantial particularity under capitalism.[101] The value-form, he repeatedly intimates, produces a universal abstraction that paradoxically has particularized substantiality. That is, as capitalism begins to revalue social relations through a process of formal abstraction, the value-form intimately articulates abstract equality with vigorously produced particularities. Indeed, as I argue in the introduction, Marx's work on slavery in the United States reveals that one such particularity is race: "The business in which slaves are used is conducted by *capitalists*. The mode of production which they introduce has not arisen out of slavery but is grafted on to it."[102]

In the first volume of *Capital*, Marx describes mercantilism or "the system of protection" as one of the many systems that revalues social relations under capitalism by instituting the value-form. He suggests that mercantilism has "the objective of manufacturing capitalists artificially in the mother country," adding in a footnote to this passage that mercantilism's "artificial manufacturing" eventually "became a temporary necessity in the international competitive struggle."[103] He thus represents mercantilism as one of the systems that works to transform, control, and manage the development of capital for the nation-state.[104]

Marx does not exactly explain how mercantilism "artificially manufactures" capitalists. Yet in part 8 of *Capital*, vol. 1, he does offer a comprehensive account of how other systems, such as the enclosure movement and colonialism, grouped under the name "so-called primitive accumulation," conduct a similar artificial manufacturing of capitalists as well as wage laborers.[105] He argues that when capitalism first emerged as an economic and political force, it worked to break down current ways of giving value to social relations, while simultaneously instituting new ways of giving value to social relations; "so-called primitive accumulation" is a historical articulation of this process of devaluing and revaluing.[106] He mocks the name "primitive accumulation" as "so-called" because it comes from the classical or bourgeois economists, such as Smith, who use it as a name for their myth about capitalism emerging from frugal man's peaceful and spontaneous decision to abstain from obsessive conflict, consumption, and debauchery and begin saving and accumulating capital: "This [classical account of] primitive accumulation plays approximately the same role in political economy as original sin does in theology. . . . Its origin is supposed to be explained when it is told as an anecdote about the past. Long, long ago there were two sorts of people; one, the diligent, intelligent and above all frugal élite; the other, lazy rascals, spending their substance, and more, in riotous living. . . . Thus it came to pass that the former sort accumulated wealth, and the latter sort finally had nothing to sell except their own skins."[107] "As a matter of fact," Marx corrects, "the methods of primitive accumulation are anything but idyllic."[108]

The centerpiece of Marx's account of primitive accumulation is his interpretation of the English enclosure movement. When English peasants lived on common lands, Marx explains, they were in possession of their means of production. Beginning in the fifteenth century, fractions of the English nobility began to force those peasants from their lands by violent legal and extralegal measures; that is, they began to "enclose" the common lands with laws depriving the peasantry of any rights to land, carving up land into large, private holdings, and ceding those holdings to noble oligarchs and the rising bourgeoisie. Consequently, the peasants had to begin working for others who did own the means of production; that is, the peasants had to become free wage laborers.

Freedom takes on a quite precise meaning here for Marx: "The free workers are therefore free from, unencumbered by, any means of production of their own."[109] The transformation of peasant producers into wage laborers "appears, on the one hand, as their emancipation from serfdom and from the fetters of the guilds, and it is this aspect of the movement which alone exists for our bourgeois historians. But, on the other hand, these newly freed men became sellers of themselves only after they had been robbed of all their own means of production."[110] These peasants become free, then, in the sense that they have been forced from their particular political, agricultural, and familial identities and transformed into formally and abstractly equivalent bearers of labor power. As wage laborers they are the free economic subjects of capitalism because they have been freed from their former particularities and are now "free" to sell their labor like any other laborer. This freedom is "anything but idyllic."

However, this is not the only aspect of the enclosure movement's transformation of the English peasantry that Marx examines. As masses of these "freed" peasants slipped into poverty and vagabondage, laws to criminalize vagabonds and paupers emerged. Not only were these peasants broken away from their particular, rural, economic, and social identities and conditions of production and transformed into mobile, abstractly equal wage laborers. They also became vagabonds who often had to steal to survive, and who were systematically reparticularized as lazy, dirty, undisciplined criminals by draconian legal discursive practices of vagabondage and theft, which Marx calls the "bloody legislation against the expropriated": "Thus were the agricultural folk first forcibly expropriated from the soil, driven from their homes, turned into vagabonds, and then whipped, branded and tortured by grotesquely terroristic laws into accepting the discipline necessary for the system of wage-labor."[111] Enclosure thus did not simply make all workers interchangeable and abstract subjects devoid of particularity. Rather, it began a discursive and material practice of subjection: at once the subordination by power and the creation of subjectivity.[112] The peasants became wage laborers whose formal and abstract equality was systematically supplemented by, and thus constitutively related to, their new particular identities as criminals and vagabonds.

Importantly, Marx insists that this process begun by enclosure is systematic and reiterative, in that the laws to expropriate the peasants and then criminalize them transformed the very identities of the peasants by being repeatedly and incessantly applied to them. Writes Marx:

> It is not enough that the conditions of labour are concentrated at one pole of society in the shape of capital, while at the other pole are grouped masses of men who have nothing to sell but their labour-power. Nor is it enough that they are compelled to sell themselves voluntarily. The advance of capitalist production develops a working class which by education, tradition and habit looks upon the requirements of that mode of production as self-evident natural laws. The organization of the capitalist process of production, once it is fully developed, breaks down all resistance. . . . The silent compulsion of economic relations sets the seal on the domination of the capitalist over the worker. . . . This is an essential aspect of so-called primitive accumulation.[113]

Capitalism here emerges not simply as the creation of formally and abstractly equal wage laborers exploited by capitalists. Those wage laborers must be systematically and relentlessly subjectified within discursive practices that naturalize the historical articulation of their formal and abstract equality with their new, particular identities.

There are other origin stories for the emergence of capitalism, and this is not the place to rehearse those debates. Rather, I am interested here in the morphology of Marx's interpretation of enclosure as one of the systems that, like mercantilism, artificially manufactures capitalists and wage laborers. If, as Marx suggests, mercantilism is, like enclosure, also a systematic devaluing and revaluing of social relations, then we could say that it too works both to abstract subjects into formal equality and constitutively to supplement that equality with new social particularities—in this case, race ("the mode of production which [capitalists] introduce has not arisen out of slavery but is grafted on to it"), nation ("manufacturing capitalists artificially in the mother country"), and gender ("in the mother country"). That is, Marx suggests that enclosure helped to instantiate capitalist relations of production by "freeing" peasants from their social and political particularities, forcing them into conditions of formal and abstract equality as wage laborers, and incessantly supplementing that equality with new social and political particularities such as criminality and vagabondage. Similarly, we can suggest that mercantilism "manufactured capitalists artificially" by "freeing" workers in the North Atlantic region from social and political particularities, forcing those workers into conditions of formal and abstract equality as wage laborers, and incessantly supplementing that equality with new social and political particularities such as codified racial, national, and gender identities.

In other words, pushed out of a racially and nationally enclosed North America and into marine vagabondage, black mariners like Briton Hammon, Olaudah Equiano, Venture Smith, John Jea, Boston King, and George Henry found their efforts to claim the mobility of that vagabondage increasingly difficult as the sea was also enclosed within increasingly reiterated, particularistic identities articulated with formal egalitarianism.

If we read the late eighteenth- and early nineteenth-century articulation of race, nation, equality, and gender so prevalent in the mariner narratives from this perspective, the story of the rise and decline of black mariners no longer appears as a story of a generally construed, progressive egalitarianism being contradicted by a generally construed, regressive racism and nationalism. Rather, and paradoxically, the subjection of national citizens as formally and abstractly equal to one another and to citizens of other nations depends upon the vigorous and substantial subjection of subjects by the interdependent codification of race, nation, and gender. The study of mercantilism allows us to map a genealogy of this subjection that was at once a subjugation and a subjectification, at once the subordination by power and the creation of subjectivity. That is, this study lets us trace the emergence of a specific, historical articulation that enclosed the North Atlantic zone within capitalist relations of production that worked to push black mariners off the sea.

CHAPTER 2
Racial Governmentality:
The African Colonization Movement

> Nothing is more certainly written in the book of fate than that these people are to be free. Nor is it less certain that the two races, equally free, cannot live in the same government.
>
> *The Autobiography of Thomas Jefferson*

> You propose my returning to Africa with Bristol Yamma and John Quamine. . . . but why do you hon'd sir, wish those poor men so much trouble as to carry me so long a voyage? Upon my arrival, how like a Barbarian shou'd I look to the Natives; I can promise that my tongue shall be quiet for a strong reason indeed being an utter stranger to the language of Anamaboe.
>
> *Letter from Phillis Wheatley to John Thornton*

*O*laudah Equiano tells us in the last chapter of his narrative that "I had suffered so many impositions in my commercial transactions in different parts of the world, that I became heartily disgusted with the seafaring life, and was determined not to return to it, at least for some time."[1] A few pages later, he explains that in 1786, "On my return to London in August, I was very agreeably surprised to find, that the benevolence of government adopted the plan of some philanthropic individuals, to send the Africans from hence to their native quarter, and that some vessels were then engaged to carry them to Sierra Leona; an act which redounded to the honour of all concerned in its promotion, and filled me with prayers and much rejoicing."[2] Equiano soon began lobbying for governmental and popular support of Sierra Leone's establishment as an independent, Christian, capitalist nation-state to be populated by blacks from Britain and the United States, as well as those liberated from the slave trade, and he was eventually appointed "Commissary on the part of the Government" to Sierra Leone. Equiano's turn to the Sierra Leone project is a strikingly direct engagement in the very discourses of racial and national particularization that he had tried to avoid with his transatlantic mercantile endeavours. Whereas on the sea he had sought a freedom outside national and racial enclosures, with Sierra Leone he sought to institutionalize a geographically enclosed, racially and nationally particularized freedom. Yet Equiano ultimately became embroiled in internecine disputes among white British supporters of Sierra Leone, and was even accused of financial improprieties—charges he vigorously denied. Disillusioned, he abandoned the Sierra Leone project just as he had abandoned his "perquisites and ventures."[3]

In 1780, a mariner and coastal shipping entrepreneur from Dartmouth, Massachusetts, named Paul Cuffe, along with six other free men of color,[4] petitioned the revolutionary legislature of their state: "We apprehand ourselves to be Aggreeved, in that while we are not allowed the Privilege of freemen of the State having no vote or Influence in the Election of those that Tax us yet many of our Colour (as is well known) have cheerfully Entered the field of Battle in the defence of the Common Cause and that (as we conceive) against a similar Exertion of Power (in Regard to taxation) too well Known to need a recital in this place."[5] In calling for relief from taxation without representation, these petitioners expose the new nation's hypocritical white settler colonial rule over people of color who had just helped it to overthrow British colonial rule. As the petition continues, Cuffe and his allies also reveal the importance maritime labor had in their struggle for freedom: "We have not an equal chance with white people neither by Sea nur by Land therefore we take it as a heard ship that poor old Negroes should be Rated which have been in Bondage some thirty some fourty and some fifty years and now just got their Liberty some by going into the serviese and some by going to Sea and others by good fortan and also poor Distressed mungrels."[6] In effect, maritime labor put them in the position to write their petition, both by garnering them a modicum of freedom and by setting limits on the exercise of that freedom. By 1808 Cuffe had turned away from his coastal ventures as well as his efforts to participate in U.S. citizenship, at least in part because of the increasing racial harassment he endured in ports along the eastern seaboard. In January 1811, he sailed his ship *Traveller* to Freetown, Sierra Leone, with a commercial cargo of beef, bread, and flour in search of a new trade route. As a British settlement of freed blacks, Sierra Leone held the promise of transatlantic black exchange. Upon his return to the United States and until his death in 1817, he vigorously sought to stimulate interest in another Christian, capitalist settlement of black Americans in West Africa under the control of black Atlantic diasporans. Though Liberia would soon become that settlement, the firm control of its white leadership systematically disenfranchised the black settlers, making Liberia an early example of U.S. imperialism rather than black Atlantic independence.

As Cuffe and Equiano indicate, the decline of black mariners on the North Atlantic in the early nineteenth century coincided with the rise of one of the most extensively discussed and debated policy proposals of the colonial and antebellum periods, a proposal commonly known as "colonization": a state and/or privately funded plan to appropriate territories in Africa or the Americas to which British and American blacks could be transported.[7] The appropriated territories were, under many of the proposals, to become formally free and independent nation-states, although many British and U.S. colonizationists envisioned these new nation-states as informal political, economic, and ideological colonies. For black mariners like Cuffe and Equiano colonization was an emancipatory strategy to which they seem to have turned once they despaired of finding freedom in the merchant marine trade. Yet by 1820, when U.S. colonizationists had focused on their own settlement of Liberia, black opposition to colonization coalesced in the United States, and public figures such as David Walker, Maria W. Stewart, James Forten, and Richard Allen vigorously denounced the plan. Over one hundred years later, after many ideological transformations, debates over back-to-Africa proposals were still a significant part of the racial landscape in the United States.

In this chapter, I examine two crucial moments in the discursive history of the colonization movement's early years in the United States, between the 1770s and the 1830s: Thomas Jefferson's foundational advocacy; and David Walker and Maria W. Stewart's opposition, itself foreshadowed by Phillis Wheatley. This early period of the movement challenges today's predominant, historical understanding of colonization as primarily a proslavery deportation project—that is, as a mechanism for expelling free blacks and rebellious slaves who might incite a desire for freedom among slaves. From its origins in the 1770s until the 1830s, the project was primarily planned and supported by a complex and uneasy coalition of free and enslaved blacks as well as white abolitionists (most of whom were northerners) and slaveholders who were vaguely "troubled" by the existence of slavery (many of whom were Virginians such as Jefferson). The colonization projects envisioned by these disparate interests were not simply deportation schemes, but rather multiphase, decades-long resettlement projects meant to establish a Christian nation-state of free black Americans in the image of, closely allied with, and even controlled by the United States. The following pages do not attempt a comprehensive history of the movement in its many varied aspects, advocates, and opponents. Rather, I focus on one crucial and overlooked discursive strand of colonization that was particularly pronounced during this early period: the representation of colonization as consistent with, indeed as the completion of, the American Revolution's emancipatory promise of universal equality.

I trace this articulation of colonization with emancipation to the writings of Thomas Jefferson, who was one of its earliest and most sustained advocates. Although some pamphlets advocating colonization appeared before Jefferson first wrote of the proposal, his over forty years of persistent and detailed advocacy, archived primarily in his personal correspondence, undoubtedly make him one of the project's founding fathers, a distinction with which early nineteenth-century texts on colonization often credit him.[8] Jefferson was manifestly troubled by the contradiction between the American Revolution's apparently victorious struggle for freedom and the persistent unfreedom of slavery. In his personal correspondence he often figured this contradiction as the obscured or misdirected light of Enlightenment freedom; though America was meant to have fully captured that light for the first time in human history, slavery showed how elusive it still was.

His fellow white settlers had turned to revolution to capture the light of free-dom held by British colonial rule, and though Jefferson was well aware that black Americans could also make such a revolutionary claim to freedom, he was terrified at that prospect. Colonization thus emerges from his writings as a desirable alterna-tive; rather than a revolutionary claim to freedom, Jeffersonian colonization offers a technical, utilitarian, governmental one. As the epigraph to this chapter indicates, Jefferson confidently prophesied black freedom: "Nothing is more certainly written in the book of fate than that these people are to be free."[9] Yet that future freedom was so threatening that he represented it as self-evidently consistent with racial and national separation: "Nor is it less certain that the two races, equally free, cannot live in the same government." As we will see, colonization articulates these two, conflictual claims, of-fering a systematic resolution of the apparent contradiction between future black free-dom and the hierarchical codification of race and nation. Importantly, this systematic resolution did not take the form of a simple state mandate. In fact, the U.S. govern-ment offered only lukewarm official support for colonization, ceding the scheme to public officials and private citizens sponsored chiefly by private organizations—in particular, after 1816, the American Colonization Society. Though many coloniza-tionists, including Jefferson, pressed for U.S. government funding, the resolution they pursued was much more intensive and extensive than any late eighteenth- or early nineteenth-century state could command from on high. The Jeffersonian strand of colonization set out to transform the very way citizenship was lived.

By making freedom dependent upon territorially discrete racial populations orga-nized into distinct nations, colonization sought to teach American subjects to under-stand themselves as such populations. Thus, Jeffersonian colonization was not a simple deportation or transportation scheme. Rather, it represented blacks and whites as ra-cially and nationally codifiable members of distinct, calculable populations that could be manipulated like numbers on a ledger or statistics in a census table. This manipula-tion was not envisioned simply as a one-time, vertical exercise of power by the United States against black Americans, but rather as a systematic reformation of citizenship that demanded the participation of the very populations it addressed. Indeed, this ref-ormation was continual, even ritualistic, involving as it did an extended, decades-long project of enumerating all black American subjects, calculating the value of all slaves, compensating slaveowners for their human property, securing territory outside the boundaries of the United States, gradually transporting emancipated black Americans to that territory, recognizing their independence as a nation, and maintaining U.S. governmental supervision of that nation so as to facilitate the spread of American capitalism and Christianity.

To understand this pervasive and diffuse form of subjection, in which Americans would be continually subjugated to and subjectified within racially and nationally codified egalitarianism, I turn to Michel Foucault's work on the Enlightenment prob-lematic of government. By theorizing a form of modern power that did not simply emanate from a single, sovereign source, but rather that was so dispersed as to require the lived, embodied participation of the subjects to whom it was addressed, Foucault's notion of governmentality captures the "colonizing trick" that Walker so precisely named in my epigraph to the book: the production, "imperceptibly" and "by persuasion," of a utilitarian, exploitative "procedure" like colonization as freedom. In turn, by reading colonization as a form of racial governmentality, we can read into Foucault's work on Enlightenment biopolitics a racial formation about which he was often silent. Though colonization itself never fully accomplished its goals, it helped to forge a racial governmentality that would become ensconced in the discursive practices of imperial U.S. citizenship. In particular, this diffusion of racial governmentality restricted and controlled the free democratic exchange and agonism that liberalism is fond of seeing in civil society, articulating equality with the hierarchical codification of race and nation.[10]

In the 1820s and 1830s, David Walker and Maria W. Stewart launched a critique of precisely this Jeffersonian strand of colonization discourse. Indeed, Phillis Wheatley's 1774 letter to colonizationist John Thornton, also quoted in the epigraph to this chapter, prophesies Stewart's and Walker's intervention.[11] Reversing the proposal's imperial terms—"how like a Barbarian shou'd I look to the Natives"—Wheatley suggests that she has little to teach West Africans—"I can promise that my tongue shall be quiet for a strong reason indeed being an utter stranger to the language of Anamaboe"—and much yet to tell the Anglo-American world: as her letter to Thornton continues: "Now to be serious, this undertaking appears too hazardous, and not sufficiently Eligible, to go—and leave my British & American Friends." Refusing colonization's supposedly emancipatory effort to send blacks out of Britain and America as imperial agents of Anglo-American capital and Christianity, Wheatley makes clear that she intends to struggle over the meaning of freedom *in* the Anglo-American world. She suggests, indeed she "can promise," that her "tongue" will articulate Anglo-American freedom. When Walker and Stewart pick up Wheatley's prophecy and challenge colonization's emancipatory promise in the 1820s and 1830s, they do not only acknowledge the power of Jefferson's precise vision of equality articulated with racial and national hierarchies. They also produce a "black enlightenment" discourse in response to and at odds with Jeffersonian colonization.[12] Or, perhaps more precisely, as Fred Moten has written in a different context, they produce "a black radical tradition in apposition to enlightenment."[13]

As a scheme to deport blacks from the United States, colonization has looked to many contemporary critics like the antithesis of American ideals of freedom and equality. By contrast, in this chapter I suggest, as did Wheatley, Walker, and Stewart, that we place the Jeffersonian strand of colonization discourse firmly within the "principle of reason" that founded, and continues to echo throughout, the United States.[14] I also suggest that we can find in the work of these critics a vision of freedom and equality that exceeds Jefferson's racial governmentality.

Colonization as Emancipation

"Colonization" is, at first glance, a curious term for a proposal often represented today as a white nationalist scheme to deport black Americans. From the late sixteenth through the nineteenth centuries, the words "deportation" and "transportation" were commonly used in English to describe forced expulsions of an individual, class, or group from a community, colony, or nation-state.[15] The terms "colonization" and "emigration" had been used since at least the seventeenth century to describe the more or less voluntary efforts of Europeans to establish economic and political outposts around the globe. "Colonization" thus suggests a relative degree of voluntary activity not suggested by "deportation" or "transportation."

How, then, might we account for the widespread application of the term "colonization" to U.S. proposals for the resettlement of black Americans? First, these proposals were different from deportation or transportation proposals because many early colonizationists were at least as concerned with the development of black Americans in their new location as they were with the details of the emigration or expulsion itself. They imagined colonized black Americans in a new African nation-state in the image of, and committed to the interests of, the United States.[16] Second, and perhaps more importantly, colonization promised formal equality to black Americans in the form of emancipation from slavery and national autonomy in Africa. That is, at its inception colonization was associated not with punishment or exile as much as it was with an emerging Enlightenment conception of freedom. This aspect of colonization is particularly pronounced in its early period, from the 1770s until approximately the 1830s.[17] In fact, proslavery forces did not begin to support the proposal and black Americans and white abolitionists did not begin to organize against it in substantial numbers until after the founding of the American Colonization Society (ACS) in 1816–17.[18] Between the 1770s, when the first North American colonization proposals emerged, and the founding of the ACS, black and white antislavery forces made up the great majority of colonizationists.[19]

This periodization is certainly somewhat artificial and schematic; some proslavery forces did support colonization before the 1830s, and after 1816 proslavery and antislavery arguments vied with each other for political and ideological control over the movement. My point is that up through the early years of the ACS's existence, colonization was predominately represented as a necessary and logical extension of emancipation; this period thus foregrounds the complicity between colonization and emerging Enlightenment conceptions of freedom. The sense of voluntary emigration carried by the word "colonization" should be read as a trace of this complicity. Though perhaps counterintuitive in today's terms, in the late eighteenth and early nineteenth centuries colonization's fusion of expulsion and emigration, of emancipation and racial separation was self-evident to many of its advocates.[20]

As opposed historical analyses as those of Winthrop Jordan and Henry Noble Sherwood make this point explicitly—without, however, pursuing its wider implications. Writes Jordan in *White Over Black*, his epochal account of the origins of U.S. white supremacy: "What was striking in this proposal [in its early period] was that fervent equalitarianism led directly to Negro removal"; writes Sherwood in his apologia for white colonizationists: "During the last quarter of the eighteenth century deportation was regarded not as a punishment for crime nor as a means to prevent an increase in the number of free negroes, but as the logical outcome of manumission."[21] Jordan's suggestive adverb "directly" and Sherwood's passive construction "was regarded" both beg the genealogical questions we must consider here: how did "fervent equalitarianism" "lead directly" to colonization? How did colonization come "to be regarded" as "the logical outcome of manumission"? How, in effect, did colonization come to be valued "directly," "logically," and self-evidently as emancipatory? When Walker writes in his *Appeal* of "some friends to the sons of Africa" being drawn "imperceptibly" into colonization, as we saw in the epigraph to the book, he refers to precisely this self-evidence.[22] The task, he suggests, is to sketch a genealogy of this striking self-evidence of emancipatory colonization.

Walker's *Appeal* also urges an analysis of what can be called the imperial form of colonization's articulation with emancipation. The persistently global terms of his text illustrate the two interrelated levels—domestic and foreign—on which early colonizationists operated.[23] As I have mentioned, a crucial aspect of colonization during this period was the concern of its advocates with the status and development of African Americans in their new location. The emphasis of colonization was not on returning Africans who had been taken from Africa to their "homeland," as much as it was on establishing settlements of Christian, black *Americans* in "uncivilized" and "undeveloped" regions of the globe. This imperial vision sought not only to form a racially and nationally particular, white American nation, but also to begin spreading the supposedly universal and exemplary elements of white America: its Christianity, its capitalist economy, and its governmental system of national statehood. Thus, colonized black Americans were represented not only as racially particularized subjects to be separated from white America, but also, paradoxically, as abstract bearers of American national form to be sent as global agents of American universality and exemplarity to Africans from whom black Americans were also in some sense distinct. I will examine this aspect of colonization in more detail later in this chapter. For now, however, I simply want to emphasize that the term "colonization" carries the trace of these dual, interrelated roles—racial purification of a domestic space and imperial power over foreign spaces—and that these roles give colonization a complexity that the terms "deportation," "transportation," or "exile" fail to capture.

Unfortunately, most twentieth-century historians of colonization have neither addressed the genealogical question of colonization's articulation with emancipation, nor examined the imperial form of colonization, nor considered the specificity of pre-1816 colonization discourse in any detail.[24] Instead, they have been concerned with determining whether post-1816 colonization, considered in a domestic framework, could be characterized as either essentially liberal and abolitionist or conservative and proslavery. The question is not an easy one to answer, however, because the proposal brought together an odd, shifting, and uneasy coalition of free black, proslavery white, and abolitionist white advocates.[25] In the face of this complexity, most historical accounts have offered what might be called "political interest" based explanations of colonization. That is, they have explained colonization by dividing its advocates into distinct groups—such as proslavery whites, black nationalists, and abolitionists—each of which is said to have viewed colonization as an effective means of realizing its particular political interests. These historical accounts differ only over which group tended to dominate the discussions and the actual efforts at colonization. As a result, colonial and antebellum colonization has often been represented in one of two ways: first, as a proposal without substantial or genuine support among black Americans that was a tool of proslavery or racially nationalistic whites who managed to dupe some naive free blacks and antislavery whites into cooperating with them, and whose real interest was to deport the free black population to keep them from inciting a desire for freedom among enslaved blacks;[26] or second, as a proposal of early or protoblack nationalists who, out of their desire for autonomy, worked tactically and warily with proslavery whites.[27]

These historical accounts are not quite "wrong." There certainly were proslavery forces who advocated colonization as a way to deport free blacks whom they saw as a threat to the slave system—especially, as I have mentioned, after 1816. Many anticolonizationists as well as some colonizationists pointed this out at the time. In addition, black colonizationists such as Equiano and Cuffe were well aware of these proslavery interests, and their tactical discussions of autonomy certainly influenced later black nationalists such as Martin Delany. Nonetheless, these contemporary explanations miss something of the texture of the early colonization movement. By reducing colonization to the rational pursuit of self-evident interests by autonomous political actors, such explanations fail to consider what it was about the colonization movement that conjoined contradictory interests. Consequently, such explanations also fail to consider carefully the articulation of colonization *with* emancipation. By seeking to determine whether colonization was genuinely emancipatory or not, these histories actually generalize and dehistoricize freedom by suppressing its historically specific articulation *with* colonization. These historical accounts thus fail to address the questions Walker's *Appeal* posed in 1829, and to which I will now turn: What notion of "freedom" is rendered by colonization, and how does that rendering become self-evident to colonizationists?

Jefferson's Claim to Colonization

Three years after David Walker's *Appeal* was published, the Massachusetts Sabbath School Union published an anonymously authored, 252-page procolonization text that exemplifies precisely this articulation of colonization with emancipation and traces it to Jefferson.[28] *Claims of the Africans: or the History of the American Colonization Society* (1832) offers a melodramatic and propagandistic history of the early years of the ACS in the form of a conversation among six members of the fictional Granville family: Mr. Granville or "Pa," Mrs. Granville or "Mother," the three Granville children (Charles, Janette, and Clara), and their Aunt Caroline. The text moves freely between a moderate critique of the slave trade, slavery, and polygenesist (or nonenvironmentalist) racism, and a white nationalist account of the United States.[29] Colonization, in turn, functions as the governmental or institutional link between these two positions by articulating abolitionism with white nationalism. In the words of Pa:

Mr. G: The men who composed [the ACS], were eminent for their talents and the high offices they sustained, and were too deeply concerned for the welfare of their country, to be much affected by the doubts of the faint hearted, or the taunting sneers of the ignorant. They felt that they were laboring for future generations, that the cause was approved of heaven and would prosper; therefore they persevered in their efforts, to enlighten the public sentiment and raise funds. (11)

As work for the future—"they were laboring for future generations"—colonization simultaneously functions as proof of the consistency of freedom with racial and national particularity, and as the utilitarian rendering of that very consistency. That is, the discourse of colonization articulates freedom with race and nation by codifying those concepts; in turn, the discourse of colonization naturalizes this articulation by representing itself as a merely technical, governmental realization of the necessary relationships among freedom, race, and nation.

Claims opens with Mr. Granville asking his son Charles and daughter Janette how they plan to celebrate the coming Fourth of July. When they express their desire to celebrate with drumming, fiddling, cannon fire, toasting, and singing, Mr. Granville suggests that "there ought to [be] a sermon, or an address, as well as singing," and declares his intention to "use my influence to have . . . an address and collection in favor of the American Colonization Society" (5–7). The text thus begins by representing colonization as exemplary of, or internal to, U.S. freedom itself. Asked by the children what the ACS does, Mr. Granville declares that "It has done, and is still doing great things, and you ought to become acquainted with its history; but it will take me a long time to tell you all I know concerning it; however, after school you may come down to the office, and if I am disengaged, I will begin this afternoon" (8–9). Throughout the rest of the text, Mr. Granville, with the occasional help of Mrs. Granville and Aunt Caroline, narrates the history of the ACS and the philosophy of colonization to the persistently eager Charles, Janette, and Clara. The text thus tutors the children, and by implication its readers, in colonization's emancipatory promise.

The account of the children's first visit to their father's office exemplifies this structure:

The children went to school, but they almost counted the hours and minutes before they should be dismissed, and be at liberty to visit their father at his office, a privilege they were seldom allowed to enjoy.

At length the happy moment arrived, and they were delighted to find him alone, sitting by his large table with a new map of Africa unrolled and spread upon the table, and a chair set for each of the little guests. After they were seated, Mr. Granville said, "I suppose the first question you wish to ask is, 'What is the design of the Colonization Society?'"

Charles and Janette together. Yes, Pa'. (8)

The reader is here called upon to identify with the position of the children, to sit eagerly and openly at the foot of their enlightened and knowledgeable father in expectation

of the true meaning of freedom and independence, a meaning institutionalized in colonization. To secure this interpellative structure, some of the chapters conclude with
study questions, such as these from chapter 1: "When was the Colonization Society
formed? Where? What was its object? Who first went to Africa to select a plan for a
colony?" (19). The study questions call upon the reader to remember the lessons of
the chapter, to internalize Pa's truths and thus, in what amounts to a textual Independence Day celebration, ritualistically to become proper and worthy national citizens.
The reader too is urged to "be at liberty" in and through Pa's words.

To perform this textual ritual, the reader must come to understand the necessary
and self-evident relationship between abolitionism and racial-national separation. Thus,
the text repeatedly decries the injustices not only of the slave trade, but also of slavery.
Chapter 5, in which Mrs. Granville traces the beginnings of slavery in the United States
to the arrival of captured Africans at Jamestown in 1620, begins with an epigraph of
common abolitionist verse: "Fleecy locks and black complexion/ Cannot forfeit nature's claim;/ Skins may differ, but affection/ Dwells in black and white the same" (72).
That chapter goes on to decry the "wickedness" of slave traders (73), and chapter 7
classes those slave traders with the "white monsters" who continue to enslave Africans
"in a foreign clime" (119). Later, Aunt Caroline emphasizes that "The [American
Colonization] Society have from the first, framed all their 'measures with reference to
the *entire* suppression of the slave trade, and to a gradual and prudent, but complete
emancipation of those now held in slavery'" (218).[30] In addition, Mr. and Mrs. Granville repeatedly debunk nonenvironmentalist racisms, as in the following exchange
from chapter 11: "*Mrs. G.* Do you not believe all the free people of color would be
of the same mind [as whites], were they equally enlightened and intelligent? *Mr. G.*
I have no doubt but they would" (240). These passages effectively suggest that blacks
in the United States are latently or potentially free and equal to whites.

Yet this latent freedom and equality can only be made manifest in Africa, as Mrs.
Granville explains:

> I do not see what inducement [black Americans] can have to remain in this country, for
> they can never rise here to the level of white men. Whereas, if they would go to the land
> of their fathers, they would soon be elevated to posts of honor and trust, if they were
> moral and educated . . . Some of the most intelligent and enterprising of this class were
> very anxious to find some spot on the globe where their complexion would be no ob-
> stacle in their pursuit of happiness and a state of political independence, years before the
> formation of the Colonization Society. (81–82)

As both "the land of their fathers" and a "spot on the globe where their complexion
would be no obstacle," Africa is here figured as the merely practical and self-evident
realization of a latent freedom and equality. However, Africa is paradoxically also
the very condition of possibility for that latency in the first place, since equality and
freedom would "never rise" from latency and become manifest anywhere else. The
latency of black freedom and equality would thus never have been knowable without

the practicality of colonization in Africa. In effect, the figure of "Africa" *performs* the very latency of black freedom and equality.

Aunt Caroline echoes this argument by supposedly quoting the black American colonizationist J. B. Russwurm:[31]

> "I consider it a mere waste of words to talk of enjoying citizenship in the United States; it is utterly impossible in the nature of things; all, therefore, who pant for this, must cast their eyes elsewhere. The interesting query now arises, where shall we find this desirable spot? If we look to Europe, we find that quarter already overburdened with a starving population; if to Asia, its distance is an insuperable barrier, were all other circumstances favorable. Where then shall we look so naturally, as to Africa?" *Charles*. I think he must have been a sensible man. *Caroline*. He was so; and a man who had received a college education. If all our colored population were to obtain learning, they would never remain in the United States in such a debased condition, but would line our shores, till they were taken, and conveyed to the *natural home of the African* where, upon the land of their ancestors, they might breathe the air of liberty, and live respected and honored by all nations. (164–65)

These passages represent blackness and whiteness as vague, irreducible essences whose proximity necessarily produces conflict and the eventual subjugation of blackness. "Complexion" is represented as a sign of natural ("in the nature of things," "look so naturally as to Africa," "natural home") affiliation ("the land of their fathers," "the land of their ancestors"). This cultural essentialism was pervasive in the colonial and antebellum periods, predating even the racial science that arose in the 1830s.[32] According to *Claims*, racial proximity could threaten the very existence of the latent freedom and equality of black Americans extolled elsewhere in the text, and in turn threaten the very possibility of universal freedom.

Without the solution of colonization, *Claims* suggests, the problem of the incompatibility of blackness and whiteness would make universal freedom impossible and lend credence to the proslavery position that Africans were justly enslaved in the United States. The "practicality" and "sensibility" of colonization keeps cultural essentialism from threatening the promise of universal freedom. The proposal's technical feasibility thus actually performs the articulation of emancipation with racial separation. In turn, the proposal protects "citizenship in the United States" from the "debased condition" of "our colored population," and that population is transformed into the racially codified "African" national citizen-subject merely formally equal to whites—"breath[ing] the air of liberty, and liv[ing] respected and honored by all nations."

Just as Walker warned, here the discourse of emancipation and equality is not used simply in a disingenuous manner, as an empty and cynical screen for a more fundamental racialist interest. Rather, the "colonizing trick" of *Claims* performs a very specific conception of freedom, one of formal and abstract equality articulated with racial and national codification. This conception achieves its full rhetorical force in the analogy, made repeatedly in *Claims*, between the colonies of Plymouth and Jamestown and the colonies of Sierra Leone and Liberia. In the midst of chapter 5, as the text attempts to downplay the disasters that actually befell the initial settlements in Liberia, Charles suggests to his mother that "The African colony had a very melancholy beginning," to which she replies, "True, my son, but not so much as the Plymouth colony, in New England" (86). Similarly, in chapter 8 Charles says to his Aunt Caroline, "I wonder the Society have not been discouraged, and abandoned the colony. It seems as if half who go die," to which she replies,

> Why, Charles, I am surprised to hear you express such cowardly sentiments. You must look over your history of the several States again, and see what Plymouth was ten years after the landing of the Pilgrims. That little colony, after struggling ten years, could number only three hundred inhabitants, and Liberia has already almost two thousand!
>
> Let us look at Jamestown in Virginia; that colony was a continued scene of riot, disorder, famine, and desolation, the twenty-five first years of its existence. In 1585, when the settlement was first attempted, almost five hundred colonists were landed, well supplied with provisions and all needful stores. . . . But being an idle, intemperate, and dissolute set of people, "their time and provisions were consumed in riot; their utensils were stolen, or destroyed. . . ."[33] Within the term of six months, of their whole number, sixty only survived. . . . Why, I would ask, should we expect to plant a colony without the loss of some lives and much treasure, any more than those who have gone before us? (155–57)

The analogy grants black Americans equality *with* European Americans on the condition that the former recognize their essential and irreducible racial difference *from* the latter. What is more, this equality is a formal and abstract one, for black Americans are considered equal only in the sense that they can become equivalent to each other as rationally abstracted, constituent members of a new African civil society. The text equates black Americans and white Americans as similarly abstract, calculable units of separate populations—"Plymouth . . . could number only *three hundred inhabitants*, and Liberia already has *almost two thousand*," "Almost *five hundred colonists* were landed," "of their *whole number, sixty only* survived" (my italics). Yet this formal and abstract equality exists only to the extent that it is articulated with codified racial difference, for the civil society into which black Americans could be rationally abstracted must be racially, nationally, and geographically distinct from the United States—it must be a new, *African* civil society.

The analogy between North American colonies and African colonies also foregrounds the imperial form of African colonization. As numerable members of racially particularized populations, colonized black Americans and white Americans become abstractly equivalent bearers of, and global agents for, American universality and exemplarity. Consider how the following tax proposal made by Caroline amplifies this imperial form of colonization: "If only one half of the money that has been spent in the United States for ardent spirits every year, were spent in carrying back to Africa the free colored people, and purchasing and sending back the slaves, there would not be left in the United States a single colored person at the end of six or seven years. Or if a tax of *nine cents* were levied upon every white person in the United States, it would pay for sending to Liberia at least fifty thousand colored people a year, so long as the tax should be paid" (219–20). Colonization here relies upon a racially particular, white domestic space with absolute power over black Americans. Yet that domestic space can be abstractly penetrated by a tax in the interest of creating a foreign space itself abstractly equivalent to, but racially and geographically distinct from, the domestic space. Once again, colonization is paradoxically both the proof of the consistency of universal freedom with racial-national particularity, and the rendering of that very consistency.

Though we can glimpse from this text the lineaments of emancipation's articulation with racial-national codification, we have to turn to other, earlier texts to trace the emergence of what Caroline calls colonization's "practicality"—to trace the genealogy, that is, of colonization's emancipatory self-evidence. In *Claims*, this "practicality" derives simply from the force of a rhetorical imperative, as we saw above: "*Charles.* I think he [Russwurm] *must have been* a sensible man [for advocating colonization]" (165; my italics). *Claims* does, however, point the way to this genealogy when it frames itself, in its first few pages and again in its final few pages, with references to Thomas Jefferson as the intellectual founder of colonization. Immediately upon the children's arrival in his office in chapter 1, Mr. Granville explains:

> Now, children, I have mentioned the names of all these [ACS] officers, that you may see how important the object of the society was, in the estimation of many of the first men in the nation, nine of whom lived in slave holding States. Indeed, it may be said to have originated in the south, and the legislature of Virginia passed several resolutions in favor of colonizing, a great many years ago. President Jefferson and President Monroe were always friendly to the scheme, and wrote and spoke of it in the highest terms of approbation, on a variety of occasions. (10)[34]

Toward the end of the text, Mrs. Granville echoes her husband in the midst of a conversation with Caroline about the evils of slavery: "*Caroline.* O we do not know the excesses which unprincipled men are left to commit, when placed in circumstances to unite in their own persons, *party, judge, and executioner. Mrs. G.* I do not wonder that President Jefferson said, 'I tremble for my country, when I remember that God is just—that his justice cannot sleep forever'" (212–13).[35]

Jefferson's name appears ritually in texts on colonization from this period, for he was correctly regarded as one of the proposal's earliest and most influential supporters. Despite Jefferson's role as a founding father of colonization, Jefferson scholars rarely even mention his long advocacy of and copious writings on the proposal.[36] When his advocacy is discussed, it is inevitably placed in the context of the frequently examined relationship between his role as a founding father of liberalism and his defense of racism or his role as a slaveowner. Most accounts of this relationship inevitably generate one of three positions.[37] First, Jefferson is said to be an enlightened liberal whose racism and slaveownership were unfortunate but aberrant or atavistic when one considers his entire legacy.[38] Second, Jefferson's racism and slaveownership are said to be moral outrages and thus signs of the limits or contradictions of his liberalism.[39] Third, Jefferson is said to have been a benevolent but realistic or pragmatic slaveowner who did his best for his slaves and who grappled honestly with the overwhelming complexities of "the peculiar institution."[40] To the contrary, Jefferson's long and passionate advocacy of colonization suggests that colonization was by no means inconsistent with or contradicted by what has been called Jeffersonian liberalism. Rather, any account of such liberalism needs to consider how Jefferson could combine both his distrust of strong, centralized government and his dogged advocacy of a massive, publicly and privately sponsored scheme to enumerate, deport, and resettle black Americans in Africa, and then to surveil and control that resettlement after deportation.

"With Respect to Everything External"

Jefferson tells us in his *Autobiography* that on February 7, 1779, as a member of the Virginia House of Delegates, he supported an amendment to a slavery bill calling for "the freedom of all [slaves] born after a certain day, and deportation at a proper age."[41] Anxious about the possibility of black revolt against the injustices of slavery, an institution that exposes to the world how incomplete and fragile the Enlightenment is in America, Jefferson declares colonization the only reasonable response: "If the contrary is left to force itself on, human nature must shutter at the prospect held up." In query 14 of the *Notes on the State of Virginia* (composed 1781–82, published in 1787), entitled "The administration of justice and description of the laws?" he offers a more extensive description of "deportation"—which in a few years he would refer to as "colonization"—to an account of the same amendment:

> An amendment . . . was prepared . . . directing, that [slaves] should continue with their parents to a certain age, then be brought up, at the public expence, to tillage, arts or sciences, according to their geniusses, till the females should be eighteen, and the males twenty-one years of age, when they should be colonized to such place as the circumstances of the time should render most proper, sending them out with arms, implements of household and of the handicraft arts, feeds, pairs of useful domestic animals, &c. to declare them a free and independent people, and extend to them our alliance and protection, till they shall have acquired strength; and to send vessels at the same time to other parts of the world for an equal number of white inhabitants; to induce whom to migrate hither, proper encouragements were to be proposed.[42]

Between these *Notes on the State of Virginia* and a letter written to Miss Fanny Wright just before his death (Aug. 7, 1825, vol. 10, 343), Jefferson wrote repeatedly in his published writings and private letters about his strong belief in and desire for colonization as emancipation, making it arguably his most consistently articulated policy proposal.[43] He would eventually add to and alter the plan, variously suggesting Africa, the West Indies, and western North America as sites for colonization, proposing different ways to raise money for the project, altering the requirements for emancipation, calling for "Germans" or simply "white laborers" to replace colonized blacks. Yet the essential structure would remain the same from the *Notes* to the Wright letter:

gradual, full emancipation of all slaves followed by the forced deportation of all blacks from the territorial boundaries of the United States and their subsequent incorporation into a formally independent nation-state that would nevertheless be economically and politically dependent upon the United States.

Jefferson began advocating colonization at a crucial moment in U.S. history, a moment during which he and his fellow American elites were struggling to formulate in theory and formalize in practice the ideas of the Enlightenment. Consequently, colonization is situated in his writings as part of this greater struggle to respond to the call of reason, to capture and render or represent the light of the Enlightenment in philosophical, political, and juridical concepts and institutions. By considering Jefferson's writings on colonization in this larger allegorical context, we can garner a more precise understanding of colonization's claim to freedom. I begin, then, with the writings' anxious struggle over the Enlightenment's unfinished journey from Europe to the United States.

Jefferson had great faith in America's superiority over Europe, and he clearly thought the Enlightenment was destined to shine brightest in the United States. He was convinced that Europe was mired in the corrupt inequalities of the ancien régime, and his vision of an agrarian republic involved leaving the dirty work of industrialization to England and the continent—"let our work-shops remain in Europe," he wrote in query 19 of the *Notes on the State of Virginia*.[44] Nonetheless, his letters look to Europe as a source of, if not the final destination for, this light. When they give vent to anxieties about the Enlightenment's incomplete arrival in the United States, the letters also figure a certain anxiety over European judgment, an anxiety marked by the phrase mentioned at the beginning of this section from the *Autobiography*: "Human nature must shutter at the prospect held up."

A letter sent in 1786 to James Madison from Paris can be read as an allegory of this struggle, an allegory in which the Enlightenment's failure to shine fully on the United States takes the form of an ambivalent mixture of admiration for and anxiety in the face of Europe, the Enlightenment's putative origin (Feb. 8, 1786, vol. 4, 192–97).[45] The letter opens with an enumeration of letters exchanged and expected, an implicit acknowledgment of the unsure lines of communication across the Atlantic: "Dear Sir,—My last letters have been of the 1st & 20th of Sep. and the 28th of Oct. Yours unacknowledged are of Aug. 20, Oct. 3, & Nov. 15. I take this the first safe opportunity of enclosing to you the bills of lading for your books, & two others for your namesake of Williamsburgh & for the attorney which I will pray you to forward" (lines 1–7). This recognition of the possibility of communicative misfire between Europe and the United States—that is, of the possibility that Madison may never even see this letter, that "the first safe opportunity" may not be safe enough—resonates throughout the entire letter as a vague sense of *im*possibility.

Nonetheless, the letter places great weight on certain transatlantic communications, particularly those involving unequal exchanges of prestige, knowledge, technical skill, the arts, and primary goods. He continues: "I thank you for the communication of the remonstrance against the assessment. Mazzei who is now in Holland promised me to have it published in the Leyden gazette. It will do us great honour" (lines 7–11).

The rest of the letter's opening paragraph elaborates on the importance of honorable representations of the United States in Europe. After telling Madison of his "great pleasure" that the Virginia Assembly has agreed in principle to federal regulation of their commerce, Jefferson writes:

> The politics of Europe render it indispensably necessary that with respect to everything external we be one nation only, firmly hooped together. Interior government is what each state should keep to itself. If it could be seen in Europe that all our states could be brought to concur in what the Virginia assembly has done, it would produce a total revolution in their opinion of us, and respect for us. And it should ever be held in mind that insult & war are the consequences of a want of respectability in the national character. As long as the states exercise separately those acts of power which respect foreign nations, so long will there continue to be irregularities committing by some one or other of them which will constantly keep us on an ill footing with foreign nations. (lines 18–33)

The revolutionary tactics on which Jefferson places so much importance here are quite different from those of 1776, though both seem to be part of one process, one movement toward "total revolution." The postindependence task is to fabricate a singular "national character," the absence of which threatens not only armed conflict, but also "insult." This character is first and foremost an "external" one, an outward appearance or surface that, though not substanceless, is nonetheless neither autonomous nor intensive. It is not autonomous because it only exists to the extent that it is "seen in Europe," to the extent that it alters "foreign" "respect" and "opinion"; and it is not intensive because a terrain of "interior government" is reserved for "each state to [keep to] itself." The revolutionary goal is still, as it was in 1776, to differentiate an internal political, economic, and ideological space from an external one, to forge an "independent union." Yet the very failure of that differentiation, the fact that it has fallen short of being "total," calls forth new and different tactics. Jefferson holds out hope here that the business unfinished by the armed, political revolution, that which kept it from realizing "total revolution," could be completed on the level of organization and representation. Yet the true test of that completion, the eyes in which it will be interpreted, ironically lie in a "Europe" that threatens "our states" and "national character" with low opinion, lack of respect, insult, and war. This passage figures a mutual watching and being watched, an exchange of glances across the Atlantic, between the old world and the new, that continues to exert a diffuse and unsettling power despite the formal independence accomplished by the Revolution.

This power is carried into the next paragraph, in which Jefferson frets over the fate of a lost rough draft of his *Notes on the State of Virginia*:

> I have been unfortunate here with this trifle. I gave out a few copies only, & to confidential persons, writing in every copy a restraint against it's publication. Among others I gave a copy to a Mr. Williamos. He died. I immediately took every precaution I could to recover this copy. But by some means or other a bookseller had got hold of it. He employed a hireling translator and was about publishing it in the most injurious form possible. An Abbé Morellet, a man of letters here to whom I had given a copy, got notice of

this. He had translated some passages for a particular purpose: and he compounded with the bookseller to translate & give him the whole, on his declining the first publication. I found it necessary to confirm this, and it will be published in French, still mutilated however in it's freest parts. I am now at a loss what to do as to England. Everything, good or bad, is thought worth publishing there; and I apprehend a translation back from the French, and a publication there. I rather believe it will be most eligible to let the original come out in that country; but am not yet decided. (lines 37–58)[46]

Despite his most rigorous efforts, Jefferson fails in Europe to control his representation of the United States. One chance mishap, Mr. Williamos's death, triggers a chain of chaotic events, sending his *Notes* careening down a dangerous and circuitous path; the death, a lost text, a futile pursuit, the violence of translation, and the uncontrollability of mechanical reproduction overpower "every precaution" as well as all "confidence" and "restraints," and put Jefferson "at a loss." Likely to be "mutilated however in its freest parts," the *Notes* risks losing its very purpose, its documentation of America's unique claim to freedom and independence, thanks to the continuing power of inept French and English booksellers and translators. As Jay Fliegelman has shown, Jefferson was always anxious about making his writings public in America, and this concern over the premature publication of the *Notes* has at least as much to do with the potential reaction of Americans as it does to that of Europeans.[47] In this passage's depiction of the circuitous wanderings of the *Notes*, then, we can read an allegory of the Enlightenment's troubled journey from Europe to the United States.

After all, Europe still claims a certain fascination for Jefferson as a source of the Enlightenment. As he proceeds to tell Madison of his recent book purchases in Europe, Jefferson offers an image that contrasts with the difficult birth of his own book:

I have purchased little for you in the book way, since I sent the catalogue of my former purchases. I wish first to have your answer to that, and your information what parts of those purchases went out of your plan. You can easily say buy more of this kind, less of that &c. My wish is to conform myself to yours. I can get for you the original Paris edition in folio of the Encyclopedie for 620 livres, 35. vols.; a good edn in 39 vols 4to, for 380#; and a good one in 39 vols 8vo, for 280#. The new one will be superior in far the greater number of articles: but not in all. And the possession of the ancient one has moreover the advantage of supplying present use. I have bought one for myself, but wait your orders as to you. (lines 59–73)

This excitement about the consummate embodiment of the Enlightenment's promise, the "Encyclopedie," seems to displace the anxiety about the fate of the *Notes*. Unlike the young *Notes*, which continues to risk being "mutilated however in its freest parts," the "Encyclopedie" is a more mature embodiment of knowledge, possessing a "superiority" that continues to make Europe powerful to Jefferson. The Enlightenment has passed from Europe to the United States, and yet not fully; it is passing, in a sense, still arriving and not yet resting, waiting just as Jefferson awaits Madison's "orders."

The excitement becomes even clearer in the rest of the letter's third paragraph, which adds technology, politics, and the arts to the list of Europe's claims to the light of the Enlightenment. After celebrating the technological prowess of French watchmakers, Jefferson discusses at length a statue Houdon, a French sculptor, is to make of George Washington (lines 87–110). He then recommends that a bust of Count Rochambeau be placed in the "new capitol" next to "that of Gates, Greene, Franklin" in honor of his similar contribution (lines 137–45), and notes "one new invention" he has encountered in Paris: "a mixture of the arts of engraving and printing, rendering both cheaper" (lines 158–70).[48] He also makes a recommendation that the Marquis de Lafayette be given land in the United States in honor of his contribution to the Enlightenment.[49] In fact, Jefferson justifies this gift of land on the grounds that "the day [may] come when it might be an useful asylum to him" (lines 122–23). That this day—in which European political upheavals would be so intense as to make clear to enlightened luminaries such as Lafayette that the United States was their new, proper home—has clearly not yet arrived, that it is still to come, is precisely the source of the letter's ambivalence, alternately boastful and anxious, over the traffic of the Enlightenment from Europe to the United States.

Jefferson's final comments to Madison, given in a postscript, only deepen this ambivalence: "P.S. Could you procure & send me an hundred or two nuts of the peccan? they would enable me to oblige some characters here whom I should be much gratified to oblige. They should come packed in sand. The seeds of the sugar maple too would be a great present" (lines 173–78). Still an economic satellite of Europe, sending primary goods to France and receiving knowledge, the arts, and political luminaries from the same, Jefferson's United States is still struggling to secure its share of the Enlightenment.

Calculating Freedom

As persistently as textual ambivalence surfaces throughout Jefferson's correspondence, so too does a meticulous formulation of its resolution, a formulation that seeks to capture and render the light of the Enlightenment. Consider, for example, a letter Jefferson wrote to the Marquis de Lafayette on December 26, 1820 (vol. 10, 179–81).[50] This exemplary speech act—in which a representative of the United States responds to a representative of France about the way Europe strikes the United States and the way both have been struck by the light of the Enlightenment—is shot through with moments of "infelicity," or what J. L. Austin would call "non-serious," "parasitic," or "non-ordinary" interruptions of ordinary, direct communication.[51] Jefferson declares that he knows just what is "going on" in France and in the United States, evincing a confident tone that pervades the letter. Yet, in the process of trotting out many of the rhetorical conventions of Enlightenment discourse, the letter stages a figural drama in which the trope of national unity emerges to offer a coherent and felicitous resolution to the conflict between enlightenment and slavery.

In his letter to Lafayette, Jefferson attempts nothing less than the task of representing the Enlightenment. Confident that the United States has the potential to improve on Lafayette's old world, Jefferson is also fearful that the Missouri Crisis will wreck this potential and demonstrate that American politics are not better than those of

Europe.[52] The letter has five sections: first, Jefferson's lament about his failing health (lines 1–9); second, Jefferson's concerns with the state of affairs in France, and Europe in general (lines 9–26); third, Jefferson's attempt to reassure Lafayette about conflicts between Spain and the United States over Spain's colonies in the Americas (lines 26–48); fourth, Jefferson's assurance that "things are going well" in the United States, and that the resolution of Missouri's entrance into the union as a slave state will in fact further the cause of emancipation (lines 49–65); and fifth, a discussion of some diplomatic business, and a salutation remarking once again on his failing health (lines 66–83). From the tired and failing body of the opening lines, through mixed metaphorics to the "anxiously wished" emancipation of the closing lines, the apparently confident and optimistic tone of the letter is coupled with parasitical ambiguity, discomfort, and struggle.

This complexity is especially evident in its unwieldy metaphorics. In the second section, and in the span of less than two hundred words, Jefferson shuttles through six distinct tropes, moving from light to wind to volcanic rumblings to bowels to explosions and finally to disease and infection, all in an effort to render the twists and turns of enlightenment. He begins this section with the classic trope of light: "In the meantime your country has been going on less well than I had hoped. But it will go on. The light which has been shed on the mind of man through the civilized world, has given it new direction, from which no human power can divert it" (lines 9–15). The last sentence of this passage couples the most lofty goals and desires with utterly ambiguous references and syntax. The source of the Enlightenment's light—so often played by God—is here passive and unknown, though implicitly nonhuman given the last phrase.[53] Also, the light's rays are immediately bent and refracted, their proper course almost indecipherable. Does the light pass from this unknown source to "the mind of man" and then "through the civilized world," or "through the civilized world" and then onto "the mind of man"? And what of the brilliance the light might lose as it passes "through"? If the mind of man is struck second, how can we know that the light is pure and uncorrupted? The antecedent of "it" in "has given it new direction" is also ambiguous. It apparently refers to "your country," that is, France, and yet "the light," "the mind of man," and "the civilized world" are also potentially "given new direction" by the Enlightenment. If it is possible to give the light new direction, if the light has the potential to be misdirected, then surely the light itself is imperfect—capable, at the very least, of being corrupted and misdirected by "the mind of man" through which it must pass. And if the light itself is capable of being corrupted and misdirected, then how could we possibly determine what that truth is beyond the shadow of a doubt? How could "the people" be represented in perfect accordance with "self-evident truths" if those truths could always already be refracted?

Despite Jefferson's confidence in the progressive development of "things" (line 9) and the steady dilution of "evil" (lines 60–61), this second section of his letter suggests that the light of Enlightenment truth is always capable of being misdirected as well as more perfectly directed. This truth mingles with imperfect nontruths, each new direction with other potential misdirections, every proper destination with improper arrivals. Jefferson's rhetoric suggests that the light itself, not God or Nature or even Man, has the nonhuman power to direct the Enlightenment, to give itself a new and more proper direction, for he does not invoke an all-knowing figure who directs the light as an implement or tool, as an official would a flashlight to illuminate what is going on. The light sustains itself, it directs and misdirects itself. This light with a life of its own belies an insecurity expressed by the letter, an anxiety about where the light is coming from and where it is going.

Toward the end of section two of the letter, the tropic movement slips into the violent and unpredictable language of revolution. Jefferson lectures Lafayette about "the volcanic rumblings in the bowels of Europe, from north to south, . . . [which] threaten a general explosion, and the march of armies into Italy cannot end in a simple march" (lines 17–21). Here the source of enlightenment remains underground, deep within the entrails of the earth, powerful and elusive because it is hidden from sight. Jefferson then adds to this the ambiguous power of disease and infection: "The disease of liberty is catching; those armies will take it in the south, carry it thence to their own country, spread there the infection of revolution and representative government, and raise its people from the prone condition of brutes to the erect altitude of man" (lines 21–26). This last tropic movement invests the light with revolution's volatile duality, its power both to poison autocratic evil and immunize the body politic, allowing healthy representative government to grow if administered properly.

This wild tropic movement—from pure and impure light to invisible breeze to hidden rumblings to cathartic disease—captures precisely the difficulty of rendering enlightened representations of the "good society." With characteristic eighteenth- and early nineteenth-century rhetorical verve, Jefferson gives us a representation of political truth that disseminates far beyond his confident tone. Perhaps most importantly, this letter exposes the possibility that the pure light of enlightenment might have an unpredictable life of its own.

The next paragraph of the letter, however, quite suddenly displaces the ambivalence figured with this wild tropic movement by offering a historically suspect but rhetorically confident allegory of American unity. He begins with a remark that parries section 1's "your country has been going on less well than I had hoped" (lines 10–11): "With us things are going on well" (line 49). The "things" to which he refers are the acquisition of Florida in 1819 and the pending entrance of Missouri into the Union as a slave state. Both events were fought over bitterly during the period, and ended up as victories for proslavery forces—thanks in part to Jefferson's support—since under Spanish control Florida had become a refuge for escaped slaves, and with Missouri on their side the slave states would hold their own against the free states in Congress and in presidential elections.[54] Yet Jefferson offers a different picture:

> The boisterous sea of liberty indeed is never without a wave, and that from Missouri is now rolling towards us, but we shall ride over it as we have over all others. It is not a moral question, but one merely of power. Its object is to raise a geographical principle for the choice of a President, and the noise will be kept up till that is effected. All know that permitting the slaves of the South to spread into the West will not add one being to that

unfortunate condition, that it will increase the happiness of those existing, and by spreading them over a larger surface, will dilute the evil everywhere, and facilitate the means of getting finally rid of it, an event more anxiously wished by those on whom it presses than by the noisy pretenders to exclusive humanity. In the meantime, it is a ladder for rivals climbing to power. (lines 49–65)

The confident unity represented by "we" and "All" makes it possible to figure the United States as a powerful and sturdy ship riding the "boisterous sea of liberty," and as an expert knowledgeably formulating the elements of a "finally" free solution: "It will increase the happiness of those existing, and by spreading them over a larger surface, will dilute the evil everywhere." These figures displace the difficulty of "a moral question" with the calculable clarity of questions "merely of power."

By representing the United States in excessively confident terms, this letter positions Europe as something of a judge. That is, if Jefferson's enlightened country receives a light refracted by its irreducible passage through Europe, then any development of the Enlightenment in the United States must be carried out under the watchful eye of Europe. To confirm the conviction that the United States is the rightful heir of this light, its proper home, its new and better world, the United States must show Europe that "things are going on well." Subjected to this field of visibility, Jefferson paradoxically figures a unified and powerful national identity as a coherent and felicitous response to the infelicities of refraction and surveillance the letter itself nonetheless rhetorically proliferates.

This moment in the letter to Lafayette represents a crucial transformation in Jefferson's work. This transformation is locatable not so much diachronically—say, in the year of this letter, 1820—as it is rhetorically at nodal points, reiterated ritually throughout Jefferson's correspondence from the 1780s through to 1820s, when the ambivalent oscillation of light, surveillance, and judgment gives way to a governmental problem, a problem of power and of knowledge: "It is not a moral question, but one merely of power . . . All know that permitting the slaves of the South to spread into the West will not add one being to that unfortunate condition, that it will increase the happiness of those existing." That is, the ambivalence of the "disease of liberty" gives way not to an ambiguous "moral question," but rather to a confident and calculable figuration of national power and unity. Although the text suggests that "All know" slavery is a self-evident and calculable problem, it is rather the self-evident and calculable representation of slavery that produces the figure of a powerful "All" who can know in the first place. That is, the "All" who "know" are themselves effects of the self-evident and calculable rhetoric of this predicate phrase: "that permitting the slaves of the South to spread into the West will not add one being to that unfortunate condition, that it will increase the happiness of those existing." This predicate retroactively renders the problem of slavery knowable to the confident, powerful, and unified subject "All." Jefferson's text here turns the "moral problem" into a tactical problem of discrete, manipulable populations, the solution to which is calculably and self-evidently knowable.

These nodal points in Jefferson's writings bear witness to the rise of what J. L.

Heilbron and his research group have called *"l'esprit géometrique,"* which they translate as "the quantifying spirit": "The later 18th century saw a rapid increase in the range and intensity of application of mathematical methods," Heilbron writes, a thesis that "amounts to specifying the time and surveying the routes by which what may be the quintessential form of modern thought first spread widely through society." They argue that this spirit was more than just a narrow, mathematical prowess or ingenuity. Rather, they see an increasingly pervasive "passion to order and systematize as well as to measure and calculate."[55] In fact, Heilbron draws the phrase *"l'esprit géometrique"* from a 1699 essay on the usefulness of mathematics in which Bernard le Bovier de Fontenelle, secretary of the Paris Academy of Sciences, writes that "A work on ethics, politics, criticism, and, perhaps, even rhetoric will be better, other things being equal, if done by a geometer." Over the next one hundred fifty years throughout Europe and North America, the wide, literary, and social terrain named by Fontenelle would become subject to this quantifying spirit, particularly after 1760 when Fontenelle's own method, rooted in Greek geometry, would be superceded by the more precise methods of analysis and algebra.[56]

As Theodore M. Porter has shown, the rise of statistical thinking after 1820 is rooted in this earlier quantifying spirit. Statisticians—who in the early nineteenth century were called "statists"—made great headway persuading intellectuals and the general public that "aggregate numbers and mean values" were valuable representations of otherwise variable objects: "Statistical writers persuaded their contemporaries that systems consisting of numerous autonomous individuals can be studied at a higher level than that of the diverse atomic constituents. They taught them that such systems could be presumed to generate large-scale order and regularity which would be virtually unaffected by the caprice that seemed to prevail in the actions of individuals."[57]

This quantifying spirit was especially captivating in the United States, as Patricia Cline Cohen has shown. More than one early nineteenth-century writer called Americans "a calculating people," and by the 1840s numeracy had become a popular obsession, as Americans incessantly calculated "electoral returns, population counts, cotton production figures, and mileage of railroad tracks," as well as "facts about prostitution, pauperism, and alcohol consumption," church membership, school attendance, and economic resources.[58] The rise of numeracy in the United States can also be seen in the increasing preference for arabic numerals over roman numerals, in the growing centrality of arithmetic to education, and in the flourishing of jobs requiring skill in mathematics.[59] Again, this penchant for calculation was no mere practical skill. It constituted what Cohen has called "a naïve infatuation with numbers" that actually changed the way people thought about the world around them, giving them new measures of truth and new images of the real.[60] Jefferson in particular must be considered a prophetic avatar of this infatuation. His obsessive penchant for using quantitative data even in contexts not usually subjected to scientific epistemology prefigured later, nineteenth-century statistical thinking.[61] As his passionate faith in the census reveals, he was especially devoted to a kind of population thinking[62] that used the census not simply as a tool, but rather as a hermeneutic, a calculable way of depicting the real that identified new problems and possibilities.

Indeed, Jefferson makes clear throughout his correspondence that the proper object of government is "the people" figured very precisely as a "population" of numerable and manipulable units. Consider just two examples. In a letter to William Short (Oct. 3, 1801), Jefferson justifies a tactical embrace of "false principles" in U.S. foreign relations with Europe in the following terms: "To be entangled with [Europe] would be a much greater evil than a temporary acquiescence in the false principles which have prevailed. Peace is our most important interest, and a recovery from debt. We feel ourselves strong, & daily growing stronger. The census just now concluded shows we have added to our population a third of what it was 10 years ago" (vol. 8, 98). Tactical government action here functions for Jefferson as a method of managing the new American nation, itself represented as a multiform population concerned with growth, strength, peace, and national security. His public and private advocacy of and faith in the census as the most important raw representation of "the people" offers a precise image of both the object and the subject of governmental organization: a calculable image of abstract, discrete, and manipulable population units.

In a letter to Baron Von Humboldt (Dec. 6, 1813), Jefferson reiterates his faith in the technical means of representing a coherent and enlightened American population. Anxious about conflicts with Spain and the future of Mexico, Jefferson declares:

> But in what ever governments [the countries of New Spain] end they will be *American* governments, no longer to be involved in the never-ceasing broils of Europe. The European nations constitute a separate division of the globe; their localities make them part of a distinct system . . . America has a hemisphere to itself. It must have its separate system of interests, which must not be subordinated to those of Europe. The insulated state in which nature has placed the American continent, should so far avail it that no spark of war kindled in the other quarters of the globe should be wafted across the wide oceans which separate us from them. And it will be so. In fifty years more the United States alone will contain fifty millions of inhabitants . . . and the numbers which will then be spread over the other parts of the American hemisphere, catching long before that the principles of our portion of it, and concurring with us in the maintenance of the same system. (vol. 9, 431)

Full of imperatives and modal commands, this letter reads more like a manifesto than a personal communication with the "dear friend" to whom it is addressed. And yet precisely the anxiety that gives to an opinion the syntax of a command suggests that, however much Jefferson wants to see "America" as unique, he cannot see the United States except in relation to how it is seen by others. Faced with this relationship, the letter represents the United States as a discrete "system," within a separate "quarter of the globe," made up of abstract and calculable "inhabitants" or "numbers."

Such nodal points—represented in the letter to Lafayette by the figures of the "All" who "know," the well-designed ship, and the clever expert or scientist; in the letter to Short by the figure of the enumerated American "population"; and in the letter to the baron by the figure of a discrete "system" of abstract and numerable "inhabitants"—translate the ambivalence of enlightenment into an ordered, systematic practice of government. They respond to this ambivalence by subjecting the United States to the "the quantifying spirit" of transparent, calculable, and tactical power, a subjection that paradoxically subjectifies the United States as an "All" who "knows" how to calculate "the means of finally getting rid of" slavery, understood as a problem of populations.

How can we account for this turn from the ambiguities of enlightenment, which seem to plague the correspondence, to population thinking and the rhetoric of calculation and quantification? As figured in the letters to Lafayette, Short, and the Baron, this turn figures a power that simultaneously subjects and subjectifies, that is both productive and regulative, and that actively renders what it subjects. As sites of active, translative, transformative textual work, the nodal points in Jefferson's texts reflect less a sovereign, centrally controlled, and unidirectional authority than the reflexive mode of power and knowledge Michel Foucault has thematized. That is, they show how a mode of power "produces reality" as well as "domains of objects and rituals of truth."[63] If Jefferson was a forerunner of the early nineteenth-century statists, it is not because he carried out state edicts like a bureaucratic functionary, but because he expressed a systematic, calculable mode of thought that would pave the way for the modern state's often diffuse power.

In *Discipline and Punish*, Foucault glimpsed this productive mode of power in the late eighteenth-century realm of criminality, when "the entire economy of punishment" began to be "redistributed" in Europe with the "disappearance of torture as a public spectacle" and the emergence of "a new theory of law and crime, a new moral or political justification of the right to punish" (7). "Punishment," Foucault argues, went from being the most visible and spectacular aspect of criminality "to become the most hidden part of the penal process" (9) as "a whole set of assessing, diagnostic, prognostic, normative judgments concerning the criminal [became] lodged in the framework of penal judgment" (18–19). Foucault's effort "to study the metamorphosis of punitive methods on the basis of a political technology of the body . . . in which punitive measures are not simply 'negative' mechanisms that made it possible to repress, to prevent, to exclude, to eliminate; but . . . are linked to a whole series of positive and useful effects which it is their task to support" (24), locates a reflexive mode of power in which punishment came to mean a multiform, systematic field of "discipline" that itself would "reform" and "free." Subjects subjected to discipline became subjects at precisely the moment of their subjection.

One of Foucault's central figures for this mode of power is Jeremy Bentham's Panopticon, an "architectural apparatus" for which "power should be visible and unverifiable. Visible: the inmate will constantly have before his eyes the tall outline of the central tower from which he is spied upon. Unverifiable: the inmate must never know whether he is being looked at any one moment; but he must be sure that he may always be so" (201). The Panopticon figures the "composition" of "mechanisms of power" (199–200) in which "a real subjection is born mechanically from a fictitious relation . . . [for h]e who is subjected to a field of visibility, and who knows it, assumes responsibility for the constraints of power; he makes them play spontaneously upon himself; he inscribes in himself the power relation in which he simultaneously plays both roles; he becomes the principle of his own subjection" (202–3). Thus, for Foucault the Panopticon is "the architectural figure" (200) for a mode of power that creates subjects as reflexive structures that allow power to take effect.

In Jefferson's texts, the figure of enlightenment plays precisely this panoptic role. Subjected to the visible and unverifiable power of light, a field of visibility in which slavery is a contradictory and frightening prospect "held up" for all to see, the United States becomes an anxious site of reflexive power. Yet what does it mean when an emerging nation-state, rather than an individual prisoner, becomes the principle of its own subjection? Foucault's work on governmentality offers some insight. Already in the final chapter of *The History of Sexuality*, Foucault begins to move from the panoptic modality of power in the sphere of criminality to other spheres by shifting from the realm of bodies to the realm of populations.[64] That is, in the words of Colin Gordon, Foucault begins to suggest that "the same style of analysis . . . that had been used to study techniques and practices addressed to individual human subjects within particular, local institutions could also be addressed to techniques and practices for governing populations of subjects at the level of a political sovereignty over an entire society."[65]

The History of Sexuality argues that the seventeenth century marks a shift in mechanisms of power from the era of sovereignty, in which "the sovereign exercised his right of life only by exercising his right to kill, or by refraining from killing" (136) and thus practiced a "right to take life or let live" (138), to the "modern" era that witnesses a "power bent on generating forces, making them grow, and ordering them" (136), "a power whose highest function was perhaps no longer to kill, but to invest life through and through" (139). This "modern" era is thus characterized by "an explosion of numerous and diverse techniques for achieving the subjugation of bodies and the control of populations, marking the beginning of an era of 'bio-power'" (140). Explaining this notion of "bio-power," Foucault continues: "A power whose task is to take charge of life needs continuous regulatory and corrective mechanisms. It is no longer a matter of bringing death into play in the field of sovereignty, but of distributing the living in the domain of value and utility. Such a power has to qualify, measure, appraise, and hierarchize" (144). Thus bio-power, in Gordon's words, refers to "forms of power exercised over persons specifically in so far as they are thought of as living beings: a politics concerned with subjects as members of a *population*." In Ann Laura Stoler's words, bio-power signifies "the regulations of the life processes of aggregate human populations."[66]

In a series of lectures delivered in 1978 entitled "Security, Territory and Population" and "The Birth of Biopolitics," or as he later retitled them in one of the lectures, "The History of 'Governmentality,'" Foucault reiterates this historical shift and develops his analytic shift. The emergence of a codifiable and calculable category of "population," and the attendant professionalization of knowledges that produced that codifiability and calculability, puts into effect a diffuse, active, and multidirectional form of power. The problems that fields of knowledge such as statistics were said to address were themselves given a particular, "problematic" form by those very fields of knowledge.[67]

The 1978 lectures on governmentality argue that the very idea of political discourse underwent a massive restructuring at precisely the historical moment in which Jefferson is writing. As he did in the last chapter of *The History of Sexuality*, Foucault argues that the period between the sixteenth and the eighteenth centuries in Europe marks a shift in the idea of governing and government. Political treatises giving governmental advice to the prince or king give way to political treatises that are not yet self-proclaimed works of political science, but rather are searching for a new model of legitimation for government. Foucault suggests that the idea of government "explodes" onto the scene during this period as a problem in new and pressing ways. The new treatises deemphasize the a priori and self-generating justification of the prince or king's legitimacy and his consequent sovereignty over a certain territory that contains his subjects. Instead, they theorize a multifaceted "art of government" capable of legitimizing itself via its ability to tactically govern *"things."*

The emergence of a "government of things," Foucault argues, entails a shift in the object of government from a territory containing inhabitants to "things" with multiple and varied needs.[68] Whereas the family previously served as a model for governing a state itself legitimated by the figure of the prince or king, the new treatises recognize a need for a more flexible and complex model of government, a model within which "the family," for example, would be just one among many objects of address for the government. Foucault refers in particular to the metaphor of the ship—popular in this period of governmental treatises, as we saw in Jefferson's letter to Lafayette—as a figure for this new object of government:

> What does it mean to govern a ship? It means clearly to take charge of the sailors, but also of the boat and its cargo; to take care of a ship means also to reckon with winds, rocks and storms; and it consists in that activity of establishing a relation between the sailors who are to be taken care of and the ship which is to be taken care of, and the cargo which is to be brought safely to port, and all those eventualities like winds, rocks, storms and so on; this is what characterizes the government of a ship. . . . What counts essentially is this complex of men and things; property and territory are merely one of its variables.[69]

This redefinition of government thus involves the emergence of "a new kind of finality" or a new goal of governing:

> For instance, government will have to ensure that the greatest possible quantity of wealth is produced, that the people are provided with sufficient means of subsistence, that the population is enabled to multiply, etc. . . . In order to achieve these various finalities, things must be disposed—and this term, *dispose*, is important because with sovereignty the instrument that allowed it to achieve its aim—that is to say, obedience to laws—was the law itself; law and sovereignty were absolutely inseparable. On the contrary, with government it is a question not of imposing law on men, but of disposing things: that

is to say, of employing tactics rather than laws, and even of using laws themselves as tactics.[70]

By shifting his analytic focus from the study of structures and institutions (such as the state) with essential and inherent "properties and propensities" to practices and deployments of power with a "plurality of specific aims," Foucault locates a governmental realm within which power operates diffusely and reflexively.[71]

Foucault's account of a governmental modality of power allows us to interpret Jefferson's notion of government more precisely than theories of oppressive and unidirectional ideology or hegemony and counterhegemony could. Jefferson's correspondence in effect dramatizes *subjection* to a field of visibility characterized by the visible and unverifiable light of the Enlightenment that is simultaneously *subjectification* within a calculable pursuit of that light. That is, subjected to an Enlightenment that he cannot fully locate in Europe or the United States, but that seems to judge America's unenlightened elements, Jefferson's texts rhetorically subjectify "America" by rendering it as a calculable and controllable population. The nodal points in Jefferson's texts that translate the ambivalence of "mutilation however in it's freest parts" (from the February 8, 1786, letter to Madison) into an enlightened "question . . . merely of power" and calculable national unity (from the December 20, 1820, letter to Lafayette), can thus be interpreted as expressions of what Foucault calls "governmentality."

Jefferson's preoccupation with slavery and the light of Enlightenment evinces his effort to define the conditions of possibility for governing the United States as a legitimate nation; he is concerned, in other words, with giving the United States the same status as the lofty European polities, but also with defining its essential difference. Responding to a persistent anxiety over slavery as a sign of the Enlightenment's frustrating refraction in the United States, a refraction all-too-visible to his European rivals, Jefferson turns to this art of government to enlighten the United States. Gone is the self-assuredness of absolute difference defined by revolution, so forcefully presented in the Declaration of Independence—a difference in kind between colony and nation. Having joined the world of burgeoning nations by the force of revolution, Jefferson's America begins to face differences in degree, differences to be interpreted by means of a new art of government. It is within this shift of interest, this reformulation of emancipation by a revolutionary become nation builder, that we can locate Jefferson's letters on colonization.

Racial Governmentality

Jefferson's discourse on colonization addresses itself directly to the disposal of populations. More than that, his discourse on colonization paradoxically renders the very idea of a racially and nationally codified population as that which it seeks to address. In this section, by reading a crucial passage on colonization from Jefferson's *Autobiography* along with the letters on colonization echoed by that passage, I trace a racial governmentality, addressed to the problem of population, running throughout Jefferson's writings. It is this racial governmentality that conjoins a discourse of emancipation with a discourse of racial and national codification. For as we will see, a power that, in Foucault's words, "distributes the living in the domain of value and utility," that "invests life" with qualifiable, measurable, appraisable, and hierarchizable value, can be said to render a freedom both conditioned upon and limited by the articulation of race and nation.[72] In turn, this interpretation of Jefferson's racial governmentality locates a historically specific racial formation in the very notion of governmentality, attending to a mode of power—racism—that Foucault famously neglected.[73]

Writing in 1821 about a debate in the Virginia House of Delegates in 1779, Jefferson offers an extremely condensed summation of his colonization discourse in this passage from his *Autobiography* to which I have repeatedly referred in this chapter:

> The bill on the subject of slaves was a mere digest of the existing laws respecting them, without any intimation of a plan for a future & general emancipation. It was thought better that this should be kept back, and attempted only by way of amendment whenever the bill should be brought on. The principles of the amendment however were agreed on, that is to say, the freedom of all born after a certain day, and deportation at a proper age. But it was found that the public mind would not yet bear the proposition, nor will it bear it even at this day. Yet the day is not distant when it must bear and adopt it, or worse will follow. Nothing is more certainly written in the book of fate than that these people are to be free. Nor is it less certain that the two races, equally free, cannot live in the same government. Nature, habit, opinion has drawn indelible lines of distinction between them. It is still in our power to direct the process of emancipation and deportation peaceably and in such slow degree as that the evil will wear off insensibly, and their place be pari passu filled up by free white laborers. If on the contrary it is left to force itself on, human nature must shutter at the prospect held up. We should in vain look for an example in the Spanish deportation or deletion of the Moors. This precedent would fall far short of our case.[74]

As we have seen throughout this chapter, Jefferson is here concerned with the fact that slavery in the United States is "held up" for the world to see as a glaring challenge to the promise of universal freedom. The inadequacy of "the Spanish deportation or deletion of the Moors" tells us that the United States cannot follow antiquated European "precedents," even when analogies suggest themselves; and yet the very act of referring to Spain suggests that Jefferson is looking to Europe again, finding both a surveillance of "our case" and an insufficiently enlightened solution.[75]

How, then, does Jefferson respond to this "prospect held up"? In this *Autobiography* passage, he articulates a dilemma I mentioned at the beginning of this chapter: "Nothing is more certainly written in the book of fate than that these people are to be free." The fact of emancipation for slaves has the structure of something already written in the future, something that "will have been"—the structure, that is, of the future anterior. Jefferson is familiar with this structure, for he made use of it as the tense of revolution when he wrote, in the Declaration of Independence, "we . . . solemnly publish and declare, That these United colonies are, and of right ought to be Free and Independent States." Both the Declaration of Independence's "are and ought to be" and the *Autobiography*'s "written in the book of fate that these people are to be free" figure what Jacques Derrida has called the "fabulous retroactivity" of the people inventing themselves in the very utterance of their independence: we will have been free once we say "we are free."[76]

Jefferson is, however, not willing to consider this means of emancipating the slaves; in fact, we know he was terrified about the prospect of a black revolution. In the *Autobiography* passage, he prophecies that "worse will follow," and that "human nature must shutter" if colonization is not adopted and slavery "is left to force itself on"—a fearful prophecy that resonates throughout his writings. In the *Notes on the State of Virginia*, for example, he recognizes that two discrete revolutionary possibilities exist in the colonies, and registers his terror of one:

> The whole commerce between master and slave is a perpetual exercise of the most boisterous passions, the most unremitting despotism on the one part, and degrading submissions on the other. . . . of the proprietors of slaves a very small proportion indeed are ever seen to labour. And can the liberties of a nation be thought secure when we have removed their only firm basis, a conviction in the minds of the people that these liberties are of the gift of God? That they are not to be violated but with his wrath? Indeed I tremble for my country when I reflect that God is just: that his justice cannot sleep for ever: that considering numbers, nature and natural means only, a revolution of the wheel of fortune, an exchange of situation is among possible events: that it may become probable by supernatural interference! The Almighty has no attribute which can take side with us in such a contest.[77]

Jefferson prophecies emancipation as a race war, a "contest" pitting white Americans against justice, the Almighty, and black Americans. Freedom for enslaved black Americans is the inevitable but terrifying effect of a just and wrathful God and "the wheel of fortune." Of course, the previous turn of that wheel made possible his own claim to the "my country" for which he trembles at the inevitability of another turn. In a July 14, 1793, letter to Monroe, Jefferson again invokes that other revolution which he cannot countenance: "I become daily more & more convinced that all the West India Islands will remain in the hands of the people of colour, & a total expulsion of the whites sooner or later take place. It is high time we should foresee the bloody scenes which our children certainly, and possibly ourselves (south of the Potommac) have to wade through, & try to avert them.—We have no news from the continent of Europe later than the 1st of May" (vol. 6, 349–50). Here, the Haitian revolution authorizes the prophecy of a dangerously revolutionary response to freedom's nonarrival in the United States. This vision of "bloody scenes" seems to prompt the reference to Europe in the very next sentence, as if Europe is silently poised to watch and to judge the "bloody scenes" to come. As in the *Autobiography* passage, Jefferson commits himself to "averting" this prophecy.

In an August 28, 1797, letter to St. George Tucker, Jefferson also writes about two mutually exclusive revolutions. Referring to Tucker's abolitionist pamphlet "Dissertation on Slavery," he writes:

> You know my subscription to it's doctrines; and to the mode of emancipation, I am satisfied that that must be a matter of compromise between the passions, the prejudices, & the real difficulties which will each have their weight in that operation. Perhaps the first chapter of this history, which has begun in St. Domingo, & the next succeeding ones, which will recount how all the whites were driven from all the other islands, may prepare our minds for a peaceable accommodation between justice, policy & necessity; & furnish an answer to the difficult question, whither shall the coloured emigrants go? and the sooner we put some plan underway, the greater hope there is that it may be permitted to proceed peaceably to it's ultimate effect. But if something is not done, & soon done, we shall be the murderers of our own children. The 'murmura venturos nautis prodentia ventos' has already reached us; the revolutionary storm, now sweeping the globe, will be upon us. (vol. 7, 167–68)

This letter shifts the grammar of Jefferson's commitment to "justice" away from the fabulously retroactive "are and ought to be" of the Declaration of Independence and the *Autobiography* passage. Instead it offers, on one hand, the prophetic threat of the Haitian revolution and, on the other hand, the practical and technical terms of "something . . . soon done," a "compromise between the passions, the prejudices, & the real difficulties," and a "peaceable accommodation between justice, policy & necessity." Emancipation is here not the effect of revolutionary force; it is not rendered by the fabulous retroactivity of a speech act the utterance of which invents the utterer. Rather, "emancipation" is a practical question—"whither shall the coloured emigrants go?"—for which he must "furnish an answer"—a "mode," "plan," "provision," or "operation" to be put into "ultimate effect."[78]

In the *Autobiography* (1821), *The Notes on the State of Virginia* (1781), and the letters to Monroe (July 14, 1793) and Tucker (Aug. 28, 1797), we can trace a concerted refiguration of "freedom" from the revolutionary, future anteriority of the Declaration of Independence to the *problem* of a future, fearful revolution, on the one hand, and the *solution* of colonization as a practical, governmental project on the other. Rhetorically, then, the very refiguring of the Declaration's fabulous retroactivity as, in the case of slavery, a prophetic problem to be practically solved gives the danger Jefferson is seeking to "avert" a form quite different from the "long train of abuses and usurpations" to which the Declaration of Independence responds with the "right . . . to throw off such a government." Derrida has argued that the fabulous retroactivity of a revolutionary declaration is an ethical act because it embraces and maintains the undecidability and underivability of its "right."[79] The Declaration of Independence thus maintains within itself a trace of the unfoundability of its foundation, a trace one can read in the conjunction of a constation, "are," and a prescription, "ought to be."[80] In his writings on colonization, however, Jefferson can be said to "avert" that ethical scene by figuring the futurity of justice at once prophetically and practically. That is, for this prophecy to be a strictly decidable, solvable problem, a problem avertable with enough effort and "foresight," the prophecy itself must have been given a form susceptible to a practical solution. In effect, the solution formulates the problem. What, then, is the problem colonization produces?

In lieu of a revolutionary solution, Jefferson attempts to derive emancipation from a governmental system, a technical, utilitarian art of government: "the two races, equally free, cannot live in the same government," he says in the *Autobiography* passage. This solution, this art of government meant to capture freedom, involves the practical manipulation of discrete, racially and nationally calculable and codifiable population units; consequently, this art of government must itself render the calculable and codifiable racial and national forms of the population to be manipulated. Again in the *Autobiography* passage, where he writes of "indelibly" separated "races"—colonized black Americans, imported "white laborers"—he gives the population units a visible and discrete form subject to manipulation. As we will see in chapter 3, unlike the discursive practices directed toward Indians at the turn of the nineteenth century—which represented hierarchical cultural differences as differences in cultural strength, differences in degree that could be assimilated and incorporated—these "indelible lines of distinction" codify a difference in kind that demands spatial separation. Similarly, in a letter to Monroe (Nov. 24, 1801) he asks, "Could we procure lands beyond the limits of the US to form a receptacle for these people?" (vol. 8, 104), and, answering himself in the next paragraph, writes "The West Indies offer a more probable & practicable retreat for them. Inhabited already by a people of their own race & color; climates congenial with their natural constitution; insulated from the other descriptions of men; nature seems to have formed these islands to become the receptacle of the blacks transplanted into this hemisphere" (105). This question and its answer do not only "objectify" black Americans, but more precisely render them as abstract, "naturally" and "practicably" manipulable units of a discrete population.

The famous letter to Jared Sparks advocating colonization epitomizes the "problem of population" Jefferson's proposal addresses (Feb. 4, 1824, vol. 10, 289–93). It begins, "In the disposition of these unfortunate people, there are two rational objects to be distinctly kept in view" (289). Immediately, the clarity and practicality of the solution is the measure of its feasibility. But this clarity and practicality reflects the calculability of "the problem" itself:

> And without repeating the other arguments which have been urged by others, I will appeal to figures only, which admit no controversy. I shall speak in round numbers, not absolutely accurate, yet not so wide from truth as to vary the result materially. There are in the United States a million and a half of people of color in slavery. To send off the whole of these at once, nobody conceives to be practicable for us, or expedient for them. Let us take twenty-five years for its accomplishment, within which time they will be doubled. Their estimated value as property, in the first place, (for actual property has been lawfully vested in that form, and who can lawfully take it from the possessors?) at an average of two hundred dollars each, young and old, would amount to six hundred

millions of dollars, which must be paid or lost by somebody. To this, add the cost of their transportation by land and sea to Mesurado, a year's provision of food and clothing, implements of husbandry and of their trades, which will amount to three hundred millions more, making thirty-six millions of dollars a year for twenty-five years, with insurance of peace all that time, and it is impossible to look at the question a second time. I am aware that at the end of about sixteen years, a gradual detraction from this sum will commence, from the gradual dimunition of breeders, and go on during the remaining nine years. Calculate this deduction, and it is still impossible to look at the enterprise a second time. (290–1)

The letter continues incessantly in this vein. While this discourse certainly borrows from that of the "business" of slavery, representing black Americans as nonhuman commodities, this dehumanization also overlaps and interacts with a certain populizing discourse: "The establishment of a colony on the coast of Africa, which may introduce among the aborigines the arts of cultivated life, and the blessings of civilization and science. By doing this, we may make to them some retribution for the long course of injuries we have been committing on their population. And considering that these blessings will descend to the '*nati natorum, et qui nascentur ab illis,*' we shall in the long run have rendered them perhaps more good than evil" (290). Black Americans are no more granted "humanity" in some general or simply positive sense in this passage than they are only reduced to commodities in the previous passage. Rather, in both passages Jefferson's discourse invests black Americans with a common, racial identity on the level of their existence as aggregate, abstract beings—on the level, that is, of their existence as a discrete population. It is this discursive production of a calculable black population that allows Jefferson to blend the dehumanizing force of the traditional discourse of slavery—"The estimated value of the new-born infant is so low, (say twelve dollars and fifty cents,) that it would probably be yielded by the owner gratis"—with the Enlightenment discourse of universal freedom—"By doing this, we may make to them some retribution for the long course of injuries we have been committing on their population."

In turn, colonization takes on an imperial form in this letter when he writes to Sparks that "a colony on the coast of Africa" will grant "retribution" both to "aborigines," in the form of "the arts of cultivated life, and the blessings of civilization and science," and to "people of color in [U.S.] slavery" in the form of "an asylum to which we can, by degrees, send the whole of that population from among us" (290). On the one hand, colonization discourse gives deportation value by positing a hierarchical racial difference between black Americans and white Americans in the process of representing black Americans as objects of expulsion. On the other hand, colonization also values U.S. colonialism in Africa by positing an abstract equivalence between white Americans and colonized black Americans as abstract bearers of American imperialism. That is, on one hand, colonized black Americans are racially different from and subject to white Americans, and thus equated with "aborigines," on the level of racial particularity. On the other hand, colonized black Americans are represented as equivalent to white Americans, and thus different from "aborigines," on the level of formal and abstract equality. Colonization discourse renders this paradox consistent, self-evident, and "rational."[81]

These manipulable representations are echoed in the analogy Jefferson draws repeatedly between colonized black Americans and "imported" "white laborers" or, often, "Germans." For instance, in the *Autobiography* passage he writes that the "place" of colonized black Americans can "be pari passu filled up by free white laborers." This analogy simultaneously constructs an abstract equivalence between "free white laborers" and colonized black Americans and codifies a racial and national difference between white and black populations. If "the two races, equally free, cannot live in the same government," Jefferson here calculates what, precisely, "the two races" share "equally," or what form of being "free" is common to both, as well as what, precisely, their governmental difference consists in.[82]

I am not suggesting here that Jefferson is a benevolent liberal who failed to overcome antiquated prejudices, nor that Jefferson's representation of colonization as genuinely emancipatory is simply a false ideological surface masking a traditional, dehumanizing and objectifying discourse of slavery. To the contrary, we ought to read both his liberal language and his objectifying language as overlapping and interacting to produce a hybrid, liberal racism driven by the governmental investment of subjects with life as populations to be enumerated, regulated, and manipulated—"we shall in the long run have *rendered* them perhaps more good than evil," Jefferson writes to Sparks. His art of government articulates race, nation, and equality by offering a solution (the enumeration, emancipation, deportation, and resettlement of black Americans) to a problem (the conflict between formally and abstractly equal populations with hierarchically ordered racial particularities) retroactively created by the terms of the solution itself. Colonization is thus not simply a utilitarian response to racial conflict; rather, colonization is embedded in a discourse that also produces that very conflict as one between racially codifiable and calculable population units whose formal and abstract equality conditions and is conditioned by their hierarchically ordered racial and national particularities. Colonization paradoxically responds to and creates the racial calculability of populations.

Yet colonization discourse does more than this. One of the most distinctive aspects of Jeffersonian colonization is that which distinguishes it most radically from a project to deport or transport black Americans out of the United States. As he says in the *Autobiography* passage quoted above, Jefferson does not adapt to a U.S. context the kind of "deportation" practiced by the Spaniards against the Moors. Black Americans precisely must not be "deleted," as he suggests the Moors were. Rather, he expresses a need to surveil and to regulate colonized black Americans after deportation, and he represents that need as absolutely necessary, self-evident and realistic—a representation that many abolitionists shared with him at least through the 1830s.

The 1824 letter to Sparks mentioned above exemplifies Jefferson's concern that the United States keep watch over black Americans long after their deportation and emancipation. When Jefferson writes that by establishing "a colony on the coast of

Africa, which may introduce among the aborigines the arts of cultivated life, and the blessings of civilization and science . . . we shall in the long run have rendered them perhaps more good than evil," the "rendering" to which he refers also includes a continuing system of surveillance and control:

> In the disposition of these unfortunate people, there are two rational objects to be distinctly kept in view. First. . . . Under this view, the colonization society is to be considered as a missionary society, having in view, however, objects more humane, more justifiable, and less aggressive on the peace of other nations, than the others of that appellation.
>
> The second object [of colonizing black Americans], and the most interesting to us, as coming home to our physical and moral characters, to our happiness and safety, is to provide an asylum to which we can, by degrees, send the whole of that population from among us, and establish them under our patronage and protection, as a separate, free and independent people. (vol. 10, 290)

In this letter, colonization displaces older, missionary practices due to the former's "rational," "more humane, more justifiable, and less aggressive" objectives. These objectives involve, on one hand, granting colonized black Americans formal equality and independence—treating them as a "free and independent people"—while, on the other hand, maintaining a system of regulation and control over them—"to provide an asylum to which we can, by degrees, send the whole of that population from among us, and establish them under our patronage and protection, as a separate . . . people." Yet this passage secures the modernity of those objectives—their quality of being "more humane, more justifiable, and less aggressive" than missionizing—by repeatedly declaring their visual self-evidence: "are . . . to be distinctly kept in view," "Under this view." The self-evident rationality and modernity of colonization thus depends on the declarative reiteration of its clarity or "distinctness." This reiteration of colonization's self-evidence turns the articulation of formal equality with control and regulation into a "rational" formula for freedom.[83]

This regulatory sentiment is echoed in a letter to Dr. Thomas Humphreys: "I concur entirely in your leading principles of gradual emancipation, of establishment on the coast of Africa, and the patronage of our nation until the emigrants shall be able to protect themselves" (Feb. 8, 1817, vol. 10, 76–77). The vision of continuing "patronage" casts America's proposed gift to black Americans less as an ethical and just act that expects no return than as an unequal exchange in which formal equality would be paid for in perpetuity by the maintenance of a colonial system of hierarchical racial and national particularity.

Jefferson also represents this articulation of formal equality with continuing regulation and control in economic terms. For example, in a letter to Rufus King from July 13, 1802, he writes: "We might for this purpose [of paying for the colonization of slaves from the United States], enter into negotiations with the natives, on some part of the coast, to obtain a settlement, and by establishing an African company, combine with it commercial operations, which might not only reimburse expenses but procure profit also" (vol. 8, 161–62). Similarly, Jefferson writes to Monroe on June 2, 1802, "and if leave can be obtained to send black insurgents there, to inquire further whether the regulations of the place would permit us to carry or take there any mercantile objects which by affording some commercial profit, might defray the expenses of the transportation" (vol. 8, 153). By bringing independent black Americans in Africa into the economic orbit of the United States as a peripheral nation-state, these continuing "commercial operations" would construct and maintain both a separation of Americans from Africans, and a continuing dependency of Africans on Americans.

The fact that colonization must continue beyond deportation, that it must proceed "in such a slow degree," as he says in the *Autobiography* passage, suggests that it not only produces and responds to, but also maintains the very terms of the crisis it represents. Colonization can be said to demand the iteration and reiteration of the calculable difference, the production and maintenance of a difference in kind, between discrete, racialized populations. That is, when Jefferson argues that the United States must keep a watchful political and economic eye over the new black American state in Africa, it seems that colonization must continue to work transatlantically after deportation so that it can maintain this calculable difference.

Colonization thus institutionalizes its claim to complete the emancipatory promise of the American Revolution in a continual, systematic, transatlantic ritual of racialization. This reiterative aspect of colonization indicates that imperial U.S. citizenship does not demand the assimilation of difference to a homogeneous national norm, but rather depends on the active production of a particular kind of difference—the calculable racial difference of a population. Yet this reiterative aspect of colonization also indicates that imperial U.S. citizenship is not animated simply by the desire to rid America of racial others. Rather, African colonization schemes precisely sought to keep alive the very racial distinction they calculated in the first place through post-deportation surveillance and control. Colonization's reiterative art of governmentality continually articulates the formal and abstract equality between populations with the racially and nationally codified particularities of those populations.

Thus, colonization's governmentality consists not only in centralized power and control (buying slaves and land, deportation), but also in a systematic, reiterative, decentralized, diffuse political reason, a calculation of society whereby people would come to be understood as discrete, calculable members of a racially and nationally codified population. In effect, colonized black Americans are to be objects of an experiment in Enlightenment governmentality; they are to be rendered, represented, and maintained "free" by the United States. When Foucault writes in *The History of Sexuality* that "I do not envisage a 'history of mentalities' that would take account of bodies only through the manner in which they have been perceived and given meaning and value; but a 'history of bodies' and the manner in which what is most material and most vital in them has been invested" (152), the manner of investment, in the case of colonization, is this reiterative and calculable political reason. In Jefferson, then, colonization can be understood not as an aberration of liberal principles of freedom, but rather as a liberal, governmental articulation of formal and abstract equality with racial and national codification by means of a well-regulated, diffuse, and responsibilized society.

This results not in a withdrawing of government from civil society, but in a dispersion of governmentality across a society itself created by governmental political reason. When he writes in the *Autobiography* passage that "Nothing is more certainly written in the book of fate than that [our slaves] are to be free. Nor is it less certain that the two races, equally free, cannot live in the same government," he suggests that formally and abstractly, as population units, black Americans and white Americans are equally free. White nationalist racism "is no less certain," however, because the freedom of these population units is conditioned upon the production and maintenance of their "indelible" racial codification.

A Barbarian to the Natives

On October 30, 1774, Phillis Wheatley penned an early objection to colonization (quoted in the epigraph to this chapter) in a letter to John Thornton, an English merchant, philanthropist, and colonizationist. Thornton had asked her to go to Anamaboe, a Gold Coast slave-trading town, and serve with two black missionaries, Bristol Yamma and John Quamine, in Samuel Hopkins's 1773 project to Christianize Africa with colonized slaves from the Americas.[84] As I mentioned at the beginning of this chapter, Wheatley skillfully deflects this request with a few powerful sentences that open the door to what would become a decades-long, black American struggle to counter what I have called the colonization movement's Jeffersonian articulation of formal equality with racial and national codification. How might we begin to interpret this struggle?[85]

Wheatley's words are especially strong given their immediate context. Many of her letters to Thornton from the period are filled with gracious greetings and salutations as well as cautious compliments and agreements, coupled with subtle assertions of her differences with Thornton.[86] For instance, just before his letter on colonization, Thornton had accused Wheatley of privileging her literary work over her spiritual work, an accusation that reflects his own Calvinistic and anti-intellectual doctrine of free grace:[87]

> When I want you to have increasing views of redeeming Love, I did not mean, that you should be able to talk more exactly about it . . . it is very possible to talk excellently of divine things, even so as to raise the admiration of others, and at the same time, the heart not be affected by them. This is the common deception among the people of God. The kingdom of heaven is not in word, but in power. . . . When I wish you to have increasing views of redeeming Love, I would have you thrown into silent wonder and adoration of the wisdom and goodness of God.[88]

Uncomfortable with Wheatley's turn to words, Thornton tries to withdraw them from her, to halt her intellectual pursuits and push her into silent affect: "I would have you thrown into silent wonder and adoration." In response, in the same letter quoted in the epigraph to this chapter, Wheatley writes:

> I will endeavour to compensate it by a strict Observance of hers [her mistress, Susanna Wheatley] and your good advice from time to time, which you have given me encourage-

ment to hope for—What a Blessed source of consolation that our greatest friend is an immortal God whose friendship is invariable! from whom I have all that is *in me* praise worthy in mental possession. . . . The world is a severe schoolmaster, for its frowns are less dang'rous than its smiles and flatteries, and it is a difficult task to keep in the path of Wisdom.[89]

Wheatley goes out of her way to assure Thornton that she recognizes his concern, without accepting his call to silence. Indeed, by reminding Thornton that God is the source of her intellect too—"from whom I have all that is *in me* praise worthy in mental possession"—she subtly refuses to silence her words. What is more, her final sentence, while apparently agreeing with Thornton's warning about the spiritual emptiness of flattery for excellent "talk" about "divine things," also allows her to be cautious about Thornton were *he* to become the "severe schoolmaster" offering her "smiles and flatteries" in exchange for her silence.

In the epigraph passage, by choosing to stay with "my British & American Friends" rather than go with two men she does not know to a place she has never been as a missionary among people whose language she does not speak, Wheatley proceeds to challenge Thornton's—and indeed the colonization movement's—assumption of racial affiliation: "You propose my returning to Africa with Bristol Yamma and John Quamine." In complicating the colonizationists' notion of a return to Africa, she goes beyond acknowledging the limits of her own knowledge; with the phrase "Upon my arrival, how like a Barbarian shou'd I look to the Natives," Wheatley undermines colonization's imperial aspirations. Read with the passages quoted above, Wheatley's ethical silence in the face of "the Natives" displaces Thornton's "silent wonder" in the face of God, emphasizing that she still has much to say in the Anglo-American world that has become her home.

Wheatley was not always so critical of colonization. She writes approvingly of colonization to Hopkins on February 9, 1774, though by declining to participate due to "the return of my asthmatic complaint" and "the sickness of my mistress" she perhaps registers implicit reservations.[90] She also writes effusively about missionary work to Samson Occom on February 11, 1774.[91] However, in a subsequent letter to Hopkins written on May 6, 1774, we read a criticism similar to the one she voices to Thornton:

I am very sorry to hear, that Philip Quaque has very little or no apparent Success in his mission. Yet, I wish that what you hear respecting him may be only a misrepresentation. Let us not be discouraged, but still hope, that God will bring about his great work, tho' Philip may not be the instrument in the Divine Hand, to perform this work of wonder, turning the African "from darkness to light." Possibly, if Philip would introduce himself properly to them, (I don't know the reverse) he might be more Successful, and in setting a good example which is more powerfully winning than Instruction.[92]

By recommending Quaque "introduce himself properly" rather than engage in "Instruction," and by acknowledging the limits of her knowledge about "the African" with the parenthetical "I don't know the reverse," Wheatley again troubles the racial and imperial claims of the colonization movement. Communication between blacks on either side of the Middle Passage, she suggests, is no simple or direct matter. Wheatley thus challenges the white colonizationist's assumption that the black Atlantic is homogeneous, as well as the black colonizationist's assumption that "the Natives" are inferior to the diaspora.

Working with figures of silence and speech, these letters depict an Atlantic world riven with difference and inequality. Race and nation are not simply isomorphic conditions for community and communication, as the colonizationists would have it: black Africans, white British and Americans. Rather, black diasporans speak directly to the "British & American" communities into which they have been forced, communities that, if they can learn to listen, may also have much to learn from "the Natives."[93]

The period in which David Walker and Maria W. Stewart offered their critiques of colonization was very different from Wheatley's 1770s. By the late 1820s and 1830s, the colonization discourse developed systematically by Jefferson just a few years after Wheatley wrote to Thornton and Hopkins had reached the level of what Foucault would call a dense discursive formation. The British colony of Sierra Leone had been well established, the ACS's settlement in Liberia was under way, and the society had chapters in many states. In the United States, conflicting groups of free blacks, moderate and radical white abolitionists, and proslavery forces were using newspapers, magazines, public speaking tours, town meetings, and congressional debates on the federal and state levels to sell colonization to free and enslaved blacks as well as white slave owners, philanthropists, missionaries, and abolitionists.

Wheatley's black community in Boston in particular had transformed since the end of the eighteenth century, reaching almost two thousand by 1830 out of a total population of just over sixty thousand. Concentrated in neighborhoods such as the north slope of Beacon Hill and organized into churches, mason halls, and societies such as the Massachusetts General Colored Association, blacks in Boston led a strong abolitionist movement that published influential newspapers such as *Freedom's Journal* and that worked alongside, if at times in conflict with, the city's prominent white abolitionists. Of course, blacks in Boston were class stratified and at times politically at odds with one another in ways Walker and Stewart are explicit about. Yet even this active debate and outright conflict testifies to a sizeable, politically active community that was more extensive than in Wheatley's time.[94]

In their own conjuncture Walker and Stewart echo Wheatley's ironic coupling of silence with speech, expanding that coupling into an anticolonization discourse that neither simply repeats or reverses the terms laid out by Jefferson nor offers an absolute opposition or alternative to those terms. Rather, Walker and Stewart intervene directly in the dense discursive formation of Jeffersonian colonization, appropriating its terms in a struggle to disarticulate the imperial form of its racial governmentality. In particular, by signifying on silence as a dis- and rearticulatory strategy, they recall the classical figure *articulus*—the use of a series of single words separated by commas, and thus silent pauses, for a dramatic, staccato effect—to which I referred in the introduction. Both Walker and Stewart's texts repeatedly figure silences that have the effect of clearing spaces or intervals, within this dense discourse, from which to generate an incalculable existence that lies beyond Jefferson's racial governmentality.[95]

These silences take a number of forms. At times, the figure of silence is literal, as when Walker writes, "What our brethren could have been thinking about, who have left their native land and home and gone away to Africa, I am unable to say" (55), and Stewart declares, "My Respected Friends, I feel almost unable to address you; almost incompetent to perform the task" (30). At other times, they proliferate rhetorical questions. For example, Walker asks in a footnote, "Why do the Slave-holders or Tyrants of America and their advocates fight so hard to keep my brethren from receiving and reading my Book of Appeal to them?—Is it because they treat us so well?—Is it because we are satisfied to rest in Slavery to them and their children?—Is it because they are treating us like men, by compensating us all over this free country!! for our labours?—But why are the Americans so very fearfully terrified respecting my Book?" (72). Writes Stewart, turning her audience toward a gendered sense of spiritual education: "What if I am a woman; is not the God of ancient times the God of these modern days? Did he not raise up Deborah, to be a mother, and a judge in Israel [Judges 4 : 4]? Did not queen Esther save the lives of the Jews? And Mary Magdalene first declare the resurrection of Christ from the dead?" (68). Combining such questioning with ironic paralepsis and a call for intellectual activity, Stewart writes elsewhere, "And shall Afric's sons be silent any longer? Far be it from me to recommend to you either to kill, burn, or destroy. But I would strongly recommend to you to improve your talents; let not one lie buried in the earth" (29). Toward the beginning of the *Appeal,* Walker offers his own irony: "I declare, it is really so amusing to hear the Southerners and Westerners of this country talk about *barbarity,* that it is positively, enough to make a man *smile*" (13). The stark silence of this "smile" is nonetheless "declared" so precisely as to urge a reinterpretation of the racial distinction between civility and barbarity. By peppering their texts with such active silences, Walker and Stewart urge an anticolonizationist practice of reinterpretation. Having cleared space for questions and new interpretations, they then examine colonization's power and eventually use its own language against it.

For instance, Walker's *Appeal* directly challenges Jefferson's influential theories of race, nation, and equality. In article 1, Walker asks:

> Has Mr. Jefferson declared to the world, that we are inferior to the whites, both in the endowments of our bodies and our minds? It is indeed surprising, that a man of such great learning, combined with such excellent natural parts, should speak so of a set of men in chains. I do not know what to compare it to, unless, like putting one wild deer in an iron cage, where it will be secured, and hold another by the side of the same, then let it go, and expect the one in the cage to run as fast as the one at liberty. So far, my brethren, were the Egyptians from heaping these insults upon their slaves, that Pharaoh's daughter took Moses, a son of Israel for her own. (10)

Countering Jefferson's claims to the world with worldly claims of his own, Walker makes "a man of such great learning, combined with such excellent natural parts" seem provincial and homely, unaware even of the differences between classical and contemporary slavery. With his deer metaphor, Walker seizes the inductive reasoning Jefferson himself proliferates in his *Notes on the State of Virginia*, making Jefferson play the part of faulty reasoner.

In turn, he opens up the very revolutionary promise Jefferson so feared:

> And those enemies who have for hundreds of years stolen our *rights*, and kept us ignorant of Him and His divine worship, [Jesus] will remove. . . . How would they like for us to make slaves of, and hold them in cruel slavery, and murder them as they do us?—But is Mr. Jefferson's assertions true? viz. "That it is unfortunate for us that our Creator has been pleased to make us *black*." We will not take his say so, for the fact. The world will have an opportunity to see whether it is unfortunate for us, that our Creator *has made us* darker than the *whites*.
>
> Fear not the number and education of our *enemies*, against whom we shall have to contend for our lawful right; guaranteed to us by our Maker; for why should we be afraid, when God is, and will continue, (if we continue humble) to be on our side? (12)

Subjecting the patronizing, colonizationist image of "unfortunate" blacks needing white tutelage to ridicule, Walker then paints a different image for the world to see, an implicitly revolutionary one, a specter of just black vengeance. What is more, Walker derives this image of revolutionary justice not from a problem of population—in fact, he explicitly puts aside the question of "number"—but rather from an incalculable natural law ("our lawful right; guaranteed to us by our Maker").

The *Appeal* proceeds to stress the importance of reading Jefferson in order to understand and then to seize the terms of his discourse. Again in article 1:

> Here let me ask Mr. Jefferson, (but he is gone to answer at the bar of God, for the deeds done in his body while living,) I therefore ask the whole American people, had I not rather die, or be put to death, than to be a slave to any tyrant, who takes not only my own, but my wife and children's lives by the inches? Yea, would I meet death with avidity far! far! ! in preference to such *servile submission* to the murderous hands of tyrants. Mr. Jefferson's very severe remarks on us have been so extensively argued upon by men whose attainments in literature, I shall never be able to reach, that I would not have meddled with it, were it not to solicit each of my brethren, who has the spirit of a man, to buy a copy of Mr. Jefferson's "Notes on Virginia," and put it in the hand of his son. For let no one of us suppose that the refutations which have been written by our white friends are enough—they are *whites*—we are *blacks*. We, and the world wish to see the charges of Mr. Jefferson refuted by the blacks *themselves*, according to their chance; . . . Our sufferings will come to an *end*, in spite of all the Americans this side of *eternity*. Then we will want all the learning and talents among ourselves, and perhaps more, to govern ourselves.— "Every dog must have its day," the American's is coming to an end. (14–15)

Positioned as the representative of "the whole American people," Jefferson is also the representative of a murderous oppression, a violence at once of calculating reason— "by the inches"—and of passion—the "deeds done in his body." The reference to "my wife" surely recalls the slavemaster's sexual power over his slaves, and perhaps even specifically Jefferson's well-known relationship with Sally Hemmings. Walker also seems to equate the embodied violence of "servile submission" with the discursive violence of "very severe remarks," taking each as seriously as the other. Consequently, the specter of black justice plays out in words too, as he at once describes and en- acts a polemic, a war of words whose stake is the very continuing existence of "the American." Again provincializing Jefferson and/as the American, the passage enlists the world in this struggle. When Walker finally calls on blacks "to govern ourselves," then, his practice of government is not so much the production of discrete, calculable members of a racially and nationally codified population subject to manipulation, as it was for Jefferson—though it is a gendered practice, passed from father to son, a practice Stewart will challenge below. Rather, "to govern" consists, for Walker, in a critique of Jeffersonian reason that would bring an end to "the American" and usher into existence an as yet unspecified, future freedom.

A crucial element of governing, then, is a critique of Jeffersonian governmentality:

> But let us review Mr. Jefferson's remarks respecting us some further ... do you know that Mr. Jefferson was one of as great characters as ever lived among the whites? See his writings for the world, and public labours for the United States of America. Do you believe that the assertions of such a man, will pass away into oblivion unobserved by this people and the world? If you do you are much mistaken—See how the American people treat us—have we souls in our bodies? Are we men who have any spirits at all? I know that there are many *swell-bellied* fellows among us, whose greatest object is to fill their stomachs. Such I do not mean—I am after those who know and feel, that we are MEN, as well as other people; to them, I say, that unless we try to refute Mr. Jefferson's arguments respecting us, we will only establish them. (15)

Walker calls for a refutation of Jefferson's subjection of blacks to mere racial embodi- ment, as well as a rejection of black subjectification within that embodiment. Being treated by whites as bodies without souls apparently leads some to live as if they were soulless and "swell-bellied." We thus encounter Walker's account of what Saidiya V. Hartman has called scenes of subjection: a "barbarism of slavery" expressed by "the forms of subjectivity and circumscribed humanity imputed to the enslaved," where even the formally free can be enslaved in a "swell-bellied humanity."[96] This embodied enclosure is at once material and discursive, and consequently demands a discursive practice in response, a critical interruption of Jefferson and a remaking of bodies with words that themselves embody "spirits" and "souls."

Walker begins his critique of colonization in article 4 by distinguishing this Jeffersonian discursive practice from the discourse of proslavery colonizationists such as Henry Clay and Elias B. Caldwell. Speaking of Clay, Walker writes that "I have been for some time taking notice of this man's speeches and public writings, but never to my knowledge have I seen any thing in his writings which insisted on the emancipation of slavery, which has almost ruined this country" (52). Similarly, "The real sense and meaning of the last part of Mr. Caldwell's speech is, get the free people of colour away to Africa, from among the slaves, where they may at once be blessed and happy, and those who we hold in slavery will be contented to rest in ignorance and wretchedness, to dig up gold and silver for us and our children. Men have indeed got to be so cunning, these days, that it would take the eye of a Solomon to penetrate and find them out" (52). Such cunning colonizationists, "a gang of slave-holders" (55), wear their interests on their sleeves, he suggests.

By contrast, black and liberal white colonizationists present different problems. To requote a passage I referred to above: "What our brethren could have been thinking about, who have left their native land and home and gone away to Africa, I am unable to say. This country is as much ours as it is the whites, whether they will admit it now or not, they will see and believe it by and by" (55). If these "brethren" must go, he directs them not to Liberia, but to England or Haiti (56). Yet Walker clearly prefers that black Americans claim their place in the United States. As he approvingly quotes Richard Allen's critique of colonization, "'I have no doubt that there are many good men who do not see as I do, and who are for sending us to Liberia; but they have not duly considered the subject—they are not men of colour.—This land which we have watered with our *tears* and *our blood*, is now our *mother country*, and we are well satisfied to stay where wisdom abounds and the gospel is free'" (58). Allen's figuration of blood counters its racialization, representing it as a sign of human labor and material servitude rather than of hierarchically codified identity. For Walker via Allen, when blood is shed under conditions of struggle, it functions as a historical claim to a material territory. For colonizationists, by contrast, blood is an invariable, material sign of a racial identity that corresponds to a specific territory, regardless of material histories; thus, black blood must be returned to its original, proper territory, Africa. Walker wrests the figure of blood from colonization's racial territorialization, writing just before the Allen quote: "Oh! my Lord how refined in inequity the whites have got to be in consequence of our blood"; in the footnote to this passage, he continues, "The Blood of our fathers who have been murdered by the whites, and the groans of our Brethren, who are now held in cruel ignorance, wretchedness and slavery by them, cry aloud to the Maker of Heaven and of earth, against the whole continent of America, for redresses" (54). The oxymoron "refined in iniquity" makes the shedding of black blood the sign of historically specific, white American injustice. What is more, both blood and groans actually cry out in this passage, forming a discourse that is thoroughly material. This articulation interrupts colonization's territorialized, static, and codified understanding of race by suggesting that the very meaning of a racial figure such as blood is a changeable effect of struggle.

In turn, Walker figures his literate practice of resistance as a more shining Enlightenment than that practiced by white Americans:

I will give here a very imperfect list of the cruelties inflicted on us by the enlightened Christians of America.—First, no trifling portion of them will beat us nearly to death, if they find us on our knees praying to God,—They hinder us from going to hear the word of God—they keep us sunk in ignorance, and will not let us learn to read the word of God, nor write—If they find us with a book of any description in our hand, they will beat us nearly to death—they are so afraid we will learn to read, and enlighten our dark and benighted minds. (65)

Severing whiteness from enlightenment, Walker figures a practice of reading and interpretation so powerful that it is prohibited by the very people who seem to extol it. Again, the intertwining of words and bodies becomes the medium of Walker's practice of freedom, and an alternative to the racial graft I discussed in the introduction. As Walker reiterates a few pages later,

Remember Americans, that we must and shall be free and enlightened as you are, will you wait until we shall, under God, obtain our liberty by the crushing arm of power? Will it not be dreadful for you? . . . And wo, wo, will be to you if we have to obtain our freedom by fighting. Throw away your fears and prejudices then, and enlighten us and treat us like men, and we will like you more than we do now hate you, and tell us now no more about colonization, for America is as much our country, as it is yours. (69–70)

Signifying on the "are and ought to be free" of the Declaration of Independence, which claimed a white settler separation *from* Britain, Walker's "must and shall be free and enlightened as you are" makes a black claim *on* a freedom not limited to formal and abstract equality. This enlightenment's equality—"treat us like men"—is a continuing, material recognition, an ethical relation to the other and an acknowledgment and interruption of the racial graft that founded America.

It is in this context, then, that Walker challenges his readers to address "the colonizing trick" to which I referred at the beginning of the introduction: the procolonizationist "friends to the sons of Africa, who are laboring for our salvation, not in words only but in truth and in deed," are perpetuating slavery, he claims, for they are seeking a merely formal equality bound irrevocably to hierarchical racial and national codification (67–68). "Colonizationists speak of America being first colonized," he declares, recalling *The Claims of the Africans'* analogy between Jamestown and Liberia,

but is there any comparison between the two? . . . We were *stolen* from our mother country, and brought *here*. We have *tilled* the ground and made fortunes for thousands, and still they are not weary of our services. *But they who stay to till the ground must be slaves.* Is there not land enough in America, or "corn enough in Egypt?" Why should they send us into a far country to die? See the thousands of foreigners emigrating to America every year: and if there be ground sufficient for them to cultivate, and bread for them to eat, why would they wish to send the *first tillers* of the land away? (57)

Exposing the use of the term "colonization" for this forced deportation and resettlement scheme, Walker undoes the movement's articulation of race, nation, and equality.

If the "friends to the sons of Africa" really want freedom for black Americans, they will not pursue a racially territorialized equality, he argues. Rather they will practice an equality of mutual recognition and material difference, an equality that remains open to a practice of freedom understood as a hermeneutic of seizing and reformulating the Enlightenment.

The year after David Walker's death, his fellow Bostonian Maria W. Stewart published her pamphlet *Religion and the Pure Principles of Morality, The Sure Foundation On Which We Must Build* in *The Liberator* of October 8, 1831. Over the next two years, Stewart would deliver a series of speeches throughout Boston, occasionally referring explicitly to Walker as an honored predecessor.[97] While in many ways Stewart shares a struggle with Walker, she also writes in different directions, expanding the anticolonizationist discourse I have been tracing in this section. For instance, she explicitly complicates Walker's self-assuredly masculinist circuits of intellectual activism, speaking directly to and for the black women Walker mostly ignores. In fact, as Lora Romero has pointed out, the only reference to a woman as an active political subject in the *Appeal* comes in article 2, where Walker inveighs for pages against "the *ignorant* and *deceitful actions* of this coloured woman," a *"notorious wretch"* whom he says turned on a group of black men who rose up against their slave driver (23–26).[98] By contrast, while offering strong criticisms of the entire black community in Boston, Stewart foregrounds the role of women in the political debates of the day, and opens up a much more nuanced sense of gender than Walker is able to offer. In addition, she ritually invokes the Jeffersonian scene of enlightenment, surveillance, and calculable populations we have encountered throughout this chapter in order to prophecy future, incalculable equalities.

Repeatedly, Stewart figures "justice," "knowledge," and "freedom" as "purity" and "light," as in this passage from an 1833 address: "But it is of no use for us to boast that we sprung from this learned and enlightened nation, for this day a thick mist of moral gloom hangs over millions of our race" (58). Unlike Jefferson, however, Stewart labors to delink the figure of enlightenment from the figure of national whiteness. Consider the following passage from her "Farewell Address" to Boston:

> What if such women as are here described should rise among our sable race? And it is not impossible. For it is not the color of the skin that makes the man or the woman, but the principle formed in the soul. Brilliant wit will shine, come from whence it will; and genius and talent will not hide the brightness of its lustre. But, to return to my subject; the mighty work of reformation has begun among this people. The dark clouds of ignorance are dispersing. The light of science is bursting forth. Knowledge is beginning to flow, nor will its moral influence be extinguished till its refulgent rays have spread over us from East to West, and from North to South. (70)

"Our race" is not essentially unenlightened, but rather conditionally shrouded by "a thick mist of moral gloom," a subjection that has subjectified blackness as servitude. "Our sable race" can be "brilliant" and will "shine" with "the brightness of its lustre."

"The light of science" can "burst forth" from blackness, and "refulgent rays" are neither racially nor nationally nor gender delimited. Stewart's "East to West" and "North to South" are thus filled with the potentiality of an alternative global enlightenment.

In fact, Stewart at times explicitly seizes the calculable language Jefferson uses to capture and enclose the light of enlightenment in racial and national forms, in order to break open those enclosures. On July 14, 1832, she writes in *The Liberator*, "Many bright and intelligent ones are in the midst of us; but because they are not calculated to display a classical education, they hide their talents behind a napkin" (44). Similarly, in Boston's Franklin Hall, she declares on September 21, 1832, that "Few white persons of either sex, who are calculated for anything else, are willing to spend their lives and bury their talents in performing mean, servile labor" (46). Whereas for Jefferson calculation is a method that makes the essential characteristics of a population visible and subject to manipulation, for Stewart calculation figures a variable process of subject formation, an education in particular kinds of labor—here, gendered domestic labor—that does not simply add new skills to an already formed subject, but rather transforms the very subjectivity of that subject. To be educated to service work is not simply to learn how to fold napkins; rather, it is to learn how to hide all one's other talents and to show the world only the servile work of napkin folding, perhaps even to come to believe in oneself as simply a napkin folder. The napkin, however, is a small and flimsy covering, and Stewart suggests here that these talents are likely to be uncovered, to exceed their enclosures. If Jefferson's quantifying spirit claimed to uncover the truth of populations, for Stewart subjects are subjected to calculation, they are made into populations through calculation and, potentially, can escape from its enclosures.

Indeed, the very racial characteristics Jefferson claims to calculate are, to Stewart, as they were to Walker, incalculable and changeable effects of struggle: "We will tell you that too much of your blood flows in our veins, too much of your color in our skins, for us not to possess your spirits" (40); "I am a true born American; your blood flows in my veins, and your spirit fires my breast" (46). Racial and national codification is denaturalized in this miscegenated scene, implicitly fraught with a sexual violence that is not reducible to the repressive regime it nonetheless enforces. Transforming the mixed blood that figures a white slavemaster's rape into a fiery spirit, Stewart claims an unpredictable potentiality that cannot be constrained by codified racial identity.

Similarly reiterating and rewriting Jeffersonian discourse, Stewart repeatedly declares that judgmental eyes are watching this enlightenment. Yet those eyes are not of a captious Europe on white America and a benevolent but wary white America on juvenile black Americans, as they were with Jefferson. Rather, the white gaze is a violent one, the slavemaster's gaze directed at blacks on the block: "But the most high God is still as able to subdue the lofty pride of these white Americans as He was the heart of that ancient rebel," she claims in the midst of a critique of "the colonizationists;" "They say, though we are looked upon as things, yet we sprang from a scientific people" (61). Provincializing "these white Americans" and their commodifying gaze by subjecting it to the more capacious power of God, Stewart then claims the "scientific" mantle from them.

This white gaze is limited in what it can see, and Stewart constantly works to widen its perspective and shift its view. For instance, addressing "the fair daughters of Africa" in *The Liberator* on October 8, 1831, Stewart again foregrounds the sexual violence of the white American gaze, implicating white women in that violence: "How long shall a mean set of men flatter us with their smiles, and enrich themselves with our hard earnings; their wives' fingers sparkling with rings, and they themselves laughing at our folly? Until we begin to promote and patronize each other. Shall we be a by-word among the nations any longer? Shall they laugh us to scorn forever?" (38). Echoing and expanding the admonition Wheatley directed at Thornton above—"The world is a severe schoolmaster, for its frowns are less dang'rous than its smiles and flatteries, and it is a difficult task to keep in the path of Wisdom"—Stewart opposes the exploited, sexualized black labor that puts "sparkling" "rings" on "their wives' fingers" to a mode of exchange in which black Americans would no longer participate in their own subjection: "to promote and patronize each other." She also challenges the scene of antebellum domestic labor, a labor that sustains sexualized and gendered forms of white domesticity, with a string of rhetorical questions answered silently. Yet the questions themselves have already rearticulated the terms in which they might be answered. For in these passages Stewart subjects the white American gaze to a global judgment—"Shall we be a by-word among nations any longer?"—that sees through the racial nation's enclosures: "Shall they laugh us to scorn forever?" It is as if the silent spaces between these questions have given her room, a certain freedom of movement, to disarticulate the Jeffersonian Enlightenment that subjected black Americans to continual surveillance and control. As Stewart asks in an address to "The Afric American Female Intelligence Society" of Boston: "Shall we be a hissing and a reproach among the nations of the earth any longer? Shall they laugh us to scorn forever?" (54). These questions immediately generate answers: "And O, my God, I beseech thee to grant that the nations of the earth may hiss at us no longer! I suffer them not to laugh us to scorn forever!" (55). Representing the "American" nation neither as a naturally racial form nor as an exemplary, imperial horizon, this global reframing of white nationalism represents the self-evident articulation of race with nation we saw in colonization discourse as a dubious, even violent articulation subject to critique.

Elsewhere, Stewart casts herself and other black Americans as the observers and, potentially, the critics. As she demands of an audience at Boston's African Masonic Hall in 1833, "Cast your eyes about, look as far as you can see; all, all is owned by the lordly white" (59); "When I cast my eyes on the long list of illustrious names that are enrolled on the bright annals of fame among the whites, I turn my eyes within, and ask my thoughts, 'Where are the names of our illustrious ones?'" (56). In the July 14, 1832, essay from *The Liberator* mentioned above, she articulates a similar vision, addressed this time to black men in particular: "O, how I long for the time to come when I shall behold our young men anxious to inform their minds on moral and political subjects—ambitious to become distinguished men of talents—view them standing pillars in the church, qualifying themselves to preach the everlasting gospel of Our Lord Jesus Christ—becoming useful and active members in society, and the future hopes of our declining years" (44). Acknowledging a critical black gaze, Stewart exhorts her Boston community to cast that gaze about in a ritual of subjectification that would transform the auction block into "standing pillars in the church." Yet *this* ritual of subjectification differs from the calculable subjection of the "bright and intelligent ones . . . in the midst of us" as "mean, servile" laborers that Stewart challenged above. Working against a power that subjects ("willing to spend their lives and bury their talents," "How long shall a mean set of men flatter us with their smiles"), Stewart here invokes a subjectivity that at once turns inward ("I turn my eyes within, and ask my thoughts," "young men anxious to inform their minds," "qualifying themselves") and outward ("view them standing pillars . . . becoming useful and active members in society"). Stewart thus does not appeal simply to an external enlightenment, as either an oppressive or a saving light, nor does she simply trace the subject's captivation by his or her own subjection. Rather, Stewart depicts a looking and a speaking within that is also a looking and a speaking "in society," figuring a space that at once escapes the gaze of enlightened subjection and shines forth with another, "illustrious" light. Crucially, Stewart does not calculate the future that such a light will expose, as Jefferson had done. Rather, she imagines a critical and open-ended practice, an inward turning and outward shining life of interpretation that leads to "future hopes."

When she addresses colonization directly, as she often does, she draws on this counterarticulation of Enlightenment discourse. "The colonizationists are blind to their own interest," she declares in the 1833 African Masonic Hall address, "for should the nations of the earth make war with America, they would find their forces much weakened by our absence; or should we remain here, can our 'brave soldiers' and 'fellow citizens,' as they were termed in time of calamity, condescend to defend the rights of whites and be again deprived of their own, or sent to Liberia in return?" (61). Colonization is "blind" to the extensive articulation of blackness and whiteness, an articulation forged in the manner of the racial graft I discussed in the introduction: at once violently and constitutively. Though "deprived of their own rights" when they were grafted onto a white nation, blacks have nonetheless become part of the national body, such that it would be "much weakened by our absence." For Stewart, following Wheatley, this violent and constitutive joining makes the colonizationists' rhetoric of return absurd, as her ironic use of "in return" suggests: resettlement in Liberia constitutes yet another deprivation of rights rather than a restoration of affiliation.

Consequently, when Stewart speaks of equality, it is not in the calculable terms of populations. Rather, equality is offered as a potential fraught with violence:

> Life has almost lost its charms for me; death has lost its sting; and the grave its terrors [I Corinthians 15:55]; and at times I have a strong desire to depart and dwell with Christ, which is far better. Let me entreat my white brethren to awake and save our sons from dissipation and our daughters from ruin. Lend the hand of assistance to feeble merit; plead the cause of virtue among our sable race; so shall our curses upon you be turned

into blessings; and though you should endeavor to drive us from these shores, still we will cling to you the more firmly; nor will we attempt to rise above you; we will presume to be called your equals only.

The unfriendly whites first drove the native American from his much loved home. Then they stole our fathers from their peaceful and quiet dwellings, and brought them hither, and made bond-men and bond-women of them and their little ones. They have obliged our brethren to labor; kept them in utter ignorance; nourished them in vice, and raised them in degradation; and now that we have enriched their soil, and filled their coffers, they say that we are not capable of becoming like white men, and that we can never rise to respectability in this country. They would drive us to a strange land. But before I go, the bayonet shall pierce me through. (63–64)

This passage is framed by the deadly racial violence that founded America ("Life has almost lost its charms for me," "The unfriendly whites first drove the native American from his much loved home") and the deadly racial violence that would accompany colonization's development of America ("before I go, the bayonet shall pierce me through"). If Jefferson's liberal, racial governmentality thrives by ignoring this framework, then Stewart's "equality" emerges from it. Emphasizing the constitutive social relations forged out of racial violence, she offers a popular, nongovernmental articulation of race and equality, a conjunction of racial difference and mutual, ethical recognition. The "clinging" she invokes is neither a servile nor a masterful one; rather, it is a presumption of and a demand for an incalculable equality. Such recognition is no mere formal equality sustained by codified identities, but rather a substantial, living, embodied equality "to be called."

Fred Moten has written that "the black radical tradition is in apposition to enlightenment. Appositional enlightenment is remixed, expanded, distilled and radically faithful to the forces its encounters carry, break and constitute."[99] An apposition is a grammatical construction in which two words, phrases, or clauses referring to the same person or thing and holding the same syntactical relationship to the words around them are set next to one another, without a coordinating conjunction. For example, in this passage from Walker's *Appeal*—"If any of us see fit to go away, go to those who have been for many years, and are now our greatest earthly friends and benefactors— the English. If not so, go to our brethren, the Haytians, who, according to their word, are bound to protect and comfort us" (56)—the words "our greatest earthly friends and benefactors" and "the English" are in apposition, as are "our brethren" and "the Haytians." As a figure for an equivalence that is neither strictly factual (as a sentence like "our friends and benefactors are the English" would suggest) nor mechanistic (as a phrase like "Haytians as our brethren" would suggest), the appositive maintains a certain tension between the two terms it silently links as well as a potential difference alongside the equivalence it implicitly asserts. As such, the appositive is very close to the classical figure *articulus* I mentioned above and in the introduction. Walker may view "the English" as "friends" or "benefactors" and "the Haytians" as "brethren," but the good work of the English and kinship of the Haytians are not eternal, static, or essential features.

Even further, however, the appositive's lack of a coordinating conjunction creates a potential break or rupture between the linked terms, an uncoordinated gap that makes room for the very remixing, expanding, and distilling to which Moten refers. For Moten, the black radical tradition seems to be in apposition precisely because of the tension or difference it maintains between blackness and enlightenment even as it makes a claim to both blackness and enlightenment: "This tradition is concerned with the opening of a new Enlightenment, one made possible by the ongoing improvisation of a given Enlightenment."[100] Thus, in Walker's passage, the very meaning of the good work of the English and the kinship of the Haytians remains open, subject to modulation and resignification. One could imagine, for instance, both a sincere and an ironic meaning of "our greatest earthly friends and benefactors—the English," in which the English are at once recognized for their abolitionist commitments and implicitly held accountable or even mocked for their "earthly" failure to live up to their own stated friendship and good work. One could read "our brethren—the Haytians" as both a recognition of and a claim on kinship, in which the radicalism of the Haitian Revolution is both celebrated and held to account, such that "our brethren" are at once honored and urged to remember the continuing enslavement of North American blacks.

When Stewart spoke to Boston's Afric-American Female Intelligence Society of America in the spring of 1832, she invoked a globe full of people rising up against their oppressors. Among other examples, she included this: "Look at the Poles, a feeble people! They rose against three hundred thousand mighty men of Russia; and though they did not gain the conquest, yet they obtained the name of gallant Poles" (54). "The Poles" and "a feeble people" are in apposition here, allowing her to argue both sincerely that a "feeble people" can disrupt their subjection as "gallant" people and ironically that the Poles were never the "feeble people" they have been thought to be. This example becomes exemplary precisely because of the simultaneously sincere and ironic rupture between "the Poles" and "a feeble people," such that the example becomes for her audience the enlightened sign of an alternative future.

I want to suggest not only that Walker and Stewart's texts make use of apposition, but also that their entire anticolonization discourse, particularly the kind of freedom it proffers, is appositional in the following sense. The freedom Walker and Stewart seek is no formal and abstract equality that would equate, to borrow from my discussion of Marx in the introduction, a coat with linen, tailoring with weaving, or disparate citizens with one another. Such a formal equality is decidedly not appositional; it equates two different terms with a coordinating conjunction so calculably precise that it codifies the identities of the two terms, making them seem natural and necessary: as Marx writes, "20 yards of linen = 1 coat, or: 20 yards of linen are worth 1 coat."[101] By contrast, as we have seen, throughout their texts Walker and Stewart invoke silences that, like the silence between appositives, allow a certain play of meaning. This play of meaning breaks the calculable and codifiable character of formal equality. Walker's and Stewart's texts return again and again to this break, I suggest, because it offers a certain freedom to rearticulate the terms of the Enlightenment, a freedom to imagine an equality that does not calculate and codify difference.

Thus, the colonizationists' distinctly Jeffersonian, calculable and codifiable claims—"America is white," "Africa is black"—are broken and rearticulated by an appositional sentence such as this, which we saw above, from Walker's *Appeal*: "'Every dog must have its day,' the American's is coming to an end" (15). The day of the American's end is the beginning not of black emancipation in Africa, but rather of America's emancipation from white governmentality. When Stewart offers a critique of "the Colonization Society" in her speech at the African Masonic Hall, she similarly resorts to apposition: "But, ah, methinks [the colonizationists'] hearts are so frozen toward us they had rather their money should be sunk in the ocean than to administer it to our relief: and I fear, if they dared, like Pharaoh, king of Egypt, they would order every male child among us to be drowned. But the most high God is still as able to subdue the lofty pride of these white Americans as He was the heart of that ancient rebel" (61). Figuring "the colonizationists" with the apposition "Pharaoh, king of Egypt," she ruptures the "pride of these white Americans" without surrendering America to them. In fact, just a few pages later she declares to the colonizationists, as we saw above, "still we will cling to you the more firmly; nor will we attempt to rise above you; we will presume to be called your equals only" (63). This presumption of equality not only emerges out of the apposition "Pharaoh, king of Egypt," it is also itself appositional, figuring as it does an uncoordinated equivalence, a clinging of one to the other.

Finally, the echo of Wheatley's own active and ironic silences in this appositional discourse comes to the fore in this passage from Walker's *Appeal*, to which I also referred above: "Remember Americans, that we must and shall be free and enlightened as you are, will you wait until we shall, under God, obtain our liberty by the crushing arm of power?" (69). This sentence signifies not only on the Declaration of Independence, as I argued earlier, but also on the final two lines of Wheatley's most well-known poem, "On being brought from AFRICA to AMERICA," lines fueled by apposition: "Remember, *Christians*, *Negros*, black as *Cain*, / May be refin'd, and join th' angelic train." Wheatley certainly addresses her imperative to "*Christians*," telling them that "*Negroes*, black as Cain" may also claim enlightenment. Yet her use of apposition also makes these lines address both "*Christians*, [and] *Negroes*," linked as objects by italics. In this sense, "*Christians*" and "*Negroes*" are reminded that they are both "black as *Cain*" and may find themselves together, appositionally, on the road to an other enlightenment. Borrowing once again from Moten, in conclusion, the colonizationists' articulation of race, nation, and equality is refigured by these appositional texts. Walker and Stewart, after and through Wheatley, stage an encounter with Jefferson's Enlightenment that remains radically faithful to its forces, while carrying and breaking those very forces, constituting them as a reclaiming of the claims of the Africans.

CHAPTER 3

Biloquial Nation:
Charles Brockden Brown's National Culture

The path was narrow, steep, and overshadowed by rocks. The sun was nearly
set, and the shadow of the cliff above, obscured the passage almost as much
as midnight would have done: I was accustomed to despise danger when it
presented itself in a sensible form, but, by a defect common in every one's
education, goblins and spectres were to me the objects of the most violent
apprehensions. These were unavoidably connected with solitude and darkness,
and were present to my fears when I entered this gloomy recess. These terrors
are always lessened by calling the attention away to some indifferent object.
I now made use of this expedient, and began to amuse myself by hallowing
as loud as organs of unusual compass and vigour would enable me. I uttered
the words which chanced to occur to me, and repeated in the shrill tones of
a Mohock savage . . . "Cow! cow! come home! home!" . . . These notes were of
course reverberated from the rocks which on either side towered aloft, but the
echo was confused and indistinct.

Memoirs of Carwin, the Biloquist

Toward the beginning of Charles Brockden Brown's uncompleted novel, *Memoirs of Carwin, the Biloquist*, the protagonist relates "events . . . which ascertained my
future destiny." Rushing home one day with the news that his father's cows have escaped their field, he takes a shortcut through an unfamiliar rocky pass; in its dark enclosure, he confronts "terrors" and "violent apprehensions" of "goblins and spectres."
His response is to "[hallow] as loud as organs of unusual compass and vigour would
enable me . . . the words which chanced to occur to me, . . . repeat[ing] in the shrill
tones of a Mohock savage. . . . 'Cow! cow! come home! home!'"[1] Once the echoes of
these tones in the rocky passage suggest to Carwin the possibility of becoming a "biloquist," Brown's word for a ventriloquist, *Memoirs of Carwin* proceeds to tell the story
of the escapades into which biloquism leads him. Serialized in *The Literary Magazine*
between 1803 and 1805, *Memoirs of Carwin* is the prequel for Brown's first completed
novel, *Wieland; or, the Transformation: An American Tale* (1798), providing the story of
Carwin's life before he appears as a crucial character in *Wieland*. Since the scene in the

139

rocky passage contains the only appearance of "a Mohock savage" in either text, the figure appears to be incidental; however, "a Mohock savage" is in fact foundational to the plots of both texts, since its "shrill tones" and their echoes produce Carwin's biloquism, which in turn motivates his lifelong misadventures. It is a tenuous foundation, however, since the "Mohock savage" appears not as a character but as the echo of ventriloquized "tones" that only "chanced to occur" and could never have been understood by their bovine addressee. As I will suggest in this chapter, "a Mohock savage" can be read as a tenuous foundation for more than these two plots.

Throughout his life, Brown sought to represent himself as a founder of the proper national literary aesthetic. Literary critics and historians have obliged him for two hundred years, often representing *Wieland* as the first American novel. But this hold on foundational status that Brown and *Wieland* have long maintained is as tenuous as it is persistent. The familiar critical narrative that positions Brown as the founder of American literature overlooks not only William Brown Hill, whose novel *The Power of Sympathy* was published in 1789, nine years before *Wieland*, but also a lengthy list of literary predecessors who raise the very question of what "American" and "literature" might mean: Olaudah Equiano, Phillis Wheatley, J. Hector St. John de Crèvecoeur, Samson Occom, to name just a few of the most well known. *Wieland*'s foundational status as the first American novel can be challenged not only by *The Power of Sympathy* and a host of protonovels and quasi novels but also by the ambiguous status of *Memoirs of Carwin*, which tells of events prior to those of *Wieland* and, although it was published after *Wieland*, seems to have been written before or during *Wieland*'s composition.[2] Indeed, Brown seems to have intended *Memoirs of Carwin* to be part of *Wieland* itself, but could not control Carwin's story and thus had to abandon and reconceive it.[3]

In "a Mohock savage," then, we have not only a tenuous foundation for the plot of *Memoirs of Carwin* but also a figure for the tenuousness of an American literary aesthetic itself. A reading of this figure, in turn, opens up a constitutive relationship between aesthetics and politics—in particular, the politics of white settler colonialism at the turn of the nineteenth century. Thus, I read Brown's "Mohock savage" in *Memoirs of Carwin* as a necessary, and necessarily tenuous, condition of possibility for American literary aesthetics. In the first part of this chapter, I show how early scholarship on Charles Brockden Brown, starting with his own representations of himself, labors to produce a narrative of the "natural" emergence of American literature, a narrative that replaces the violent history of white settler colonialism with an aesthetic call to incorporate scenes of "wild" America into tales of white colonial life. At the turn of the nineteenth century, while Brown was writing, the U.S. government worked vigorously to assimilate Iroquois communities, including Mohawks, by forcibly converting them into discrete yeoman families on privately owned plots of land. Brown's vision of a national literary aesthetic articulated this assimilation and conversion policy in the cultural sphere. The twentieth-century debate in Brown scholarship over whether Brown's work is a conservative defense of tradition, a liberal celebration of modernity, or a bit of both reproduces this narrative of cultural assimilation, I argue, for this debate systematically fails to consider how the discursive practices of white settler colonialism helped to produce the very distinction between the traditional and the modern.

In the rest of this chapter, I offer a close reading of *Memoirs of Carwin*, suggesting that Carwin's two judgments in the rocky passage—first, to utter "the shrill tones of a Mohock savage," and then to master the echoes of those tones and turn them into biloquism—can be read as aesthetic judgments founded on a discourse of cultural assimilation. As we will see, Immanuel Kant's own foundational account of aesthetic judgment also grounds itself on a tenuous invocation of the figure of the Iroquois, and a reading of this Brown-Kant conjuncture directs us to a foundational intersection of aesthetics and politics. Rather than adjudicate the question of whether *Memoirs of Carwin* celebrates or criticizes modernity, I attempt to limn the racial and national forms that make that question possible in the first place. Finally, I reevaluate the apparent critique of modernity offered by the rest of *Memoirs of Carwin*, showing how the foundational figure of the "Mohock savage" continues to echo throughout the text, leading it into plot complexities from which it cannot recover. Thus, though the transformation of white settler colonialism into national culture ostensibly split politics from aesthetics, allowing the purity of the latter to emerge from the impurity of the former, I show how the political continues to echo in the aesthetic. Crucially, Brown's work demands a reading practice that can hear such echoes without attempting to master and control them, without subjecting them to an absolute historical or theoretical closure.

As we move from African colonization to Indian assimilation, then, we witness a sharp distinction between black and Indian racial formations around the turn of the nineteenth century. Whereas colonization represented blackness as fundamentally inassimilable and sought to nationalize whiteness by producing a racially and nationally codified, geographic distinction between white U.S. citizens and black Americans, U.S. governmental and literary discursive practices around 1800 vigorously pursued the forced assimilation of Indian racial form to whiteness. This distinction is crucial not only for the normalization and emergent hegemony of white racial formation, but also for—to use a contemporary term with roots in the eighteenth century—people of color as well. As Jack D. Forbes has shown, miscegenation was the norm among people of color, and it is colonial discursive practices that ultimately worked to draw (often ambiguous and always changing) distinctions among such racial identities as African, Indian, and Mexican.[4] Indeed, codified racial identities are not originally pure forms that subsequently become mixed; rather, racial identity is originally hybrid, and "purity" is an effect of subsequent discourses and policies of codification.

To be sure, the inassimilablity of blackness and the assimilability of Indianness at the flashpoints of African colonization and Brown's literary nationalism were not exclusive tendencies. As we see in Walker's and Stewart's texts, African Americans articulated an alternative American identity that rejected inassimilability—though not in the name of assimilation, but rather in the name of a variegated black globality. Some nineteenth-century white abolitionists like John Brown also articulated their own visions of an egalitarian nation of blacks and whites in North America, and white slavemasters notoriously practiced their own, violent assimilation through miscegena-tion. In addition, right through the eighteenth and early nineteenth centuries there were those, such as Benjamin Rush, who argued against the assimilation of Indians, and indeed such arguments would take the reigns of U.S. governmental policy by the 1830s, when removal and reservations institutionalized Indian inassimilability. As we will see in the next chapter, the U.S.–Mexico War and the Yucatán's Caste War of 1847 subsequently drew on black and Indian racial formations to codify Mexican identity. The distinction—produced by the early colonization movement and Brown's literary nationalism—between inassimilable black and assimilable Indian racial forma-tions highlights just two of the many flashpoints that contribute to the history of impe-rial U.S. citizenship. Though each flashpoint gained a certain hegemony as it flared up at its moments of danger, to paraphrase Benjamin, it is precisely the often ambivalent, always violent waxing and waning of racial formations that keep imperial U.S. citizen-ship in motion and in struggle.

The Foundational Form of Charles Brockden Brown

By 1830, both *Wieland*, published with the subtitle *An American Tale*, and Brown are widely represented by critics as the beginning of modern American literature, even though *Wieland* was not the first novel and Brown not the first fiction writer in the United States.[5] As Cathy Davidson explains:

> Almost immediately after Brown's death in 1810, his friends and fellow writers began promoting a complete edition of his novels, and in 1827 that demand was fulfilled to become another American first. . . . In 1824, John Neal turned Brown's life into a type of the "plight of the American writer," praised abroad, neglected at home. By 1830, Charles Brockden Brown became the first American novelist to be cast, in the best Romantic tradition, as the moody iconoclast, appreciated by the "intelligent, the cultivated, and the reflecting classes of society" but, of course, spurned by the philistine masses. . . . That very iconography of the neglected great author serves to encourage contemporary read-ers not to make the same mistake.[6]

In fact, Brown himself formulated the nationalist and foundationalist terms of his own reception in the preface to his 1799 novel *Edgar Huntly, or Memoirs of a Sleep-Walker* and in his prospectus for the lost novel *Sky-Walk*:

> America has opened new views to the naturalist and politician, but has seldome furnished themes to the moral painter. That new springs of action, and new motives to curiosity should operate; that the field of investigation, opened to us by our own country, should differ essentially from those which exist in Europe, may be readily conceived. The sources of amusement to the fancy and instruction to the heart, that are peculiar to ourselves, are equally numerous and inexhaustible. It is the purpose of this work to profit by some of these sources; to exhibit a series of adventures, growing out of the condition of our country, and connected with one of the most common and most wonderful diseases or affections of the human frame.

One merit the writer may at least claim; that of calling forth the passions and engaging the sympathy of the reader, by means hitherto unemployed by preceding authors. Puerile superstition and exploded manners; Gothic castles and chimeras, are the materials usually employed for this end. The incidents of Indian hostility, and the perils of the western wilderness, are far more suitable; and, for a native of America to overlook these, would admit of no apology.[7]

He, therefore, who paints, not from books, but from nature, who introduces those lines and hues in which we differ, rather than those in which we resemble our kindred nations beyond the ocean, may lay some claim to the patronage of his countrymen.[8]

Paradoxically, Brown calls for the systematic and normative construction of "America's" natural and essential difference: if this difference exists in "nature" but requires an artist who "introduces those lines and hues" to make it visible to "his countrymen," then it is both natural and constructed. "New springs of action, and new motives to curiosity" seem to be immanent for "America," and yet they are invisible unless artists intervene and do what they "should." The prescriptive "should" indicates that while the natural and essential difference "grow[s] out of the condition of our country," growth itself depends upon a particular, active involvement of "our country" and its writers. This involvement is systematic because the prototypical American writer will subject "equally numerous and inexhaustible" "sources" "to profit"; it is normative because that system promises to render an exceptional and exemplary America by aesthetically transforming white settler colonialism. That is, in Brown's prescription, the figure of "a native of America" supplants Native Americans, themselves reduced to scenes of "Indian hostility" and "western wilderness" that the new "native" merely witnesses, records, and incorporates into his originality. The early construction of Brown's foundational status thus secured a naturalized narrative of national literary development.[9]

This narrative of U.S. literary development was, in turn, part of a wider assimilationist discourse on eastern Native Americans at the turn of the nineteenth century. Literary magazines of the period were filled with programmatic calls for the founding of an authentic American culture derived not from Europe, but from "indigenous"—that is, white settler colonial—sources, thereby turning white colonists into the proper subjects of America and invoking Native Americans only as obstacles or backdrops.[10] Writes Michael T. Gilmore,

Calls for a distinctively American literature, commencing with the outbreak of hostilities in 1775, dramatically increased in frequency and volume after the signing of the Treaty of Paris. "America," said Noah Webster in 1785, "must be as independent in *literature* as she is in *politics*, as famous for *arts* as for *arms*." The poet Philip Freneau echoed the sentiments of many when he urged an import tax on the works of foreign writers to teach his compatriots that "native manufactures" deserved protection in letters as well as in coaches and firearms.[11]

If Freneau's proposal echoes the racial-nationalism of Hamilton's mercantilism, discussed in chapter 1, the echoes of the "shrill tones of a Mohock savage" allegorically render a racial nation not so much by ritually excluding nonnatives as by ritually as-similating Indians into a white nativism.

Indeed, theories of redness as a racial form that could "become white" as opposed to unchangeable blackness, which also proliferated during this period, schematize this ritual of assimilation.[12] Consider Jefferson's distinctions among blackness, redness, and whiteness in query 14 of *Notes on the State of Virginia*:

> Whether the black of the negro resides in the reticular membrane between the skin and scarf-skin, or in the scarf-skin itself; whether it proceeds from the colour of the blood, the colour of the bile, or from that of some other secretion, the difference is fixed in nature, and is as real as if its seat and cause were better known to us. And is this difference of no importance? Is it not the foundation of a greater or less share of beauty in the two races? Are not the fine mixtures of red and white, the expressions of every passion by greater or less suffusions of colour in the one, preferable to that eternal monotony, which reigns in the countenances, that immoveable veil of black which covers all the emotions of the other race?[13]

In its effort to locate race on or beneath the surface of the body, this passage is re-markably prescient of the American racial science that would take center stage in the 1830s and 1840s. Yet the insistence that redness could be fused with whiteness differs markedly from that later period, when removal policy would represent a pervasive disbelief in the assimilability of Indians. In Jefferson's turn-of-the-century, the desire to assimilate Indians into white America remained strong.

As Elisabeth Tooker has argued, the 1790s also saw a sudden rise in archeological interest in Native American cultures in general, and Iroquois cultures in particular, since "the new nation was seeking to establish its identity as one separate from England, as a country with its own history."[14] We witnessed a graphic depiction of this archeological interest in the introduction when I considered Thomas Jefferson's description of digging through an Indian gravesite or "barrow." By representing grave robbing as untroubled scientific inquiry, query 11 of the *Notes on the State of Virginia* establishes white settler culture's claims to science and to history: Indian incivility au-thorizes Jefferson's treatment of Indian remains as objects, and yet those very objects give civilized North America an antiquity that measures up to European history. That is, by objectifying Indian remains, Jefferson subjectifies Indians as the geographical ancestors of white settlers. Indians are thus assimilated to the historical narrative of America's development, a narrative whose protagonist and author is the white set-tler. Furthermore, Jefferson claims that this North American antiquity links North American history to European history when he suggests that "the aboriginal inhabi-tants of America" originally migrated from Europe, thereby turning the narrative of America's development into a narrative of global white civility.

Together, these cultural discourses—literary, physiognomic, and archeological—found the nation by recasting its violent white settler emergence as a practical and intellectual process of assimilation. Colonialism emerges from these discursive prac-tices as intellectually superior, curious, and open to incorporating Indian raw material.

Rather than violently appropriating Indian spaces and lives, white settler colonialism seems to be intelligently making a cultural space for and giving aesthetic life to the Indian.

This effort to incorporate the Indian into a unique American culture animated not only cultural work, but also governmental colonial policy toward Iroquois in particular, who had a history of organized resistance to and strategic engagement with Anglo-American colonization in the eighteenth century and who had long held positions of strategic interest to white colonists. Alliances with the British during the American Revolution led many Iroquois, after the Revolution, to British reservations in Canada, and those who remained in the United States were treated as a conquered people with no rights to land. With Thomas Jefferson's administration, however, a renewed emphasis was put on forced assimilation and economic, political, and social conversion. The U.S. government began privatizing communal reservations and assigning small land plots to individual Iroquois families in an effort to convert them into yeoman farmers and to reduce the amount of land they held. To accelerate the social, political, and economic assimilation of Iroquois, economic relations between whites and Iroquois were expanded and subjected to new regulations by means of the Trade and Intercourse Acts as well as congressional oversight of trading factories where Indians obtained European and U.S. goods and technology.[15] At the turn of the nineteenth century, then, particularly with regard to Iroquois, nationalist cultural and governmental policy coalesced around discursive practices of racial assimilation.

Remarkably, through the mid–twentieth century Brown scholars failed to question Brown's naturalized narrative of national literary development or to place it in this wider scene of U.S. colonial discourses and practices. Fred Lewis Pattee's statement in his introduction to a 1926 edition of *Wieland* and *Memoirs of Carwin* is typical: "With Brown began not only a native American literature, but a literature created for the first time in America for mere literature's sake. With him began a literary period."[16] The use of "native American" as an adjective for white settler colonials figures this transformation of white settler colonialism into an aesthetics of assimilation. As Davidson shows, before the age of New Criticism Brown scholars also invariably coupled uncritical representations of Brown's foundationality with criticism only of Brown's aesthetic "flaws": his Latinate prose, his uneven character development, his plot inconsistencies or indeterminacies.[17] Such aesthetic judgments further secure the naturalized narrative of national literary development by exposing an *under*development in need of refinement.

Some contemporary scholarship still slips all too easily into this uncritical nationalism and developmentalism. For instance, Bernard Rosenthal's use of the term "native American" in the following passage reproduces both Pattee's and Brown's rhetorical assimilation of Native Americans:

> If the idea of Brown as progenitor of American fiction eventually collapses for want of substance, the impulse to find him interesting for what he foreshadowed accords with the milieu in which Brown wrote. In his own day Brown's belletristic contemporaries made

much of how America's literature would develop and who would be the first to write a native American literature worthy of national recognition and, always implicitly, of British
approval. . . . If his use of the wilderness and of Indians in *Edgar Huntly*, and of urban
plagues in *Arthur Mervyn* and *Ormond*, employ American Settings, the heart of what
Brown claims for himself is the wish to be a "moral painter," and such a task quickly tran-
scends nationality. . . . At a time when his contemporaries clamored for an American
literature . . . his own interests lay with problems more metaphysical than geographical.[18]

By taking up the "impulse" of "the milieu in which Brown wrote," Rosenthal repeats
that milieu's naturalization of national literary development. The particularity of
white settler colonialism is occluded with the conflation of "wilderness" and "Indians"
and with the figure of "native Americans." This occlusion enables an unproblematic
"nationality" that can in turn be "quickly transcended" by "problems more metaphysical than geographical." U.S. nationality thus becomes the condition of possibility for
universality. As we will see in this chapter, the "metaphysical" and the "geographical" cannot be so easily disentangled. Similarly, James D. Hart's *The Concise Oxford
Companion to American Literature* singles out *Memoirs of Carwin* as "hackwork," and
writes that "Although Brown was appreciated by Keats, Shelley, and Scott, and even
influenced his own master, Godwin, he failed to achieve his aims because of his haste,
immaturity, stilted language, fascination by the pathological, and inability to master
completely the Godwinian plot structure."[19] This normative, aesthetic narrative of
national literary development still finds adherents.[20]

For the most part, however, studies of Brown following Davidson's have increasingly challenged some of the terms of these earlier accounts, ushering in something of
a renaissance in Brown criticism. The criticisms of Brown's aesthetic "flaws" have been
tempered, and Brown's representations of the complex social, historical, and economic
shifts that were taking place in the postrevolutionary United States have been emphasized.[21] Some critics argue that Brown ultimately celebrates "the glorious American
republican experiment."[22] Other critics argue just the opposite: that Brown's skepticism
about Godwinian radicalism leads him to represent Godwin's advocacy of absolute
individual freedom from external constraints as sure to provoke social anarchy and
individual depravity, and that Brown, in turn, advocates a reinstitution of traditional
ethical constraints.[23] Still other critics suggest that Brown's texts do not take a defini-
tive position for or against postrevolutionary social, historical, and economic shifts but,
rather, allegorize the very disruption, trauma, and ambivalence of these shifts.[24]

This scholarship to some extent undoes the earlier nationalist and foundationalist
criticism by offering a more precise account of the conflictual sociohistorical context
that influenced Brown. Even more promising, in the past few years scholars have
begun to consider the specific implications of the white settler colonial discursive
practices within which Brown's work is set.[25] This chapter contributes to this recent
scholarship by placing Davidson's eloquent emphasis on the readerly ambivalence of
Brown's texts in the context of white settler colonialism.

Davidson's reading of Brown's *Arthur Mervyn* concludes with the argument that

Brown can be said neither to celebrate modernity nor to reject it: "Take your pick: America the corrupt or America the beautiful. There is ample evidence for either reading. . . . [B]oth stories are latent within the text and both are possible within the nation that the text evokes" (251–52). This formulation begs a crucial, genealogical question: how could the "pick" between these particular two stories have been made possible in the first place? That is, whether we represent Brown as a modern who celebrates the Enlightenment, as a traditionalist who fears its excesses, or as a writer whose texts ambivalently stage a complex conflict between moderns and traditionalists, we still must account for the question of how the precise terms of this conflict—tradition and modernity, corruption and beauty—themselves accrue value. By looking closely at *Memoirs of Carwin*, a text either ignored by critics or still spoken of mostly in terms of its aesthetic "flaws," I will consider the conditions of possibility for the terms of this conflict.[26] The plot of *Memoirs of Carwin* easily lends itself to the reading of Brown as a conservative critic of Godwinian modernization; however, a reading that remains fixed on the white settler colonial debate between white settler traditionalism and white settler radicalism necessarily ignores the foundational figure of "a Mohock savage" and the discursive practices of which it is a trace. My reading of *Memoirs of Carwin* suggests that the very distinction between the modern and the traditional is itself made possible by an allegory of aesthetic assimilation.[27]

Carwin's First Judgment

In his plausible account of the relationship between *Wieland* and *Memoirs of Carwin*, Pattee contends that Brown had originally meant for *Wieland* to offer each of its characters' points of view on the tale's mysteries, a standard gothic plot device; however, Carwin's point of view seems to have taken "possession of Brown and hurried him to such lengths that it became too unwieldy for inclusion in the novel."[28] As a text whose composition seems to have forced a separation from its original context, *Memoirs of Carwin* represents both a break from and a rewriting of *Wieland*. In *Wieland*—narrated in the first person by an unsure Clara Wieland whose name is not even mentioned until chapter 5, and who constantly struggles against being overwhelmed and confused by the gothic events of the narrative—Carwin appears as a grotesque, clownish, and enigmatic figure, an English traveler who "was an adherent to the Romish faith" and had "transformed" himself into a Spaniard but who later claims that "America . . . is my native soil" (79, 227). In *Memoirs of Carwin*, however, Carwin—now the confident narrator—is far less enigmatic, and he unambiguously becomes an American from the first sentence:

> I was the second son of a farmer, whose place of residence was a western district of Pennsylvania. My eldest brother seemed fitted by nature for the employment to which he was destined. His wishes never led him astray from the hay-stack and the furrow. . . . My character was the reverse of his. My thirst of knowledge was augmented in proportion as it was supplied with gratification. The more I heard or read, the more restless and unconquerable my curiosity became. My senses were perpetually alive to novelty,

my fancy teemed with visions of the future, and my attention fastened upon every thing mysterious or unknown. (281)

In these first sentences, a retooled Carwin naturally leans toward the modern, the cosmopolitan, the enlightened. The "reverse" of his farming brother, he appears as a new American citizen: white, male, free, and devoted to a progress that would overcome old-fashioned, agrarian, moral constraints, accumulate knowledge, and master the unknown. *Memoirs of Carwin*, then, emerges immediately as a national allegory, told from the perspective of a citizen-subject who understands himself to be truly "unconquerable" in his modernity.[29]

The first few pages of *Memoirs of Carwin* foreground the ethical and aesthetic framework of this national allegory, as Carwin is placed at the very threshold of a passage from the old morality and lifestyle of his father to the new possibilities held out by the signs of enlightened modernity: books, experimentation, knowledge. Carwin describes a life in which he struggles to escape the punishments of his father and brother who surveil his every act, and who represent "limits," "watchfulness," "unenlightened desire," "[r]eproaches and blows, painful privations and ignominious penances" (282). He responds to these constraints by turning them into a motivation for his development:

> I exerted all my powers to elude his watchfulness. Censures and stripes were sufficiently unpleasing to make me strive to avoid them. To affect this desirable end, I was incessantly employed in the invention of stratagems and the execution of expedients.
>
> My passion was surely not deserving of blame, and I have frequently lamented the hardships to which it subjected me; yet, perhaps, the claims which were made upon my ingenuity and fortitude were not without beneficial effects upon my character. (282)

Paradoxically, Carwin's internal "passion" subjects him as if it were an external force, like his father: "the hardships to which it subjected me." This internal and external "passion" in turn makes "character" the site of Carwin's emergence as a modern subject. The figure "character" thus gathers and contains the excessive, paradoxical conflict of internal and external forces. Carwin is simultaneously made into a subject and subordinated by power in this conflict. His life under threat of punishment becomes the incentive for an "incessant" development of this natural "character," which in turn leads him to the epochal events in the rocky passage.

However, rather than reading Brown's narrative as an allegorical evaluation of Carwin's individual "character"—of whether that character is good, bad, or a bit of both, allowing us, as Davidson puts it, to "take our pick"—I would like to consider a prior question. How does the opposition between tradition and modernity, secured by the phrase "the reverse of his," become individualized and naturalized as a matter of "character"? The epochal events in the rocky passage—Carwin's rite of passage from the traditional to the modern—offer an answer.

Carwin begins to narrate his rite of passage as follows: "In my fourteenth year, events happened which ascertained my future destiny. One evening I had been sent to bring cows from a meadow, some miles distant from my father's mansion. My time was limited, and I was menaced with severe chastisement if, according to my custom, I should stay beyond the period assigned. For some time these menaces rung in my ears, and I went on my way with speed" (282–83). Confronted with an "accident"—the escape of the cows from his father's field—Carwin responds by transgressing his responsibility to his father. He does not conform to paternal authority and return to report this accident; instead, he is consumed by his apparently natural "thirst of knowledge" and immediately seeks to understand the accident, to subject it to a reasoned inquiry: "It was my *duty* to carry home the earliest tidings of this accident, but the first suggestion was to *examine* the cause and manner of this escape" (283; my italics). In keeping with his future-leaning "character," Carwin opts for charting the accident by subjecting it to a regime of detached, empirical observation and reasoned experimentation, to produce understanding.

Carwin's investigation is soon interrupted by fear of his father, causing him to head home. Due to his still active powers of observation, however, he "discovers" what appears to be a shortcut: "a narrow pass which . . . would conduct me, though not without danger and toil, to the opposite side of the ridge." He sets out on a path toward that pass, setting the scene for his transformation:

> The path was narrow, steep, and overshadowed by rocks. The sun was nearly set, and the shadow of the cliff above, obscured the passage almost as much as midnight would have done: I was accustomed to despise danger when it presented itself in a sensible form, but, by a defect common in every one's education, goblins and spectres were to me the objects of the most violent apprehensions. These were unavoidably connected with solitude and darkness, and were present to my fears when I entered this gloomy recess. (284)

Moving from accident to reasoned examination to a gothic terror of the spectral and the unknown framed in an ethical and aesthetic scene, the text precipitates a terrifying moment of indecision. Critically, as we will see later, this is a universal moment, since it is attributed to "a defect common in every one's education."

In response, Carwin makes the first crucial judgment of his life:

> These terrors are always lessened by calling the attention away to some indifferent object. I now made use of this expedient, and began to amuse myself by hallowing as loud as organs of unusual compass and vigour would enable me. I uttered the words which chanced to occur to me, and repeated in the shrill tones of a Mohock savage . . . "Cow! cow! come home! home!" . . . These notes were of course reverberated from the rocks which on either side towered aloft, but the echo was confused and indistinct. (284–85, Brown's ellipses)

Imperceptibly, by "chance," Carwin turns his terror into an indifferent, objective posture enabling a self-generated, aesthetic amusement: as he soon explains, "My terrors were quickly supplanted by delight" (246). He will quickly decide (again spontaneously, due to his "thirst of knowledge") to master this echo, a judgment that makes him a "biloquist." But before we consider that second aspect of this scene, how might we characterize and account for Carwin's first, aesthetic judgment: his "indifferent," objective "attention" and the resulting amusement and "delight"? From what source or fund does this judgment emanate? What determines the specificity of this utterance and its power to dispel terror?

If we take Carwin at his word, we might say that he draws on his natural "character." That is, we might say that he generates this force of will out of a capacity available to every subject who "thirsts" to overcome the constraints of tradition, paternal authority, unreason, and educational defects.[30] Carwin's impulse to call "attention away to some indifferent object" would be the sign of this character, the mark of his will to leave the terror of tradition behind. In turn, amusement, indifference, objectivity, and eventually delight would be the marks of this character's success. From this perspective, "the shrill tones of a Mohock savage" would be an incidental detail, mere "words which chanced to occur" to Carwin.

We cannot say that Carwin's character is natural here, however. This passage shifts ambivalently between passive and active voices: "are always lessened," "were of course reverberated," and "were quickly supplanted" on the one hand, and "I now made use," "began to amuse myself," "I uttered . . . and repeated," on the other. Carwin seems both passively manipulated by his character and actively in control of its power to influence his circumstances. The construction "terrors were quickly supplanted by delight" is especially ambivalent, since the passive voice suggests that Carwin has been a mere vehicle for a natural transformation, while the verb "to supplant" suggests an active overturning, even a rooting out or an uprooting of established beliefs and affects. "Delight" sustains and deepens this ambivalence, for it is both the cause and the effect of this supplanting, both that which takes the place of the uprooted and that which uproots. Carwin's first judgment in the rocky passage is thus characterized by an odd blend of nature and will; his character is ambivalently composed of a passive, natural tendency to let delight supplant terror and an active, willful desire to choose indifference, expedience, objectivity, and amusement over terror. Carwin is no longer merely making inductive, empirical determinations. Rather, paradoxically, it seems to be in his nature to supplant the terror of tradition with reasonable, aesthetic judgment.

It is here that Brown, a tenuous founder of American literary aesthetics, intersects with Immanuel Kant, whose own foundational account of aesthetic judgment—*The Critique of Judgement*, published in 1790, just eight years before Brown began to write *Memoirs of Carwin*—explores the emergence of modern aesthetics and, indeed, civilized culture itself. That is, Carwin's act of judgment uncannily resembles Kant's ideal act of aesthetic judgment, and Carwin himself uncannily resembles Kant's abstract and universal subject of judgment. These resemblances work on a number of levels. Although Rand B. Evans and Allan Gardner Smith have argued that German idealists in general, and Kant in particular, did not directly influence U.S. conceptions of mind and psychology until the 1840s, Smith establishes that Brown was one of the earliest critics of his contemporaries' devotion to a rationalist-sensationalist psychology that blended John Locke's extreme sensationalism with the rationalism of the Scottish Common Sense school, a psychology Kant too can be said to have challenged.[31] In addition, both *Memoirs of Carwin* and *The Critique of Judgement* replace rationalist-sensationalist psychology with an account of aesthetic judgment as paradoxically in the nature of human will. In turn, these accounts invoke the apparently incidental figures of the "Iroquois" and the "Mohock" to control this paradox, and therefore they can be read allegorically as founding themselves on a particular racial formation. I would like to consider each of these levels of intersection or resemblance in some detail, in order to construct a genealogy of Carwin's "character."

Whereas Locke had argued that ideas were the result of external impressions made upon the senses, Francis Hutcheson initiated the Scottish School's argument that a universal and innate sense of right structured human thought, providing a rational framework for sensationalism and moderating its mechanistic tendencies by opening up a space for "free will." English physician Erasmus Darwin and American physician Benjamin Rush became two of the most influential proponents of this rationalist-sensationalist conception of human thought, and both influenced Brown, as Smith has established.[32] Yet, Brown seems not to have been satisfied with the optimism of this conception, for his novels repeatedly place characters who explicitly advocate sensationalist, rationalist, and sensationalist-rationalist positions in mysterious and gothic circumstances for which they cannot account and that often drive them into grave misconceptions, delusions, or even homicidal madness. Brown's complex representations of social and mental life thus present important challenges to reigning rationalist and sensationalist conceptions.

Kant also challenged these conceptions by arguing that in and of themselves sensations cannot give knowledge, but rather that the transcendental unity—or the intuitions of time and space together with the categories—conditions knowledge a priori[33] and thus is that which orders perception and experience for knowledge, but does not access perception and experience in any direct or unmediated manner.[34] *The Critique of Judgement* in particular makes this argument when it deduces the universality of aesthetic judgment for both an abstract subject and for a social faculty of "taste." For Kant, this abstract and universal subject of judgment exhibits "the proper mental mood for a feeling of the sublime" (115), which "does not reside in any of the things of nature, but only in our own mind, in so far as we may become conscious of our superiority over nature within, and thus also over nature without us" (114). Kant's deduction of the universality of this "proper mental mood," or "the necessity of that agreement between other men's judgements upon the sublime and our own" (116), shows how "culture" itself is possible:

> The proper mental mood for a feeling of the sublime postulates the mind's susceptibility for ideas, since it is precisely in the failure of nature to attain to these [ideas] . . . that there is something forbidding to sensibility. . . . In fact, without the development of moral ideas, that which, thanks to preparatory culture, we call sublime, merely strikes the untutored man as terrifying. He will see in the evidences which the ravages of nature give of her dominion, and in the vast scale of her might, compared with which his own is diminished to insignificance, only the misery, peril, and distress that would compass

the man who was thrown to its mercy. So the simple-minded, and, for the most part, intelligent, Savoyard peasant, (as Herr von Sassure relates,) unhesitatingly called all lovers of snow-mountains fools. And who can tell whether he would have been so wide of the mark, if that student of nature had taken the risk of the dangers to which he exposed himself merely, as most travellers do, for a fad, or so as some day to be able to give a thrilling account of his adventures? But the mind of Sassure was bent on the instruction of mankind, and soul-stirring sensations that excellent man indeed had, and the reader of his travels got them thrown into the bargain. (115–16)

Like Kant's Sassure and the Savoyard peasant combined, Carwin forms a judgment that "instructs" his "simple-minded," "peasant" sensibility in a feeling for the sublime and "the development of moral ideas," thereby opening himself up to the properly "cultural," "soul-stirring sensations" of the "excellent man": Carwin's "delight." Just as Carwin's "character" or "thirst of knowledge" is represented as latent in *Memoirs of Carwin*, so too does Kant's description of the "Savoyard peasant" as "intelligent" but "untutored" suggest a latent, modern character. What, then, makes this "agreement between other men's judgements upon the sublime and our own" possible?

For Kant, the faculty of judgment prescribes laws a priori, most importantly, for "estimates that are called aesthetic, and which relate to the beautiful and sublime, whether of nature or of art" (5). The faculty of judgment is crucial because it "forms a middle term between understanding," which prescribes laws a priori for the faculty of knowledge and is assigned to a Critique of Pure Reason, "and reason," which prescribes laws a priori for the faculty of desire and is assigned to a Critique of Practical Reason (4).[35] Consequently, the "correct employment" of the faculty of judgment "is so necessary and universally requisite that it is just this faculty that is intended when we speak of sound understanding" (5).

For this "correct employment" of the faculty of judgment to be possible, a subject must become "disinterested," according to Kant:

It is quite plain that in order to say that the object *is beautiful*, and to show that I have taste, everything turns on the meaning which I can give to this representation, and not on any factor which makes me dependent on the real existence of the object. Every one must allow that a judgement on the beautiful which is tinged with the slightest interest, is very partial and not a pure judgement of taste. One must not be in the least prepossessed in favour of the real existence of the thing, but must preserve complete indifference in this respect, in order to play the part of judge in matters of taste. (43)

Aesthetic judgment thus formalizes a specific object of aesthetic production in order for that object to become exemplary. That is, aesthetic judgment involves a formalization of the particular such that it comes to represent a universal; a singular instance gains universality through aesthetic judgment. Importantly, this process does not happen to or in the object, but rather animates the subject who judges: "Everything turns on the meaning which I can give to this representation, and not on any factor which makes me dependent on the real existence of the object." Thus, the subject who "correctly employs" the faculty of judgment is not only disinterested but is, in fact, a subject abstracted from all particularities, a universal or formal and abstract subject.[36]

In turn, for Kant "taste" is the social aspect of the faculty of judgment, or the universal and abstract subject's ability to communicate its judgment with its fellow subjects: "the faculty of estimating what makes our feeling in a given representation universally communicable without mediation of a concept" (153). Taste allows the universal and common appreciation of "fine art," which in turn "advances" culture toward sociality (166). Thus, although aesthetic estimates "do not of themselves contribute a whit to the knowledge of things, they still belong wholly to the faculty of knowledge" because when "correctly employed" by a subject and shared among like subjects they form the social faculty of taste, a necessary (though not sufficient) condition for "common human understanding" (5–6; 152–53). Culture, as the communication of a correctly employed faculty of judgment, enables proper sociality as well as knowledge in the most universal sense (6). Without a correctly employed faculty of judgment, as we saw above, "that which, thanks to preparatory culture, we call sublime, merely strikes the untutored man as terrifying," thereby inhibiting the faculties of judgment, knowledge, and desire alike, as well as culture and knowledge (115).

In sum, Kant suggests that the individual's ability to transform a merely sensual awareness of the material particularity of an object into a critical faculty of disinterested judgment regarding the formal universality of an object (its beauty), and to communicate that judgment with fellow subjects who judge similarly, is the condition of possibility for a society's ability to generate an unprejudiced critical faculty of universal, rational communicability and, as Kant writes, "*sensus communis*," or "common" or "public sense" (82–83, 151–53). Kant's theory of culture, then, posits a human faculty of aesthetic judgment that develops universality from particularity; "culture" names a formal and abstract equality among subjects, a formal and abstract equality that subjects produce, via the faculty of taste, out of differences and particularities.

Let me suggest, then, that Carwin sheds the premodern constraints and fears of his early years through a Kantian aesthetic judgment. In the rocky passage, we see Carwin move from a universal but premodern, guilty, and terrified conscience to an abstract, impartial, and universal posture of judgment (from "a defect common in *every one's* education" to "These terrors are always lessened by calling the attention away to some *indifferent object*"), a transition from which he spontaneously generates an aesthetic attitude: "I . . . began to *amuse* myself" and "My terrors were quickly supplanted by delight" (285–86, my italics). The text suggests that we the readers, whom Carwin addresses in a personal but universal sense with his "Memoirs" and with the pronoun "you" (287, 314, 337), will understand or even identify with (see ourselves in) his actions because, at least potentially, we share with him both the "defect common in every one's education" and the latent faculty of judgment.[37] For Brown and for Kant, Carwin and the Savoyard peasant can become modern, universal, and abstract subjects by correctly employing their latent faculty of judgment. Premodern, asocial particularity—figured by Carwin's "terrors" (285) and the Savoyard peasant's "terrifying . . . misery, peril, and distress" (115)—is thus transformed into universality, or *"sensus communis,"* by a disinterested, aesthetic judgment understandable by other universal and abstract subjects similarly capable of disinterested judgment.

Yet this faculty of judgment conceals a paradox. How can subjects produce culture by means of a faculty of judgment that produces subjectivity? More specifically, how does a latent human nature produce the culture that differentiates humanity from nature? This paradox is controlled in both texts by the differentiation of subjects who can access the universality of judgment—figured by Carwin and the Savoyard peasant—from subjects who cannot. Indeed, Brown and Kant differentiate Carwin and the Savoyard peasant from uncannily similar, racially particularized figures who are barred from universality. Although these racialized figures apparently emerge incidentally, casually, or by chance, I want to suggest that their very incidental appearances give their differentiation from potentially universal subjects that much more strength: some subjects have the ability to activate the nature that differentiates them from nature because, clearly and self-evidently, other subjects cannot. The differentiation of potentially universal subjectivity from necessarily particular subjects is thus also a deferral or a displacement: the human nature that allows culture to differentiate humanity from nature textually defers or displaces its natural particularity to figures who are represented as even more natural.[38]

In *The Critique of Judgement*, the figure for racialized particularity is "Iroquois," and it appears at two key moments in the text. First, in order to argue that "the delight which determines the judgement of taste is independent of all interest," Kant distinguishes between impure, interested, or partial judgments and pure, disinterested judgments. For the former, he gives four examples, the second of which is the figure "Iroquois":

> If any one asks me whether I consider that the palace I see before me is beautiful, [first example] I may, perhaps, reply that I do not care for things of that sort that are merely made to be gaped at. Or [second example] I may reply in the same strain as that Iroquois *sachem* who said that nothing in Paris pleased him better than the eating-houses. I may even go a step further [third example] and inveigh with the vigour of a *Rousseau* against the vanity of the great who spend the sweat of the people on such superfluous things. Or, in fine, [fourth example] I may quite easily persuade myself that if I found myself on an uninhabited island, without hope of ever again coming among men, and could conjure such a palace into existence by a mere wish, I should still not trouble to do so, so long as I had a hut there that was comfortable enough for me. (43)[39]

Although "all this may be admitted and approved," these are all examples of impure judgments, and thus they do not address "the point now at issue," because, as I quoted above, "Every one must allow that a judgement on the beautiful which is tinged with the slightest interest, is very partial and not a pure judgement of taste" (43). Whether one disapproves of gaping at lavish objects or innocently devours objects of pleasure, whether one challenges the exploitative conditions of production of such objects or utopically opts out of these conditions, one remains "dependent on the real existence of the object" and so has not ascended to the level of taste: the level, that is, of objectivity, indifference, disinterest, and civility (43). To a certain extent this passage equates all of these examples of dependency, valuing (or devaluing) "that Iroquois *sachem*" as much as it values (or devalues) the anonymous cynic, the critic Rousseau, and the utopian castaway. Yet we must also notice the subtle differences among these examples. Only the "Iroquois *sachem*" is completely uncritical here. Although the criticisms of the cynic, the critic, and the utopian are impure in their dependence on the object, perhaps even naive in their particularistic concerns, the "Iroquois *sachem*" in Paris looks only to satisfy his most immediate desires. Although the "Iroquois *sachem*" can come to Paris and stuff himself full in the eating houses, he cannot even generate the distance from those pleasures that Frenchmen such as Rousseau can. He is depicted as locked in his particularity, a state even clearer in the German. The "I" who is modulated throughout these examples *becomes* the cynic, the Rousseauian critic, and the utopian: *"ich liebe . . . nicht"* [I do not care for], *"ich kann . . . schmählen"* [I may inveigh], *"ich kann mich . . . überzeugen"* [I may persuade myself]. The "Iroquois *sachem*," however, is held at a distance from that "I": *"oder, wie jener irokesische Sachem: ihm gefalle . . . nichts besser"* [or, like that Iroquois sachem: nothing pleased him better].[40] Whereas Kant allows his authorial voice to perform the roles of cynic, Rousseauian critic, and utopian with the use of the first-person conditional "I may," he balks when it comes to the Iroquois sachem, instead using the third-person past tense. This verbal oscillation forges a certain, provisional equality between the authorial voice and the examples of the cynic, the critic, and the utopian, with whom Kant deigns to identify if only fleetingly, and a certain, matter-of-fact hierarchy between that voice and the Iroquois sachem, in whose role the text's "I" prefers not to imagine itself. In addition, because they are more personal and conditional, the claims about the cynic, the critic, and the utopian are more tentative, perhaps even more unsure than the claim about the Iroquois sachem, which is offered as fact.

Later in *The Critique of Judgement*, Kant again uses the figure "Iroquois" as an example of premodern, preaesthetic forms of judgment:

With no one to take into account but himself a man abandoned on a desert island would not adorn either himself or his hut, nor would he look for flowers, and still less plant them, with the object of providing himself with personal adornments. Only in society does it occur to him to be not merely a man, but a man refined after the manner of his kind (the beginning of civilization)—for that is the estimate formed of one who has the bent and turn for communicating his pleasure to others, and who is not quite satisfied with an Object unless his feeling of delight in it can be shared in communion with others. Further, a regard to universal communicability is a thing which every one expects and requires from every one else, just as if it were part of an original compact dictated by humanity itself. And thus, no doubt, at first only charms, e.g. colours for painting oneself (roucou among the Caribs and cinnabar among the Iroquois), or flowers, seashells, beautifully coloured feathers, then, in the course of time, also beautiful forms (as

in canoes, wearing-apparel, &c.) which convey no gratification, i.e. delight of enjoyment, become of moment in society and attract a considerable interest. Eventually, when
civilization has reached its height it makes this work of communication almost the main
business of refined inclination, and the entire value of sensations is placed in the degree
to which they permit of universal communication. At this stage, then, even where the
pleasure which each one has in an object is but insignificant and possesses of itself no
conspicuous interest, still the idea of its universal communicability almost indefinitely
augments its value. (Kant, 155–56)[41]

Here, "The Iroquois" who uses "cinnabar" is not "convey[ing] . . . delight of enjoyment" to fellow Iroquois but, rather, is merely expressing a solipsistic, affective "interest" in cinnabar as a "charm" for "oneself." Although "in the course of time" the
emergence of "canoes, wearing-apparel, &c" signals a certain development, this is not
a social moment but a "moment in society" still anterior to civilization proper; the
very development represented by this moment locks these canoe makers and apparel
wearers within an underdevelopment that can only foreshadow their assimilation
or destruction.[42] When this particularistic "interest" of particular Iroquois in the
merely sensory quality of the "charm" is formalized over time, it can be communicated to others and enable "civilization." In effect, formalization revalues "sensations,"
"charms," and "interest," transforming them into universal, "refined inclination."
Finally, we must note a hierarchical distinction that has emerged between these two
passages—the elite "Iroquois *sachem*" of the first and the common "Iroquois" of the
second—though I will wait until later in this chapter to read that difference.

Why might the Iroquois have become the figure for racialized particularity in
these texts?[43] Iroquois played an important role in the imaginations of the colonial
Dutch, French, British, and independent Americans, as each constructed their colonizing projects around fantasmatic understandings of the individual tribes and the
collective alliance. From the seventeenth century, the Iroquois were represented in
Dutch, French, British, and U.S. colonial discourses as a politically savvy and militari-
ly brutal empire.[44] This dual interpretation of the Iroquois as a politically advanced
federation but a socially barbaric or underdeveloped people persists with remarkable
consistency, continuing to appear in the twentieth century due in large part to the
legacy of nineteenth-century anthropologist Lewis H. Morgan.[45] As members of both
the Iroquois Great League of Peace and the Iroquois Confederacy, Mohawks seem
to have been represented as particularly "barbaric" Iroquois in British and U.S. colonial discourses, as a look at the dissemination of the word "Mohawk" or "Mohock"
shows.[46] The earliest reference is given in the *Oxford English Dictionary* as a text
by P. Vincent (1638), which includes the sentence "He went with forty men to the
Mohocks, which are cruel, bloody cannibals." This link with savagery and cannibalism
is repeated again and again throughout the seventeenth, eighteenth, and nineteenth
centuries, and it is even fed back into Europe and applied to European "undesirables";
the *Oxford English Dictionary* takes eighteenth-century, English uses of Mohock and
Mohawk to mean "a class of aristocratic ruffians who infested the streets of London

at night in the early years of the 18th century."[47] This generative displacement of the name Mohock is a lexical map of the text of colonialism, tracing the manner in which colonialism produces coherent and normative racial and national formations for the colonies and the metropole.

As I mentioned, this representation of Mohawks as simultaneously dangerous and admirable, as objects of idealization, aestheticization, and assimilation, was important to governmental and cultural discursive practices alike. Understood in this context, Brown's figure of the "shrill tones of a Mohock savage" can no longer be taken as incidental to his allegorical critique, celebration, or ambivalent evaluation of U.S. modernization. Carwin's apparently spontaneous decision to imitate these "shrill tones" and then turn them into an exemplary instance of aesthetic judgment is no mere natural result of his "character." Rather, Carwin's judgment in the rocky passage allegorizes the very assimilation policy being directed against Iroquois at the turn of the nineteenth century, drawing specifically on colonial discourses about Mohawks. The figurative incorporation of "the shrill tones of a Mohock savage," through a formal and abstract judgment turning terrifying objects into indifferent ones, represents Mohawks as assimilable, particularized antecedents of American national identity. Carwin's emergence as a developed and modern subject of America—whether Brown is critical of that emergence or not—is itself initiated by that subject's prior racial formation. That is, the very distinction between traditional nature and modern culture is made possible by distinguishing both from "a Mohock savage," who represents a prior nature subject to aesthetic assimilation.

"A Mohock savage" can thus be said to figure the source or fund of pure particularity from which Carwin generates his Kantian judgment in the rocky passage and his subsequent universal and abstract subjectivity, as "Iroquois" figures the source or fund from which the Savoyard peasant could do so with proper "tutoring."[48] For Kant and Brown, the condition of possibility for the potential movement of Carwin and the Savoyard peasant to universality and civilized sociability is an absolutely particular figure. The formal modernization of subjectivity is represented as the systematic deferral of particularity, resulting in a fundamental racial differing of civilized from uncivilized subjects. For Brown, this development entails a specific assimilation or incorporation of the uncivilizable, a transformation of particularity into universality through an aesthetics of assimilation. Kant's text does not emphasize this specific scene of assimilation, just as it does not express the need to specify which Iroquois tribe he is invoking. That the figures "Iroquois" and "Mohock" seem incidental in each text—"words which chanced to occur to" Carwin (284); and to Kant, "not the point now at issue" but merely "*exempli gratia*" (43, 155)—is precisely the mark of their pure particularity and thus their self-evident difference from and deferral within universality.[49]

Let me now pick up Carwin where I left him after his first judgment in the rocky passage and turn attention to his second judgment: his decision to master the echo of "the shrill tones of a Mohock savage" and become a biloquist. This second judgment inaugurates a series of elaborate displacements of Carwin's initial racial and national formation. As I have suggested thus far, the iteration of a racial formation founds

Brown's national allegory; as I will suggest presently, a concealed reiteration of that racial formation sustains it.

Carwin's Second Judgment

As quickly as it is mobilized in *Memoirs of Carwin*, the figure of the "Mohock" is subsumed by another: the echo. For after Carwin hears the first "confused and indistinct" echo of his initial "Mohock savage" utterance, he proceeds, shored up with a newfound confidence, through the rocky passage:

> I continued, for some time, thus to beguile the way, till I reached a space more than commonly abrupt, and which required all my attention. My rude ditty was suspended till I had surmounted this impediment. In a few minutes I was at leisure to renew it. After finishing the strain, I paused. In a few seconds a voice as I then imagined, uttered the same cry from the point of a rock some hundred feet behind me; the same words, with equal distinctness, and deliberation, and in the same tone, appeared to be spoken. I was startled by this incident, and cast a fearful glance behind, to discover by whom it was uttered. The spot where I stood was buried in dusk, but the eminences were still invested with a luminous and vivid twilight. The speaker, however, was concealed from my view.
>
> I had scarcely begun to wonder at this occurrence, when a new occasion for wonder, was afforded me. A few seconds, in like manner, elapsed, when my ditty was again rehearsed, with a no less perfect imitation, in a different quarter . . . Five times was this ditty successively resounded, at intervals nearly equal, always from a new quarter, and with little abatement of its original distinctness and force. (285)

The more distinct echoes of his call puzzle him and renew his terror, until he makes the second crucial judgment of his life and, once again, banishes his terrors:

> A little reflection was sufficient to shew that this was no more than an echo of an extraordinary kind. My terrors were quickly supplanted by delight. The motives to dispatch were forgotten, and I amused myself for an hour, with talking to these cliffs: I placed myself in new positions, and exhausted my lungs and my invention in new clamours.
>
> The pleasures of this new discovery were an ample compensation for the ill treatment which I expected on my return. By some caprice in my father I escaped merely with a few reproaches. I seized the first opportunity of again visiting this recess, and repeating my amusement; time, and incessant repetition, could scarcely lessen its charms or exhaust the variety produced by new tones and new positions. . . . My reflections were naturally suggested by the singularity of this echo. To hear my own voice speak at a distance would have been formerly regarded as prodigious. To hear too, that voice, not uttered by another, by whom it might easily be mimicked, but by myself! I cannot now recollect the transition which led me to the notion of sounds, similar to these, but produced by other means than reverberation. Could I not so dispose my organs as to make my voice appear at a distance? (285–87)

Carwin surmounts his subjection to the authority of his traditional father by "play[ing] the part of judge in matters of taste" (Kant, 43) with his second crucial judgment: he decides to master the echo and to teach himself to become a willful producer of the echo's pleasure and delight. This second judgment is structured much like the first. "Naturally" and spontaneously, without being able to "now recollect the transition," Carwin focuses only on the "extraordinary" "singularity of this echo," eschewing mere mimicry in favor of what Kant might have called "genius," or the "innate mental aptitude" that can be neither learned nor mimicked but *through which* nature gives the rule to art" (168): "Hence, where an author owes a product to his genius, he does not himself know how the *ideas* for it have entered into his head, nor has he it in his power to invent the like at pleasure, or methodically, and communicate the same to others in such precepts as would put them in a position to produce similar products" (169). Carwin draws on this rich fund of the echo, reaping a profit from it by subjecting it to his control.

With this second judgment, however, Carwin also begins to drift from Kant's aesthetic ideal and to become more of the scientist, or one who seeks the "power to invent the like at pleasure, or methodically" (Kant, 169), by engaging in "incessant repetition" and asking such practical questions as, "Could I not so dispose my organs as to make my voice appear at a distance?" (Brown, 287). Invoking the language of scientific investigation and mastery even more insistently, Carwin continues:

> From speculation I proceeded to experiment. . . . A certain position of the organs took place on the first attempt, altogether new, unexampled and as it were, by accident, for I could not attain it on the second experiment.
>
> You will not wonder that I exerted myself with indefatigable zeal to regain what had once, though for so short a space, been in my power. Your own ears have witnessed the success of these efforts.[50] By perpetual exertion I gained it a second time, and now was a diligent observer of the circumstances attending it. Gradually I subjected these finer and more subtle motions to the command of my will. What was at first difficult, by exercise and habit, was rendered easy. I learned to accommodate my voice to all the varieties of distance and directions.
>
> It cannot be denied that this faculty is wonderful and rare, but when we consider the possible modifications of muscular motion, how few of these are usually exerted, how imperfectly they are subjected to the will, and yet that the will is capable of being rendered unlimited and absolute, will not our wonder cease? (287–88)

For Carwin, the echo suggests an opportunity to rewrite a chance occurrence as a mastered invention. Faced with a second moment of judgment in this rocky passage, one provoked by an echo of his first judgment, he responds with a will to mastery and control, a rewriting of his initial judgment in the idiom of scientific biloquism.

Carwin at this point resembles Kant's "immortal" Newton more than his "poetic" genius. As Kant explains this distinction:

> So all that *Newton* has set forth in his immortal work on the Principles of Natural Philosophy may well be learned, however great a mind it took to find it all out, but we cannot learn to write in a true poetic vein, no matter how complete all the precepts of

the poetic art may be, or however excellent its models. The reason is that all the steps that Newton had to take from the first elements of geometry to his greatest and most profound discoveries were such as he could make intuitively evident and plain to follow, not only for himself but for every one else. On the other hand no *Homer* or *Wieland* can show how his ideas, so rich at once in fancy and in thought, enter and assemble themselves in his brain, for the good reason that he does not himself know, and so cannot teach others. In matters of science, therefore, the greatest inventor differs only in degree from the most laborious imitator and apprentice, whereas he differs specifically from one endowed by nature for fine art. No disparagement, however, of those great men, to whom the human race is so deeply indebted, is involved in this comparison of them with those who on the score of their talent for fine art are the elect of nature. The talent for science is formed for the continued advances of greater perfection in knowledge, with all its dependent practical advantages, as also for imparting the same to others. Hence scientists can boast a ground of considerable superiority over those who merit the honour of being called geniuses, since genius reaches a point at which art must make a halt, as there is a limit imposed upon it which it cannot transcend. This limit has in all probability been long since attained. In addition, such skill cannot be communicated, but requires to be bestowed directly from the hand of nature upon each individual, and so with him it dies, awaiting the day when nature once again endows another in the same way—one who needs no more than an example to set the talent of which he is conscious at work on similar lines. (169–70)

Kant's comparison between the Greek poet Homer and the eighteenth-century German poet Christoph Martin Wieland speaks not only to the neoclassicism of German aesthetics but also to Kant's emphasis on "the talent for science" over "the talent for fine art." Science seems to name the "transcendence" of fine art, thus reminding us that Kant himself privileged understanding and a critique of pure reason, as well as reason and a critique of practical reason, over aesthetic judgment and its critique.[51] Genius is here characterized by a solipsism haunted by death, whereas science has a transmissibility that pushes it beyond art. It would seem to be Carwin's own effort to proceed "from speculation . . . to experiment" that pushes him beyond the limits of genius and toward the scientific practice of the "diligent observer of circumstances," who through "exercise and habit" is able to consider "all the varieties of distance and direction" and all "the possible modifications of muscular motion" (287–88). In turn, this push gives Carwin an "unlimited and absolute" power more akin to Kant's Newton than to Kant's Wieland (288).

Of course, Carwin's biloquism eventually pushes the life of another Wieland beyond his own limits and toward depraved, homicidal insanity in Brown's other novel about Carwin, *Wieland*. Indeed, even in the context of *Memoirs of Carwin*, the scientific elements of biloquism begin to make trouble for the poetic, suggesting that Carwin's shift from aesthetic judgment to scientific practice figures the rationalism about which Brown was so skeptical. Jay Fliegelman has argued a similar point:

Brown's novel of authority misrepresented and authority imagined is a terrifying post-French Revolutionary account of the fallibility of the human mind and, by extension, of democracy itself. Ventriloquism and religious enthusiasm, the novel's [i.e., *Wieland*] dramatic devices, seem with a sardonic literalness to call into question all possible faith in the republican formula *vox populi, vox Dei*—the voice of the people is the voice of God. . . . Carwin's ventriloquism, like mesmerism or the new eighteenth-century concern with "social conditioning," transformed coercion into an inner voice that rendered the outer one unnecessary—a profane surrogate for the Christian conscience or Quaker "inner light" through which God himself performed his ventriloquism.[52]

Carwin's biloquial misadventures in *Memoirs of Carwin* and *Wieland* articulate a Brownian critique of "all possible faith in the republican formula *vox populi, vox Dei*": a critique, that is, of the very rational universality Brown's Carwin and Kant's Newton or Wieland represent. More importantly, however, I want to suggest that the reproducible and reiterative aspect of scientific biloquism, which, by definition, aesthetic genius cannot perform, is called forth by the concealed racial and national form of Carwin's character. For if Carwin's utterance of the "shrill tones of a Mohock savage" retroactively conditions his "character" or "thirst of knowledge," and thus figures the iterative, cultural assimilation of Mohawks being sought in the newly independent United States of the 1790s, then the "incessant" scientific *re*iterability of Carwin's mastery over the echo of those "shrill tones" figures the *maintenance* required by any policy of assimilation. That is, the condition of possibility for maintaining the universal and natural cast of Carwin's national identity, and thus for concealing its particular racial and national formation, is the systematic and continuing reproduction of its natural universality: "I *learned* to accommodate my voice," Carwin explains (my italics). More so than "fine art," scientific biloquism, as a figure for the maintenance of mastery over the echo of "the shrill tones of a Mohock savage," is made necessary by the racialized terms of Brown's national allegory.

Indeed, by describing Carwin as a biloquist and not a ventriloquist here, Brown seems to have coined a term, and in the process to have performed an important substitution and displacement of "fine art" by "science." The *Oxford English Dictionary* gives *Memoirs of Carwin* and *Wieland* as the first uses of "biloquist" and "biloquial" in the English language, whereas "ventriloquism" has a history dating back to the sixteenth century. "Ventriloquism," meaning voices coming from the *venter* or the belly, suggests voices from an unknown origin, or some deep and unlocatable interiority.[53] This unknown origin resonates with the fact that ventriloquism was often understood in the seventeenth and eighteenth centuries to indicate possession by evil spirits or by Satan. Its unknown, satanic quality undoubtedly gave the word "ventriloquism" an antirational, premodern feel for Brown. By coining the term "biloquism," he suggests a merely doubled voice, a single copy alongside a single original, no matter how many forms the "copy" might take (for Carwin biloquizes many different animal and human voices). In fact, Brown repeatedly emphasizes that Carwin's voices were produced by "a certain position of the organs" of the mouth, or a precise "concurrence of teeth, palate and tongue," making them a mere trick of the mouth rather than an unknown, supernatural or preternatural emanation from the *venter* (287–88). Brown's Carwin in effect tames the gothic text of "goblins and spectres" implicit in the word "ventriloquism" by producing a "biloquial" skill of his own mastery out of his natural "thirst of knowledge." "Biloquism," more precisely than the superstitiously tinted word "ventriloquism," figures a universally reiterable and learnable practice that could reproduce the citizen-subject by preserving the assimilated echo of the Mohock savage, turning the memory of its threatening particularity into a formal practice of modern citizenship.

Thus, although biloquism can be read as a figure for Carwin's dangerous rationalism, and in turn as part of Brown's critique of Godwinism, the fact that biloquism emerges from Carwin's mastery of the echo of "the shrill tones of a Mohock savage" indicates the prior, concealed racial formation of that critique. That is, Brown's very critique of Godwin is itself conditioned upon the naturalized emergence, assimilation, and continuing mastery of the "Mohock savage." Nonetheless, this incorporation and mastery cannot be said to be absolute, for as the plot of *Memoirs of Carwin* develops, one can still hear echoes of this figure.

As soon as Carwin masters the echo of "the shrill tones of a Mohock savage," he leaves his family and sets out to make a life for himself. Yet he finds it nearly impossible to resist using his biloquism to deceive people into following his wishes, despite his sense that such deception leads him into unethical territory. In one of his earliest experiments with his new-found skill, Carwin makes the voice of Ariel, from Shakespeare's *The Tempest*, appear to sing from the sky at a garden party. The scene begins with a woman singing some of Ariel's songs to the assembled guests:

> On a subsequent occasion a select company was assembled at a garden, at a small distance from the city. Discourse glided through a variety of topics, till it lighted at length on the subject of invisible beings. From the speculations of philosophers we proceeded to the creations of the poet. Some maintained the justness of Shakspear's *[sic]* delineations of aerial beings, while others denied it. By no violent transition, Ariel and his songs were introduced, and a lady, celebrated for her musical skill, was solicited to accompany her pedal harp with the song of "Five fathom deep thy father lies" . . . She was known to have set, for her favourite instrument, all the songs of Shakspeare *[sic]*. . . . She ended and the audience were mute with rapture. (297; first ellipsis Brown's, second ellipsis mine)

In *The Tempest*, Ariel sings "Five fathom deep thy father lies"—actually, "Full fadom five thy father lies"—in the midst of the scene that first conveys the differences between Caliban and Ariel (act 1, scene 2). After asking Prospero for his freedom and being rebuffed, Ariel is forced by Prospero into meekly thanking him for rescuing him from imprisonment by the witch Sycorax. Prospero forces Ariel's gratitude in an exchange that highlights Prospero's role as master, as he repeatedly commands Ariel to "Speak!" in response to his rhetorical questions. At this moment, Caliban enters and curses Prospero for enslaving him and decries his inability to free himself. Caliban then exits, and Ariel returns to do Prospero's bidding and to lure Ferdinand to him with "Full fadom five thy father lies." Ariel's song makes Ferdinand think a god is tell-ing him about the death of his father, Alonso, and thus Ferdinand is lured slowly into Prospero's grasp. When Brown reproduces this song at the garden party of *Memoirs of Carwin*, the guests disregard the fact that Ariel is a slave to Prospero and instead appreciate the song as an object of beauty. Enraptured by a song a slave performs ac-cording to his master's bidding, sublating Ariel's airy slavery to an invisible object of aesthetic judgment, the guests formalize the text of colonialism in just the way Carwin does in the rocky passage.

By invoking Ariel in an allegory of U.S. identity itself made possible by a racial formation—the "shrill tones of a Mohock savage"—Brown mobilizes a trope that Roberto Fernández Retamar diagnosed in his epochal article "Caliban: Notes Toward a Discussion of Culture in Our America." In what amounts to a genealogy of one element of the text of colonialism in the Americas, Fernández Retamar argues that the name "Carib" was conflated with the word "cannibal" soon after Columbus publicized the supposedly cannibalistic practices of the Caribs in his *Diario de Navegación*.[54] From Columbus's *Diario de Navegación* to Mannoni's *Psychologie de la Colonisation* and beyond, Fernández Retamar continues, the figure of the Carib as cannibal has been opposed to the figure of the Arauaco or Taino Indian whom Columbus described as "peaceful, meek, and even timorous and cowardly."[55] For Fernández Retamar, the couplet has consistently been used in colonial discourse to suggest that the colonized peoples of the Americas were either irredeemable beasts who ought to be exterminated, or noble savages who could be assimilated into modernity as slave laborers or later as cooperative "employees" of the institutions of colonization (for example, temporary allies against other enemies, native colonial administrators, and the national bourgeoisie).

In Shakespeare's *The Tempest* in particular, Fernández Retamar suggests, the figure of the Carib-cannibal anagramatically became Caliban, and the figure of the Arauaco became Ariel.[56] In Fernández Retamar's reading, Caliban, the colonized subject who resists his subjection to the end and suffers dearly for it, is opposed to the airy and sublime Ariel, a cooperative slave who, through his "peaceful, meek, and even timorous" ways, is awarded his freedom by his master Prospero. Fernández Retamar calls on us to read for the appearance of this couplet in colonial discourse and to at-tend to its role in discourses and practices of colonization. Though he gives credit to Latin American revolutionaries and intellectuals such as Jose Martí and Simón Bolívar, among others,[57] Fernández Retamar's own reading helped to initiate a series of efforts to reclaim Caliban as a figure for resistance in the midst of colonialism and neocolonialism.[58] Though his very ability to speak is subjected to Prospero's mastery in *The Tempest*, Caliban continues to resist Prospero and thus, for Fernández Retamar, becomes the sign of the possibility of using the language and practices of the colonizer against colonization.

The appearance of Ariel in *Memoirs of Carwin* is all the more interesting given Fernández Retamar's reading of the Carib-Caliban and Arauaco-Ariel couplet. As we have seen, Mohawks came to be known as cannibals by colonists in North America, and the very name "Mohock" acquired many of the associations the Carib-Caliban figure did. Thus, when Carwin cannot help but intervene in the garden party's scene of rapture, by making Ariel sing another song, we must keep track of the echoes of the Caliban-Mohock figure. The scene continues:

> The pause continued, when a strain was wafted to our ears from another quarter. . . . The sound proceeded from above. At first it was faint and scarcely audible; presently it reached a louder key, and every eye was cast up in expectation of beholding a face among the pedant clusters. The strain was easily recognised, for it was no other than that which Ariel is made to sing when finally absolved from the service of the wizard.
>
> > *In the Cowslips bell I lie,*
> > *On the Bat's back I do fly . . .*
> > *After summer merrily, &c.*
>
> Their hearts palpitated as they listened: they gazed at each other for a solution of the mystery. At length the strain died away at distance, and an interval of silence was succeeded by an earnest discussion of the cause of this prodigy. One supposition only could be adopted, which was, that the strain was uttered by human organs. That the songster was stationed on the roof of the arbour, and having finished his melody had risen into the viewless fields of air. (297–98) (Brown's ellipses)

Carwin chooses to sing the song Ariel sings when Prospero announces his intention to set Ariel free (act 5, scene 1, lines 86–87: "Quickly, spirit!/ Thou shalt ere long be free").[59] By choosing this song, Carwin once again assimilates the "Mohock savage" by turning the colonized subject into an object for wonder. What is more, he has now rewritten "the shrill tones of a Mohock savage," the Brownian figuration of Caliban, as the "peaceful, meek, and even timorous" Ariel; in *The Tempest*, after Ariel sings this song, Prospero replies, "Why, that's my dainty Ariel!" (act 5, scene 1, line 95). More so than even *The Tempest*, *Memoirs of Carwin* completely displaces the figure of Caliban. Carwin develops the Caliban-Mohock into Ariel, just as he has developed his biloquial skill since his first encounter with the echo in the rocky passage. From cannibalistic and savage Caliban-Mohock to sublime Ariel, Carwin performs a forceful rewriting of the text of colonialism in the Americas by formalizing a figure for the troubling and resistive colonized subject, and all that "by no violent transition" (297).

Of course, Carwin's performance turns Ariel from a pure object of enrapture to an object of enrapture and wonder, even superstition, among the guests at the garden part, and this biloquial performance later causes problems for Carwin. The guests initially seem thrown into an extremely rational consideration of the mysterious voice: "an earnest discussion of the cause of this prodigy." In turn, this extreme rationalism paradoxically precipitates a renewed superstition: "That the songster . . . had risen into the viewless fields of air." This extreme and unstable rationalism at the heart of the modernizing narrative can once again be read as Brown's critique of the dangers of modernization and the dissolution of traditional, institutional constraints. In fact, this garden party becomes the occasion for Carwin to meet Ludloe, a Godwinian character who leads Carwin into increasingly elaborate perils throughout the rest of *Memoirs of Carwin*, as I will discuss in the next section. Carwin's biloquism leads him out of his family's provincial existence and into a thoroughly modern and cosmopolitan world, a freedom of movement figured by the song Carwin invokes from *The Tempest*, which actually reads: "Where the bee sucks, there suck I, / In a cowslip's bell I lie; / There I couch when owls do cry. / On the bat's back I do fly / After summer merrily. / Merrily, merrily shall I live now, / Under the blossom that hangs on the bough" (act 5, scene 1, lines 88–94). Yet *Memoirs of Carwin* increasingly depicts the dangers of such moderni- zation. In effect, biloquism becomes a figure for such dangers as *Memoirs of Carwin* becomes a cautionary tale of modernity's excesses.[60]

However, this cautionary tale does not extend to America's white settler colonial history, nor to U.S. colonial policy toward the Iroquois at the turn of the nineteenth century. For *prior* to Brown's use of biloquism to critique modernization, *Memoirs of Carwin* turns the echo of "a Mohock savage" into Ariel. That is, it is not the trouble- some Caliban who appears and spooks the garden party audience into a superstitious fear that questions the very possibility of culture's universal communicability. Rather, it is Carwin's mastered Caliban, the airy Ariel whose enslavement is utterly erased in *Memoirs of Carwin*, displaced by aesthetic rapture and scientific mastery. If Caliban had spoken through Carwin, the assimilation of the figure of the Mohock might have been troubled by unassimilated "savagery." Yet the Brownian critique of modernity is not voiced by the colonized Caliban-Mohock, and so cannot question America's white settler colonial formation. Rather, by assimilating the "Mohock savage" into Carwin's "character" and transforming that character into biloquism, *Memoirs of Carwin* con- structs an early American debate between white settler traditionism and white settler modernity, a debate enjoined by Brown's critics ever since. The very terms of that debate are themselves made possible by Brown's allegory of assimilation and transfor- mation. Perhaps Brown's text explicitly urges us, in Davidson's terms, to take our pick between America the corrupt and America the beautiful. However, we must also learn to read carefully and critically for the echo of the racialized condition of possibility for that choice itself.[61]

Finally, the difference between "the Iroquois" and "that Iroquois *sachem*" in *The Critique of Judgement* can be read. Recalling the passages, Kant writes:

> And thus, no doubt, at first only charms, e.g. colours for painting oneself (roucou among the Caribs and cinnabar among the Iroquois), or flowers, sea-shells, beautifully coloured feathers, then, in the course of time, also beautiful forms (as in canoes, wearing-apparel, &c.) which convey no gratification, i.e. delight of enjoyment, become of moment in so- ciety and attract a considerable interest. (155–56)

> If any one asks me whether I consider that the palace I see before me is beautiful . . . I may reply in the same strain as that Iroquois *sachem* who said that nothing in Paris pleased him better than the eating-houses. (43)

Hierarchies within Iroquois communities reappear, through the lens of a European philosopher, as the difference between an Iroquois leader in Paris (who, though not refined and not even critical, can humorously encounter and even comment on a

European eating house) and common Iroquois, who do not even exist in the same epoch as civilized man, and who are linked to Columbus's name for El Gran Carib Island's unwelcoming inhabitants: "the Caribs." Ariel is welcome to eat in Paris, but Caliban must never even go there. The question of beauty can only be posed once "Caliban" becomes "Ariel," once "the Iroquois" becomes "that Iroquois *sachem,*" once "a Mohock savage" becomes the sublime voice of a biloquized Ariel. In turn, the question of biloquism's value can only be debated with civilized terms like *tradition* and *modernity* if the assimilation of that "Mohock savage" remains forgotten.

The Biloquial Picaresque

How can we read the critique of modernization toward which *Memoirs of Carwin* seems to move if it—like the very discursive practices of modernization in the United States around 1800—is made possible by the assimilation and reiterated mastery of the "Mohock savage"? As it attempts to chart the course of a critical allegory without directly addressing the foundational figure of the "Mohock savage," *Memoirs of Carwin* spins out of control, as if it were haunted by that foundational figure.

The last half of *Memoirs of Carwin* focuses on the relationship between Carwin and Ludloe, and in particular on Ludloe's efforts to involve Carwin in a secret society with a utopian scheme to start a Godwinian community on a remote Pacific island. It is, however, somewhat absurd to say that the rest of this novel "focuses" on anything. After the garden party scene, *Memoirs of Carwin* veers into a dense thicket of plots, subplots, and themes through which the reader is pulled at breathtaking speed—until all comes to a screeching halt with the novel's truncated conclusion. Consider the plot of the novel's final sixty pages.

After the garden party, Carwin's aunt dies and her will names her servant Dorthy as "her sole and universal heir" (299). On the verge of using his biloquism to imitate his dead aunt's voice and frighten Dorthy into giving him some of his aunt's riches, Carwin meets Ludloe. Ludloe promptly showers Carwin with attention and affection, as well as lessons in his vaguely Godwinian philosophy of "absolute equality," elitist anticapitalism, radical individualism, and ends-justify-the-means morality. Carwin implicitly falls in love with Ludloe, and readily agrees to Ludloe's suggestion that the two travel to Ireland, Ludloe's homeland, especially since Ludloe promises to pay for all of Carwin's expenses. In Dublin, the two continue to discuss books, politics, and morality, and then decide that Carwin must travel to Spain to improve himself, since "books alone were insufficient to impart knowledge" (311). While in Spain, Carwin adopts Catholicism and practices his biloquism frequently. Carwin and Ludloe continue their discussions by mail, though Carwin never reveals his biloquial skill. When Carwin serendipitously expresses his own interest in pursuing a utopian scheme modeled on the English colonization of North America and the Jesuit colonization of South America—though avoiding the "erroneous notions" (318) of each—Ludloe immediately calls Carwin back to Dublin.

Ludloe then reveals that he is a member of a secret, fraternal society involved in just such a utopian scheme, and offers Carwin entrance into the society on two conditions: that he never reveal the society's existence to anyone else; and that he give to Ludloe a "confession" that discloses "every fact in his history, and every secret of his heart" (324). Any violations of either of these conditions would be punished by death. While Carwin struggles with whether to reveal his biloquism during this confession, Ludloe suddenly urges Carwin to marry Mrs. Bennington, a widow and a relative of Ludloe, in order to attain social and economic stability adequate to involvement in the secret society—even though, as Ludloe explains, marriage may well be sexual slavery for women. The two thus formulate a scheme to effect this marriage. After nearly accidentally killing a woman whom he attempts to save from robbers by using his biloquism—and discovering later that this woman was none other than Mrs. Bennington—Carwin begins his confession, having decided that he will not reveal his biloquism. After confessing for hours, Ludloe tells Carwin that he has made important omissions, and that Carwin must begin again, since "The whole truth can only be disclosed after numerous and repeated conversations" (354). The novel breaks off with Carwin about to meet Mrs. Bennington, unsure over whether to confess his biloquism, and in a state of bewilderment over Ludloe's power.

The excess and ambivalence of this part of the novel offer a striking example of what Cathy Davidson has called the "picaresque novel in early America," which

> overflows its own ostensible boundaries, brimming with unreconciled contradictions, with simultaneous pictures of different Americas imposed one upon the other, and even with different constructs of the cosmos all concurrently entertained. Its whole is both more and less than the sum of its parts. Indeed, the picaresque always contains a surplus of its own measure and that excess is its margin of safety.
>
> The picaresque constructs its own politics or *polis*, a crazy quilt of American attitudes and practices. The loosest subgenre of all, it hovers ever on the edge of a formalistic collapse under the burden of its own inclusiveness. (164)

Indeed, when Carwin travels to Spain—the land of the picaresque's origins—he performs this genre to perfection. As he wanders from Barcelona to Sevilla, he encounters various people and places, engaging in biloquial misadventures but pursuing no particular goal: "Man was the chief subject of my study, and the social sphere that in which I principally moved; but I was not inattentive to inanimate nature, nor unmindful of the past" (312).

For Davidson, the mobilities that characterize the early American picaresque on the level of form as well as the level of plot are restricted to male characters, and as a result are decidedly gendered: "The female simply does not have the same freedoms—to journey, to judge, to have her judgments heeded—as does the male, and that is a fact of picaresque fiction almost as much as it is a fact of sentimental fiction" (179). Yet *Memoirs of Carwin* complicates Davidson's account. The homosocial relationship between Ludloe and Carwin sexualizes the picaresque in ways that exceed the binary between male freedom and female unfreedom. When the Mrs. Bennington subplot intervenes to mediate this relationship and apparently restore a gendered order, Ludloe and Carwin explicitly discuss marriage as a form of sexual slavery. Thus, rather than being just an instance of a genre that posits a gendered freedom, *Memoirs of Carwin* explicitly thematizes the volatile sexualizing and gendering of freedom. That is, the very themes of fraternal desire and women's rights emerge within *Memoirs of Carwin*'s ambivalent but skeptical allegory of modernization. How do we account for the fact that the picaresque form of *Memoirs of Carwin* opens up the very questions that Davidson says the early American picaresque tends to foreclose?[62]

In Carwin's relationship with Ludloe, Brown condenses a dizzying array of the period's overlapping, conservative concerns. As a dangerous Irishman who travels freely between Ireland and the United States, Ludloe figures nativist positions on immigration. As an advocate of a radically egalitarian secret society, a critic of marriage as "sexual slavery," and a morally unscrupulous character tied to an Ireland-Spain axis, Ludloe figures conspiratorial views about the influence of Catholicism, Illuminatism, Masonry, and Jacobinism on the American masses. As a powerful man who deftly brings Carwin under his psychological control and toward his fraternal society, Ludloe figures the period's widespread fears over the desires let loose by unrestricted fraternity—fears examined so carefully by Dana D. Nelson in *National Manhood*.[63] Finally, as a foreigner who enlists the naive Carwin in his political schemes, Ludloe figures the vulnerability of the United States as an aspiring imperial power becoming an independent player in the world system. Brown's apparent inability to settle even on a spelling of Ludloe's name—he shifts back and forth between "Ludloe" and "Ludlow" throughout the novel—offers an immediate index of the ambivalence condensed into this character.

Throughout all these concerns, however, biloquism functions as a consistent if volatile center of gravity. The text suggests, without ever explicitly stating, that as a guest at the garden party Ludloe found out about Carwin's biloquism and that, in turn, Ludloe sees it as a powerful resource for his secret society's efforts to enlist mass support as well as a way of keeping Carwin under his control. At first a figure for the assimilation and reiterative mastery of the Indian, after the garden party biloquism becomes a figure for Carwin's vulnerability to Ludloe and all his dangers. This shift effectively maps a national terrain. Having first figured the consolidation of a domestic space through the assimilation and mastery of Indian "savagery," biloquism then figures the vulnerability of that domestic space to a foreign space of social and political radicalism. Indeed, the novel takes a decidedly international turn with the introduction of Ludloe after the garden party, as if to allegorize supposedly naive America's emergence onto the international scene. In turn, biloquism transposes those geographic borders onto the citizen-subject by depicting Carwin as a character literally inhabited by a power that makes his own naive desires vulnerable to the manipulative, radical, foreign, homosocial desires of Ludloe. As a figure of internal and external borders under multiple threats, biloquism seems to make Carwin's borders vulnerable to all that Ludloe represents.

Though he often expresses his desire for Ludloe ("I felt myself removed to a comfortless and chilling distance from Ludloe. I wanted to share in his occupations and views" [309]), Carwin nonetheless resists that desire, and the figure for his resistance is his biloquism ("I persisted in the resolution of concealing *one thing*" [348]). Though

Ludloe often professes his own love of Carwin ("I love you. The first impulse of my love is to dissuade you from seeking to know more" about the secret society [322]) he also makes Carwin's total confession a condition of that love ("I cannot be deceived; and let sincerity be henceforth the rule of your conduct toward me, not merely because it is right, but because concealment is impossible" [354]). Consequently, after the first round of confession, in which Carwin has failed to mention his biloquism, Ludloe reiterates his total commitment to Carwin and again implores him to reveal any further secrets he may have hidden. Carwin muses in response: "You cannot easily conceive the emphatical solemnity with which this was spoken. Had he fixed piercing eyes on me while he spoke; had I perceived him watching my looks, and labouring to penetrate my secret thoughts, I should doubtless have been ruined" (352). Clearly, Carwin must reveal his biloquism in order to secure his relationship with Ludloe, to enter Ludloe's fraternal organization, and to realize his utopian society's "growth into a nation" (317). However, the text also suggests that Carwin would never have desired that relationship, longed for that organization, or imagined that society if his biloquism had not spurred Ludloe's interest in the first place. As Carwin explains, Ludloe was adept at covertly forming Carwin's desires: "It was his [Ludloe's] business to make every new step appear to be suggested by my own reflections" (311).

The homosocial desires circulating between Carwin and Ludloe become so unwieldy, however, that they solicit further control. Consequently, the subplot involving Mrs. Bennington invokes the exchange of women; says Ludloe, "The marriage I now propose to you is desireable, because it will make you independent of me" (333). Indeed, the text explicitly thematizes this exchange, allowing Ludloe and Carwin to debate whether marriage is an unjust institution, a woman's "contract of servitude" to a man; as Ludloe declares, "This relation is *sexual*. Your slave is a woman; and the bond, which transfers her property and person to you, is. . . . *marriage*" (331; Brown's ellipsis). Ludloe sets aside this critique of marriage, however, in the name of the wealth and independence it will give Carwin—wealth and independence that will facilitate his involvement in the fraternal organization. The marriage, as a heteronormative container for Carwin's sexual desire, thus allows Carwin to enter the fraternal society with merely fraternal desires.

Carwin, on the other hand, is not sure what to believe, since he "had never had any intellectual or sentimental connection with the sex" and consequently "was accustomed to regard the physical and sensual consequences of the sexual relation as realities, and every thing intellectual, disinterested, and heroic, which enthusiasts connect with it as idle dreams" (334). Inexperienced, Carwin is open to suggestions—in this case Ludloe's suggestions—on matters of love and marriage: "I am yet a stranger to the secret, on the preservation of which so much stress is laid, and it will be optional with me to receive it or not" (334). Fearful of the "danger" women may pose, Carwin nonetheless "resolved to see the lady" on Ludloe's urging (334–35).

By associating a radical critique of marriage with a character who is so unprincipled that he is willing to put aside the critique for his own gain, the text makes the critique itself suspect. Even more, however, the text again suggests that Carwin's biloquism, desired by Ludloe, has led him deeper into unscrupulous territory—the territory of Ludloe's radical critique and unprincipled behavior, the one inseparable from the other. In fact, it is biloquism that initially links Carwin to Mrs. Bennington. While taking a stroll one evening, Carwin stumbles into a group of thieves robbing a woman in her carriage. When he uses his biloquism to scare the robbers away, he also causes the thieves to fire a pistol that, in turn, scares the woman's horses. Carwin later finds out that he "did more harm than good," as the woman, who was none other than Mrs. Bennington, was injured by the horses: "What an ill-omened interference was mine!" Carwin laments (338). Carwin's guilt over this biloquial mishap seems to lure him further into Ludloe's marriage scheme by making Carwin feel responsible for the injured Mrs. Bennington.

According to *Memoirs of Carwin*, then, the excessive energy and power of Ludloe's fraternal desire, his secret society, and his critique of marriage derive from the figure of biloquism. Without Carwin's biloquial skill, the text suggests, Ludloe would never have taken an interest in Carwin, would never have tried to lure him into his secret society, and would never have urged him both to enter into a marriage and to acknowledge marriage's injustice. Consequently, the text implies that to escape from these perils Carwin must control his biloquism to such an extent that it loses its ambivalent status as at once in him and other than him. Were Carwin fully to incorporate those "shrill tones of a Mohock savage," making them one with his voice rather than a volatile double of his voice, finally integrating the other into a mastered self, he would be shored up against all that threatens his integrity. *Memoirs of Carwin*'s anxious and furious excesses reveal a frustrated desire that motivates the terms of Brown's critique of modernization: a desire for the conclusion of white settler colonialism, a desire for the complete assimilation of those "shrill tones of a Mohock savage." *Memoirs of Carwin* figures excessive fraternal desire and unscrupulous foreign radicalism as modern threats to the new and naive nation-state and citizen-subject by deriving those threats from a discrete and identifiable source: biloquism, itself a figure for the incomplete white settler colonial assimilation of the Indian. The text's complicated intertwining of multiple themes and plot twists generates an array of conservative fears, and then derives those fears from white settler colonialism's unfinished business.

I would like to return to Kant once more before I conclude this chapter. In a footnote to her reading of the *Critique of Judgement*, Gayatri Chakravorty Spivak writes that in Sarah Koffman, Genevieve Lloyd, and Beverley Brown's reading of Kant, "The treatment of (the theme and figure of) woman is shown to be demonstrated abundantly by Kant's text, even if often in the ruse of disavowal. As I hope to show, the figure of the 'native informant' is, by contrast, foreclosed. Rhetorically crucial at the most important moment in the argument, it is not part of the argument in any way. Was it in this rift that the seeds of the civilizing mission of today's universalist feminism were sown?"[64] In other words, Koffman, Lloyd, and Brown show how Kant invokes woman in order to distance her from man's capacity for judgment. Kant disavows woman in the sense that he invokes her in order to argue against her inclusion within the sphere of reason, thereby refusing to recognize the challenge she presents to man represented as the normative subject. For Spivak, however, Kant distances "the figure of the 'native informant'" in a more absolute way. She shows how Kant's apparently incidental invocations of "New Hollanders" and "Tierra del Fuegans"—we could add "Iroquois" and the "Iroquois *sachem*"—exclude "the native" or "man in the raw" from the subjectivity in question in the *Critique of Judgement* without ever offering an explicit argument to that effect. The "native" is man before culture, and so is not yet a full subject. This "native," though "rhetorically crucial," is represented as incidental to the question of judgment. The "native" is foreclosed, then, in the sense that it is excluded from the symbolic world of subjectivity altogether—so excluded that there is no need to articulate an argument for that exclusion, as there is a need to articulate an argument for woman's distance from judgment.[65]

With her question at the end of this passage, Spivak suggests that feminism capitalizes on the difference between disavowal and foreclosure when it sets out to win the argument for inclusion in the exercise of reason without considering how that argument will continue to foreclose the "native." Feminism may win inclusion for woman alongside man, but that reason may still be one that forecloses "natives" until they conform to the universal of civility. Included in civility, women are also enlisted in universality's "civilizing mission," its multiform efforts to remake or eliminate "natives" locked in uncivilized particularism.

By thematizing women's rights in *Memoirs of Carwin*, Brown returns to a question he had already examined in *Alcuin: A Dialogue* (1798), leaving Brownian critics to debate for years what Brown's position on this political issue of his day really was.[66] Yet *Memoirs of Carwin's* explicit thematization of women's rights also emerges from what we could call, with Spivak, the foreclosure of the figure of the "Mohock savage," its reiterative assimilation and mastery by Carwin's biloquism. Thus, any interpretation of Brown's truncated allegory of gender in *Memoirs of Carwin* must consider how both a Brownian critique of gender inequality and a Brownian caution against the excesses of such a critique share a "civilizing mission."

By attending to the biloquial echoes of those "shrill tones of a Mohock savage," I hope to have reframed the terms in which Brown's work has long been set. With the figure of biloquism, *Memoirs of Carwin* makes the mastery and assimilation of the Indian the condition of possibility for its allegorical comparison of traditional and modern values. The text thus opens and sustains a debate on the advantages and perils of modernization in America by attempting to close down any critical consideration of white settler colonialism. When we engage in the former debate on its own terms—by, for instance, considering whether *Memoirs of Carwin* is for or against nativism, for or against women's rights—we implicate ourselves in the foreclosure of the latter. By tracing the deep and constitutive relationships between the assimilative drive of white settler colonialism and the emergence of a national debate over modernization, we reframe the latter debate within the racial and national conditions of its emergence.

Motivated by a reading of the figure of "a Mohock savage," I have offered an argument about a historically specific articulation of aesthetics with politics. Strictly speaking, however, this is a forced reading, even an impossible reading. It is forced because in order to argue for the articulation of aesthetics with politics I move across registers, back and forth from the literary historical to the literary to the philosophical to the political. It is impossible because the figure that both motivates the reading and toward which the reading moves is, precisely, a figure, and though figures may be a part of some now accepted understandings of literature, they are not properly a part of literary history, philosophy, or politics. Even if figures were accepted in such disciplines, in a certain sense this reading would still be impossible because figures by definition turn from the truth, and so cannot strictly speaking ever found a turn toward the truth, even my attempt to turn toward a historically specific articulation of aesthetics with politics. In a sense, then, my switching of registers both enables this reading and covers over its impossibility. As Derrida emphasizes, "There is no politics without 'action' or without an 'active' text," and so because of my reading's foundation in the figure of "a Mohock savage" and despite its movement toward a historically specific articulation of aesthetics with politics, the very notions of a "figure" and of "politics" make that articulation perpetually dis- and rearticulable, beyond any claims to hermeneutic or historical closure. Such dis-and rearticulations—"the political" in a most radical sense—at once give possibility and impossibility to my reading. Finally, before even these impossibilities is the impossibility of using a figure such as "a Mohock savage" as a foundation for a reading of that which it is an effect: a reading of white settler colonialism and the articulation of aesthetics with politics.[67] To its end, then, this chapter provokes the tension between aesthetics and politics.

CHAPTER 4

Ambivalent Alliance: The U.S.–Mexico War and the Caste War of Yucatán

LAGUNA, March 25, 1848.

DEAR COMMODORE: I send you an official despatch *[sic]*, by which you will see that things are daily getting worse in Yucatan, and that the Spanish race is about abandoning the country to the *aborigines.* I shall do all I can for the preservation of lives. Property has already been abandoned by these miserable fugitives. Why could not a few thousand troops, who will remain idle during the armistice, be sent here to "roll back the tide of victory?" The war-whoop of these ruthless Indians would have no terrors to those who have conquered the red men of our own territory. I sincerely believe that three thousand of our troops, either regulars or volunteers, would, in a month, with the *prestige* which they possess, drive every Indian in Yucatan into the bay of Honduras. I hope you will approve of my course, and that I shall soon see the "Scorpion" again, and hear from you.

Please give my regards to Captain Mackenzie, and believe me as, sir, truly yours,

A. BIGELOW.

Commodore Perry.

P.S—A subscription is now going on among the inhabitants of this place to send up barges with provisions to relieve these unfortunates.

Letter from Commander A. Bigelow to Commodore M. C. Perry

*A*s we saw in the previous chapter, when Carwin turned his superstitious "terrors" into the "delight" of biloquism by mastering "the shrill tones of a Mohock savage," abstract equality among U.S. citizens was dependent upon the forcible assimilation of Indian particularity. Charles Brockden Brown's turn-of-the-century flashpoint was thus characterized by materially and representationally violent efforts to modernize the Indian. In the epigraph to this chapter, when Commander A. Bigelow, senior U.S. naval officer at the port of Laguna de Términos in the Mexican state of Yucatán, calls on Commodore Matthew Perry, who was commanding the Home Squadron in the Gulf of Mexico, to send U.S. troops to defend Yucatecan Creoles against a massive Maya insurgency, he unwittingly marks a transformation in U.S. citizenship. By arrogantly declaring that "The war-whoop of these ruthless Indians would have no terrors to those who have conquered the red men of our own territory," Bigelow suggests that, by the flashpoint Michael Rogin has called "the American 1848," Brownian modernization efforts had long since been abandoned.[1] Between 1815 and 1848, the assimilative logic of civilization policy largely gave way to a policy of eradication: war, removal, and reservations. As Reginald Horsman has carefully shown, by 1830 "neither the mass of the American people nor the political leaders of the country believed that the Indians could be melded into American society."[2] Whereas to Carwin "the shrill tones of a Mohock savage" were sounds worthy of imitation and mastery, to Bigelow an Indian "war-whoop" is neither terrifying nor powerful nor admirable; it is always already "conquered," utterly debased, thoroughly uncivilized and uncivilizable.

However, Bigelow's letter still carries a trace of civilization policy's assimilative logic. When he distinguishes "the Spanish race" from *"aborigines,"* Bigelow stops short of characterizing the Yucatecan Creoles as white, blending the centuries-old Black Legend—which set Spaniards off from European white civility—with early nineteenth-century accounts of Mexicans as a "mongrel" people, part Spanish and part Indian.[3] The Mexican nation is racially bifurcated in this letter: Spanish-almost-white and aboriginal nonwhite. In turn, Bigelow's patronizing references to "miserable fugitives" and "unfortunates," who too readily abandon their property in the face of "these ruthless Indians," make the Yucatecan Creoles seem like underdeveloped juveniles in need of tutoring from fearless U.S. whites. Bigelow appears to imagine that by "driving every Indian in Yucatan into the bay of Honduras," the United States will help the Yucatecan Creoles develop white civility. Seen from the Yucatán, it would seem that "the American 1848" has not so much rejected assimilative logic for eradicative logic, as Rogin and Horsman suggest, as it has blended elements of both logics.[4]

When Bigelow asks "Why could not a few thousand troops, who will remain idle during the armistice, be sent here," he places this blend in a precise context. "The armistice" to which he refers is the cessation of hostilities in the U.S.–Mexico War with the preliminary signing of the Treaty of Guadalupe Hidalgo on February 2, 1848. By March 25, when the letter was written, the U.S. Congress, the Mexican Chamber of Deputies, and the Mexican Senate had already voted to ratify slightly different versions of the treaty. With the U.S. military occupying Mexico City, all sides awaited the exchange of ratifications and final negotiations, which would take place in Querétaro on May 26.[5] As Bigelow's letter makes clear, however, this armistice was hardly a peaceful period in Mexico. Since mid-1847, Yucatán had been embroiled in the largest and, ultimately, perhaps the most successful Indian uprising in the postconquest history of the Americas: the so-called Caste War of 1847. What began as a factional conflict between Yucatecan Creoles who wanted independence from Mexico and those who wanted to remain a state within Mexico had, by 1847, turned into a race war of these two, hastily united factions against the Maya majority who had long been oppressed by Spanish and then Creole minority rule.

Petitioned by Yucatán Commissioner Justo Sierra O'Reilly to come to the aid of "the white race" in Yucatán, President Polk sought congressional approval for aid to the Creoles, including U.S. military occupation of the peninsula with an eye to eventual annexation. Yet Sierra and Polk's efforts met resistance in a U.S. Congress confused about the racial and national status of these Yucatecan Creoles. In fact, for much of the spring of 1848, debates raged in Congress and the U.S. press about the Creoles' status and, in turn, about the racial and national form of U.S. citizenship. Was it in the interest of U.S. citizens to aid citizens of Yucatán? How were the citizens of Yucatán different from the Mexican citizens with whom the United States was still technically at war or from the untrustworthy Spanish citizens of the Black Legend? For that matter, who *were* the citizens of Yucatán? As many in the United States pointed out, the Maya had themselves been granted citizenship rights after Mexican independence in 1821, and if at least some Creoles were racially mixed, how exactly were Maya to be distinguished from Creoles? If U.S. aid led to the annexation of Yucatán, would the United States find itself incorporating hundreds of thousands of savage Indians and not-quite-civilized Creoles who expected citizenship rights? Just as most Americans had come to the conclusion that Indians north of the Rio Grande had to be "removed" rather than "civilized," that Indians and whites were fundamentally and eternally different, that the rights of white citizens depended upon the explicit denial of Indian rights, the possibility of U.S. intervention in the Caste War cast that conclusion in doubt. Consequently, the conjuncture of the U.S.–Mexico War and the Caste War reproduced a deep ambiguity in the racial and national form of U.S. citizenship.

Though the idea of full-scale military occupation died, informal U.S. aid—including arms and hundreds of volunteer U.S. soldiers—did reach the Creoles, helping them to accomplish some of what Commander Bigelow envisioned: it rescued the Creoles from the brink of annihilation and exile, rolling back the tide of Maya victory just enough to let the Creoles reoccupy the north and west of the peninsula. Far from being driven into the Bay of Honduras, however, the Maya effectively destroyed the peninsula's exploitative sugar industry, and held the eastern forest zone for another sixty years, until the Mexican Revolution.

Thus, as the U.S.–Mexico War fed into the Caste War, an ambivalent and uneven alliance formed. Yucatecan Creoles, who saw themselves as civilized whites engaged in a race war against savage Indians, were aided by the United States in their war against the Maya. Yet, as we see from Bigelow's letter, while many in the United States also saw the Maya as savage Indians, most saw the Creoles as not fully civilized and not quite white. In turn, this ambivalent alliance between U.S. whites and Yucatecan Creoles effectively foreshadowed the uneven economic development that would emerge from the Caste War. As we will see, in lieu of formal occupation and annexation, the U.S. government and U.S. businesses turned to informal aid for and, eventually, private investment in Yucatán, which turned out to be much less costly and more profitable than direct occupation and annexation. In effect, the Caste War of 1847 taught U.S. capital the advantages of neocolonial development over colonial development.

In this chapter, I examine this articulation of the U.S.–Mexico War and the Caste War. I argue that the Caste War provoked a dilemma for U.S. citizenship, a dilemma dramatized by Bigelow's ambivalent blend of racial assimilation and eradication: how far and in what manner can U.S. citizenship extend its reach? I trace the emergence and management of this dilemma from three interlinked archives: first, U.S. and Mexican government documents on the Caste War; second, the explosion of U.S. popular fiction about the war during the 1840s and 1850s; and third, the Treaty of Guadalupe

Hidalgo, particularly article 9 of the treaty, which promises "all the rights of citizens" to Mexicans annexed by the United States.

As a number of literary critics, historians, and legal scholars have argued in recent years, the Civil War has long overshadowed the U.S.–Mexico War in nineteenth-century scholarship.[6] These critics have shown how the U.S.–Mexico War was not simply a trial run for the Civil War, how it was not a war fought primarily over slavery, and how it did not only affect black and white racial formations. Rather, the U.S.–Mexico War foregrounds differential relationships among multiple racial, national, gender, and class formations forged in part by U.S. expansionism. Building on this scholarship, I want to suggest that recent attention to the U.S.–Mexico War itself has overshadowed not simply the Caste War, but particularly the constitutive relationship *between* the U.S.–Mexico War and the Caste War. This overshadowing has resulted in an erasure of a crucial flashpoint in mid-nineteenth-century North America, a transnational flashpoint that had two crucial effects on U.S. citizenship: it transformed U.S. imperialism from white settler colonialism to neocolonialism, and it produced white, Indian, Mexican, and, eventually, Chicano racial formations that blended the assimilative mode of civilization policy with the eradicative mode of removal policy.

My readings of these three archives suggest that the U.S.–Mexico War can no longer be considered just a "border war," either in the geographic sense of the territories wrested from Mexico and annexed by the United States, or in the metaphorical sense of the subsequent, racially and nationally hybrid identity formations produced in annexed California, Texas, New Mexico, and Arizona. Rather, these archives bear witness to the complex, hemispheric interplay between social conflict in the United States and social conflict in Mexico, conflict that reached beyond the emerging U.S.–Mexico border to the Yucatán peninsula. To the extent that this border paradigm has represented Chicanos as sharing the same history of subjugation to U.S. imperialism as that of Mexican citizens or indeed all Latinos, it must be revised by a transnational, hemispheric paradigm that takes into account the war's subjection of Chicanos, their subordination by the power of white nationalism and their production as formally enfranchised subjects of U.S. imperialism. That is, a crucial consequence of moving beyond the border paradigm is the recognition that Mexican Americans and later Chicanos have been at once racially excluded from full participation in U.S. citizenship and enfranchised, albeit ambivalently, on the imperial side of the international division of labor.

As I argue toward the end of the chapter, this articulation of race, nation, and equality is most strikingly figured by article 9 of the Treaty of Guadalupe Hidalgo. Though article 9 has often been understood as a broken promise due to the postwar history of discrimination against Mexican Americans and Chicanos, both that discrimination and the postwar, neocolonial relationship between Mexico and the United States might more precisely be understood as the paradoxical fulfillment of article 9's promise. Read in the context of contemporaneous government documents and the novelettes, article 9 can be seen to articulate a racially and nationally codified equality. Thus, in promising to recognize Mexicans annexed by the United States as fellow citizens equal on the national stage, article 9 offers them a formal and abstract equality whose universality is conditioned upon assimilation to white nationality. In turn, in promising to recognize Mexico as a fellow nation-state equal on the world stage, the treaty as a whole offers Mexicans a formal and abstract equality whose universality is conditioned upon dependent, comprador status in the world-economy. The Treaty of Guadalupe Hidalgo's promise of "all the rights of citizens" is, in effect, fulfilled by the incessantly reiterated demands of racial assimilation, presented to Mexican Americans and Chicanos, and national compradorization, presented to Mexican citizens, precisely because that promise offers a restricted equality conditioned upon racial and national codification.

I begin this chapter with a brief account of the Caste War itself. I then interpret each of these three archives—the Caste War documents, the novelettes, and the treaty—explaining how they bear witness to the impact the articulation of the U.S.–Mexico War and the Caste War had on U.S. citizenship.

Articulating the Wars

A series of economic and political transformations brought Yucatán to its 1847 flashpoint.[7] Between Mexican independence in 1821 and the beginning of the Caste War in 1847, relatively large-scale, commercial agriculture spread from the northwest of the Yucatán peninsula to much of the region, incorporating new sectors into an extensive, diversified economy supplemented by a strong subsistence base. This transformation had a markedly negative impact on the large and diverse Maya communities of the Yucatán peninsula. Though the Maya had been deeply integrated in and transformed by the capitalist world-economy over the centuries since the conquest, this early nineteenth-century period saw a new and vigorous attack on Maya social and economic practices. As Gilbert M. Joseph has shown so precisely, the new agroindustries, especially the rapidly spreading sugar industry, imposed a harsher labor regime than the Maya were accustomed to and initiated new and more extensive seizures of land that disrupted the corn production so crucial to Maya subsistence and religion.[8] What is more, whereas Maya in the northwest of the peninsula had long been integrated into Creole-controlled relations of production through cattle and corn industries, the growth of sugar plantations between 1821 and 1847 saw some of the first, direct Creole appropriation of the land and labor force of the so-called frontier Maya in the forests of the peninsula's south and east.

Politically, the Creole elite of Yucatán long held ambivalent and conflictual relations with central Mexican authorities and among themselves, and during the 1830s and 1840s these conflicts broke into open defiance of central Mexico and sometimes violent conflict among Yucatecan elites. In 1846, Governor Miguel Barbachano agreed to join Mexico in the war against the United States, and his decision reignited smoldering tensions between Creole elites in his own seat of power, the capital Mérida, and the state's other major city, Campeche. Unwilling to line up against the United States, whose warships had recently taken Tampico and Veracruz, and with whom Campeche was closely tied through Gulf trade networks, Campechano Creole leader Domingo Barret led a revolt against Barbachano and Mérida, calling for Yucatecan independence and neutrality in the war with the United States. As had often happened in past intra-elite struggles, Barret recruited and armed the peninsula's Maya majority to do much of his fighting, promising to give them relief from discriminatory governmental and religious tax systems. This time, however, the Maya were in a position to press their own demands.

In January 1847, a Maya battalion allied with Barret attacked the regional city of Valladolid. The attack lasted for days, killed most of the city's Creoles, and drove the rest out of the city as refugees. The extent of the destruction went well beyond Barret's tactical goals, and made clear to Creoles on both sides of the conflict that the Maya could exploit Creole factionalism for aims unrelated to the intraelite struggle. In particular, based on letters written from Maya leaders to Creole officials between 1847 and 1852, the Maya seem to have been fighting not only to halt the encroachment of the exploitative sugar industry on the eastern forest zone, but also for the elimination of caste distinctions such as discriminatory church dues and land allotment, debt peonage, and the legally sanctioned physical abuse of Maya by mestizos and Creoles.[9] These demands—which the letters tend to call "*libertad,*" freedom or liberty, rather than equality—are coupled with a demand for a certain Maya autonomy within Yucatán. The Maya call for the elimination of caste distinctions was not, then, a call for mere formal equality, or what Marx would have called "political emancipation,"[10] but rather a call for two different visions of liberty: a liberty from discriminatory codifications of identity and a liberty for the continuing exercise of Maya difference. This is a freedom that is not necessarily conditioned upon assimilation to a normative, Mexican or Yucatecan racial form, and thus could be at odds with Mexico's hegemonic, nineteenth-century racial ideology of *mestizaje* and its complementary romanticization of the Indian as the brave and noble ancestor of the Mexican.[11]

The Creole elite clearly had no interest in Maya concerns, however, and government officials and newspapers began to speak hyperbolically of a full-scale race war brewing on the eastern frontier zone. The Creole factions quickly put aside their differences and organized violent, indiscriminate reprisals against the Maya—even executing Maya caciques who had traditionally defended Creole interests. More than any Maya actions, this Creole response turned the conflict into a "caste" or race war by July 1847. A powerful Maya force, previously armed by the Creoles themselves as well as by British arms dealers in Belize, nearly drove the Creoles and their mestizo allies off the peninsula by May 1848. When the Maya abruptly stopped their assault at the outskirts of Mérida and withdrew their forces—for reasons still unclear—the Creoles counterattacked and, thanks in part to U.S. aid, retook the developed regions in the north and west of the peninsula.[12] Though skirmishes between Creoles and Maya would continue for decades, the Maya rebellion had terminated the spread of sugar plantations to the frontier region of the east and south, and continued to hold off further development in that region until the Mexican Revolution.

As the voice of Yucatecan Creole interests stationed in Washington, D.C., Justo Sierra O'Reilly was the primary lens through which the Polk administration viewed these events. In a series of letters written between November 24, 1847, and June 16, 1848, Sierra sought to drum up support in Washington for the Creoles. Yet Sierra's letters differ markedly from those of other government officials, both Mexican and U.S., stationed in or near Yucatán. These other officials usually try to explain the multi-form racial and national logics of Yucatán by describing Creole and Maya factions, alliances and conflicts with central Mexico, and the variable role of mestizos. These explanations in turn provoke silent or annoyed confusion from U.S. officials more accustomed to the binary racial logics of the United States: white vs. black, civility vs. barbarism. By contrast, Sierra consistently casts the conflict in those stark, bi-nary terms. Read in the context of letters from other government officials in Yucatán, Sierra's letters appear remarkably tactical in their single-minded effort to construct a pan-American whiteness—set against both a pan-American Indian barbarism and the threat of European recolonization—that would be recognized in Washington.

For instance, when Yucatán Secretario General José R. Nicolni wrote to Com-modore Perry on February 1, 1848, he began "with the object of informing you of the state which the atrocious war, declared by the Indians against the other races, has brought on."[13] This opening acknowledgment of a plurality of races in Yucatán ("the other races") foregrounds precisely the racial ambiguity that made the Caste War complicated in the United States, and that Sierra's letters skirt. The letter initially at-tempts to simplify this plurality by frequently distinguishing between the "barbarians" and "'civilization,' whose empire has been attacked," a distinction that reflects the Creole elite's attachment to racialized civility. Yet Nicolni eventually amplifies the am-biguity of racial formations in Yucatán when he tries to explain why his government's troops have been unable to defeat these "barbarians." After declaring that a shortage of troops led the government "to order into active service all the existing (military) militia forces, in order to partially meet the grave exigencies of the moment," Nicolni writes of his troops' failures:

> Your honor, knowing people as you do, cannot be ignorant of the fact that armies can-not be created by improvisation; and that, although enthusiasm may, now and then, lead armed citizens to do prodigies in moments of effervesence, when their valor appears to be indomitable, this exaltation, leading people, as it does, into a state of violence, cannot last long; and, therefore, their valor is like electricity, which can only work with rapidity.
>
> The soldier of this class is of very little use in a long-lasting and tiresome war; in the bush and mountain war, which those barbarians are waging against us.
>
> This class of military people, whose profession is not war; who have no hopes of pro-motion; have other interests; other affections, which, as soon as the enthusiasm is passed, must operate rather too freely upon their spirits; do away with their fortitude; diminish their resignation, and finally lead them to abandon those ranks, in which they do not like to remain any longer. Only those who have no exact idea of human nature will be surprised at those facts.[14]

Where Bigelow saw cowardice in the Yucatecan troops, a cowardice that cast doubt on the racial identity of those troops, Nicolni describes a "class" distinction. Although the fleeting "enthusiasm" and "effervesence" Nicolni sees in his troops certainly can be a drawback in a war fought on the "barbarians'" turf of "bush and mountain," these qualities do not overwhelm his faith in his troops' essential civility. "This class" is still made up of "people" rather than "barbarians"; they are not uncivilized but rather free spirits; their failures are not evidence of savagery but rather "of human nature." Certainly, Nicolni's sense of class is inflected by the nineteenth-century Mexican racial ideology of *mestizaje*, and he likely understood these troops as undercivilized mestizos.[15] However, by foregrounding their "human nature," he signals the Creoles' variegated understanding of racial difference, an understanding that granted civility to *mestizos* in order to emphasize Indian barbarity.

Shortly after Nicolni sent his letter, Commander Bigelow forwarded an article from *La Union*, a newspaper published in Mérida, which explained "that the captain-general and commander of the naval station, informed of the state of this country in consequence of the sanguinary war waged by the Indians against the whites, negroes, and mestizos, had resolved to send a vessel of war, in order to obtain more correct information of the true situation, not only of the Spaniards, but also of the natives and other foreigners residing in Yucatan."[16] The proliferation of racial and, in Nicolni's terms, "class" forms in this article again reflects *mestizaje*. The racial distinctions between "whites," "mestizos," "Spaniards," and "other foreigners" bleed into each other, and the terms cohere as separate categories only provisionally by virtue of a range of shifting cultural practices. Are the "Spaniards" to whom the article refers just "the whites," or are they also "negroes" or "mestizos"? Are the "Spaniards" "foreigners," and who are the "other foreigners"? Similarly, in a letter to Secretary of the Navy John Mason, Commodore Perry enclosed a statement from the governor of the island of Carmen in Yucatán that decried "the cruel war which the Indian population of the department are waging against all those who are not of their race."[17] Although the racial ambiguity of "all those" was self evident, and often entirely unambiguous, to many Yucatecos and Mexicans, it was a source of great confusion for U.S. officials.

This confusion is reflected in a long and detailed letter from A. McKenney to Commodore Perry summarizing the Caste War. Undated, though probably written in mid- to late March 1848, the letter begins by describing the Indians as "a class of serfs," who, after Mexican independence, "were recognized as citizens, enjoying equal rights and immunities with the other races."[18] After blaming central Mexico and its "immoral troops" for imposing "military despotism" and "tyranny" on Yucatán, McKenney proceeds to trace the splits among Creole factions on the peninsula.[19] Though McKenney seeks to establish a fairly clear set of distinctions between tyrannical Mexicans, white Yucatecos, and Indians, his ambiguous reference to "other races" alongside the Indians as well as his references to factions among the Creoles foreshadow the breakdown of his distinctions over the course of the letter.

Once he comes to the Maya offensive of 1847, the racial and national forms of the factions in the Caste War become thoroughly scrambled. The neutrality of Yucatán in the U.S.–Mexico War, he explains, gave pretexts to partizans of General Santa Anna for frequent disorderly movements and pronunciamentos in the capital in favor of Mexico, which, although suffocated by the government troops, have caused immense injuries to the State, demoralizing the people, and producing, finally, the insurrection of the Indians, who were stimulated to these acts of rebellion by the movers of these disorders.

In the mean time, the Indians, encouraged by the division of the whites, and stimulated by a few reprobates (whites) who resided among them, threw off all disguise and boldly took the field, proclaiming destruction to all the other races. Tihosuco was taken, and many of its citizens were inhumanly butchered; and the women after being violated, were carried into hopeless captivity. The town was burnt and razed to the ground, and the most appalling atrocities committed.[20]

It would seem that not only Indians, but also Mexicans—Santa Anna—and whites— the Yucatecan "reprobates (whites)"—can wear the "disguise" of civility in Mexico, for they directly "stimulated" the "Indians . . . to these acts of rebellion." Clearly disgusted at "deserters who abandoned their flag" in the face of Maya offensives, McKenney concludes his letter with a warning: "Among those reputed as whites, there are many of mixed blood whose sympathies are decidedly with the Indians, and there are fears that they may be induced to take part with them, which would render the destruction of the country inevitable."[21] McKenney's initial racial distinctions have been destroyed by the end of this letter, as the referents of "they" and "them" in the phrase "they may be induced to take part with them" are entirely ambiguous. Does he mean that "those reputed as whites" who are really "of mixed blood" will be induced to join the "Indians"? Might those few whites who are not "of mixed blood," the "reprobates," also be so induced? Or is it the Indians who might be induced to "take part" in rebellion with the true and/or false whites? As in the Bigelow letter with which this chapter began, McKenney struggles and fails to turn what Nicolni sees as "class" distinctions into clear-cut racial divisions in order to preserve the link between civility and whiteness.

Sierra's letter to Buchanan on March 7, 1848, typifies his contrasting, tactical approach to Washington. From the first sentence of the letter, he paints the Caste War in stark tones:

SIR: In some of my anterior notes I made known to the government of the U. States, through the channel of the Secretary of State, the horrible and incalculable evils and misfortunes which the people of Yucatan were suffering from a war forced upon them by the barbarous indian tribes who live on the Eastern frontier of Yucatan, who have evidently been armed and incited thereto by some secret power. This savage and exterminating war has assumed such a formidable aspect that I can in compliance with my duty, no longer refrain from invoking frankly, and conclusively, the sympathy and humanity of this highly civilized republican government, in favor of that people who are every way worthy of a better fate. In the name of humanity and civilization, I am compelled to demand that this government will dictate all such measures as may be within its power, and if possible by a prompt intervention put an end to this war which threatens to produce the most lamentable consequences to the american policy.

. . . It is not necessary that I should remind the Honble Secretary of State that humanity, civilization, and sound policy all unite in exacting this duty at the hands of the U. States; prompt aid, given with that alacrity and good will which I believe is characteristic of the intelligent, free, civilized, and above all eminently religious people of this country, would produce the most beneficial results and at once put a stop to a war which otherwise might become general.[22]

The United States should intervene, he argues, because barbarism threatens not only Yucatecan Creoles but civilization itself. This letter makes use of a trope Sierra repeats again and again in his correspondence to Washington. When he writes of a "war which threatens to produce the most lamentable consequences to the american[23] policy," and then warns vaguely of an Indian war "which otherwise might become general," Sierra figures a space of *pan-American* interest. The phrase "The american policy" plays on the ambiguity of the adjective "American," which in U.S. English tends to refer to the United States but in Latin American Spanish tends to refer to the hemisphere. Whereas the former meaning would speak more narrowly to the interests of the United States as an imperial power in the Americas, the latter meaning posits a community of interest shared by U.S. and Yucatecan citizens alike. The similarly ambiguous suggestion of a "general" war growing out of the Caste War amplifies the latter meaning of "american," suggesting that this Maya uprising might spread to the rest of Mexico, or North America, or indeed the entire Americas. Sierra apparently hopes to rally a pan-American civility against the general threat of Indians in the Americas.

This pan-American civility emerges more explicitly as a *racial* formation in a letter Sierra wrote to Buchanan on April 3, 1848. He begins by describing "The war of the barbarians" as "an atrocious and cruel war in which neither sex nor condition is spared by those savages," and proceeds to rehearse dramatic scenes of "white families" being killed by the "hundreds" as well as his familiar charges against British arms suppliers.[24] After lamenting that "The works which the civilization of three hundred years and the efforts of our forefathers had erected, have already appeared wherever has been set the impious step of the accursed race which today returns with fire and blood the immense benefits it has received from the people of Yucatan," he concludes:

In sum, Mr. Minister, the country is on the point of being lost, and the white race on the point of being extinguished by the savages, unless it encounters the sympathy, protection and support of civilized people.

The people of Yucatan will not allow themselves to be assassinated and destroyed without trying every recourse within their power to prevent it. They must, therefore, appeal to foreign power, invoking in their behalf the rights of humanity, and the sympathy which a cultured and Christian people must feel for another which is equally so. And to what people are we to have recourse, but to that of the powerful republic which stands at the front of American civilization, and to which we openly declare such great esteem, and from which we expect our future prosperity and growth?[25]

Sierra makes clear that the Yucatán's "savages" are not simply a local threat, but rather a threat to the white civility of the entire hemisphere, for the "civilization of three hundred years" to which he refers is not simply Yucatecan nor even Mexican civilization, but an "American civilization," a civilization of the Americas. The cost of activating this pan-American racial trope also becomes clear in this passage: Sierra is more than willing to become a comprador member of this American civilization, a client of the United States "from which we expect our future prosperity and growth."

When Sierra refers to "the impious step of the accursed race which today returns with fire and blood the immense benefits it has received from the people of Yucatan," he also speaks to the United States in the language of its transition from civilization policy to removal policy: the Indians refuse to be grateful for all the Creoles' efforts to civilize them, he claims. As early as February 15, 1848, Sierra used this argument to spark Washington's interest in the plight of Yucatán:

> Noble & philanthropic, liberal & broad, is the political principle which has ever been dominant in Yucatan. Our constitution & our laws have secured to the indigenous race the same identical rights which they give to all the other citizens. Our policy has always been to alleviate the social condition of the Indians, improving it by civil & religious instruction & spreading amongst them all the benefits of civilization in the same way & to the same extent as our means & resources permitted us to do in behalf of our own race. Many of them have, thus, been called into public life, who have succeeded in throwing off the brutal stupidity which has been & is their characteristic. And so well has the object of this policy been attained in one point of view, that we have finally made ourselves the mark of the hatred, the envy & the savage ferocity of the eastern Indians, who have declared against us a war of extermination.[26]

Even when he cites evidence of Indian assimilation—"Many of them have, thus, been called into public life, who have succeeded in throwing off the brutal stupidity"— Sierra negates that evidence with the phrase "which has been & is their characteristic." The sentence effectively removes the civility attained by the Indians "who have succeeded" when it declares that "brutal stupidity" not only "has been" but still "is their characteristic."

Sierra then augments the pan-American relationship he has just posited by invoking the very trope of "America" we see in the March 7 and April 3 letters. After warning of that "occult and mysterious power" in Europe that might be helping the Indians, he writes: "But there are some circumstances of which it is superlatively important that the Govt & people of the U. States should be apprized, occupying as they do the vanguard of the freedom & civilization of the American nations, and bound as they are, from the immense power which they possess to prevent the catastrophe, to preserve Yucatan from becoming the prey of rebellious savages."[27] Plural though "the American nations" are, they share a common "freedom & civilization" whose guardianship and patronage Sierra is willing to place in the hands of "the U. States."

Sierra's effort to articulate the U.S.–Mexico War and the Caste War provokes a dilemma: how far beyond its borders and in what manner can U.S. citizenship extend its reach? We can trace this dilemma by comparing President James K. Polk's December 1847 State of the Union Address, composed before Sierra's intervention, to Polk's April 1848 Message to Congress proposing a bill to intervene on behalf of Yucatecan Creoles.

On December 7, 1847, Polk devoted most of his annual Congressional Message, or State of the Union Address, to the U.S.–Mexico War. This is not surprising, since party politics were at a boil, the personal ambitions of U.S. leaders were raging, and negotiations with Mexico were at a turning point.[28] Though it contains no mention of the Caste War, the 1847 State of the Union Address is notable for its representation of the U.S.–Mexico War as a struggle for U.S. citizenship itself. Delivered to "Fellow-citizens of the Senate and of the House of Representatives," the address begins its summary of the causes of the war by decrying "the wanton violation of the rights of person and property of our citizens committed by Mexico, her repeated acts of bad faith, through a long series of years, and her disregard of solemn treaties, stipulating for indemnity to our injured citizens."[29] Polk proceeds to charge Mexico with "invading the territory of the State of Texas, striking the first blow, and shedding the blood of our citizens on our own soil."[30] The only "indemnity" for "the just and long deferred claims of our citizens against" Mexico, the only reparation for "our citizens, who hold just demands against her," the only way of discharging "our duty to these citizens," "our own citizens," is to wrest land from Mexico.[31] Arguing against the "no territory doctrine" being advocated by some in Congress, whereby the war would end with only Texas being annexed, Polk represents the annexation of further Mexican territory as the only way to repair the injured bodies of U.S. citizens. Indeed, these bodies seem to be bleeding precisely because Mexico unjustly continues to hold onto its own land.

In fact, the claims to which Polk refers argue just that: white settlers, many of them U.S. citizens, had squatted on land in the northern Mexican territories and had subsequently claimed ownership of that land, as well as a desire to be annexed by the United States. In turn, when Northern Mexican colonists asserted their prior rights to this land, and when the Mexican government asserted its prior colonization of these territories, the squatters called on the United States to defend their claims. Polk's argument suggests that prior to Spanish and Mexican colonization, this land somehow embodied U.S. citizenship; Mexico's prior claim thus emerges as an injurious expropriation of the apparently primordial right of U.S. citizens to North America. What is more, by posing this conflict as a struggle between U.S. colonists and Mexican colonists, Polk discursively removes North American Indians—viewed as savage obstacles to colonization by both sets of colonists—from the land altogether.

Yet Polk goes further than this in his State of the Union Address. Arguing that it is just and realistic to demand territory from Mexico as a condition of peace, Polk declares:

> There is another consideration which induced the belief that the Mexican Government
> might even desire to place this province [of New Mexico] under the protection of the

Government of the United States. Numerous bands of fierce and warlike savages wander over it, and upon its borders. Mexico has been, and must continue to be, too feeble to restrain them from committing depredations, robberies and murders, not only upon the inhabitants of New Mexico itself, but upon those of the other northern States of Mexico. It would be a blessing to all these northern states to have their citizens protected against them by the power of the United States. At this moment, many Mexicans, principally females and children, are in captivity among them. If New Mexico were held and governed by the United States, we could effectually prevent these tribes from committing such outrages, and compel them to release these captives, and restore them to their families and friends.

In proposing to acquire New Mexico and the Californias, it was known that but an inconsiderable portion of the Mexican people would be transferred with them, the country embraced within these provinces being chiefly an uninhabited region.[32]

Polk's sharp distinction between "fierce and warlike savages" on the one hand, and innocent, law-abiding Mexican and U.S. citizens on the other hand, is consistent with the discursive practices of Indian removal so pervasive in the mid-century United States. Initially, it describes Mexicans in much the way Bigelow describes Yucatecos in his letter: as helpless victims, here "principally females and children" who need to be protected by the virile "power of the United States." By sketching a scene of white men saving brown women and children from even browner savages (to reformulate Gayatri Chakravorty Spivak's well-known formulation),[33] Polk represents annexation as the paternalistic mission of U.S. white nationalism. Yet Polk steps back from even this paternalism in the next paragraph when he downplays the very existence of Mexicans in New Mexico: "but an inconsiderable portion of the Mexican people would be transferred with them, the country embraced within these provinces being chiefly an uninhabited region." After invoking Mexicans in order to racialize Indians as savages subject to removal, Polk then removes Mexicans to open New Mexico to settlement by white U.S. citizens. By subjecting Mexicans to this discursive removal, Polk indian- izes them, laying the groundwork for a white nationalist settlement policy in territo- ries acquired from Mexico.

Indeed, this indianization of the Mexican is a crucial U.S. trope during the U.S.–Mexico War; it allows whiteness to be withdrawn from Mexicans and, in turn, supplements the formal and abstract equality of U.S. citizenship with whiteness. Polk amplifies this tropology later in his State of the Union Address, when he explains why Major General Taylor was directed to seize supplies for U.S. troops from Mexican citizens without remuneration:

While the war had been conducted on our part according to the most humane and liberal principles observed by civilized nations, it was waged in a far different spirit on the part of Mexico. Not appreciating our forbearance, the Mexican people generally became hos- tile to the United States, and availed themselves of every opportunity to commit the most savage excesses upon our troops. Large numbers of the population took up arms, and, engaging in guerilla warfare, robbed and murdered in the most cruel manner individual soldiers, or small parties, whom accident or other causes had separated from the main body of our army; bands of guerrilleros and robbers infested the roads, harassed our trains, and, whenever it was in their power, cut off our supplies.

The Mexicans having thus shown themselves to be wholly incapable of appreciating our forbearance and liberality, it was deemed proper to change the manner of conducting the war, by making them feel its pressure according to the usages observed under similar circumstances by all other civilized nations.[34]

Attempting to whip up outrage at popular resistance to an invading army, Polk suggests that the invasion's "humane and liberal principles" revealed Mexicans to be "savage" "guerrilleros and robbers," nearly indistinguishable from the previous passage's "fierce and warlike savages" who "wander" over New Mexico. The innocent Mexican "women and children" who were the victims of Indians in New Mexico are removed completely from this passage, as they were from the second paragraph of the previous passage. Here, however, Mexican innocents are replaced by "individual soldiers, or small parties" of innocent U.S. troops, even innocent U.S. "trains" and "supplies," who, rather than being engaged in warfare, are "harassed" by "savage excesses" such as "murder" and "robbery." Polk withdraws civility from Mexicans, constructing a clear-cut distinction between savage, indianized Mexicans and U.S. white civility, and casting the entire Mexican population as an obstacle to the full exercise of U.S. citizenship. He thus indianizes the Mexican along the lines of the eradicative or removal logic Rogin and Horsman have chronicled.

As Polk himself notes, he had already made many of these points in his address to Congress on May 11, 1846, when the war had just begun, and in his 1846 State of the Union Address.[35] Indeed, the account of citizenship in the 1847 address is notable precisely because it is the last gasp of Polk's clear-cut distinction between Mexicans and U.S. citizens, his last figuration of Mexicans as objects of mere removal or eradication. When he delivered the 1847 address, Polk was already considering intelligence that would soon cause him to revise his account of U.S. citizenship. Thirteen days before the 1847 address, on November 24, Secretary of State James Buchanan received Sierra's first letter referring to the beginning of a Maya revolt in Yucatán, or what Sierra calls "a savage war on the white race."[36] Over the next four months, the administration received increasingly alarming information from Yucatán, transmitted by Sierra as well as by U.S. naval officials in the Gulf of Mexico and newspaper reports. On April 29, 1848, almost five months after his 1847 State of the Union Address, Polk forwarded much of this information to Congress, along with a presidential message announcing that "the Indians of Yucatan are waging a war of extermination against the white race." Polk's April 1848 message to Congress conforms so remarkably to the discourse of Sierra's letters that it seems likely Sierra's correspondence facilitated a certain informal, discursive alliance, if not a formal, governmental one, with the administration.

In the April message, Polk recommends that the United States "occupy and hold military possession" of the Yucatán as soon as troops can be spared from the rest of Mexico in order "to prevent Yucatan from becoming a colony of any European power . . . and, at the same time, to rescue the white race from extermination or expulsion from their country."[37] Since the Yucatecan Creoles had offered their sovereignty in exchange for aid from France, England, Spain, or the United States, Polk invoked the Monroe Doctrine to assert U.S. strategic interests in the region; in the subsequent congressional debate on Polk's recommendation, this would be referred to as the "policy" argument for the military occupation of Yucatán. Polk's second argument—his call "to rescue the white race"—would be referred to as the "humanity" argument for occupation.

It is this second argument that makes such a marked departure from the account of citizenship Polk offers in his 1847 State of the Union Address. Quite suddenly, not even five months after his suggestion that U.S. white citizenship was directly threatened by the very existence of Mexicans who, like Indians, require removal, Polk has asked Congress to consider a transnational, racial alliance with a select group of Mexican citizens. The Yucatecan Creoles, though not yet fellow citizens—we know that Polk and his allies hoped to annex Yucatán much as Texas had been annexed—are represented as fellow members of "the white race." Though the "policy" argument certainly met great opposition in Congress, the "humanity" argument provoked wholesale ambivalence, confusion, and consternation about the racial and national form of U.S. citizenship. When Polk delivers his April 29 message to Congress, he clearly hopes to cement the pan-American racial alliance Sierra has offered so insistently. Before it can be formalized, however, this alliance will begin to fray in Congress.

"The position of Yucatan is peculiar," wrote Secretary of State Buchanan to Sierra on December 24, 1847, in a letter included among the documents Polk sent to Congress in the spring of 1848 as it debated a bill to occupy Yucatán and aid the peninsula's Creoles in the Caste War.[38] Buchanan was referring specifically to Yucatán's ambiguous, on-again-off-again relationship with Mexico, an ambiguity he used to deny Sierra's request to lift the U.S. military blockade of Laguna de Terminos, a crucial entrepot for Yucatecan trade. Yet Buchanan's phrase could also serve as an epigraph for the entire congressional debate over the Yucatán bill, encapsulating the crisis precipitated by Polk and Sierra's proposed pan-American racial alliance. Congress would find Yucatecan racial and national formations to be so peculiar and ambiguous that it would fail to reach consensus on the bill. Although U.S. aid was already finding its way to Yucatán, and more would arrive even after the bill faltered, the inability of Congress to reach consensus on a formal bill to occupy the peninsula signifies a turning point in this mid-century conflict. Although the peculiarity and ambiguity of racial and national formations in Yucatán soured Congress on occupation and annexation, the U.S. aid that did arrive helped to turn the tide of the war in the Creoles' favor, and laid the groundwork for U.S. neocolonialism, or an imperialism freed from permanent military and settler occupation.

The House of Representatives only debated Yucatán intervention on April 29, after which it referred the matter to the Committee on Foreign Affairs, where it died.

However, during that one day of debate House members raised fundamental questions about Polk's proposed alliance. According to the *Congressional Globe*, after the president's message was presented a dispute broke out over whether the message should be referred to the Committee on Territories or the Committee on Foreign Affairs. In other words, the House members were initially unclear about the status of Yucatán itself: was it a foreign nation-state on par with the United States, or was it an underdeveloped territory whose inhabitants needed to be tutored before they could be considered equal to those of the United States? Polk's message was itself unclear on this score: on the one hand, he proposed occupying Yucatán as a territory, and only later considering the possibility of its statehood; on the other hand, Polk presented the Creoles as fellow members of pan-American white civility.

Representative Julius Rockwell of Massachusetts asserted Yucatán's territorial status, citing Texas as a precedent: "If anything was to be done with relation to acquiring the territory, it should be done in the form of a territorial government. Such was the condition of that people, such their intellectual and social state, that this was the only fit way in which any portion of the territory of Mexico could ripen into a State."[39] However, this assimilation model, resonant with the civilization policies so recently supplanted by removal policy in the United States, is immediately questioned by Joseph R. Ingersoll of Pennsylvania, who also cites Texas: "When an appeal came from Texas, at the time that General Woll issued his proclamation threatening extermination by internecine war, we listened to her invocation, and hastened to the assistance of suffering humanity, though it might be we viewed the Texans as more nearly allied to ourselves." Though Ingersoll says he is ultimately persuaded to give some aid to "the Yucatanese" in their struggle "against savages that thirsted for the blood of the Yucatanese," his suggestion that Texans who rose up against Mexico are "more nearly allied to ourselves" questions whether the Creoles are worthy of an alliance with the United States.[40] Immediately, other members of the House cast this question of worthiness in explicitly racial terms.

Alexander H. Stephens of Georgia responds with a call for more specific information on the conflict and more time to debate the matter, questioning the Creoles' racial worth: "Suppose it true that the Spanish white population of Yucatan, as they were called, should propose to this Government to sell out their country, if we would protect them; suppose this was so, (and he was not going to prejudge the case,) did it not involve a grave question? Was it not a new question? . . . He was not prepared to do it without some reflection" (the parenthetical "he" seems to be Stephens; the *Congressional Globe* occasionally adopts the third person voice).[41] The newness of the question, its difference from previous U.S. interventions—such as the annexation of Texas, to which Rockwell and Ingersoll refer—seems to be this supposition that "the Spanish white population of Yucatan" was indeed white, when they might in fact only be "called" white. Stephens needs more information so that he can reflect further on this "question."

Even the nuanced critique of the Yucatecan Creoles' elitism offered by Joseph M. Root of Ohio opposes the occupation of Yucatán in racialist terms. Root declares that an alliance with Yucatecan Creoles would be an alliance "with the aristocracy of Yucatan" and that the United States is "going to oppose the democracy" by entering into such an alliance with a "minority." The people these Yucatecans called "'a lawless mob'" "were, after all, the 'native Americans' in Yucatan" and, as an oppressed "majority," Root asserts, deserved U.S. aid more than the "Spanish aristocracy" did. He even sarcastically criticizes the Creole claims to civility, naming their racial interests: "These aristocrats were to surrender us the country if we would but attack the majority, who were cruelly oppressing them, the minority. This seemed to be the only reason why we should attack the native Yucatanese, unless, indeed, it was on account of their *color*." Root's criticism is not, however, a critique of white nationalism. As he argues (again in the *Congressional Globe*'s third person voice):

> Who were the Spaniards that were so infinitely [the Maya's] superiors? Mr. R. imagined they were about equal to the Mexican; and if there was anything under the face of heaven meaner than a Mexican "greaser," he should like to know it. He felt more like taking sides against such fellows than against the poor Indians. . . . That country contained two distinct races, at war with each other; and we were called to take part with one of them, and to destroy their enemies. Now, Mr. R. admitted that his sympathies were, first, in favor of the white race; but those who went on this ground must show him better samples of the white man than these Spaniards before they would get up his sympathies very high.[42]

Root makes explicit the white nationalism implied by Rockwell, Ingersoll, and Stephens. The Indians of Yucatán may be the oppressed, democratic majority and the Creoles the oppressive, aristocratic minority, but neither are fully worthy of Root's "sympathies" nor, consequently, of an alliance with the United States. Such "sympathies" and such an alliance could only be worthwhile if the two parties in the alliance were equal "samples of the white man."

Polk and Sierra's proposed pan-American racial alliance ran aground in the House on the shores of Yucatán's "peculiar" racial and national forms. In effect, House members could not recognize the whiteness Sierra saw in his fellow Creoles and Polk saw through Sierra. The same failure of recognition would characterize the much longer Senate debate. Between April 29, when Polk's message and its accompanying documents were laid on the table, and May 17, when a report of an armistice between the Creoles and the Maya reached the floor, more than a dozen Senators would challenge the alliance on racial grounds.

The Senate debate began on May 4, when Polk's main congressional supporter, Edward A. Hannegan from Indiana, sent a bill authorizing "temporary occupation of Yucatan" from the Committee of Foreign Affairs, which he chaired, to the Senate for consideration:

> SEC. 1. *Be it enacted, &c.*, That the President of the United States be, and he is hereby, authorized to take temporary military occupation of Yucatan, and to employ the army and navy of the United States to assist the people of Yucatan in repelling the incursions of the Indian savages now overrunning and devastating that country.

SEC. 2. *And be it further enacted,* That the President be, and he is hereby, authorized and empowered to furnish, on such terms and conditions as he may deem proper, to the white population of Yucatan, such arms, ammunition, ordnance, and other military means as they may need, to enable them to resist and repel the Indian hostilities now waged against them, and to restore peace and security to their country.

SEC. 3. *And be it further enacted,* That the President be, and he is hereby, authorized and empowered to accept the services of an equal number of volunteer troops to supply the place of such as may be withdrawn from their present duty by virtue of this act, provided their services shall be required; the same to be raised for service during the war with Mexico, agreeably to the provisions of the acts of May 13, 1846, and March 3, 1847.[43]

The bill reflects Sierra's letters and Polk's April address quite precisely. The Caste War is represented as a conflict between two, starkly opposed forces: "the people of Yucatan" who are also "the white population of Yucatan," and "the Indian savages." The Caste War is explicitly articulated with the U.S.–Mexico War by the suggestion that U.S. troops be raised to fight the Maya in "the same" way troops were raised to fight Mexicans. The bill's proposed alliance between the United States and Yucatán thus seeks to separate the Yucatecan Creoles from Mexicans and Indians. Though there is no mention of the Monroe Doctrine in the bill, Polk's address and Hannegan's opening arguments present Polk's "policy" and "humanity" grounds for U.S. intervention.

Initially, John C. Calhoun of South Carolina and John J. Crittenden of Kentucky simply attempt to postpone the debate by calling for more "information" on "both the origin and the character of the war," especially given that the administration examined intelligence from Yucatán for months before recommending intervention.[44] However, when Polk does send more intelligence, and Hannegan insists on immediate action, the whiteness of the Creoles comes under attack. A measure of the skepticism with which the bill's attempt to equate the United States with "the white population of Yucatan" is met can be found just three days into the debate. On May 5, Hannegan tries to "withdraw the appeal to humanity altogether" and "take higher ground. Let us say to the people of Yucatan, that we will act—we will preserve you from destruction—we will prevent the seizure of your territory by any foreign Power."[45] But Hannegan's belated attempt to shift the debate to Polk's "policy" argument also fails, as senator after senator insists on returning to the "humanity" argument.

Skepticism about the Creoles' racial form is reflected in the inconsistency in the terms the senators use to describe the Yucatecan Creoles. In one speech, John M. Clayton of Delaware refers to them as "suffering people," "Creoles," "these Yucatecos," "the white race in Yucatan," and "the Spanish race;" similarly, he shifts among terms for the Maya, at times calling them "Indians" and at other times "Mexican Indians." Senator James D. Westcott of Florida struggles with the binary distinction itself, referring to "the Spanish and Mexicans and half Indians that reside" in Yucatán.[46] Lewis Cass of Michigan refers at one point to "the two races of Spanish and of aboriginal descent," and later distinguishes between "Indians" and "the white race."[47]

This inconsistency develops into explicit arguments against the whiteness of the Creoles on a number of occasions. For instance, Calhoun rejects comparisons between the Yucatán and Texas, calling Texans "'bone of our bone and flesh of our flesh'" and Yucatán "a worthless country" ruled by "the Spanish or white race, and in that we include the mixed races" who are "not very elevated in their sentiments, nor very well informed on political subjects," though "they are far better informed, and far more elevated in sentiment, than the Indian race can possibly be."[48] Though they deserve some aid, "It is now clear that the white population, including the mixed race, is so prostrated and feeble, and the Indians so powerful, that not a hope remains of reestablishing the permanent ascendency of the former."[49] Consequently, "the white population of Yucatan have, in a great measure, themselves to blame. The factious conflicts—fierce and maniacal—in which they have been engaged to the last have involved them in these frightful calamities."[50] By repeatedly collapsing distinctions between "the white race" and "the mixed races," and raising doubts about the "sentiments" and political development of the Creoles, Calhoun disdains Polk and Sierra's pan-American white civilization. Any population foolish enough to grant citizenship to Indians, Calhoun suggests, could not possibly be equal to U.S. citizens. These Creoles are not just politically inexperienced; they are racially suspect.

Calhoun's attack on the Creoles is echoed by other Senators as they repeatedly raise the issue of the Maya's citizenship rights in Yucatán. Some suggest, as Root did in the House debate, that the Maya, because they are the majority and because they suffered under Spanish and then Creole rule, might have legitimate grievances. Says Crittenden, supported in the midst of his speech by Clayton:

> For three hundred years they have governed these people, and been teaching them religion, and giving them knowledge and education. And now they come and tell us that these people are still savages, when church and state have had them under their direction for three hundred years. They must have been very badly governed, and the government must have been a very unjust one, at least a very unparental one, if, after three hundred years of subjection, they are still in their savage state. . . . The relation which they sustain in Yucatan, is not the relation which the savages of our country have borne towards us. These people are citizens. There is no such thing as slavery there in the legal sense of the term.
>
> Mr. CLAYTON, (in his seat.) They have the right of suffrage.
>
> Mr. CRITTENDEN. They enjoy civil rights; but such civil rights and such enjoyment of them as the laws of Spanish colonization have left to the conquered people of South America. A state of subjugation, I acknowledge; but what are these people attempting to do in Yucatan more than has been done by these people in Guatemala, which we have considered as a Government, and to which we send a diplomatic agent? What are they doing, would but what has been successfully done by the people of Guatemala about twenty years ago, when one of their chiefs, at the head of the Indian population—who would be better understood in this country if we were to call them native Mexicans, or the aboriginal inhabitants of the country—throwing off the yoke of the Spaniard,

established a government for themselves? They have risen up against the descendants of the Spaniards, by whom they were first conquered, have overthrown them, and have governed that country very well from that time to the present. I know of no difference between these Indians and those who are termed savages in Yucatan; but I may be mistaken. I wish a great deal more information than I now have, before I can venture to vote for this bill.[51]

By erasing Mexican independence and collapsing Spaniard into Creole with the repeated phrase "for three hundred years," Crittenden casts doubt on the white civility of Sierra's government. In addition, though the Maya are "citizens," they are still themselves beneath white civility, for they seem to deserve a more "parental" government than they have been given rather than a government of their own. Crittenden does tentatively suggest that the Maya might eventually deserve their own government—posing that possibility in the form of a question, and qualifying that question with "but I may be mistaken. I wish a great deal more information than I now have." However, the supporting analogy to Guatemala complicates the status of the Yucatecan Creoles more than it recognizes the civility of the Maya. The Guatemalan independence movement of the 1820s to which Crittenden refers was itself a Creole-led movement. To call those leaders an "Indian population" or "native Mexicans, or the aboriginal inhabitants of the country" is to scramble already unstable distinctions among Yucatecan Creoles, Guatemalan Creoles, Mexicans, the Maya of Yucatán, and the Maya of Guatemala. Crittenden's argument thus functions more to cast doubt on the worthiness of the Creoles than it does to vindicate the Maya of Yucatán or Guatemala, for he certainly does not raise the possibility of intervening on the latter's behalf.

The existence of a probably successful, possibly just Indian majority revolt in Yucatán makes other senators anxious about the potential annexation of the peninsula, to which Polk referred obliquely in his April 29 message. John M. Niles of Connecticut goes so far as to compare the Maya revolt with the revolts against aristocracy raging in Europe, particularly in France. As with Root in the House, however, the argument functions less to rally support for the Maya than it does to cast doubt on the worthiness of Sierra and his government:

> Mr. Sierra seems to avoid going into the origin of the controversies. Traced to its source, I think it will be found that this war at present existing in that country is one of the deplorable evils resulting from their divisions. Sir, is it not improbable that the degraded native population of that country, who for three long centuries have been in a state of complete subjugation, and whose natural characteristic, according to Mr. Sierra, is stupidity, should, of their own accord, after having endured oppression so long, from some strange feeling newly sprung up in their breasts, unite their strength, and form an offensive league against their ancient oppressors? Sir, there are, there must have been, other causes of this difficulty, of which we at present know nothing. . . . I saw an article in a paper published at Merida, in which the superior class are speculating upon the probabilities of receiving aid from this country. Nothing short, says the writer, of annexation will be of any use to them.[52]

Niles's reference to unknown "other causes" raises questions about Polk and Sierra's account of the Caste War as a race war, and works to keep the Creoles at arm's length. As he proceeds to express disdain at the Creoles' interest in annexation, he also questions whether they are worthy of becoming annexed subjects of the United States. After reading from the Nicolni letter discussed earlier in this chapter, Niles declares:

> Here the Governor [of Yucatán] says that these Indians have become terrible enemies. Mr. Sierra states that they are vastly superior to his own people. In all the accounts which we have had of this cruel war, with all its terrible devastations, I have never seen any account of the first battle that has been fought or the first stand that has been made by the white population of that distracted country. It appears that they have a small force in the field, but whether it is that they are afraid to fight I know not, I cannot say; as yet they appear to have had no skirmish, nor made any resistance, however slight, to the desolating progress this formidable people are continuing. Now, sir, if we engage in this war, we assume upon our hands no small undertaking. I know our soldiers are brave, and probably one thousand of our troops would oppose a more formidable resistance to the incursions of these Indians than the whole military force of Yucatan.[53]

Niles generalizes Nicolni and Sierras's acknowledgment that the Maya fight better in forests than the Creoles' troops do with the damning sentence "Mr. Sierra states that they are vastly superior to his own people." Followed by a sharp distinction between the cowardice "of the white population of that distracted country" and the bravery of U.S. troops, this passage hollows out racial distinctions between the Creoles and the Indians. Consequently, neither population emerges as worth the risk of annexation. Faced with the choice between exterminating the Maya for the Creoles and incorporating both Maya and Creole citizens into a new territory of the United States, Niles opts for letting the Yucatán aid bill die.

Despite an effort by Lewis Cass of Michigan to aid Hannegan and the president with a call both to rescue Yucatán's "civilized population" and to keep the British from closing the Gulf to U.S. trade, debate over the bill ceased when Hannegan suddenly announced on May 17 that "I have received further intelligence upon which I rely with a confident assurance in my own mind of its correctness, that a treaty has been made between the contending parties in Yucatan."[54] Though this treaty had already collapsed by the time word of its existence reached the United States, Congress would permanently suspend debate on the matter. The senators seem to have been overwhelmed by the ambiguity of the Creoles' racial and national status. The vigor with which some opposed this alliance suggests that white civility was itself tenuous and vulnerable, that it would not withstand formal equivalence with potentially "Spanish," "Mexican," or "mixed" race Creoles.

At first glance, this refusal to see the Yucatecan Creoles as civilized whites would seem to reflect the shift in U.S. Indian policy, described by Rogin and Horsman, from assimilation or civilization policy to extermination or war and removal policy: once indianized, Mexicans are apparently inassimilable. However, aid from the United States would reach the Yucatecan Creoles informally, under the cover of the U.S. war with

Mexico. Polk ordered the Home Squadron to stations ships within sight of Mérida, in the hope of intimidating the Maya. The U.S. navy eventually evacuated some Creoles from the peninsula until the Maya halted their offensive, and redirected some arms from the U.S.–Mexico War to Creole forces. Hundreds of volunteer U.S. troops, many of them veterans of the U.S.–Mexico War, arrived to fight by the side of the Creoles. Though far short of full-scale occupation and annexation, U.S. aid did help turn the tide of the war in the Creoles' favor.

Rather than the sharp shift in racial ideology from assimilation to extermination, then, we can see a blend of both ideologies in this informal, uneven, ambivalent alliance between Yucatecan Creoles, who saw themselves as civilized whites engaged in a race war against savage Indians, and the United States, which also saw the Maya as savage Indians but considered the Creoles to be not fully civilized and not quite white. This informal alliance represents a desire to civilize certain Mexicans—the Creoles—who are worthy of such imperial benevolence only to the extent that they have been differentiated from other Mexicans—the Maya—who are subject to extermination. The very tenuousness of this distinction effectively steered U.S. intervention into flexible and informal channels, rather than the formal channels of occupation and annexation.

Indeed, I want to suggest that Congress's decision to reject occupation and annexation in the name of a pan-American white civility in favor of a more informal alliance set Yucatán on the path of what is today called dependent development. Shortly after the Caste War ended in 1852, with the Yucatán's sugar industry in ruins, U.S. and Mexican capital poured into the development of henequen plantations on the peninsula. A fiber used to produce rope, henequen grew more readily than sugar in the climate and geography of the peninsula's Creole-controlled northern and western lowlands. As the world market for rope made of henequen fiber quickly expanded between the 1850s and the 1880s—a result, in part, of the growth of the (increasingly white-only) merchant marine trade we encountered at the end of chapter 1—U.S. capital found itself with a foothold in an immensely profitable enterprise that required none of the volatile settlement by U.S. whites and none of the politically and financially costly military occupations by the U.S. government that had characterized U.S. white settler colonialism up to that point. By 1915, Yucatecan henequen had monopolized the world rope-fiber market, and the U.S.–based International Harvester Company had established an informal empire in Yucatán by controlling the region's dependency on a henequen monocrop economy.[55] In effect, the Caste War of 1847 taught U.S. capital the advantages of corporate, neocolonial development over colonial development. The Creoles who had desired citizenship within the United States had to settle for comprador status. The partial equivalence between U.S. citizens and Yucatecan Creoles put into effect by informal U.S. aid temporarily resolved the Senate's anxiety over U.S. citizenship, protecting both its imperial and its racial interests by exporting discursive practices that were at once assimilative and eradicative.

Ambivalent Allegories

In the midst of the Senate debate on the Yucatán bill, Jefferson Davis, Senator from Mississippi, declared that Polk needed no authorization to order a military occupation of Yucatán because the Caste War "is an incident of the Mexican war, which past legislation has declared and recognized." Davis was countered by Kentucky Senator John J. Crittenden's claim that the Caste War "is not . . . part and parcel of the Mexican war."[56] Opposed yet also the mirror image of one another—antipodes in the original sense of the word—the utterances of Davis and Crittenden epitomize the articulation of the U.S.–Mexico War and the Caste War: one war is neither the same as nor separable from the other, but rather the two wars articulate at a volatile and ambivalent flashpoint.[57] The informal alliance that emerged out of congressional inaction on the Yucatán bill can be read as a partial resolution of this volatility and ambivalence. So too can a set of popular texts published and avidly consumed in the United States at precisely the moment when the U.S.–Mexico War and the Caste War were being articulated. In fact, these texts played a crucial role in that articulation.

Between 1840 and 1860, spurred by technological advances in printmaking and decreasing postal rates, publishing houses in northeastern cities satiated the U.S. reading public with scores of cheap romances about the conflict between the United States and Mexico. These fifty- to one-hundred-page novelettes, which were often initially serialized in story-paper format, sold from 30,000 to 50,000 per title to a mostly working-class reading audience, giving many people in the United States their first representations of Mexicans, Texans, Tejanos, and Californios. The novelettes were produced under conditions similar to the quasi factories of the more well-known dime novels of the 1860s–1890s, conditions described so well by Michael Denning in his *Mechanic Accents*: groups of workers, usually women, would clip sensational stories out of newspapers, give them to editors who would mock up a plotline, and the editors would charge their authors with stretching that plot to fifty or one hundred even more sensational pages.[58]

After years of critical debasement at the hands of normative aesthetic distinctions between "high" and "low" literature, in the past few decades such popular fiction has been credited with unique insights into social formations. Indeed, at times popular fiction has been privileged for its exuberant challenges to cultural normativity, its uneven and contradictory, violent and salacious excesses shown to reveal the rough and frayed edges of race, class, gender, and nation. Yet such readings run the risk of enacting their own aesthetic normalization when they celebrate the "low" or the popular as a site that inevitably resists the necessary normativity of the "high." U.S.–Mexico War novelettes exemplify this hermeneutic dilemma.

Decidedly exuberant, violent, and salacious, these novelettes are full of incidents of racial, national, class, and gender passing and transgression—border crossings, if you will—that articulate the instability of identities during the U.S.–Mexico War period. However, the novelettes also consistently work to resolve that instability. These texts are incessant; they incessantly reiterate stock plot and character types that spin out of control and toward the unexpected only to veer back to the expected, containing their own excesses with rigorous reiterations of narrative closure, particularly in the form of weddings between "fair" Mexican women and heroic, white U.S. men. I want to suggest that these border crossings and closures allegorize the articulation of the U.S.–Mexico War with the Caste War. For while scenes of racial, national, class, and sexual drag and disguise "foreground the gaps, contradictions, and seamy underside of the ideological projects of white settler colonialism and manifest destiny," as Shelley Streeby has argued, the reiterative resolution of these scenes in remarkably precise dramas of miscegenated, heterosexual normativity ritually forecloses that underside.[59] I want to suggest that this ritual of foreclosure allegorizes the transformation of white settler colonialism and manifest destiny into neocolonial white civility, a transformation characteristic of the U.S.–Mexico War/Caste War conjuncture.[60]

Consider, for instance, *The Heroine of Tampico: or, Wildfire the Wanderer*, published in 1847 by Frederick Gleason and Maturin Murray Ballou's nationalistic Flag of Our Union Office in Boston and authored by one of the more prolific dime novel authors, Harry Halyard.[61] Initially, *The Heroine of Tampico* confronts its readers with a circus of misplaced and disguised characters. The novel opens literally in between nations, on a ship "becalmed in the Mexican Gulf" (7) and populated by racially and nationally ambiguous characters: it is a Mexican ship, but it is run by a Captain Hall, whom we are told has a "sun-tanned hand" (8), and a second officer named Maywood; below deck, we meet Doctor Almagro, "whose color was a sort of dingy yellow, which betokened their possessor to be about half Creole and half Mexican" (8), and who is attending Avaline Allerton, a "young and beautiful" woman lying ill on a "snow-white" couch next to another "young Mexican gentleman" (9), Don Vincensio de Almonte; we also meet Avaline's father, the "cunning" George Allerton who is an American merchant from the Mexican town of Tampico. Another ship approaches, populated by other ambiguous characters: this ship is run by "Spanish sailors," but carries Charles Wallingford, "a lieutenant in marine service of the U.S.," as well as Wildfire the Wanderer, who has a "grotesque appearance" with blue eyes and an "embrowned surface" "dressed in buckskin pants too short for him"; he is accompanied by Azilca, "a handsome Indian girl" who calls him "father" (13–14). These ships immediately present readers with the vertigo of North America's intertwined commercial, sexual, racial, and national relations, a vertigo that intensifies as new, disguised, and ambiguous characters are introduced and a Mexican plot against Avaline is revealed.

Yet *The Heroine of Tampico* works vigorously to tame all this instability. For instance, Avaline—the "heroine"—is revealed to have grown up in Mexico but to have been born in the United States with skin "as white as the driven snow" (28). Wildfire the Wanderer turns out to be the Harvard-educated Dr. Herbert Mandeville, who has been passing as a nomadic Indian. In the end, the four white American male protagonists—Wildfire, Charles Wallingford, his brother Henry, and the Vermonter Jedediah Starkweather— save Avaline from the clutches of Don Vincensio's treacherous designs on her body. U.S. expansionism thus consolidates white nationalist masculinity by saving white women such as Avaline from Mexican men.

However, there is more to this narrative's closure. As racial and national ambiguities are resolved, and the U.S.–Mexico War comes to an end, *The Heroine of Tampico*, like every U.S.–Mexico War novelette, concludes with the ultimate, normative figure for narrative closure, a flurry of weddings:

> In consequence of the wounds he had previously received, Charles Wallingford repaired, soon after the events related above, to New York, accompanied by Avaline Allerton, his brother Henry, and Azilca. Herbert Mandeville, too, accompanied them, he, in the meantime, having dropped forever his former title of Wildfire, the wanderer. Corporal Jedediah Starkweather is still in Mexico, and has promised us, after he reads our book, that he will send us an alfired big letter, containing some tarnal big adventurs, which, perhaps, we may venture to publish in the Flag of Our Union.
>
> We will now, dear reader, conclude our story by stating that somewhere in the vicinity of the first of January, 1847, a double wedding took place in the city of New York which was afterwards announced as follows:
>
> "Married, at _____ Church, by Rev. Mr. _____, Mr. Charles Walllingford, Lieutenant of the U.S. Marine Corps, to Miss Avaline Allerton. Also, at the same time and place, by the same clergyman, Lieutenant Henry Wallingford to Miss Azilca, adopted daughter of Herbert Mandeville, M.D."
>
> THE END. (99–100)

It is Azilca that I want to focus on here initially. We learn during the novel that Azilca is a Seminole Indian whose parents—"a Seminole chieftain . . . and his squaw"—were killed in the "Florida war," or the brutal Seminole Wars (19). She was adopted by Wildfire the Wanderer, who took pity on her despite having fought for the Kentucky rangers against the Seminoles. An object of pity in much the way the Yucatecan Creoles are in the letter from Commander Bigelow with which I began this chapter, Azilca is adopted so as to differentiate her from her parents' resistive ways. Yet before coming to Mexico, we are told, she still resists full assimilation by maintaining her native dress and talking very little; indeed, *she* seems to assimilate Wildfire the Wanderer, whose Indian guise becomes more rough, Halyard suggests, under her influence. It would seem to be her time in Mexico with Avaline, as a captive of Don Vincensio, that makes Azilca willing to assimilate, in this concluding passage, by marrying the handsome U.S. marine Henry Wallingford and, implicitly, giving her reproductive labor up to miscegenation. In turn, Wildfire is also able to regain his own white civility—"having dropped forever his former title of Wildfire, the wanderer"—once he has assured Azilca's assimilation. The figure of Azilca suggests that *The Heroine of Tampico* is able to rediscover civilization policy's assimilative logic by going to Mexico. The war with and defeat of Mexico thus become the condition of possibility for a renewed fantasy of Indian assimilation, indulged at the very moment removal policy is in full force.

What, then, of Corporal Jedediah Starkweather? He is the text's most intimate hero, as we are reminded when the narrator takes on the voice of the publisher in this conclusion and explains that he "is still in Mexico, and has promised us, after he reads our book, that he will send us an alfired big letter, containing some tarnal big adventurs, which, perhaps, we may venture to publish in the Flag of Our Union." Though he speaks a ridiculous Vermont accent throughout the novel, and often annoys the more elite characters (U.S. and Mexican alike) with his interminable, comic tales of rural life, Jedediah is also brave in battle and loyal to his compatriots. In turn, he offers the clearest, simplest, and most vigorous defenses of the United States—as well as the most violent attacks on Mexicans and Indians. Indeed, Jedediah is the vehicle through which the racial formations of Indians and Mexicans are at once most deeply intertwined and most clearly drawn. When Jedediah calls the Mexicans against whom he fights "blasted red-skins" and "red-skinned rascals," he effectively indianizes them, equating them with the Seminole Indians who also refused to be assimilated into the United States (59). Yet when he addresses Azilca as "Miss" and calls her "the awfordest puty gal that ever I set my tew eyes on," he differentiates her from resistive Indians, and acknowledges the possibility of Indian assimilation to white civility (43, 66). It is this acknowledgment, made just before the end of the novel as an approval of her marriage, and thus an endorsement of Azilca's assimilation, that ushers Jedediah into the concluding chapter. Suddenly no longer pining for his Vermont home, as he has throughout the novel, he remains in Mexico, setting out for "tarnal big adventurs" in January 1847: the very month when the Caste War ignited in Yucatán. Might we read Jedediah as one of those volunteer soldiers who fought alongside the Yucatecan Creoles against the Maya, in the name of white civility? Might *The Heroine of Tampico*'s closure open the door to a certain informal discursive alliance with Mexico, an ambivalent acknowledgment of both Mexican racial difference and pan-American civility?

Another Halyard text published one year later, in 1848, and thus after the Caste War had made its way into the very mass media from which the novelettes' plots were often clipped, suggests as much. *The Mexican Spy; or, the Bride of Buena Vista* also has a spectacularly complex plot that unravels only to be tied back up in a neat knot.[62] Yet *The Mexican Spy* goes much further in both scrambling and integrating U.S. and Mexican characters than *The Heroine of Tampico*.

The central villain of this text is Don Jose de Villa Rica, "a rich Mexican, of Castillian extraction, whose enmity to the North Americans, was only equaled by his regard for General Santa Anna" (7). The story opens in 1846 with Don Jose and Santa Anna searching for a spy to send into the U.S. camp. After Brutus, the former American slave and now consort of Don Jose, bumbles his way out of contention, Gonzardo Caspareta volunteers to be that spy, but for reasons of his own. Mexican, but educated in the United States, Gonzardo is loyal to Mexico yet hates Mexican officials such as Santa Anna, whom he considers corrupt for killing his father and confiscating his family's land. He agrees to be the Mexican spy, then, in order to carry out his own plan of revenge against Santa Anna and Don Jose. Meanwhile, the handsome U.S. hero Major Henry Rowland, with his "white looking countenance," and the Connecticut rube Pelatiah P. Shattuck, an uncanny reinvention of *The Heroine of Tampico*'s Jedediah Starkweather, are held captive in the Mexican camp.

Don Jose also has two nieces, Annabel and Blondinita, the "fair and beautiful" daughters of Don Jose's sister[63] and a Philadelphia merchant named John Blackler. Many years earlier, the ten-month-old Blondinita had been stolen by Gonzardo and brought up near Don Jose's home by Gonzardo's friend Munso, unaware of her heritage. Gonzardo had planned to raise Blondinita to marry his son, Ariamento, thereby clandestinely joining the Caspareta family with the Villa Rica family and allowing Gonzardo to regain his land. While Blondinita was being raised by Munso, Don Jose's sister died; in turn, John Blackler "almost succeeded . . . in amassing a large fortune, [but] his affairs took an unfortunate turn, and he met with many heavy losses, though he still struggled manfully against the tide of ill success, until the present troubles commenced between this country and the United States, when the failure of a large mercantile firm in Tampico, by which he lost the whole of the little property he possessed, caused him to become a poor but honest bankrupt" (88). Consequently, Annabel moved from Philadelphia to Mexico as a young woman to live with Don Jose.

The Mexican Spy thus begins with a tangled web of identities and interests: Americans held prisoner by Mexicans; a Mexican pretending to spy on Americans in order to plot against other Mexicans; an American merchant's efforts to become rich on international capital disrupted by the U.S.–Mexico "troubles," and his binational and biracial daughters crossing from Mexico to the United States to Mexico. As the action unfolds, this web initially becomes even more tangled. The middle of the text is filled with characters attempting to escape their predicaments by donning disguises: Annabel, who fell in love with Henry Rowland when the two met in Philadelphia years earlier, plots with Gonzardo to dress as a nun and pass into the Mexican camp to free Rowland;[64] Marguerita, Gonzardo's daughter, disguises herself as a "market-girl" to pass money and letters from her father to his allies (35); upon learning about her own true past, Blondinita escapes Munso's house dressed as a nun (44); Gonzardo disguises himself as a Spanish priest to track her down (46); Pelatiah and Henry dress as nuns to escape their captivity (49). Indeed, the middle chapter of the text, the seventh of fourteen, begins with an epigraph slightly misquoted from Shakespeare's *As You Like It*: "As many other manish cowards,/ That do outface it with their semblances." In *As You Like It*, these words—spoken at the end of act 1 by Rosalind when she and Celia decide to go in drag, as Ganymede and Aliena, to the forest of Arden in search of Rosalind's banished father—mediate between the comedy's initial disarray (the disruption of the royal court and the shift to Arden) and its concluding, romantic resolution (the flurry of marriages and the concluding dance that bring everyone out of the woods and back into the town).

Not surprisingly, *The Mexican Spy* also emerges from its Arden, but with a decidedly nineteenth-century romance of miscegenation. While Don Jose plots to infiltrate the U.S. camp with a spy, Don Jose's daughter Corita, "our passionate Mexican senorita" with a "dark complexion," herself seeks vainly to win the love of Rowland (7, 21). Corita's desires are foiled, however, because Rowland is in love with Annabel and her "pale" and "serene" "countenance" (9, 21). As Annabel, herself a miscegenated subject, winds her way circuitously through the text toward her own miscegenated marriage with Henry, Corita becomes increasingly bitter and evil, plotting unsuccessfully against

Henry and Annabel. Meanwhile Blondinita, Annabel's sister, who is also racially and nationally miscegenated, winds her way to marriage with Ariamento. As the bride of Buena Vista, she secures the Caspareta family's land, and allows Gonzardo to take his revenge on Santa Anna and the corrupt Mexican government. Finally, U.S. Captain Charles Blackler, the brother of Annabel and Blondinita, marries Gonzardo's daughter, Marguerita.

The text's final scene suggests that all its subjects have been returned to their proper places, in another nod to a Shakespearean trope: "Dear readers . . . we will hasten to conclude our narrative, by saying, that . . . Gonzardo Caspareta, with his band of rancheros, generously escorted all the Americans of the party out of all danger from Santa Anna and his soldiers, so that they all got safely at last to the American camp" (100). However, *The Mexican Spy* has so miscegenated its subjects that "Americans" and "Mexicans" are not so easily separable, even by so generous an escort. Blondinita and Annabel, "American by birth" but Mexican by upbringing, end up on different sides of the new racial and national divide between Mexico and the United States: Blondinita, as Ariamento's bride of Buena Vista restoring justice in Mexico, and Annabel, as Henry's American bride. Charles Blackler, who unlike his sisters never lived in Mexico despite his Mexican mother and uncle, marries Gonzardo's daughter, but we are never told whether they end up "American" or "Mexican."

The heterosexual normativity of the conclusion thus figures not so much a return to proper place, a reestablishment of temporarily crossed borders, as it does a wary transformation of propriety itself. At the conclusion of this text, Henry assimilates the biracial and binational Annabel into the white, American fold, while Ariamento assimilates the biracial and binational Blondinita into the Mexican fold; in turn, the biracial but decidedly American Charles ends up suspended between borders in his marriage with the Mexican Marguerita. Subject to assimilation but also potentially assimilative, Mexican racial and national form emerges from this text with a powerful ambivalence, a difference suspended between becoming-American and becoming-Mexican. Though Gonzardo, his son Ariamento, and his bride of Buena Vista Blondinita represent the potentially honorable side of becoming-Mexican, apparently balancing the dishonor of Santa Anna, Don Jose, and Corita, that honor has its limits. Explains the conclusion, "As for the Mexican Spy [Gonzardo Caspareta], we have also heard that he was killed at the battle of Buena Vista" (100). Like the Yucatecan Creoles with whom the United States forged a wary, informal alliance, Gonzardo leaves a not-quite-white legacy. Killed for battling the United States, he nonetheless lives on in his son's propertied marriage. Yet Gonzardo's afterlife is transformed, for his property has been returned with a difference: rather than returning Mexicans to Mexico and Americans to the United States, *The Mexican Spy* civilizes Mexico, assimilating Annabel to U.S. civility and giving whiteness to Mexico in the form of Blondinita.

Crucially, Gonzardo's not-quite-white legacy is confirmed by the two other major characters, to whose fate in the novel's precipitous conclusion we can now turn: Pelatiah P. Shattuck and Brutus. Pelatiah plays the matchmaker in the text's binational, interracial marriages even as he declares his willingness to fight to the death defending slavery. As *The Mexican Spy*'s most intimate hero, Pelatiah even more than *The Heroine of Tampico*'s Jedediah endorses the fight against bad, barbarous Mexicans and pursues the assimilation of good, civilizable Mexicans. Pelatiah thus figures the possibility incessantly reiterated by so many U.S.–Mexico War novelettes in their moments of narrative closure: U.S. white civility will be rejuvenated in Mexico, where savagery can be eradicated and civilization can be tutored. Brutus, in turn, functions as *The Mexican Spy*'s confirmation of this relationship between Mexico and the United States. A former slave from Alabama, he begins the story as Villa Rica's servant and ends the story happily choosing to return to slavery in Alabama. Brutus is a crucial character in this novel, because the extreme representation of his blackness—via the absurd dialect he speaks, the foolish minstrelsy he performs, and the glorification of chattel slavery he voices—differentiates his racial form from that of the always clever, if at times treacherous, Mexicans. I want to suggest that this differentiation, coupled with the miscegenation performed by the other Mexican characters, amplifies the ambivalent, Indian racial form of Mexicans in the novelettes. Brutus's incessant, hyperbolic reminder of black inassimilability brings into relief the different forms of indianness Mexicans can inhabit. The very possibility of Mexican assimilation to white civility is secured by the figure of Brutus. It should not surprise us, then, that characters such as Brutus, and the indianization of the Mexican he enables, appear ritually in U.S.–Mexico War novelettes.

Charles E. Averill's novelettes are much more explicitly violent and sexual than any others from the period. Consequently, their concluding flurries of weddings amplify both the ambivalence of the U.S.–Mexico War/Caste War conjuncture, and the stakes of containing that ambivalence. *The Secret Service Ship, or, The Fall of San Juan D'Ulloa* (1848) is set in 1846 during the U.S. siege on the castle of San Juan D'Ulúa near Veracruz, just after U.S. victories at the battles of Palo Alto and Resaca de la Palma and on the eve of the battle of Buena Vista.[65] As the novelette opens, Midshipman Rogers of the U.S. Navy's Secret Service ship *The Spirit of the Sea* has crept into the castle as a spy, and runs into a woman pursued by a Mexican officer with "the tall proportions and herculean frame of a gigantic man" and a "black heart" (10). As he tries to rape her, she cuts off his hand, and with Rogers's help hurls him into a "death-vault," or a pit in the floor of the castle. She turns out to be Isora la Vega, daughter of a Mexican general, "radiant with all the beauty of Mexico's sunny southern clime, matchless in the perfections of the magnificent queenly figure, the superb black eye, the glossy waves of night-hued hair, the exquisite classic contour, the rose-bud lip that modelled Cupid's bow, and the thousand graces of person, air and manner" (12). The dismembered Mexican officer, she explains, is General Ampudia, her father's rival, and the death vault is a pit filled with the rotting bodies of Ampudia's enemies, including, perhaps, her father. Isora and Rogers immediately form a transnational bond: "'O, my suffering country!'" Isora declares, "'I love thee, will sacrifice life for thee—but O, I cannot doom to ignominious death the preserver of my life! Midshipman Rogers! you come a spy of my native land's sworn enemy! but you have perilled all for me, and are safe in my honor'" (16). She promises not to turn him in, and the scene is set for their promised marriage, with which the text concludes.

Before that resolution, however, the text winds its way through myriad murders, dismemberments, imprisonments, poisonings, tortures, attempted rapes, and drag scenes. We learn that Isora has an alternate identity: Lorenzo Larasca, the "grand Chieftain" or "Queen" of an honorable band of Mexican "banditti" who are themselves fighting against both the United States and corrupt, barbaric Mexicans like Ampudia and his two evil deputies, the "twin Patagonians" Juana and Geronimo (92). The battle between Mexico and the United States increasingly becomes a sideshow to these intra-Mexican disputes. The text sets Isora and her friend Inez, among the "noblest women in Mexico" (42), along with the brave Bernardo Balsatio, who turns out to be Isora's brother, against the "black," "hellish," and "fiendish" Ampudia and the "inhuman" siblings Juana and Geronimo (28). The siblings' inhumanity takes on a quite precise, Indian form, when Geronimo declares that "'the Cannibal blood of Patagonia flows in our veins! we are, both she and I, of the race of giants,—the race which scorns connexion with the poor pigmy populace of the world, and loves to feast upon the paltry mannikins' blood and revel in their misery!'" (90). The line between civilizable and uncivilizable Mexicans could not be more clearly drawn, rooted as it is in the quantity of indianness that "flows through their veins." Which side represents Mexico's true nature remains, however, vigorously ambivalent throughout the text.

Mexico's tenuous potential is even written into its geography. As Isora declares to Rogers in Mexico City, as the U.S. military is on the verge of moving into the city: "'Oh that bleeding Mexico were as calm and sweetly peaceful as this fair city!' exclaimed the young Mexican girl, as that same day with her lover she stood admiring the beauties and splendor of the magnificent metropolis, which is probably the most superb capital on the face of the civilized globe" (88). Crucially, this passage wavers between making Mexico's potential civility available to assimilation by the United States, with the universal figure of "the civilized globe," and recognizing Mexico's independence, by granting the status of national "capital" to "the magnificent metropolis." Is Mexico's civility independent of or subject to the United States, the passage seems to ask. Again, the answer is found in the text's concluding weddings.

For most of the text, Isora crosses back and forth between her Isora and Lorenzo identities, all the while insisting on keeping Rogers at a distance: "'And why not, love, break through your fatal vow never to be mine while our countries are at war?' said her lover, tenderly, as he held her thus fondly to his bosom. 'Never, never, Rogers, while Mexico and America are foes to each other;' exclaimed the brave girl, firmly" (88). Yet when the "twin Patagonians" and Ampudia are killed and Mexico is defeated by the United States at the end of the text, she renounces her male identity and agrees to marry Rogers:

"Dearest Isora," said her lover tenderly and gladly, "we shall soon be happy, and you will be all my own, for this war that now divides us for a brief time, must now soon close beyond a doubt, and then there will be no bar of nationality between our union. It is, dearest, but an engagement fixed for an indefinite instead of a stated time, and will not last half as long probably as half the definite engagements of my own country."

"O, dear Rogers," exclaimed the happy girl, "I am so happy that peace is now again about to smile upon us. All the dark clouds that before overshadowed have now disappeared, before the bright sun of joy and happiness that rises so bright and glorious in our joyous life-horizon. Ah, dearest, I joy to think how soon we shall be indissolubly united." (100)

Then, suddenly, the narrator brings the story to a syntactically tortured close:

And so, dear reader, please to consider our hero and heroine happily wedded at the end of the war. . . . Our hero is one of those staunch American hearts which fell vanquished before the smiling attacks of Mexican's fair daughters, which yet had always conquered in the strife their brothers and their sires.

The Mexican Capital has now fallen, the halls of the Montezumas are ours, Mexico has already opened negotiations of amity; and our whole land rings with the glad intelligence that Peace is again dawning brightly the country's rainbow of promise in the nation's horizon. If indeed this be so, the campaign is over, and so is our tale, the war ended, and finished also our story of the SECRET SERVICE SHIP. (100)

The "fair" Isora "vanquished" Rogers by surrendering her masculinity and turning away from her racial and national "brothers" and "sires," thereby consolidating the white masculinity of the U.S. citizen-soldier. Miscegenation emerges here as the figure for an "indissolubly united" Mexico and the United States. Yet the text also remains tenuously attached to Mexico's inassimilable independence, vacillating wildly with Rogers and Isora's syntactically ambivalent declarations of that unity. Rogers's invokes a near-future happiness, yet he also struggles to isolate that future moment: a "war that now divides us for a brief time" is "now soon close beyond a doubt," suggesting the "now" is paradoxically both a moment of war and a moment of hopeful unity. That paradoxically divided and united "now" turns up again in the next sentence, Rogers's last words in the text, splitting what is meant to be a climactic articulation of hope into an utterly confusing attempt to isolate the precise moment of unity: "It is, dearest, but an engagement fixed for an indefinite instead of a stated time, and will not last half as long probably as half the definite engagements of my own country." Isora's final words echo this ambivalence. "Peace is now about to smile upon us," she claims, also vacillating between the present and the future. Her subsequent extended metaphor amplifies this vacillation, as it declares that "the dark clouds" "have now disappeared," and yet places the "bright and glorious" sun on the "life-horizon," about to rise.

Furthermore, the Rogers/Isora wedding is coupled with the marriage of Isora's friend and near-double throughout the text, Inez Iturbide, the daughter of the Mexican leader, to Bernardo Balsatio/La Vega, Isora's brother and another "banditti" leader thought to have been killed. Once Bernardo is freed from Ampudia's dungeon, he and Inez fall in love, and as Inez exclaims to Isora, "'O, joy! he yet lives, and soon will be here again. We meet daily, and this is our bridal day . . . ' 'your bridal day!' reiterated

Isora, in surprise. Ere Inez could reply, a manly step and then a gentle knock was heard at the door, and Inez with love's instinct flew to the door. Opening, it gave to Don Bernardo Balsatio, now looking the manly, handsome cavalier that he was, a far different appearance from the unshaven and neglected captive sufferer of San Juan de'Ulloa's [sic] dungeon" (98). This couple provides the hope of an independent Mexican civility, formally equal with but racially and nationally independent of the United States. On Averill's rendering, Mexico, at once barbaric and civil, subject to destruction and conquest as well as assimilation and independence, offers an ambivalent assurance of U.S. white civility.

Another prolific writer of U.S.–Mexico War novelettes, Justin Jones, who wrote by the name Harry Hazel, vividly foregrounds this ambivalent assurance in his texts. In *Inez, The Beautiful: or, Love on the Rio Grande* (1846), Hazel figures miscegenation as the management of U.S. citizenship's racial and national ambivalence.[66] Representing Mexican officers as "chieftains" (9) and Mexican soldiers as "half-barbarous republicans" (10), "savage beasts" (12), and "half-naked, half starved beings, wearing scarcely the semblance of humanity" (10), this text vigorously indianizes the Mexican. The figures "half" and "scarcely" suspend Mexicans between republican white civility and Indian savagery, raising the question of which way they will develop.

This question is answered by a love affair between U.S. Lieutenant Charles Devereux, "whose complexion, contrasted with the swarthy Mexicans and Spaniards . . . was light and fair" (10), and Doña Inez Olmedo, who was "not of the blood of the Anglo-Saxons, [as] the long tresses of glossy raven hair, and the large black lustrous eyes, fully indicated," but also "was not a descendant of the Aztecs, [as] the transparency of her complexion and the graceful delicacy of her limbs strongly denoted" (16). Rather, "pure Castilian blood flowed in her veins" (16). The two meet in the borderlands between the U.S. and Mexican armies, during a truce in a June 1846 battle at "Matamoras." Devereux has sneaked across the battle lines, and happens upon Don Jose Terceiro who, with his "dark features," is attempting to rape Inez: "His black, serpent-like eyes, were gazing upon the voluptuous charms which her well-moulded bust displayed—to the heavings of her bosom, and to the snowy whiteness of her uncovered neck.—It required but little to inflame the worst passions of the Castilian, and he had more than once marked Inez as a victim to his hellish lust" (14). The vacillation among figures for the Spaniard of the Black Legend, the Aztec, and the miscegenated Mexican echoes the jumble of terms the U.S. Congress applied to the Yucatecan Creoles as it debated the Yucatán aid bill. By representing both Don Jose and Inez as "Castilian," the text links these two characters even as it seeks to differentiate them so vividly. Don Jose's "Castilian" darkness exceeds the "pure Castilian blood" that Inez exhibits, suggesting that his "blood" does not run so "pure," that his "worst passions" are more than "Castilian." In turn, Inez's suggestion that being "captured by the Indians" would be "infinitely worse" than "falling into the hands of the Americans" positions her as ambivalently between indianness and whiteness, as well as potentially desiring the latter (14).

Devereux saves Inez, but after arranging to meet her again he is captured on his way back to the U.S. camp. Faced with a military trial and a near-certain execution, Devereux's own tenuous identity is secured:

And in this particular he might have been called effeminate looking; so, too, with his large blue and lustrous eyes, which many a proud beauty of the opposite sex might have envied. But here, for one of his age, all traces of effeminacy ceased;—his broad and massive brow, dark and shaggy eyebrows; a fine and manly lip, on which rested an expression of magnanimous defiance and courage, indicated the heart and soul of the man. With a nod and a smile which shew a handsome set of even white teeth, he answered the salutation of the Judge Advocate, and took the seat which had been assigned him with the utmost composure. (10)

As an officer, Devereux's effeminacy might be a mark of a class standing that kept him from being an enlisted soldier. If so, his encounter with Inez and his trial by Mexican "half-barbarous republicans" rejuvenates him, allowing him to normalize his masculinity and gather his racial and national status.

If the concluding wedding between Inez and Devereux consummates that rejuvenation, then the plot leading up to this conclusion is an extended performance of that consummation. Having decided that they cannot be together until the U.S.–Mexico War is settled, Devereux and Inez part ways. As Devereux fights on the battlefield at "Resaca del a Palma" toward the end of the text, he meets "among the little Mexican band . . . one, young and even effeminate looking, who fought beside his General with a courage, which even the equally brave Devereux could not but admire" (45). This "Mexican prodigy" with "dark eyes" fights his way through the American forces with General Olmedo, Inez's father, until the two finally surrender to Devereux. After Devereux confesses his love for Inez to her father, the "effeminate" youth steps forward: "a surprising *denouement* occurred, not intended for that time and place, in the sudden transformation of a gallant warrior into an Amazonian beauty. By some accident or other the straight and sleek black hair, which before only covered the head, now floated in curled clusters over the shoulders" (49). Of course, it is Inez herself, in drag as a young Mexican soldier, "'a second Joan of Arc!'" Devereux declares excitedly (49). Quickly, "she divested herself of her male apparel, and soon appeared in her own proper dress. 'There, I feel much easier now, and I hope I shall never have cause to wear such uncomfortable garments again'" (49). The recovery of her "effeminate looking" manner mirrors the eradication of Devereux's "effeminacy" earlier in the text. Transformed into "an Amazonian beauty" of "the land of the Montezumas," Inez's "pure Castilian blood" is indianized so that it may be assimilated by Devereux. Her disguise and unveiling pave the way for her return to propriety, but, as in Halyard's *The Mexican Spy*, a transformed propriety—or, more precisely, a propriety whose transformation is promised.

With Jose Terceiro marching off to the gallows of the victorious U.S. forces, and Inez and her father applauding American "justice," the narrative concludes abruptly:

A contract of marriage between our hero and heroine was concluded upon, but not to be consummated until peace is concluded between the United States and Mexico! The latter condition our readers may be assured is "a consummation devoutly to be wished," by both the lovers, and they may be set down, sincerely and conscientiously, as agreeing with that respectable class of citizens who embrace the strongest PEACE views.

Our hero and heroine are now in the land of the Montezumas, the one pursuing his profession according to "orders;" and the other is on a visit to a noble family in the city of Mexico, where she is passing time with her friends as pleasantly as the peculiar circumstances will permit. The illustrious General is still detained as a prisoner, though every mark of respect and attention is extended to him by the hospitable Americans, and his prison-house covers the whole length and breadth of our great and glorious Republic.

The union of our lovers, should the happy event be attended with anything remarkable, will serve us at some future time as the basis of a short sequel. (50–51)

In this denouement, the indianization of Inez carries all the ambivalence we have seen in the other discursive practices of this period. More honorable than the "dark" Jose Terceiro, Inez reveals the potential civility of Mexicans. As "an Amazonian beauty" who surrenders her masculinity to Devereux, she places that potential in the hands of U.S. white civility. Hospitable America offers itself up as, at once, a gallows for the "monstrous villain[s]" of Mexico (50), a spacious "prison-house" for "illustrious" Mexican men, and an altar of miscegenation for Mexican women. Offering both conquest and assimilation, vacillating among the execution, imprisonment, and assimilation of Mexicans, *Inez, The Beautiful* promises a new kind of "peace," one that simultaneously assimilates and conquers Mexico.

I want to suggest that a "short sequel" of sorts was written for *Inez, The Beautiful*, but not necessarily as a novelette. The new kind of "peace" Harry Hazel figures, a "peace" that articulated the formal equality of citizenship with an emerging, racial and national codification of Mexico and the United States, is embodied in the very text that brought the U.S.–Mexico War to a close: the Treaty of Guadalupe Hidalgo.

Beyond the Broken Promise

Article 9 of the treaty reads:

The Mexicans who, in the territories aforesaid, shall not preserve the character of citizens of the Mexican Republic, conformably with what is stipulated in the preceding article, shall be incorporated into the Union of the United States and be admitted, at the proper time (to be judged of by the Congress of the United States) to the enjoyment of all the rights of citizens of the United States according to the principles of the Constitution; and in the mean time shall be maintained and protected in the free enjoyment of their liberty and property, and secured in the free exercise of their religion without restriction.[67]

There is a long and varied tradition of representing article 9's promise of "all the rights of citizens of the United States" to annexed Mexicans as a "broken promise," given the extensive, postwar racial exploitation of Mexican Americans in the United States.

In particular, complex articulations of this "broken promise" discourse emerged from post–World War II Chicano and Mexican American activists who, variously in California, Texas, and the Southwest, sought to use the treaty's promise as a lever for antiracist, anticolonial struggles, often within an internal colonization framework. However, as that quite supple activist work has more recently been translated into institutionalized civil rights discourse and, in turn, into the work of literary critics on the U.S.–Mexico War period, it has at times become a more static and unidimensional call for the fulfillment of the promise of equal rights.[68] But what exactly does it mean to call for the fulfillment of article 9? What rights are promised? What kind of equality does it figure?

First of all, Latino Critical Legal scholars have produced an important body of work—so-called Lat Crit scholarship—critiquing the way the phrase "at the proper time (to be judged of by the Congress of the United States)" ultimately handed the civil rights of annexed Mexicans over to a bureaucratic, U.S. judiciary working entirely within an Anglo-U.S., English-language legal system utterly unfamiliar to most Mexicans.[69] "The proper time" turned out to be never for many annexed Mexicans; those who tried to negotiate the absurdly complex and ever-changing avenues to citizenship rights, particularly property rights, often found themselves with nothing to show for years of participation in an expensive and evasive procedure. Even when they wanted to renounce their Mexican citizenship, they often found themselves locked out by article 9's bureaucratic institutionalization.

But as we have seen from the government documents and the novelettes, the "character" of Mexican citizens was difficult to decipher at all, much less adjudicate, for the U.S. citizen whose representatives are, after all, charged with that responsibility by article 9. Indeed, the anxious ambiguity the U.S. citizen saw in the Mexican citizen is recorded by the prohibition "shall not preserve": the first step on the road to becoming a U.S. citizen is a negation, a becoming unpreserved, disposed of, lost, wasted. The Mexican citizen must negate itself and then present that negated self before the U.S. citizen's representative for judgment. Judgment of what? Judgment of the negation. But what, precisely, is to be negated? And how is that negation to be performed?

With the qualifying phrase "conformably with what is stipulated in the preceding article," article 9 refers us to article 8, which offers a certain formula for this negation:

> Those who shall prefer to remain in the said territories [previously belonging to Mexico but now belonging to the United States], may either retain the title and rights of Mexican citizens, or acquire those of citizens of the United States. But, they shall be under the obligation to make their election within one year from the date of the exchange of ratifications of this treaty: and those who shall remain in the said territories, after the expiration of that year, without having declared their intention to retain the character of Mexicans, shall be considered to have elected to become citizens of the United States.[70]

"The character of Mexicans" is here defined as "the title and rights of Mexican citizens," and it can be preserved only by an explicit utterance, an "election" or declaration of "intention" "to retain" that character. Either this explicit utterance (a declaration of "intention" to "acquire" the character "of citizens of the United States") or a failure or refusal to make any declaration (a silence on the matter) would constitute the negation of "the character of Mexicans." In the case of a failure or refusal to declare one's citizenship, U.S. citizenship would declare itself, the subject would be declared by U.S. citizenship, incorporated or assimilated by default.

Yet the significance of this "election" or declaration of "intention" is oddly unclear in article 8. Regardless of whether one retains "the character of Mexicans" or acquires that "of citizens of the United States," the article explicitly promises to protect the subject's "title" to their property, "without their being subjected, on this account, to any contribution, tax, or charge whatever." Indeed, as article 8 concludes, "In the said territories, property of every kind, now belonging to Mexicans not established there, shall be inviolably respected. The present owners, the heirs of these, and all Mexicans who may hereafter acquire said property by contract, shall enjoy with respect to it, guaranties equally ample as if the same belonged to citizens of the United States."[71] If article 8 demands an "election" of Mexican or U.S. "character," defining "character" as "title and rights," and then promises to protect "title" regardless of national identity, then the "election" of Mexican or U.S. "character" must pertain to this category of "rights." That is, the difference between Mexican and U.S. "character" must be something more than property rights, some unspecified "rights" beyond "title." This detour through article 8 thus returns us to the question provoked by article 9: exactly what is the Mexican "character"—the unspecified "rights" beyond property—to be negated by U.S. citizenship?

I want to suggest that the government documents and the novelettes I have been considering throughout this chapter give us some indication. The elusive act of ceasing to "preserve the character of citizens of the Mexican Republic," the act that would constitute a cessation of the character of Mexican citizenship, would seem to be a renunciation of the very "character" that has proven to be so anxiously ambiguous to the U.S. citizen: the variously Indian racial form of the Mexican. Indeed, because that "character" is anxiously ambiguous, the renunciation also functions as a naming, a specification, an identification of that "character." The prohibition "shall not preserve" demands the negation of an ambiguity so that the ambiguity will no longer be ambiguous, so that the ambiguity will emerge as an unambiguous, negated "character." The negation functions as an identification of that which has been negated. It retroactively produces its own, discrete object.

Now, if the negation is judged to have been fully performed (if a negation could ever be fully performed) then the "shall not preserve" gives way to a positive content: "the enjoyment of all the rights of citizens of the United States." But what does that mean? Again, the government documents and the novelettes give us an indication by pitting the indianized "character" of the Mexican against white civility, by presenting that "character" with the choice of eradication or assimilation. Forged at the conjuncture of the U.S.–Mexico War and the Caste War, "the enjoyment of all the rights of citizens of the United States" promises assimilation to white civility. It is not enough to function as if one were a white citizen. One must enjoy that white civility. As objects of desire, as enjoyable objects whose condition of enjoyment is a negation of the Mexican self, a disposal of Indian racial form, these citizenship rights would seem to entail specific obligations too. What are those obligations?

The articulation of the U.S.–Mexico War and the Caste War makes some of those obligations apparent. Let us remember that, as the ink was drying on the treaty's promise, the U.S. government sanctioned informal assistance to the Yucatecan Creoles. In particular, hundreds of U.S. citizen-soldiers—Corporal Jedediah Starkweathers, if you will—arrived in Yucatán to fight with Mexican elites in a race war against Maya who were themselves, apparently, fighting for another form of citizenship, a freedom from both eradication and assimilation. Those U.S. soldiers exercised their patriotic duty to eradicate the barbaric Maya so as to clear the path to white civility for the not-quite-white Yucatecan Creoles. The involvement of those soldiers in the Caste War performs precisely the task laid out by Bigelow in the letter with which I began this chapter: as a way to "relieve these unfortunate" Creoles from the "red men" of their territory so that they might attain the status of U.S. civility. These citizen-soldiers embody the obligations of the informal alliance between the United States and the Yucatán's Creoles, and articulate the racially and nationally specific obligations of "all the rights of U.S. citizens." By understanding themselves as obliged to kill Indians and assimilate Creoles, they conditioned the exercise of their rights upon such eradication and assimilation.

Thus, article 9's promise does not necessitate doing away with racial and national hierarchies. Rather, the citizenship offered by the treaty intensifies those hierarchies, subjecting U.S. and Mexican citizen-subjects to racial and national codification even as it formally equates them to each other. This citizenship conditions its civility on the assimilation of Mexican Americans in the United States and the formation of a comprador class in Mexico. That is, article 9's abstract equality demands the assimilation of Mexican Americans to white civility and the cooperation of Mexican elites with U.S. capital. However, since assimilation undermines Mexican American subjectivity, urging the Mexican American subject to become white, and compradorization undermines Mexican subjectivity, urging the Mexican subject to become a U.S. client, article 9 effectively promises to fracture Mexican American and Mexican subjectivities. To seek the fulfillment of article 9's promise, then, is to run the risk of endlessly pursuing these fracturing demands of racial assimilation and national compradorization, to iterate and reiterate the articulation of formal equality and white, U.S. civility. Article 9 produces and guarantees imperial U.S. citizenship. The U.S. role in the Caste War makes this reading of article 9 apparent.

Turning a Page of U.S. Imperialism

In "A Page of American History," an article published in the *American Antiquarian Society* journal in 1905, Edward H. Thompson—onetime U.S. consul to Mexico and a serious student of Maya antiquity—sets out to recall a forgotten tale: the participation of U.S. citizens in the Caste War. Assured of the whiteness of the peninsula's Creoles—"The white Yucatecon of that day, whether hidalgo or artizan, was no degenerate"—Thompson nonetheless represents those forgotten U.S. soldiers as agents of the white American's burden: "During the middle part of the last century, events were taking place in Yucatan that, had they happened in other lands or at other times, would have become subjects of epic poems. But the place of happening was on a distant, ragged edge of the American continent, more unknown, perhaps, to the average American of those times, than is the darkest spot of the Dark Continent to the citizen of today."[72] After giving a sweeping account of the events leading up to the Caste War, and a pathos-laden synopsis of the struggles of the Creoles and their brave U.S. allies against the "savage ferocity and valor" of the Maya, Thompson suddenly becomes an ethnographer.[73]

As he explains, "From now on I shall quote the statements of active participants on both sides of the struggle, statements made to me personally and noted down with great care."[74] Among the statements he records are testimonials from two surviving U.S. veterans of the Caste War, Edward Pinkus and Michael Foster. After the war, Pinkus returned wounded to Mérida, where "he was tenderly nursed back to life and health by the lady, a native of Merida, whom he afterward married. Afterward he went in and fought against the French by the side of Juarez. When peace was again declared he returned to Merida and started what was then the finest tailoring establishment in the province. He lived to see his sons grow up to be men of influence and respectability in the community."[75] Foster, in turn, "married a native of Yucatan by whom he had one son"; "at the time of making his statement, in 1904, [he was] clear in intellect but had almost forgotten his native tongue. He spoke Spanish and the native Maya tongue with far greater facility than he did the English language."[76] Though Thompson's flair for romance makes Pinkus and Foster seem like characters torn from the pages of a novelette, these stories are in many ways the very opposite of those ambivalent allegories. By describing white Americans settlers who went native after the Caste War, allowing Mexico to assimilate them, Thompson makes the Creole world of Yucatán seem more desirable than the white civility of the United States.

However, at the very end of his article, when Thompson records the testimonials of three Mayan veterans—General Naverrette, Dionisio Pec, and Leandro Poot—he puts the stories of Pinkus and Foster in context:

> I will now give the statements of those who actually fought against those men and, right here it may be well to note two interesting facts, that by a curious coincidence make me, perhaps, of all living persons, the only man who could produce these statements. Several years ago, while on an exploration into the then almost unexplored interior, I chanced upon an aged native working his *milpa* alone. I spent some time in the neighborhood investigating a hitherto unknown ruined group, and during a part of this time he worked for me.[77]

Thompson's "first interesting fact" is that he met Dionisio Pec "while on an exploration into the then almost unexplored interior [of Yucatán]," and that Pec "worked for" Thompson while he "spent some time in the neighborhood investigating a hitherto unknown ruined group." His "second interesting fact is that Leandro Poot, the younger brother of the former war chief of the rebellious Mayas, is now and has been for several years a dweller upon my plantation of Chichen. We have had many hours of pleasant and interesting conversation and the statement he gives was in this way obtained."[78]

The reason we can read Pinkus and Foster's testimonials at all, we learn here, is Thompson's presence in Yucatán as a turn-of-the-century, neocolonial agent of international capital. In fact, Thompson is well known for having used his diplomatic post and access to U.S. capital to plunder sacred Mayan sites in violation of Mexican laws against the export of antiquities. In particular, he infamously dredged the sacred *cenotes* of Chichén Itzá in a search for gold, as Thompson's own accounts of his actions in Mexico reveal and as Quetzil E. Castañeda has more recently recounted. In the contrast between the value Thompson attributed to Mayan antiquities (many of which are still housed in U.S. museums) and his negation of any contemporary Mayan claim to their own past, we can see an archeological counterpart to the simultaneous enfranchisement and negation of Mexicans expressed by the governmental and literary archives I have considered in this chapter.[79]

While Thompson was in Yucatán developing his "plantation" and raiding archeological sites, masses of Mexican laborers were slipping into often brutal poverty as production for foreign consumption increased markedly, with profits accruing to large landholders, merchants, bankers, industrialists, as well as fractions of the military and the political classes. Crucially, foreign and particularly U.S. investment in the Mexican economy boomed. As James D. Cockroft writes, "by 1897, U.S. investment in Mexico totaled more than $200 million and exceeded U.S. investment in the rest of Latin America, in Canada, in Europe, or in Asia. In the next fourteen years, this figure *quintupled*, and by 1911 U.S. investments were estimated to be greater than those of the Mexican bourgeoisie and double those of other foreign investors."[80] Along the way, landowners like Thompson made ample use of cheap wage labor and debt peonage, impoverishing peasant workers such as Leandro Poot and Dionisio Pec. Writes Gilbert M. Joseph of this conjuncture:

In the decades ahead [of the 1870s], local henequen planters became increasingly dependent upon U.S. capital, loaned first by bankers and subsequently by cordage brokers and manufacturers, most notably [the U.S.-based] International Harvester [Company]. . . .

The *yucatecos* would soon learn how onerous this lien arrangement could be. Recent scholarship has linked the brutal, regressive nature of the labor regime in Yucatán during the late *porfiriato* to the planters' pressing need for capital and their increasingly precarious position in the henequen marketing structure. Each of the rural mobilizations that took place in Yucatán during the early revolutionary era (1910–13) sought in one way or another to break the stranglehold on the regional political ecomomy that North American corporate capital (i.e., International Harvester and its satellites) had established, in close partnership with the most powerful faction of the planter class. Yet while this transnational "collaborator mechanism" provoked intense opposition at all levels of regional society, it also underwrote a strain of dependent capitalism that would seriously impede popular participation and limit the effectiveness of the later revolutionary process (1915–24).[81]

Whereas the white settlers Pinkus and Foster embody the trace of Polk's failed effort to annex Yucatán, Thompson, the proper subject of this "Page of American History," embodies the historical resolution of this mid-nineteenth-century flashpoint. Thus, his exceptionality as "the only man who could produce these statements" figures the transformation of U.S. exceptionalism from the manifest destiny of white settler colonials such as Pinkus and Foster to the corporate neocolonial development Cockroft and Joseph reference, a transformation initiated by the articulation of the U.S.–Mexico War and the Caste War of Yucatán. One cannot help but wonder if Thompson's "conversations" with Leandro Poot, his plantation "dweller," remained as "pleasant and interesting" as they seemed in 1905 when, just five years later, peasant workers became a militant spark for the Mexican Revolution.

"Yankee Universality"

Our analysis has shown that the form of value, that is, the expression of the value of a commodity, arises from the nature of commodity-value, as opposed to value and its magnitude arising from their mode of expression as exchange-value. This second view is the delusion both of the Mercantilists (and people like Ferrier, Ganilh, etc., who have made a modern rehash of Mercantilism) and their antipodes, the modern bagmen of free trade, such as Bastiat and his associates.

Capital, volume 1

*I*n the first chapter of *Capital*, volume 1, Karl Marx warns his readers not to take the well-worn distinction between free trade and mercantilism at face value. He suggests that the two economic systems are *"Antipoden"* or "antipodes"—opposed yet also the mirror image of one another—because they both share the same "delusion" about value. Both "the Mercantilists" and "the modern bagmen of free trade, such as Bastiat and his associates," operate under the assumption that "value and its magnitude aris[e] from their mode of expression as exchange-value," whereas Marx argues that "the form of value, that is the expression of the value of a commodity, arises from the nature of commodity-value."[1] In other words, by representing the exchangeability of commodities as a natural attribute of the object, and thus as the source or ground of value, both mercantilists and free traders fail to consider the multiform, potentially antagonistic social relations that produce heterogeneous commodities—chief among them the commodity labor-power—that can be exchanged as if they were equal. As we saw in chapter 1, Fernand Braudel, Immanuel Wallerstein, and Giovanni Arrighi view this very antipodal relationship through a more metahistorical lens, showing how mercantilism and free trade policies have complemented one another in the historical formation of nation-states seeking imperial power.

However, the figure "antipodes" also points toward an articulation of mercantilism and free trade that escapes both the value theory account and the world system theory account—or, rather, an articulation that can only be analyzed at the intersection of these two accounts. "Antipodes" derives from Greek and Latin words literally meaning "having the feet opposite" and referring to people who live opposite to one another on the earth, such that the feet of one mirror the feet of the other. In modern Romance languages, this anthropospatial meaning was condensed with the more abstract meaning of "antipode"—"the exact opposite of a person or thing"—to produce a figure that could be (and indeed was) deployed powerfully in colonial discourse to name an absolute difference between Europeans and those subject to European colonization.[2] Yet the term's power is an anxious and unstable one, since the very absoluteness of the difference it invokes paradoxically initiates a differential relationship—the one's meaning comes to rely on the other's counter-meaning—that threatens to become an uneasy commonality, a mirroring in which the one's feet touch the feet of the other.

In his analyses of this antipodal relationship between mercantilism and free trade scattered throughout his work, Marx gave special consideration to perhaps the most influential U.S. political economist of the later nineteenth century: Henry Charles Carey. Indeed, by offering Frédéric Bastiat as his privileged example of "the modern bagmen of free trade" in the epigraph, Marx implicitly invokes Carey. For later in *Capital*, Marx calls Carey "the secret source of the harmonious wisdom of a Bastiat," and in the "Bastiat and Carey" section of the *Grundrisse* he represents Bastiat's work as derivative of Carey's, pointing out that even Bastiat "confesses that he leans on" Carey.[3]

Born in 1793, the son of the publisher Mathew Carey, Henry Charles Carey never went to college, instead turning his familial contacts into an extensive business career. In 1835, Carey pulled out of his father's struggling publishing house to study economics, and began to drift from his own, early free trade position toward the protectionism his father had long supported. Carey's 1847 text *The Past, the Present, and the Future*, along with his 1845 pamphlet "Commercial Associations of France and England," marked the completion of his turn to a comprehensive mercantilism, encompassing not only protectionist measures such as tariffs but also extensive state investment and intervention in industrial and agricultural development, banking, and trade.[4] Yet Carey never completely abandoned his earlier classicism. In fact, he continued to criticise strong, centralized states, representing his own advocacy of state-sponsored mercantilism as a temporary measure that would eventually be abandoned once the United States had "restored" its economic "independence."

In political circles, Carey's ties to business and manufacturing interests, rather than to the prevailing classicism of academic political economists, gave his mercantilism a certain pragmatic, popular credibility against the perceived elitism of the classicists.

After the publication of *The Past, the Present, and the Future*, he became a regular contributor to *The New York Tribune* (joining Marx, who with Engels's help also wrote for the *Tribune* from exile in London during the 1850s) and began to correspond regularly with U.S. political leaders, advising them on tariffs, banking, monetary policy, economic development, and slavery. In Europe, Carey became a favorite target of John Stuart Mill's polemics, and made a particular impact on the revival of mercantilism in Germany. Carey also became well known as a liberal social reformer who embraced gradual abolition, advocated certain rights for women, children, and the poor, and never tired of critiquing European imperialisms.[5]

Paradoxically, as we will see, Carey combined this liberalism with a vigorous advocacy of U.S. imperialism. As we saw in chapter 4, when Carey published *The Past, the Present, and the Future* in 1847, the United States was in the midst of a transition from a white settler colony fitfully subject to global economic and political developments to a colonial power increasingly able to subject other countries to its national economic and political developments. *The Past, the Present, and the Future*, and the liberal, nationalistic school of political economy it helped to found, played a crucial role in this transition. As a text that oscillates between free tradism and mercantilism, *The Past, the Present, and the Future*'s odd combination of liberal, imperial, antistatist mercantilism captures the anxious, colonial power invoked by Marx's figure of the antipode.

The antipode, Marx's interpretations of Carey, and Carey's *The Past, the Present, and the Future* together offer a fitting epilogue for *The Colonizing Trick* for a number of reasons. As a figure of an intimate yet anxious and unstable relationship between apparently opposed values, and as a figure with strong colonial undertones, the antipode can also be read as a figure of the imperial U.S. citizenship whose emergence I have been examining throughout this book. For, as we have seen, imperial U.S. citizenship is animated by a notion of equality that is intimately articulated with the seemingly opposed notions of racial and national codification.

Marx was curiously unable to read Carey's antipodal logic, his odd blend of mercantilism and free trade, of liberalism and U.S. imperialism. Relentlessly critical as he often was of Carey, Marx nonetheless fails to formulate an extensive critique of Carey's work. Consequently, Marx seems at times to be taken with Carey, especially when he represents Carey as a figure for the United States in general, a country Marx often represents as the most developed example of capitalism's modernizing tendencies. "Carey's generality," Marx writes, as we will see below, "is Yankee universality." Unfortunately, Marx does not consider the rich implications of this paradoxically particularized universality.

By attending more critically to Carey's antipodal logic, his "Yankee universality," I want to show how *The Past, the Present, and the Future*, as its title suggests, draws on the past and gestures toward the future of imperial U.S. citizenship. On the one hand, Carey's text is an outgrowth of the eighteenth- and early nineteenth-century discursive practices I have examined in *The Colonizing Trick*. In fact, Carey explicitly touches on each of this book's flashpoints: he advocates mercantilism, African colonization, Indian assimilation, and the colonization of Mexico. Carey thus traces the transformation of

U.S. exceptionalism from the manifest destiny of white settler colonials to a corporate, neocolonialism—the very transformation, which emerged out of the articulation of the U.S.–Mexico War and the Caste War, I discussed in chapter 4.

Along the way, Carey represents the United States as so exceptional that it is also globally exemplary and, hence, destined to reshape the world in its image. America's exceptional exemplarity is epitomized by *The Past, the Present, and the Future*'s antipodal protagonist, the U.S. citizen who knows best how to colonize the world because he knows so well what it was like to have been colonized by, and to have wrenched independence from, the British. A close reading of the text shows that this imperial U.S. citizen is animated by the continual and systematic racial purification of both domestic and foreign spaces. However, because this text is offered in the form of an allegory, it dramatically fails to control the very systematicity it proffers. To read Carey's antipodal allegory is thus to read for the anxious and unstable power it struggles to master.

On the other hand, *The Past, the Present, and the Future* also prefigures W. W. Rostow's post–World War II theorization of political economy, *The Stages of Economic Growth: A Non-Communist Manifesto*, and Francis Fukuyama's post–Cold War theorization of political economy, *The End of History and the Last Man*. For each text, equality is a fungible figure articulated with racial and imperial interests. Each text also marks a turning point in the history of U.S. imperialism. As I argue below, *The Past, the Present, and the Future* marks the transformation of white settler colonialism into corporate neocolonialism. As other critics have made clear, *The Stages of Economic Growth* marks the transformation of corporate neocolonialism into a developmentalism seeking to assimilate the newly liberated colonial world, *The End of History* marks the ascendancy of U.S.–style neoliberalism.

"Carey, the Yankee"

In the *Grundrisse*, Marx consistently shies away from Carey's odd blend of mercantilism and free trade in an apparent rush to oppose "Carey, the Yankee," as a representative of mercantilism, to "Bastiat, the Frenchman," as a representative of free trade.[6] Again and again "Carey" is offered as a metonym for "North America" or "America" and "Bastiat" as a metonym for "France."[7] Coupled with this is Marx's tendency to privilege Carey and the United States. That is, Marx turns Bastiat's "confession" about leaning on Carey not into a reading of Carey's antipodal combination of free trade and mercantilism, but rather into a reading of the originality of both Carey and the United States:

> Carey is the only original economist among the North Americans. Belongs to a country where bourgeois society did not develop on the foundation of the feudal system, but developed rather from itself; where this society appears not as the surviving result of a centuries-old movement, but rather as the starting-point of a new movement; where the state, in contrast to all earlier national formations, was from the beginning subordinate to bourgeois society, to its production, and never could make the pretence of being an end-in-itself; where, finally, bourgeois society itself, linking up the productive forces of

an old world with the enormous natural terrain of a new one, has developed to hitherto unheard-of dimensions and with unheard-of freedom of movement, has far outstripped all previous work in the conquest of the forces of nature, and where, finally, even the antitheses of bourgeois society itself appear only as vanishing moments. That the relations of production within which this enormous new world has developed so quickly, so surprisingly and so happily should be regarded by Carey as the eternal, normal relations of social production and intercourse, that these should seem to him as hampered and damaged by the inherited barriers of the feudal period, in Europe . . . what could be more natural?[8]

Marx seems oddly content with the highly abstract and unhistorical claim that the United States "did not develop on the foundation of the feudal system, but developed rather from itself," as if he were convinced by Carey's own representation of the United States as an exceptional and exemplary land. Certainly he excoriates Carey for generalizing American harmonies, and he later mocks Carey for blaming the world market in general, and Britain in particular, for "the beginnings of this disharmony in the United States":[9] However, Marx seems to accept that "disharmony" has, indeed, just begun to appear in the United States, causing trouble for a nation rooted in relatively "happy" and unquestionably exceptional beginnings.

Such a sketch of American beginnings thrives on a suppression of the complex dynamics of American-style "primitive accumulation," dynamics Marx elsewhere writes of quite carefully: indenture, slavery, expropriation of Indian lands, Indian genocide, state-sponsored wars for continental expansion.[10] It is as if the originality Marx attributes to Carey enables and is enabled by the exceptionalism Marx attributes to the United States. When Marx goes on to write that "Carey, quite apart from the scientific value of his researches, has at least the merit of articulating in abstract form the large-scale American relations, and, what is more, of doing so in antithesis to the old world,"[11] it would seem that, for Marx, "American relations" really are the antitheses of "old world" relations, that in an even more material sense than Carey admits, the United States really is uniquely "new," even endowed with "unheard-of freedom."

Indeed, by the end of "Bastiat and Carey," Marx's emphasis on Carey's originality becomes so conflated with Carey's claims about the originality of the United States that Marx's critical reading of Carey fades entirely from the text:

Carey is rich, therefore, in, so to speak, *bonafide* research in economic science, such as about credit, rent, etc. Bastiat is preoccupied merely with pacifying paraphrases of researches ending in contrasts; hypocrisy of contentment. Carey's generality is Yankee universality. France and China are equally close to him. Always the man who lives on the Pacific and the Atlantic. Bastiat's generality is to ignore all countries. As a genuine Yankee, Carey absorbs from all directions the massive material furnished him by the old world, not so as to recognise the inherent soul of this material, and thus to concede to it the right to its peculiar life, but rather so as to work it up for his purposes, as indifferent raw material, as inanimate documentation for his theses, abstracted from his Yankee standpoint. Hence his strayings and wanderings through all countries, massive and uncritical use of statistics, a catalogue-like erudition. Bastiat, by contrast, presents fantasy history. . . . Hence both [Bastiat and Carey] are equally unhistorical and anti-historical. But the unhistoric moment in Carey is the contemporary historic principle of North America, while the unhistoric element in Bastiat is a mere reminiscence of the French eighteenth-century manner of generalizing. Hence Carey is formless and diffuse, Bastiat affected and formally-logical. The most he achieves is commonplaces, expressed paradoxically, ground and polished into facets. With Carey, a couple of general theses, advanced in schoolmasterly form. Following them, a shapeless material, compendium, as documentation—the substance of his theses in no way digested.[12]

In this passage, Marx reiterates Carey's nationalistic claims in much the same way as the young Marx copied pages and pages of classical political economists such as Smith into his "Economic and Philosophical Manuscripts" of 1844. However, whereas the 1844 text began with such reiteration, effectively inhabiting the texts of the bourgeois economists so that it could critique them from within, "Bastiat and Carey" *concludes* with such reiteration, as if Carey's "Yankee universality" came to inhabit Marx. Certainly Marx is troubled by Carey's "abstracted" argumentation, his "formless and diffuse" presentation, his refusal to "digest" his theses. Nonetheless, by the end of the "Bastiat and Carey" manuscript, Carey's priority over Bastiat is not Carey's odd combination of antipodes, his articulation of Bastiat's free tradism with mercantilism, but rather the superiority of his analysis over Bastiat's, itself a reflection of the superiority of the United States over France. Since Carey himself was fond of reiterating the superiority of the United States over France, it would seem that even Marx's polemics against Bastiat bear the trace of Carey.[13]

The Past, The Present, and The Future

What would a more critical reading of Carey's antipodal representation of U.S. superiority look like? How, in other words, might we interpret Marx's precritical but rich claim that "Carey's generality is Yankee universality"? Marx fails to read Carey's antipodal logic because he fails to read the articulation of race and nation that authorizes it. Carey's work does not simply reflect the universality of American particularity, as Marx suggests in the *Grundisse*; nor is Carey's work dismissably superficial and spurious, as Marx suggests in *Capital*. Positioning the United States at the forefront of global political and economic development, *The Past, the Present, and the Future* commits the United States to building an informal empire perpetually animated by racial purification.

Though it begins in classic nineteenth-century political economic fashion by offering an allegory of an individual "first cultivator" peacefully, harmoniously, and industriously improving the land and increasing his population without any help from a meddling central state, the text eventually falters in its attempt to represent this as an American allegory. It depicts the United States as a naturally free and harmonious land that has been forced by British colonial rule and subsequent British economic hegemony into temporarily instituting a complex mercantilist system in order to restore a free and harmonious economy. Thus, at the beginning of his text Carey argues strenuously against state intervention and in favor of free trade, which he says prevailed at "America's" beginnings, but by the end of his text he calls for comprehensive state intervention to counter British power and to create the conditions for a "return" to free trade.

However, while the British (and occasionally other European empires) are the explicit cause of America's fall from freedom and harmony, *The Past, the Present, and the Future* is increasingly troubled by a series of racially marked figures who implicitly disrupt that freedom and harmony. Initially oblivious to the histories of slavery, genocide, and continental expansionism that made white settler colonialism so powerful in North America, *The Past, the Present, and the Future* eventually resorts to a very meddling state in an effort to contain and control the histories of racial violence and exploitation that continually creep into its narrative.

This process begins in earnest in chapter 10, where Carey distinguishes between two styles of colonization—"concentration" and "centralization":

> [Concentration] looks inward, and tends to promote a love of home and of quiet happiness, and a desire for union; facilitating the growth of wealth and the preparation of the great machine of production, and enabling man [to] acquire a love of books and a habit of independent thought and action. Here each man minds his own business, and superintends the application of the proceeds of his own labour. Centralization, on the contrary, looks outward, and tends to promote a love of war and discord, and a disrelish for home and its pursuits, preventing the growth of wealth, and retarding the preparation of the great machine. Under it men are forced to move in masses, governed by ministers, and generals, and admirals: and the habit of independent thought or action has no existence.[14]

As it happens, only the United States has been permitted to pursue concentration, which Carey calls "the natural system" (296), whereas all other nations of the world have been forced into centralization by European, particularly British and French, imperialism.

Crucially, concentration is unburdened by high costs and the arbitrary, corrupt, and often violent rule of "the State" because "In time, twenty, thirty, fifty, or a hundred of these little communities, at first scattered over the land, and separated by broad tracts of forest, and deep and rapid rivers running through the most fertile lands, or by hills and mountains: are brought into connection with each other: and these numerous little pyramids now form a great pyramid, or State" (288). Concentration thus does not do away with "the State," but rather develops it with what Carey calls a "system" that is different from centralization (322). The systematic inwardness, localism, and union to which Carey refers in these passages, the celebrated "connection with each other," or what Carey repeatedly calls concentration's "strong tendency towards placing the consumer by the side of the producer" (103), figure a formal equality among citizen-subjects apparently abstracted from their particular identities.

What is more, this equality becomes, for Carey, freedom itself: "With each step in the progress of this [system], labor will become more and more productive: man will learn more and more to concentrate his thoughts and affections upon home: he will learn more and more to unite with his fellow man, and will acquire daily increasing power over the land and over himself: and he will become richer and happier, more virtuous, more intelligent and more free" (308–9). Concentration thus also refers to an individual mindset, a practice of thought in which each and every individual trains his or her mind on the same systematic process. Concentration is a vigilant state of mind, an absolute self-control, named "freedom." Thus, though Carey decries the influence of "the State," he effectively envisions the state taking up its place within each individual.

Carey continually emphasizes that this concentrated equality and freedom is "American." In chapter 11, entitled "Colonization," he writes: "The colonization of the United States differs from that of the two countries we have considered [Britain and France], in the great fact that they [U.S. colonists] desire no subjects. The colonists are equal with the people of the States from which they sprang, and hence the quiet and beautiful action of the system" (345). U.S. colonialism is exceptional, here, because its colonists colonize themselves. However, as it turns out the system of U.S. colonialism need not be limited geographically: "Nevertheless, the Yankees are the greatest colonists in the world; and there are none so ready to drive a railroad through New York or Ohio, or to seize on the profits of a speculation in opium, or in bird's-nests: but when they do so, they take care that the men who manage their concerns abroad shall be owners like themselves, directly interested in the result" (338). Marx's suggestion that "France and China are equally close to" Carey, that he is "always the man who lives on the Pacific and the Atlantic," comes into focus here. "Yankees" can "drive through New York or Ohio," exploit the opium trade in Asia, and speculate in "bird's-nests" wherever they may be profitable because "Yankees" "take care" to train local agents of that exploitation in the art of concentration, to make them into little states linked in a "great union" with the United States.

Such training may require force, Carey admits. Though "peace" is one of Carey's great watchwords throughout the text, he also admits that widespread, popular commitment to war among U.S. citizens can at times be even more valuable. Thus, as he explains in chapter 14, North American conflicts have at times been best settled by the kind of war I considered in chapter 4 (he celebrates U.S. victories over Mexico) and other times merely by political settlements backed by the threat of such a war (he lauds the annexation, by treaty, of Oregon and Maine).

In two chapters late in the book, entitled "Ireland" and "India," Carey exemplifies this global power, this domestication of the globe, by calling on each country to push for independence from Britain and to adopt the U.S. system of concentration. Carey thus declares that since the U.S. citizen knows best how to decolonize himself (this because he succeeded in gaining his independence), and he also knows best how to colonize (this because of the harmony of interests Carey claims exists in North America), nations like Ireland and India ought to take after the United States, ought to heed its advice and imitate its development. The "American," according to Carey, is the world historical subject, the subject at the end of history. Its particularity is at once and paradoxically universal, its exceptionalism at once and paradoxically exemplary: "Yankee universality."

However, to sustain the credibility of the protagonist of his narrative, the colonized colonizer, Carey must also confront the histories his text fails to keep silent, histories that threaten to turn the entire story into a nightmare of expropriation, enslavement, and brutality. For instance, Carey discusses this systematic response to Indian resistance:

> The insignificant tribe of savages that starves on the product of the upper soil of hundreds of thousands of acres of land, looks with jealous eyes on every intruder, knowing that each new mouth requiring to be fed tends to increase the difficulty of obtaining subsistence; whereas the farmer rejoices in the arrival of the blacksmith and the shoemaker, because they come to eat on the spot the corn which heretofore he has carried ten, twenty, or thirty miles to market, to exchange for shoes for himself and his horses . . . Give to the poor tribe spades, and the knowledge how to use them, and the power of association will begin. The supply of food becoming more abundant, they hail the arrival of the stranger who brings them knives and clothing to be exchanged for skins and corn; wealth grows, and the habit of association—the first step towards civilization—arises. (80)

Here, Carey implicitly invokes late eighteenth- and early nineteenth-century efforts, which I discussed in chapter 3, to transform Indians into white citizens. Carey's reference to such systematic, state-sponsored measures is strikingly at odds with his celebration of linked local polities, as well as his polemics against "centralization" and European colonialisms. In effect, Carey's admission of racialized social conflict into this narrative ("looks with jealous eyes on every intruder") calls forth a concerted, centralized response from the state, despite Carey's own apparent resistance to such a state. That is, Carey needs the state to step in and keep the colonization of North America unfolding progressively and inexorably. In the process, the racial particularity of "the first cultivator" is revealed: "The millions of acres belonging to the savage are valueless. He starves, surrounded by rich meadows, covered with the finest timber. The white man approaches, and roads are made: and land acquires some value, for which he is paid" (346–47).

When racial slavery finally emerges in his text, Carey similarly turns to the state. Though he blames the existence of slavery on England, he still needs to explain its continued growth in the midst of what he calls "the quiet and beautiful action of the system" of U.S. development (345). He thus turns to the colonization movement, which I examined in chapter 2:

> The Almighty never intended them to mix with the white race, nor is it desireable that they should do so; for as a separate and independent race of free men, they will be happier, better, and more useful, than in any other condition . . . The time is now not far distant when the whole race will be concentrated in the southern tier of States . . .

Ultimately, and at no distant period, those States will be owned and inhabited by a race of free citizens, differing in color but similar in rights, and equal in capacity to their fellow-citizens of the north. (362, 364)

Uncannily echoing Jefferson's foundational writings on colonization, Carey proposes a paradox: blacks and whites will be formally and abstractly equal, but racially and nationally particularized. He offers a liberal defense of U.S. white nationalism, an abolitionism whose "freedom" articulates equality with the hierarchical codification of race and nation.

His invocations of civilization policy, the U.S.–Mexico War, and colonization function as moments of purification and containment, in which the histories that haunt the text's image of American harmony are allowed into the open only to be contained by the power of a state whose necessity is immediately represented as incidental. If Carey's often stated placement of "the consumer side by side with the producer" figures the formal and abstract equality of citizens, then this formal equality is here seen to require a systematic and reiterative articulation with racial and national particularity.

In this context, it should not come as a surprise that, in the final fifty pages of this text that has championed free and unfettered trade among ever expanding localisms, Carey turns unabashedly to mercantilism. As it turns out, the thriving local states and the harmony on which they concentrate their attention never even existed in the United States after all: "The truest grandeur consists in the most perfect power over ourselves, our thoughts and actions, and in conceding to all men the exercise of the same powers that we desire for ourselves. The people of the United States do not exercise that power: but they may do so, and we trust they will" (450). Here, colonization as concentration slips into a mythical past and an ideal future between which the relentlessly present tense narrative of *The Past, the Present, and the Future* is suspended. Carey then confidently prophecies the arrival of the present: "Then will it become necessary to offer them inducements to stay at home: then will the people acquire power: and then may the world see an approach to peace" (457). These "inducements" necessary to make "home" homey to "them"—the "producers," "consumers," and "great and little capitalists" of the United States, whose interests are those of "the world" (457)—are, it turns out, comprehensive mercantilist policies.

As *The Past, the Present, and the Future* draws to a close, the global and domestic implications of Carey's mercantilism become clear. When Carey writes that "Concentration, even to its present extent, cannot be maintained without protection" (469), he reveals that the white citizen's formal equality must have its particularity forced and enforced:

If we desire to preserve peace, we must arrest the progress of depopulation and promote concentration upon rich soils, and that can be done only by increased protection, by aid of *a tariff that is not for revenue*—a tariff whose direct object shall be that of establishing the right of every man to determine for himself where he will live, and how he will employ his labour, or his capital, or both. What is needed is a distinct declaration of a *determination* on the part of the whole nation, farmers and planters, to pursue the course necessary for bringing the consumer of cotton, and wool, and food, to the side of the producers of those commodities: for bringing the lapstone to the hides and the food, instead of carrying the hides and the food to the lapstone: and thus to terminate the system of indirect taxation by both England and France, and to annihilate, by means of measures of peaceful but vigorous resistance, the power of those countries to disturb the world by means of fleets and armies. Were such a measure once deliberately adopted as the policy of the whole nation, evasion of its provisions would be impossible, for all, males and females, old and young, rich and poor, land-owner and labourer, would feel that their own interests were directly concerned in their enforcement. (469–70)

This liberal list of "all" notably excludes those North Americans who are struggling to trouble the "peace" Carey's "we" desires, including the black laborers who are producing the very cotton to which he refers and the Indians who occupy the land he claims. However, this is no simple exclusion to be rectified by extending the list, by giving blacks and Indians access to the equality and freedom Carey envisions. Carey's "we" or "all" is subjectified as a formally and abstractly equal "whole" precisely by being subjected to racial and national codification.

Though mercantilism is meant explicitly to guard against the "external influences" of European economic power, the system effectively institutionalizes a protective vigilance within the U.S. citizen and its state against the racialized subjects that had to be codified and differentiated from equality for the harmonious story to be told at all. Free trade among formally equal citizens would seem to need protection not only from competing imperial powers; it also requires continuing, systematic protection against the "slaves" and "savages" that the United States keeps failing to eliminate. Only after such a system has been installed will the racial and national particularity of U.S. development become applicable to the "world": "The example once set and its object distinctly avowed by the United States, it would be followed by every nation in Europe" (470), and, in turn, as we learn in the chapters on India and Ireland, by the rest of the globe.

The Past, the Present, and the Future paradoxically articulates discursive practices of free trade with discursive practices of mercantilism as antipodes at once opposed and interrelated. Consequently, the "Yankee universality" that Marx sees in Carey can be read as a sign not of the United States at the forefront of history's progressive development, either because of its efficient lack of feudalism or its peaceful avoidance of primitive accumulation. Rather, Carey's text paradoxically articulates quite precise forms of universality with quite precise forms of particularity: on one hand, formal and abstract equality with codified racial and national identities; on the other hand, U.S. exceptionality with U.S. exemplarity. "Yankee universality" names this imperial articulation of U.S. citizenship, this interpenetration of the domestic and the foreign that marks the emergence of U.S. imperialism.

Notes

Introduction

1. Walker, *David Walker's Appeal*, 67–68, 75. For a typical example of such a procolonization argument, see "Original Communications," *Freedom's Journal*, August 24, 1827. The pages of *Freedom's Journal* are filled with similar critiques of colonization, some of which were written by Walker himself.

2. On universal egalitarianism and the state/civil society distinction, see, for example, Barbalet, *Citizenship*; Keane, *Democracy and Civil Society* and *Civil Society*; Kettner, *Development of American Citizenship*; Macpherson, *Political Theory of Possessive Individualism*. On the implications of this problematic for current debates over the political efficacy of rights claims, see Wendy Brown, *States of Injury*, esp. 96–134; Glendon, *Rights Talk*; Mamdani, *Beyond Rights Talk and Culture Talk*; Spivak, "Acting Bits/Identity Talk."

3. Bailyn, *Voyagers to the West*, 4.

4. See, for example, Banton, *Racial Theories*; Blackburn, *Overthrow of Colonial Slavery* and *Making of New World Slavery*; Essed and Goldberg, *Race Critical Theories*; Goldberg, *Racist Culture*; Gossett, *Race*; Guillaumin, "Specific Character of Racist Ideology"; Horsman, *Race and Manifest Destiny*; Jordan, *White Over Black*; Stanton, *Leopard's Spots*; Vaughan, *Roots of American Racism*; Eric Williams, *Capitalism and Slavery*. The historical debate in U.S. scholarship on chattel slavery over whether race or slavery "came first" can be understood as a symptom of such progressivist conceptions of history; the impasse in this debate testifies to the mutually constitutive, simultaneous emergence of both race and slavery. On this debate, see Allen, *Invention of the White Race*; Boskin, *Into Slavery*, 101–12; Handlin and Handlin, "Origins of the Southern Labor System"; McPherson et al., *Blacks in America*; Solow and Engerman, *British Capitalism and Caribbean Slavery*; Vaughan, "Origins Debate"; Eric Williams, *Capitalism and Slavery*.

5. On the "invention of tradition," see Hobsbawm and Ranger, *Invention of Tradition*. On the modernity of the nation, see Anderson, *Imagined Communities*; Armstrong, *Nations before Nationalism*; Breuilly, *Nationalism and the State*; Gellner, *Nations and Nationalism*; Hobsbawm, *Nations and Nationalism Since 1780*; Mosse, *Nationalism and Sexuality*; Narin, *Faces of Nationalism*; Anthony Smith, *The Ethnic Origins of Nations*; Yuval-Davis and Anthias, *Woman, Nation, State*. For a counterpoint to these texts, see Hastings, *Construction of Nationhood*. U.S. historians commonly insist that U.S. nationalism and even a coherent U.S. state did not exist until well into the nineteenth century. *The Colonizing Trick* suggests that traces of both formations began to congeal in the late eighteenth century.

6. On the supplementary relationship between race and nation, see Balibar, *Masses, Classes, Ideas*, especially 191–204; Balibar and Wallerstein, *Race, Nation, Class*, especially 37–67 and 86–106. On this relationship in the Americas, see, for instance, Blackburn, *Overthrow of Colonial Slavery* and *Making of New World Slavery*, and in the United States in particular, see, for instance, Roediger, *The Wages of Whiteness*.

7. Balibar, *Masses, Classes, Ideas*, 193.

8. For examinations of the relationship between universalism and particularism, see Balibar, "Ambiguous Universality"; Balibar, *Masses, Classes, Ideas*, especially 39–59; Balibar and Wallerstein, *Race, Nation, Class*, 1–27, 37–67, 86–105; Wendy Brown, *States of Injury*, 96–134; Butler et al., *Contingency, Hegemony, Universality*; Chakrabarty, *Provincializing Europe*, esp. 47–71; Laclau, *Emancipation(s)*, 20–65; Miranda Joseph, *Against the Romance of Community* and "Performance of

Production and Consumption"; Osborne, *The Politics of Time*, 165; Postone, "Anti-Semitism and National Socialism"; Sakai, "Modernity and Its Critique"; Scott, "Universalism and the History of Feminism" and *"Only Paradoxes to Offer."*

Attentiveness to the mutually constitutive relationships between citizenship and inequality has been growing in early American literary scholarship in recent years. See, to give just a few examples, the important work of Castiglia, "Abolition's Racial Interiors" and "Pedagogical Discipline and the Creation of White Citizenship"; Castronovo, *Fathering the Nation* and *NecroCitizenship*; Hartman, *Scenes of Subjection*; Nelson, *National Manhood*; Wald, *Constituting Americans*; Rowe, *At Emerson's Tomb* and *Literary Culture and U.S. Imperialism*. For a contribution to this question, overlooked by many literary scholars, see Greene, *Imperatives*, especially 236–316.

9. Butler, *Psychic Life of Power*, 2.

10. Hartman, *Scenes of Subjection*, 4–6.

11. Moten, unpublished manuscript.

12. These revolutionary potentials have been well documented thanks to post–World War II new social history. For examples of work in this tradition, see the American Social History Project's two-volume textbook *Who Built America?*; Linebaugh and Rediker, *The Many-Headed Hydra*; Montgomery, *Citizen Worker*.

13. See Liddell, *Greek-English Lexicon*; Lindström, "History of the 'Article.'" For classical sources, see, for example, Aristotle, *Rhetoric and the Poetics of Aristotle*, 1456B, 1457A; Plato, "Timaeus" in *Collected Dialogues of Plato, Including the Letters*, 74A; Quintilian, *Institutiones Oratoriae*, especially book 9 in volume 3 and book 10 in volume 4. For an outline of this lexical history, see *Compact Oxford English Dictionary*, 118–19.

14. *Compact Oxford English Dictionary*, 118. On the colonial import of the articulate/inarticulate binary, see Rousseau's "Essay on the Origin of Languages" and Herder's "Essay on the Origin of Language," in Rousseau and Herder, *On the Origin of Language*.

15. Noah Webster, *An American Dictionary*, vol. 1 [1828]. Based on other dictionaries that use the same quotation, the reference would seem to be to Darwin's *Zoonomia*.

16. Webster, *An American Dictionary*, vol. 1 [1828]. For other similar early nineteenth-century definitions, see Barclay, *A Complete and Universal Dictionary of the English Language*; Webster, *A Dictionary of the English Language: Abridged from the American Dictionary*; Webster, *An American Dictionary* [1839].

17. Walker, *David Walker's Appeal*, 62.

18. Jefferson, *Writings*, 223.

19. Ibid., 224–25.

20. On the debate over barrows and its role in constructing an American antiquity, see Sayre, "Mound Builders." Sayre claims that in the *Notes* Jefferson dismisses the mounds as mere natural artifacts, celebrating America's natural, rather than cultural, heritage. Only after his second term as president, writes Sayre, did Jefferson adopt the widespread fascination with the archeological heritage of Native Americans. However, Sayre also admits that at the time of the *Notes* Jefferson was fascinated by Indian languages as signs of ancient American heritage. I do not see such a clear distinction between Jefferson's discussion of the mounds and his discussion of languages.

21. Jefferson, *Writings*, 227.

22. Brown, *Memoirs of Carwin, the Biloquist*, in *Wieland and Memoirs of Carwin, the Biloquist*, 282–83.

23. Ibid., 284–85.

24. Ibid., 287.

25. Ibid., 287, 288.

26. Stuart Hall, "Race, Articulation, and Societies," 336. This essay has been reprinted in Essed and Goldberg, *Race Critical Theories*, 38–68. See also Hall's "Reflections on 'Race, Articulation, and Societies'" and "On Postmodernism and Articulation." On articulation in Hall and cultural studies, see Jennifer Daryl Slack, "Theory and Method of Articulation in Cultural Studies." In their *Hegemony and Socialist Strategy*, Laclau and Mouffe offer another important reading of articulation that is akin to Hall's, though they do not consider the relationship of race to articulation, as does Hall, nor to they account for the pre-Marxian genealogy of the term itself. For an extremely suggestive interpretation of articulation as a figure for potential political movement within a contemporary black diaspora, see Edwards's "Uses of 'Diaspora.'" On the notion of articulation in Marxian theories of the state, see Jessop, *Capitalist State*, 213–20, and *State Theory*, 10–11, 193–272.

27. Frank, "Development of Underdevelopment"; Laclau, "Feudalism and Capitalism in Latin America." See also Larrain, *Theories of Development*.

28. Hall, "Race, Articulation, and Societies", 320–21. A similar argument is offered by Cedric Robinson's important *Black Marxism* (see especially pages 1–37). I discuss Robinson's work in chapter 1.

29. Ibid., 325.

30. Ibid., 325.

31. Ibid., 338. Hall cites his "Pluralism, Race and Class in Caribbean Society," in *Race and Class in Post-colonial Society* and *Policing the Crisis*.

32. A prominent example of this is Roediger's otherwise excellent study, *The Wages of Whiteness*, which seems to rely on the model of racial projection elaborated in Sartre's 1948 text *Anti-Semite and Jew*. The generality of the logic of projection to which Roediger refers—a logic we can trace to the very different historical context of Sartre's 1948—clashes with the specificity of his historical research into early U.S. working-class culture and politics. See also Kovel, *White Racism* and Rawick, *From Sundown to Sunup*. For an alternate account of anti-Semitism more akin to my approach, see Postone, "Anti-Semitism and National Socialism."

33. A prominent example of this is Lowe's important *Immigrant Acts*. For Lowe, Marx shows how capitalism and state nationalism institute a regime of universal abstraction that seeks to erase all particularities. Resistance to that regime consists in cultural productions that invoke particularities against capitalism and official state culture (24–29). This account tends to assume a necessary contradiction between capitalism as a force of universal abstraction and particularities subject to, or erased by, that abstraction. Lowe's account thus begs the question of how subjects are not only "subject to" or "subjects of" the conflict between universalism and particularism (9), but are also subjectified within the terms of that conflict, as well as the question of how multiple racial formations might be at odds with, rather than analogous to, one another.

34. Hall, "Race, Articulation, and Societies," 325–26.

35. Ibid., 328–29. Hall refers to Foster-Carter's "Modes of Production Debate."

36. Hall, "Race, Articulation, and Societies," 328.

37. Walker, *David Walker's Appeal*, 62.

38. Marx, *Capital*, vol. 1, 874.

39. The work of Negri, Postone, and Spivak on value theory has been indispensable to my interpretation of Marx in this chapter. See Negri, *Marx Beyond Marx*, and Postone, "Anti-Semitism and National Socialism" and *Time, Labor, and Social Domination*. For Spivak's work on value theory, see "Scattered Speculations," "Speculations on Reading Marx," "Poststructuralism, Marginality,

Post-coloniality and Value," "Remembering the Limits," "Limits and Openings of Marx in Derrida." See also Keenan's reading of *Capital*, "The Point Is to [Ex]Change It." For a brilliant deployment of Spivak's work in the context of a feminist politics of reproduction, see Weinbaum, "Marx, Irigaray, and the Politics of Reproduction." For a trenchant use of value theory to critique contemporary ideologies of community, see Miranda Joseph, "The Peformance of Production and Consumption" and *Against the Romance of Community*.

40. I will examine this process primarily from the perspective of what Marx calls "the simple form of value." In *Capital*, vol. 1, he argues that the value form can actually be broken down into four forms: "the simple, isolated, or accidental form of value" (139–54), "the total or expanded form " (154–57), "the general form" (157–62), and "the money form" (162–63). While he says that "we have to trace the development of the expression of value contained in the value-relation of commodities from its simplest, almost imperceptible outline to the dazzling money-form" (139), it seems clear from the argument that this "development" is synchronic; that is, the value form is simultaneously all four of these forms. Analytically, the four forms are four different ways of representing the value form that offer different perspectives on its meaning and force in the world of commodities; synthetically, the four forms render the meaning and force behind social relations such as the commodity.

41. Ibid., 142.

42. Marx, *Grundrisse*, 241–45.

43. In *Marx beyond Marx*, Negri makes this point by distinguishing Marx's starting point in *Capital*, the commodity, from his starting point in the *Grundrisse*, money. Negri expresses a decided preference for the latter: "There is so much class hatred contained in [the *Grundrisse's*] way of approaching the material! Money has the advantage of presenting me immediately the lurid face of the social relation of value; it shows me value right away as exchange, commanded and organized for exploitation. I do not need to plunge into Hegelianism in order to discover the double face of the commodity, of value: money has only one face, that of the boss" (23; see also 39). See also Rosdolsky, *Making of Marx's* Capital.

44. Marx, *Grundrisse*, 245.

45. Marx, *Capital*, vol. 1, 155.

46. For Marx's concept of a "rational abstraction," see *Grundrisse*, 85.

47. The work of the value form on citizenship can also be gleaned from the so-called early Marx, most strikingly from "On the Jewish Question" (1833) and the "Economic and Philosophical Manuscripts" (1844), in *Early Writings*, 211–41, 279–400. For a brilliant reading of the former text as an analysis of universal abstraction in citizenship, see Brown, *States of Injury*, 96–134.

48. Marx, *Capital*, vol. 1, 142.

49. Marx, *Grundrisse*, 141.

50. Marx, *Capital*, vol. 1, 164.

51. Ibid., 164–65.

52. Ibid. I follow Gillian Rose in modifying the translation of *"die phantasmagorische Form."* She notes the connection between *phantasmagorische* and the English word phantasmagoria (*Melancholy Science*, 31). However, I opt for "phantasmagoric form" because Rose's own translation, "phantasmatic form," overplays the connection between Freud's conception of the fetish and Marx's conception; by contrast, Fowkes's translation, "fantastic form," obscures the tie to phantasmagoria (Marx, *Capital*, vol. 1, 165).

53. "In Philipstal's 'phantasmagoria' the figures were made rapidly to increase and decrease in size, to advance and retreat, dissolve, vanish, and pass into each other, in a manner then considered marvellous." *Compact Oxford English Dictionary*, vol. 2, 2151.

54. Althusser, "Contradiction and Overdetermination." See also Derrida, *Specters of Marx*, and Keenan, "The Point Is to [Ex]change It," on this theme of haunting. For a crucial critique of Derrida's Marx, see Spivak, "Ghostwriting." See also Sprinker, *Ghostly Demarcations*.

55. The concept of "reification," elaborated classically by Georg Lukács, is the most prevalent such reading; see *History and Class Consciousness*, 83–222. For a deployment of this concept in the context of early U.S. literature, see Carolyn Porter, *Seeing and Being*. For a recent treatment of reification, see Bewes, *Reification*.

56. The complex developments of Marx and Engels's positions on "the national question" in Europe, especially Ireland, and in India are other important sites for such furtive attempts. See Marx's articles in the *New York Daily Tribune* on India and China from 1853, in *Political Writings Volume Two*, 301–33; his letters and passages, some written with Engels, on Ireland, in Marx and Engels, *Ireland and the Irish Question*; "The Communist Manifesto" from 1847, in *Political Writings Volume One*, 62–98; Marx and Engels's speeches on Poland from 1847–48 and their "The Demands of the Communist Party in Germany" from 1848, in *Political Writings Volume One*, 99–103 and 109–11; see also Engels's articles in *Rheinische Zeitung* on the Magyar struggle and Bakunin's "Democratic Pan-Slavism" from 1849, in Marx, *Political Writings Volume One*, 213–45.

57. Marx, *On America and the Civil War*, 104.

58. Marx, *Grundrisse*, 275.

59. Throughout the nineteenth-century United States, as Roediger has argued, the trope of "wage-slavery" performed precisely this erasure of racialization under capitalism; see *Wages of Whiteness*, 72–74, 176.

60. Marx, *Grundrisse*, 464.

61. Marx, *Collected Works*, vol. 31, 516. For the German, see *Werke*, Band 26.2, 299.

62. Marx's perspectival shift between the production perspective and the world-market perspective lays down the terms of a now classic debate over the origins of capitalism. Marxists such as Brenner, Genovese, and the early Laclau take up the production perspective, whereas members of the world-system and *dependendista* schools take up the global perspective of trade. See Brenner, "The Origins of Capitalist Development"; Frank, *World Accumulation, 1492–1789*; Laclau, "Feudalism and Capitalism in Latin America"; Wallerstein, "Rise and Future Demise of the World Capitalist System." For an excellent summary of this debate, its context and its antecedents, see Larrain, *Theories of Development*. For this debate in a U.S. context, see Fox-Genovese and Genovese, *Fruits of Merchant Capital*; Genovese, *Political Economy of Slavery*; Fogel and Engerman, *Time on the Cross*; Wallerstein, "American Slavery and the Capitalist World-Economy."

63. I would like to thank Judith Butler and Katrin Pahl for discussing this passage from Marx with me. I take responsibility for the translation.

64. Marx, *Capital*, vol. 1, 345.

65. Marx, *Grundrisse*, 107–8.

66. Ibid., 96, 108. Althusser and Balibar, *Reading Capital*, 46–48, 64–68, 97–105.

67. Webster, *An American Dictionary*, vol. 1 [1828].

68. Hinks offers the most extensive account of the circulation of Walker's *Appeal* available; see Hinks, *To Awaken My Afflicted Brethren*, 116–72. See also Wilentz, "Introduction," ix.

69. Wilentz, "Introduction," vii. See Aptheker *"One Continual Cry,"* 1, 45–53; Eaton, "A Dangerous Pamphlet in the Old South"; Harding, *There Is a River*, 92–94; Hinks "'There Is a Great Work for You to Do'" and *To Awaken My Afflicted Brethren*.

70. See Hinks, *To Awaken My Afflicted Brethren*, 112–72; Wilentz, introduction to Walker, *Appeal*, x.

71. Hinks casts doubt on the persistent suggestion that Walker was assassinated. See *To Awaken My Afflicted Brethren*, 269–71.

72. The English translation inserts "(Ranke)" here, but this is not in the German. See Benjamin, *Gesammelte Schriften*, 695.

73. Walter Benjamin, "Theses on the Philosphy of History," 255. For the German, see Benjamin, *Gesammelte Schriften*, 695.

74. Mitchell, "The Politics of Experiment," 309–10.

75. Quoted in ibid., 324.

76. Seth Moglen has done important work on what he calls "black enlightenment" in his work-in-progress on nineteenth-century African American political thought (personal communication). I borrow the term "appositional" from Fred Moten (unpublished manuscript).

77. For an example of this tendency, see Buell, "American Literary Emergence as a Post-colonial Phenomenon." For a more careful acknowledgment of the challenges attending this relationship between colonial/postcolonial studies and American literary studies, see Carolyn Porter, "What We Know That We Don't Know." For a powerful meditation upon these challenges that reaches beyond the literary, see Sharpe, "Is the United States Postcolonial?"

78. Benjamin, "Theses on the Philosophy of History," 256.

1. Racial Capitalism

1. Gales, *Annals of Congress*, 106–7. In the *Annals* of the early years of Congress, only House debates are recorded in any detail. For more of this debate, see sections under "Collection of Duties" in *Annals of Congress*, 106–867.

2. Hill, "First Stages of the Tariff Policy," 564; Taussig, *Tariff History*, 14–15.

3. Gales, *Annals of Congress*, 106–7.

4. Ibid., 164.

5. Ibid., 106.

6. Ibid., 147.

7. For an excellent account of this gendered citizenship, see Nelson's *National Manhood*. See also Isenberg, *Sex and Citizenship in Antebellum America* and Kerber, *Toward an Intellectual History of Women*.

8. Alexander Hamilton, "Report on the Subject of Manufactures," 59.

9. Equiano, *The Interesting Narrative and Other Writings*, ed. Vincent Carretta, 116; *The Interesting Narrative of the Life of Olaudah Equiano, or Gustavus Vassa, the African*, ed. Henry Louis Gates Jr., 84. Throughout this chapter I quote from the ninth edition of Equiano's narrative, originally published in London in 1794. Vincent Carretta, editor of Penguin's 1995 republication of this edition, has made the case for the 1794 text (xxix). Page citations in the text give the page number of the Carretta edition first, followed by a semicolon and the equivalent page number from the 1814 Leeds edition, edited by Henry Louis Gates Jr.

10. Nash, "Forging Freedom: The Emancipation Experience in the Northern Seaports, 1775–1820," in *Race, Class, and Politics*, 283–321. Nancy Prince's *A Narrative of the Life and Travels of Mrs. Nancy Prince* (1850) is a key text for reading black women at sea. See also the important collection *Women at Sea*, edited by Paravisini-Gebert and Romero-Cesareo.

11. For historical accounts of seafaring as a crucial avenue of employment for black men in the late eighteenth and early to mid-nineteenth centuries, see Bolster, "'To Feel like a Man'" and *Black Jacks*; Foner and Lewis, *Black Worker*, 196–241; Lemisch, *Jack Tar vs. John Bull*; Linebaugh, "All the Atlantic Mountains Shook"; Linebaugh and Rediker, *Many-Headed Hydra* and "Many-

Headed Hydra"; Nash, "Forging Freedom"; Putney, *Black Sailors*; Rediker, *Between the Devil and the Deep Blue Sea*; Gladdis Smith, "Black Seamen and the Federal Courts, 1789–1860." I have also conducted a review of eighteenth-century High Court of Admiralty (HCA) and Vice-Admiralty Court (VAC) records in the Public Record Office (PRO) at Kew, Richmond, Surrey, England where one finds numerous instances of black sailors suing for wages they have been bilked or being disciplined after racially invested conflicts. Although a close reading of these records is outside the scope of this study, the PRO and its guides to the HCA and VAC records are crucial archival and reference sources that have informed my work. I thank Marcus Rediker, whose own work sent me to the PRO. At the PRO, the HCA and VAC records are arranged by class/piece. For just a few examples of relevant HCA cases, see HCA 1/22–23, HCA 1/25, HCA 1/61, HCA 24/133 and 135–37, HCA 49/91. For a more readily available and readable collection of VAC records, see Towle, *Records*. I thank Shirley Carrie for adeptly following up on this research in London for me.

12. In addition to the texts I discuss in this chapter, the narratives of James Albert Ukawsaw Gronniosaw (1770), John Marrant (1785), Paul Cuffe (1811, 1812, 1817), William Grimes (1824, 1855), Paul Cuffe [Jr.] (1839), Moses Grandy (1844), Nancy Prince (1850), John Thompson (1856), James Mars (1864), and James L. Smith (1881) are important touchstones.

13. Statistically, for instance, by 1803 about 18 percent of U.S. seamen's jobs were filled by black men (most but not all of whom were free). In 1803, 22 percent of berths on U.S. ships sailing from Providence were held by blacks (159 of 723 berths); by 1844 that number had dropped to 11.4 percent (42 of 369). Also in 1803, 13 percent of berths from Savannah were held by blacks (47 of 367); by 1836 that number had dropped to 2 percent (5 of 240). Finally, in 1803, 16 percent of berths from New Orleans were held by blacks (93 of 585); by 1843 that number had dropped to 3 percent (40 of 1339). See Bolster, *Black Jacks*, 235–39; Putney, *Black Sailors*, 120–25.

14. Hill, "First Stages of the Tariff Policy," 461–90; Faulkner, "Development of the American System," 11; Taussig, *Tariff History*, 15.

15. Recent economic histories of mercantilism have accepted that the term itself was not used by many of the economic thinkers to whom it is attributed, and that there were vast differences among and within the mercantilist arguments and policies of different countries and different economists. Nonetheless, the term can be used analytically and nominally to indicate the emergence, beginning in early seventeenth-century England, and later developing in Europe and the United States, of a set of economic discursive practices that had the effect of systematically creating economic wealth and power within nationally defined, territorially specific economies. On this account of mercantilism, see Arrighi, *Long Twentieth Century*; Braudel, *Civilization and Capitalism*, vols. 1–3; Magnusson, *Mercantilist Economics* and *Mercantilism*; Wallerstein, *Modern World-System II* and *Modern World-System III*.

However, the term "mercantilism" has been extremely controversial, particularly among classical and neoclassical economists and economic historians, and I will offer a thumbnail sketch of this controversy here. The phrase *systéme mercantile* was apparently first used by Marquis de Mirabeau in his *Philosophie Rurale*. Adam Smith offers the first extensive account in English of what he called, from Mirabeau, "the mercantile system" in book 4 of *An Inquiry into the Nature and Causes of the Wealth of Nations*. Smith polemically and reductively defines this system as one based on a confusion of a nation's wealth with its supply of money and consequently as harmfully seeking to institutionalize a favorable balance of trade with extensive protectionist policies. He further insists that the mercantile system functions only in the interest of devious and self-interested merchants, and that it runs counter to his own economic system. Although the system

Smith advocates actually has many similarities with the mercantile systems of his day—he was by no means an opponent of significant protectionist or encouragement policies—many subsequent economists and economic historians have adopted his polemical account, further narrowing Smith's already narrow definition of mercantilism and further exaggerating the distinction between Smith's system and mercantilism. McCulloch in his 1828 introduction to *The Wealth of Nations* and Jones in his 1859 "Primitive Political Economy of England" begin this tradition. In the mid- to late nineteenth century, economists such as List and Schmoller in Germany, Cunningham in England, and Carey in the United States revive and defend mercantilism as an economic system characterized by centralized state regulation of territorially specific economies in the interest of increasing the power and wealth of national economies. See List, *National System of Political Economy*; Schmoller, *Mercantile System*; Cunningham, *Growth of English Industry and Commerce*; Carey, *The Past, the Present, and the Future*. On Carey in particular, see my epilogue and "'Yankee Universality.'"

In reaction to these arguments, neoclassical economists revive the McCulloch and Jones critique of mercantilism, thus further institutionalizing and exaggerating Smith's polemical account. In 1930, Viner extends this neoclassical polemic against a straw-mercantilism ("Early English Theories of Trade"). In 1931, Heckscher, though critical of mercantilism, defines it much more broadly as an extensive system of economic thought and practice in *Mercantilism*. Judges in 1939 and later Coleman respond that, in fact, mercantilism never even existed as a coherent system of economic thought or practice (see Judges, "The Idea of a Mercantile State"; Coleman, "Mercantilism Revisited"). On the intellectual history of the term, see Coleman, introduction to *Revisions in Mercantilism*; Magnusson, *Mercantilist Economics* and *Mercantilism*; Palgrave, *Dictionary of Political Economy*, 727–28; Pribram, *A History of Economic Reasoning*.

Many of these classical and neoclassical economic historians argue that mercantilist policies were based exclusively or primarily on the medieval theory (named bullionism or monetarism and often figured as the Midas fallacy) that a nation's money supply equals its wealth, and that there is a fixed supply of wealth in the world that consequently has to be fought over through the merchant trade. In fact, however, most mercantilists have been explicitly critical of such a theory, and have offered a diverse and much more complex range of justifications for their policies right up through the twentieth century. Consequently, mercantilism can hardly be reduced to an atavistic, medieval theory of wealth. Writes Wallerstein in a succinct footnote, "I cannot agree with Coleman's view that although mercantilism is a 'red-herring of historiography' as a label for policy, it is useful as a description of economic theories (1957, 24). I should have thought the exact opposite was true, that the theories were inconsistent because they were apologia but that countries in certain positions tend to adopt policies that we call mercantilist" (Wallerstein, *Modern World-System II*, 37). Wallerstein refers to Coleman's "Eli Heckscher and the Idea of Mercantilism." For the range of theoretical justifications for mercantilism, see Braudel, *Civilization and Capitalism*, vol. 2; Coleman, *Revisions in Mercantilism*; Magnusson, *Mercantilist Economics* and *Mercantilism*.

16. Sheridan, "The Domestic Economy," 70. In his account of the shift of power from skilled, working-class mechanics and artisans to merchants, manufacturers, speculators, and large-scale capitalists in late eighteenth-century New York City, Peskin reveals the strong link between discourses of national unity and mercantilist policies. See Peskin, "From Protection to Encouragement."

For historical studies of particular mercantilist policies and practices in North America, see Bailyn, *New England Merchants*. On the seventeenth and eighteenth centuries, see also Bridenbaugh, *Cities in the Wilderness*; Bushman, *From Puritan to Yankee*; Daniels, "Economic Development in Colonial and Revolutionary Connecticut"; Earle, *Evolution of a Tidewater Settlement System*; Earle and Hoffman, "Staple Crops and Urban Development in the Eighteenth-Century South"; Greene, *Pursuits of Happiness*; Clarence P. Gould, *Money and Transportation in Maryland*; Henretta and Nobles, *Evolution and Revolution*, 197–220; Lemon, *The Best Poor Man's Country*; Merrens, *Colonial North Carolina in the Eighteenth Century*; Isabel S. Mitchell, *Roads and Road-Making in Colonial Connecticut*; Robert D. Mitchell, *Commercialism and Frontier*; Morris, *Government and Labor in Early America*; Nash, *Urban Crucible*; Nettels, "British Mercantilism and the Economic Development of the Thirteen Colonies"; Edward G. Roberts, "Roads of Virginia, 1607–1840"; Schweitzer, "Economic Regulation and the Colonial Economy"; Walzer, "Transportation in the Philadelphia Trading Area, 1740–1755."

17. The Declaration of Independence complains about "cutting off our trade with all parts of the world" and "imposing taxes on us without our consent."

18. Gomes, *Foreign Trade and the National Economy*, 263; Taussig, *Tariff History*. More generally, see Hill, "First Stages of the Tariff Policy," 455–614, for the tariff history of British North America and the early United States. On the political contexts of this tariff history in the post-independence period, see also Fox-Genovese and Genovese, *Fruits of Merchant Capital*; Henretta and Nobles, *Evolution and Revolution*; Kulikoff, *The Agrarian Origins of American Capitalism*; Montgomery, *Citizen Worker*; Wood, *The Creation of the American Republic*.

19. Arrighi, *Long Twentieth Century*, 58–84, 239ff.

20. Arrighi, *Long Twentieth Century*, 141. Arrighi refers to Hirschman's *Strategy of Economic Development*. See also Braudel, *Civilization and Capitalism*; Magnusson, *Mercantilist Economics* and *Mercantilism*; Wallerstein, *Modern World-System II* and *Modern World-System III*.

21. Arrighi, *Long Twentieth Century*, 49.

22. Wallerstein, *Modern World-System III*, 37.

23. Ibid., 58.

24. Ibid., 38.

25. See Weeks, "American Nationalism, American Imperialism."

26. Ibid., 487.

27. Ibid., 490.

28. Arrighi, *Long Twentieth Century*, 1–84, 140–42, 223–24; Braudel, *Civilization and Capitalism*, vols. 2 and 3; Gomes, *Foreign Trade and the National Economy*, 3–37, 258–64; Mjoset, "Turn of Two Centuries"; Polanyi, *Great Transformation*, 36–42, 67–76, 278; Taussig, *Tariff History*; Wallerstein, *Modern World-System II*, 37, 56, 80–81, 98–99, 209, 236–41, 268–89, and *Modern World-System III*, 66–71, 77–87, 97–100, 122, 170–71, 196–204, 247–50; Winch, *Classical Political Economy and the Colonies*, 97.

29. Balibar and Wallerstein, *Race, Nation, Class*, 88–90.

30. Ibid., 88; Arrighi, *Long Twentieth Century*, 49.

31. See U.S. attorney general William Wirt's 1821 ruling on a case in which a customs collector at Norfolk, Virginia, challenged the legality of a free black captain's command: "Free persons of color in Virginia are not citizens of the United States, within the intent and meaning of the acts regulating foreign and coastal trade, so as to be qualified to command vessels." Benjamin F. Hall, *Official Opinions of the Attorneys General of the United States*, 506–7; also quoted in Bolster, *Black Jacks*, 172.

32. Hamer, "Great Britain, the United States, and the Negro Seamen Acts, 1822–1848" and "British Consuls and the Negro Seamen Acts, 1850–1860."

33. Bolster, *Black Jacks*, 206, 289.

34. Ibid., 225–29.

35. Ibid., 171–75. On these families, see Harris, *Paul Cuffe*; Nash, *Forging Freedom* and *Race and Revolution*, 63–65; Lamont D. Thomas, *Rise to Be a People*; Juliet E. K. Walker, "Racism, Slavery, and Free Enterprise."

36. Bolster, *Black Jacks*, 168.

37. Cugoano, *Thoughts and Sentiments on the Evil of Slavery*; Wedderburn, *The Horrors of Slavery and Other Writings*.

38. See Butler, *Psychic Life of Power*, especially 1–31.

39. Bolster, *Black Jacks*, 34.

40. Ibid., 227–28.

41. Bolster, "'Every Inch a Man,'" 149, 165.

42. Bolster, *Black Jacks*, 229.

43. Briton Hammon, *A Narrative*. Citations will be given parenthetically.

44. I borrow this phrase from Rodgers's *Wooden World*.

45. On this relative freedom, see Bolster, *Black Jacks*; Linebaugh, "All the Atlantic Mountains Shook"; Linebaugh and Rediker, "Many-Headed Hydra" and *Many-Headed Hydra*; Rediker, *Between the Devil and the Deep Blue Sea*.

46. Baker, *Blues, Ideology, and Afro-American Literature*, 19. In his reading of Foucault, Baker represents the "statement" as "the fundamental unit of discourse. [Foucault] defines the statement as a materially repeatable (i.e., recorded) linguistic function. A chart, graph, exclamation, table, sentence, or logical proposition may serve as a statement." In turn, he represents the function of statements in a "discursive formation" as follows: "The distribution and combination of statements in a discourse are regulated, according to Foucault, by discoverable principles or laws. . . . These laws of formation are referred to as a 'discursive formation.' . . . They make possible the emergence of the notions and themes of a discourse" (18). In this passage Baker refers to Foucault, *Archaeology of Knowledge*, 38, 56, 79–87. A "canon" in Baker's argument refers not simply to a selection of texts, but also to the logic of selecting, organizing, and representing those texts as a unified body of knowledge (16–26). Baker takes Miller's epochal *Errand into the Wilderness* as exemplary of traditional U.S. literary criticism, and Robert Spiller's *A Literary History of the United States* as exemplary of traditional U.S. literary history.

47. Baker, *Blues, Ideology, and Afro-American Literature*, 26.

48. Ibid., 37.

49. Ibid., 32–38.

50. Andrews, "First Fifty Years of the Slave Narrative"; Costanzo, *Surprising Narrative*, chapter 4; Foster, *Witnessing Slavery*, 15; Gilroy, *Black Atlantic*, 12; Marren, "Between Slavery and Freedom," 95.

51. Chinosole, "Tryin' to Get Over," 46.

52. Gilroy, *Black Atlantic*, 6.

53. Gilroy, *Black Atlantic*, 12. See Linebaugh, "All the Atlantic Mountains Shook"; Linebaugh and Rediker, *Many-Headed Hydra* and "Many-Headed Hydra"; Rediker, *Between the Devil and the Deep Blue Sea*. For a critique of Gilroy, see Chrisman, "Journeying."

54. See Fichtelberg, "Word between Worlds," 459–80, for another discussion of Equiano and political economy.

55. Baker, *Blues, Ideology, and Afro-American Literature*, 38.

56. Baker inadvertently indicates the source of this category mistake in a footnote: "I have

relied heavily on the works of [Eugene] Genovese for my claims about slavery in the Old South" (209)—namely, Genovese's *Political Economy of Slavery* and *The World the Slaveholders Made*. Baker thus selectively draws on just one side—Genovese's—of what has in fact been an extensive, multi-sided debate among economic historians over the relationships among slavery, mercantilism, and capitalism. The crucial texts for this debate are Fox-Genovese and Genovese, *Fruits of Merchant Capital*; Genovese, *Political Economy of Slavery*; Fogel and Engerman, *Time on the Cross*; Wallerstein, "American Slavery and the Capitalist World-Economy." As I mentioned in note 63 of the introduction, this debate can be read as the U.S. "spin-off" of an earlier debate over the global origins of capitalism, feudalism, and slavery, a debate staged most starkly between Brenner and Laclau, on one side, and Frank and Wallerstein, among others, on the other side. For a sampling of this debate, see Brenner, "The Origins of Capitalist Development: A Critique of Neo-Smithian Marxism"; Frank, *World Accumulation*; Wallerstein, "Rise and Future Demise of the World Capitalist System." For an excellent recap of this debate, see Larrain, *Theories of Development*.

57. The political economic textuality of Equiano's *Narrative* has rarely been examined. The most influential exception is Baker's *Blues, Ideology, and Afro-American Literature*. Hinds's "Spirit of Trade" offers an important account of how Equiano's ambiguous engagement with capitalist enterprise interacts with his religious and legal engagements. Unfortunately, however, it replicates Baker's conflation of "mercantile" with "mercantilism" (636, 637–38, 639), and thus does not address the constitutive relationship among racial codification, national codification, and formal equality.

Other critical studies that do touch on the figure of the economic in Equiano are Caldwell, "'Talking Too Much English'"; Fichtelberg, "Word between World"; Marren, "Between Slavery and Freedom"; Shapiro, "Mass African Suicide." Akiyo Ito's comparison of the subscriber lists of the only U.S. edition of the *Narrative* with the lists of the nine British editions shows that the *Narrative*'s U.S. subscribers tended to be artisans, while its British subscribers tended to be elite merchants and aristocrats. Though for Ito this difference indicates the relative strength of abolitionism in Britain and the United States, it also offers intriguing clues to a reception study of Equiano's mercantile discourse. See Ito, "Olaudah Equiano and the New York Artisans." On the publication history of the *Narrative*, see James Green, "Publishing History of Olaudah Equiano's Interesting Narrative."

For studies not mentioned elsewhere in this chapter of the *Narrative*'s shifting voices and its spiritual, autobiographical, and abolitionist components, see Aravamudan, *Tropicopolitans*; Baucom, "Introduction"; Carretta, "Defining a Gentleman" and "Olaudah Equiano or Gustavus Vassa?"; Elrod, "Moses"; Gates, *Signifying Monkey*; Gautier, "Slavery"; Gerzina, "Mobility in Chains"; Mtumbani, "Black Voice in Eighteenth-Century Britain"; Murphy, "Olaudah Equiano, Accidental Tourist"; Orban, "Dominant and Submerged Discourses in the Life of Olaudah Equiano (or Gustavus Vassa?)"; Potkay, "Olaudah Equiano and the Art of Spiritual Autobiography"; Potkay et al., "Forum"; Sabino and Hall, "Path Not Taken"; Wilfred D. Samuels, "Disguised Voice in *The Interesting Narrative of Olaudah Equiano*"; Valerie Smith, *Self-Discovery and Authority in Afro-American Narrative*.

58. There has been a debate over the authenticity of Equiano's representations of his West African homeland. See Acholonu, *Igbo Roots of Olaudah Equiano* and "Home of Olaudah Equiano"; Carretta, "Defining a Gentleman" and "Olaudah Equiano or Gustavus Vassa?"; Ogude, "Facts into Fiction."

59. Fichtelberg, "Word between Worlds," 469.

60. On the dynamic of the mochlos, see Derrida, "Mochlos."

61. See Bower, *America's Virgin Islands*; Creque, *The U.S. Virgins and the Eastern Caribbean*; N. A. T. Hall, *Slave Society in the Danish West Indies* and *Virgin Islands of the United States*.

62. See Blackburn, *The Making of New World Slavery*, 500–1; N. A. T. Hall, 19–23; Pedersen, "Scope and Structure of the Danish Negro Slave Trade."

63. I consulted the two-volume, 1831 Leeds edition, published by Tho.s Inchbold, housed in the John Carter Brown Library. Page references to this edition are given parenthetically. The *British Museum Catalogue* lists an 1822 edition, as does the *Dictionary of National Biography*, while Sabin lists an 1823 edition. According to the *Dictionary of National Biography*, Schroeder (1774–1853) was born at Bawdry, ran away from home as a youth, and spent three years in the merchant service. After he returned, he settled in Leeds, and became an engraver under the name of William Butterworth—also his literary pseudonym. In addition, he was apparently at one point a landlord of the Shakspere Head public-house in Kirkgate. See *British Museum Catalogue*, 817; *Compact Edition of the Dictionary of National Biography*, 1867; Sabin, *Bibliotheca Americana*, vol. 3, 185.

64. Bolster has found evidence for such cross-racial allegiances in his research on black seamen in the nineteenth century: "While by no means either color-blind or without internal frictions, Atlantic maritime culture created its own institutions and its own stratifications, which could work to the relative advantage of black men. One [nineteenth-century] observer summed it up by writing, 'The good will of "old salts" to negroes is proverbial'" ("'To Feel Like a Man,'" 1179). See also *Black Jacks*.

65. Equiano sets this scene in 1765, but, as Carretta reminds us, the Stamp Act was repealed by Parliament on 18 March 1766 (276).

66. The term "boycott" was, in fact, not coined until 1880. See "Boycott," in *Compact Oxford English Dictionary*, vol. 1, 260. See also Chasin, *Selling Out*.

67. On the history of the Stamp Act, see Gipson, "Great Debate"; Lemisch, *Jack Tar*; Edmund S. Morgan, *Stamp Act Crisis*; Edmund S. Morgan and Helen M. Morgan, *Stamp Act Crisis*; Thomas, *British Politics and the Stamp Act Crisis*; Wood, *Creation of the American Republic*.

68. See Mossman, *Money of the American Colonies and Confederation*. See also Snelling, *View of the Copper Coin and Coinage of England*. Thanks to David Hancock for pointing me toward this material.

69. The narrative was republished in 1835 and again in 1897. The 1798 edition can be found in Dorothy Porter, *Early Negro Writing, 1760–1837*, 538–58. For the 1835 edition, I have used a copy from the Schomburg Center for Research in Black Culture. I quote from this 1835 edition, giving page numbers parenthetically in the text. The 1897 edition, with the addition of Selden's compilation of oral histories of Venture Smith entitled "Traditions of Venture!," can be found in Bontemps, *Five Black Lives*, 1–34.

As has often been pointed out, the narrative appears to have had a white amanuensis: probably Elisha Niles, perhaps the printer Holt. Thus the tenuousness of authorial control that structures all texts as well as the performative ruse that structures all autobiographical texts are amplified and transformed by this racialized scene, shared by many early slave narratives. Though I am more concerned with the historical articulation performed by this text than with this question of authorship, it is worth noting that the authorial and autobiographical problematic has produced some discussion of the "authenticity" of Smith's narrative. On this and other issues relating to Smith's narrative, see Andrews, "First Fifty Years of the Slave Narrative" and *To Tell a Free Story*; Desrochers "'Not Fade Away'"; Frances Smith Foster, *Witnessing Slavery*; Philip Gould, "Free Carpenter, Venture Capitalist"; Nichols, *Many Thousand Gone*; John Sekora, "Black Message/White Envelope."

70. For the historical context of Smith's life and that of his text, see Desrochers, "'Not Fade Away.'"

71. Indeed, as Desrochers has suggested, Venture can be seen to blend traces of his African childhood into his Western life, working in a syncretic fashion to forge a more culturally complex freedom than his obsessive mercantile endeavors might suggest at first glance (51–66).

72. I have not been able to confirm John Willock's identity. The narrative has been classified by one bibliographer as an "imaginary voyage." I have consulted the John Carter Brown Library's 1798 copy, *Voyages and Adventures of John Willock, Mariner*. The first British edition, published in 1789, is *Voyages to various parts of the world*. See Sabin, *Bibliotheca Americana*, vol. 27, 484; and Gove, *Imaginary Voyage in Prose Fiction*, 391.

73. The publication date of Jea's narrative is often given as 1800, but as Hodges has argued it must have been later, though before 1817. See Hodges, introduction to *Black Itinerants of the Gospel*, 34. For Jea's narrative, I quote from Hodges's edition, giving page numbers parenthetically in the text, though I have also consulted what seems to be a first edition in the John Carter Brown Library, published by the author in Portsea and undated except for an unattributed notation in pencil on the title page which reads "1800?".

As Jea suggests on the last page of his text, he also likely had an amanuensis: "My dear reader, I would now inform you, that I have stated this in the best manner I am able, for I cannot write, therefore it is not so correct as if I have been able to have written it myself" (159). Hodges argues that the amanuensis was probably not the printer, James Williams, but does not suggest who it might have been (34).

74. See Hodges, *Black Itinerants of the Gospel*, 1–9, 18–39. For an important account of spirituality in early black literature, see Bassard's *Spiritual Interrogations*. It was Katherine Clay Bassard who taught me eighteenth-century black literature while I was in graduate school, and I am most grateful to her for sparking and guiding my early studies.

75. Jea's lack of concern with mercantile labor as a road to freedom can also be gleaned from his book of hymns, published by J. Williams in Portsea in 1816. Though many of the hymns focus on the life of sailors at sea, rather than calling on God to aid those sailors in their material labors the hymns usually call on sailors to address their spiritual life so that God will keep the forces of nature at bay. See Hodges, *Black Itinerants of the Gospel*, 164–77, and in particular hymns nos. 296 to 300.

76. For a vivid account of this pro-British sentiment, see a narrative I discuss later by King, a black preacher and mariner, entitled "Memoirs of the Life of Boston King." Born a slave in South Carolina in the late 1750s or early 1760s, by the time of the Revolutionary War King refers to Americans repeatedly and unambiguously as "the enemy" ("Memoirs," April, 157).

77. Jea does not say if the other rebellious sailors are black or not. If we assume that some were white, we need to acknowledge the kind of cross-racial solidarity of which Bolster, Linebaugh, and Rediker have written, and/or the other reasons Jea mentions for not being impressed: the typically brutal working conditions on board ships of war, and the national alliances of British sailors to their homeland.

78. Wallerstein, *Modern World-System III*, 251.

79. King, "Memoirs," March, 109.

80. Ibid., April, 158.

81. See Nash, *Race, Class, and Politics*, 289.

82. Tabili, "'A Maritime Race,'" 173.

83. Bolster, *Black Jacks*, 170.

84. Bolster, *Black Jacks*, 168. See also Bolster's "'To Feel like a Man'" and "'Every Inch a Man.'"

85. See, for example, Kerber, *Toward an Intellectual History of Women*, 159–99. See also Tabili, "Maritime Race"; Cockburn, *Machinery of Dominance*; Sonya Rose, *Limited Livelihoods*; Pringle and Game, *Gender at Work*.

86. See Nash, *Race, Class, and Politics*, 289.

87. Tabili, "'A Maritime Race,'" 173. Tabili's article traces the application of land-based racial and gender divisions of labor to the British steam-powered merchant marine, and the consequent transformations of those divisions of labor.

88. Gales, *Annals of Congress*, 164.

89. See Nelson, *National Manhood*; Isenberg, *Sex and Citizenship*; and Kerber, *Toward an Intellectual History of Women*.

90. Adam Smith, *Wealth of Nations*, vol. 1, 475.

91. Ibid., 444–45, 455.

92. Ibid., 143.

93. It is important to remember that, though we find Smith's gendered critique of merchants in the midst of a text that has become known as *the* great defense of free market capitalism, *The Wealth of Nations* offered only modest proposals for scaling back mercantilist measures, and indeed advocated significant protectionist and encouragement policies. What is more, Smith's critique of what he called the "mercantile system" was itself possible only because decades of vigorous British mercantilism had nationalized British territory and its subjects, and had thus secured British hegemony in the world-system.

94. See Mulcaire, "Public Credit," 1038, 1036.

95. Equiano, *Interesting Narrative and Other Writings*, ed. Vincent Carretta, 116.

96. To the extent that Smith's figure of the merchant is implicitly informed by anti-Semitic discourse, we might here locate a foundational intersection of two of racial capitalism's most persistent specters: blacks and Jews.

97. Bolster, "'Every Inch a Man,'" 168.

98. Henry, *Life of George Henry*. Subsequent citations will be given in parentheses in the text.

99. Balibar and Wallerstein, *Race, Nation, Class*, 50, 103.

100. Cedric J. Robinson, *Black Marxism*, 9.

101. Marx, *Capital*, vol. 1, 142, 165.

102. Marx, *Collected Works*, vol. 31, 516.

103. Marx, *Capital*, vol. 1, 932.

104. Ibid.

105. "Just as the system of protection originally had the objective of manufacturing capitalists artificially in the mother country, so Wakefield's theory of colonization . . . aims at manufacturing wage-labourers in the colonies" (ibid.).

106. See Spivak, *Outside in the Teaching Machine*, 13–14.

107. Marx, *Capital*, vol. 1, 873.

108. Ibid., 874.

109. Ibid.

110. Ibid., 875.

111. Ibid., 898, 899.

112. On subjection and the fraught simultaneity of subjugation and subject-formation, see Butler, *Psychic Life of Power*, especially 1–31.

113. Marx, *Capital*, vol. 1, 899–900.

2. Racial Governmentality

1. Equiano, *Interesting Narrative*, 220; "Interesting Narrative," 167.

2. Equiano, *Interesting Narrative*, 226; "The Interesting Narrative," 171.

3. See Equiano, *Interesting Narrative*, 325–51. On Cuffe, see Sheldon H. Harris, *Paul Cuffe*, and Lamont D. Thomas, *Rise to Be a People*.

4. As was not uncommon in the period, Cuffe's mother Ruth Moses was an Indian, yet Cuffe was represented by others, and often represented himself, as "Negro." On the historical importance of, and contemporary blindness to, histories of racial hybridity, see Forbes, *Africans and Native Americans*.

5. Aptheker, *Documentary History*, 15.

6. Ibid.

7. Jordan notes that "warhawk expansionism" between 1806 and 1816 precipitated a passionate belief in the destiny of the white settler colonization of at least the entire North American continent, and made Africa and the Caribbean the only realistic sites for colonization (*White Over Black*, 566). The Monroe Doctrine, and Jefferson's approving response to it in a letter to Monroe, Oct. 24, 1823 (Ford, *Writings of Thomas Jefferson*, vol. 10, 277), serve as markers of this shift, although Jefferson seems to have believed in such continental destiny as early as 1786, as is clear from his "observations for the article *Etats-Unis* prepared for the *Encyclopedie*" (ibid., vol. 4, 180). Throughout this chapter, all references to Jefferson's letters refer to Ford's multivolume work, unless another citation is given. I give the date of the letter, volume number, and page number in that volume.

8. See Jordan, *White Over Black*, 542–51, for detailed descriptions of the earliest proposals.

9. Jefferson, *Writings*, 44.

10. Thanks to Chris Castiglia for pointing out to me that this account of colonization functions as a corrective to the Habermasian notion of civility-as-free-critique that has predominated early American studies in recent years.

11. Wheatley, *Collected Works*, 184.

12. Seth Moglen has used the phrase "black enlightenment" in his work-in-progress on nineteenth-century African American political thought.

13. Moten, unpublished manuscript.

14. On the principle of reason, see Derrida, "Principle of Reason."

15. For example, the British practiced the deportation or transportation of "criminals" to Australia and North America, and the early English colonists in North America deported or transported from their towns or communities people who did not conform to their moral, ethical, or legal requirements. See Beatie, *Crime and the Courts in England*; Linebaugh, *London Hanged*, 17–18; Abbot Emerson Smith, *Colonists in Bondage*.

16. We might say, ahistorically, that colonization proposals were something of a hybrid of seventeenth-, eighteenth-, and nineteenth-century deportation or transportation proposals; nineteenth-century British colonialism (in the sense that they involved establishing governmental and cultural replicas of the United States on other continents through settler colonialism); and high imperialism or neocolonialism (in the sense that they involved maintaining governmental and cultural control over a "foreign" population even after that population attained formal independence and control over their own territory). It is this hybrid status—and its unaccountability within either the standard narrative of deportation/transportation or the standard narrative of colonialism, imperialism, and neocolonialism—that we must consider.

17. Jordan dates the beginning of an ideologically coherent colonization "campaign" at the 1790s, adding that the "scattering of such proposals prior even to *The Notes on Virginia*

[composed in 1781–82, published in 1787], seem to have been highly miscellaneous in inspiration and purpose" (*White Over Black*, 542, 546). My analysis of Jefferson in this chapter will suggest that, by the 1780s, a coherent *discourse* of colonization had already taken shape. Foner, who ignores the magnitude of Jefferson's contribution to colonization, dates the origins of the debate among free blacks over colonization at the late 1780s (Foner, *History of Black Americans: From Africa*, 580), but also provides evidence of free black colonization proposals being discussed as early as 1773 (ibid., 579), as do Floyd Miller, *Search for a Black Nationality*, 3–53; Moses, *Classical Black Nationalism*, 6–11; and Shick, *Behold the Promised Land*, 3–5. See also John David Smith, *Emigration*.

18. The ACS was a private, procolonization organization, many of whose members were nonetheless government officials who helped secure some government funding for the society. It was founded in 1816–17, and eventually directed the establishment of Liberia in Western Africa. The ACS took inspiration from the British Committee for the Relief of the Black Poor, founded in 1786, and the British Sierra Leone Company, founded in 1791. See Asiegbu, *Slavery and the Politics of Liberation*, on the role of these British organizations in the establishment of the colony of Sierra Leone. On the origins and early history of the ACS, see Bancroft, "The Colonization of American Negroes"; Foner, *History of Black Americans: From Africa*, 584–93; Fox, *American Colonization Society*; Shick, *Behold the Promised Land*; Staudenraus, *African Colonization Movement*. For the history of the ACS after 1816, see Beyan, *The American Colonization Society and the Creation of the Liberian State*. On Liberia in particular, see Shick, *Behold the Promised Land*; Foner, *History of Black Americans: From the Emergence*, 255–56, 290–303, and for funding of the ACS, 291–93; Fox, *American Colonization Society*; Kinshasa, *Emigration vs. Assimilation*; McCartney, *Black Power Ideologies*, chapters 2 and 3; Floyd Miller, *Search for a Black Nationality*, 54ff; Staudenraus, *African Colonization Movement*. On the early, antislavery support for colonization, see Foner, *History of Black Americans: From Africa*, 584; Foner, *History of Black Americans: From the Emergence*, 291, 295; Jordan, *White Over Black*, 566; McCartney, *Black Power Ideologies*, 17–18; Miller, *Search for a Black Nationality*, 54–90; Moses, *Golden Age of Black Nationalism*, 34–35, and *Classical Black Nationalism*, 13–14.

19. Foner, *History of Black Americans: From Africa*, 579–84; Jordan, *White Over Black*, 548–49; Miller, *Search for a Black Nationality*, vii–viii, 3–20; Moses, *Classical Black Nationalism*, 6–13.

20. Hugh Davis and Stirn also argue that even in the 1830s there was no sharp division between emancipation and colonization. See Davis, "At the Crossroads" and Stirn, "Urgent Gradualism."

21. Jordan, *White Over Black*, 548; Sherwood, "Early Negro Deportation Projects," 487, and also 507–8. In this article, Sherwood is an apologist for white colonizationists when he argues that white leaders of the movement were committed to an essential and real freedom: "The men identified with the movement were of a high order and had for their purpose the emancipation of a race and the civilization of a continent" (507). Sherwood is right, as was Walker, not to dismiss or repress the connection between emancipation and colonization. But rather than celebrate the "high," or essential and timeless, nature of the concept of freedom at the core of colonization, as Sherwood does, I argue that colonization produces a historically specific, discursively formed notion of freedom itself epistemologically inseparable from racist and nationalist commitments.

In his otherwise careful argument devoted to limning the historical character of U.S. white supremacism, Jordan to some extent echoes this Sherwood position when he claims that "No one [of late eighteenth- and early nineteenth-century antislavery advocates in the North] denounced colonization as a proslavery instrument, as the next generation was to do, for the good reason that the project was supported *only* by men of *genuine* antislavery feeling" (548; my italics). Foner also criticizes Jordan for this comment, but fails to place it in the context of Jordan's entire argument about colonization (Foner, *History of Black Americans from Africa* 585). Consider the passage immediately following Jordan's claim about "genuine antislavery feeling": "Indeed, by far the most heartfelt of the denunciations of colonization [during this early period]—and there seem to have been extremely few—came from the most vociferous proponent of slavery, William Loughton Smith . . . Colonization was an emancipationist scheme calculated primarily to benefit the emancipators. Essentially it was a means of profiting white Americans by getting rid of the twin tyrannies of Negroes and slavery" (549). Each sentence in this passage offers a somewhat different account of the articulation of colonization with emancipation. Following the Sherwood-esque claim about colonizationists' commitment to essential and true freedom, Jordan claims that true antislavery forces opposed colonization, and then claims that colonizationists were disingenuous, self-interested profiteers. This ambiguity reflects Jordan's concerted, if not entirely successful, struggle to account for the problem at the center of this chapter: colonization's emancipatory claim.

22. Walker, *David Walker's Appeal*, 67–68.

23. See, for example, ibid., 1–3, 7, 12–13, 16–18, 20, 35–37, 46, 63, 72–73.

24. Recent exceptions are Castiglia, "Abolitionisms Racial Interiors" and "Pedagogical Discipline and the Creation of White Citizenship"; Onuf, "'To Declare Them a Free and Independent People'"; Saillant, "American Enlightenment." Foner, Jordan, and Miller discuss the pre-1816 period in some detail, and they struggle to evaluate the relationships among the mixed interests of colonizationists (though they still consider the interests to be *discrete*) as well as the curious connection between emancipation and colonization. See Foner, *History of Black Americans: From Africa*, 579–94, and *History of Black Americans: From the Emergence*, 290–308; Jordan, *White Over Black*, 542–69; Floyd Miller, *Search for a Black Nationality*, 3–53.

25. The question of to what extent and in what manner enslaved blacks supported colonization is, of course, extremely difficult to document, given their strictly subaltern position. There was certainly some support, given that some of the black Americans who went to Africa had been slaves, though certainly colonized slaves might have gone simply because it was their only means of attaining freedom from their masters. A crucial source for addressing this issue is the correspondence from black settlers in Liberia; see note 85. Also, the efforts Walker went through to disseminate his *Appeal* throughout the South would seem to suggest that he had indications of support among slaves for colonization—support he risked his life to discourage. On Walker's efforts, see Aptheker, *"One Continual Cry,"* 1, 45–53; Eaton, "A Dangerous Pamphlet in the Old South"; Vincent Harding, *There Is a River*, 92–94; Hinks, "'There Is a Great Work for You to Do'" and *To Awaken My Afflicted Brethren*, 116–72.

26. See Berlin, "Slaves Who Were Free," 172–88; Beyan, *American Colonization Society*; Horton, *Free People of Color*; Kinshasa, *Emigration vs. Assimilation*; Mehlinger, "Attitude of the Free Negro Toward African Colonization."

27. See Shick, *Behold the Promised Land*; Moses, *Classical Black Nationalism*; McCartney, *Black Power Ideologies*; Floyd Miller, *Search for a Black Nationality*; Stuckey, *Ideological Origins of Black Nationalism*, 1–29. Silger offers an extended study of the multiple "motivations" of free blacks who emigrated after 1816 under the auspices of the ACS, without dismissing the importance of black opposition to emigration; see "Attitude of Free Blacks Toward Emigration to Liberia." There is another group of early twentieth-century histories that offer apologia for colonization. They argue that colonizationists were well meaning and benevolent but technically unsophisticated

enough to realize the proposal; see, for example, Bancroft, "Colonization of American Negroes"; Charles I. Foster, "The Colonization of Free Negroes in Liberia"; Fox, *American Colonization Society*; Frederickson, *Black Image in the White Mind*; Opper, "Mind of White Participants in the African Colonization Movement"; Sherwood, "Early Negro Deportation Projects" and "Formation of the American Colonization Society"; Staudenraus, *African Colonization Movement*. There is also much scholarship on colonization and its supporters, particularly Martin Delany and Marcus Garvey, from the mid-nineteenth to the mid-twentieth centuries, though this period raises issues outside the scope of my study.

28. Citations will be given in parentheses. The title page of *Claims* declares that it is "By the Author of Conversations on the Sandwich Islands Mission, &c. &c." *Conversations on the Sandwich Islands Mission* is also anonymously authored, however, and it does not indicate the other texts to which the "&c. &c." of *Claims* refers.

29. On the differences between polygenesist racisms and other forms of racism, see Gould, *Mismeasure of Man*.

30. As with much of the information about the ACS given in this text, Aunt Caroline's statement is not historically accurate: ACS members were by no means uniformly against slavery or the slave trade. It is not clear from the text what Aunt Caroline is supposed to be quoting.

31. I have not been able to trace this quotation to Russwurm himself.

32. It is important to remember that the often-discussed scientific turn of racial discourse in the United States during the 1830s and 1840s was neither a fundamental break in nor an inauguration of modern racism, but rather was substantially an elaboration of this prior culturalism. For histories of race and racism that examine the formative period before the turn to "scientific" racism, see, for example, Goldberg, *Racist Culture*; Gossett, *Race*, 3–53; Guillaumin, "Specific Character of Racist Ideology," 29–98; Stanton, *Leopard's Spots*.

33. Again, the quotation is unattributed.

34. Monroe actually suggests to Jefferson the possibility of a penal colony to which black insurrectionaries could be deported, and Jefferson expands the discussion to colonization for all black Americans. For the Monroe-Jefferson exchange, see two letters from Jefferson to Monroe, of Nov. 24, 1801 (vol. 8, 103–6), and June 2, 1802 (vol. 8, 152–54), and three letters from Monroe to Jefferson, of June 15, 1801 (Hamilton, *Writings of James Monroe*, vol. 3, 292–95), Feb. 13, 1802 (ibid., 336–38), and June 11, 1802 (ibid., 351–53).

35. The reference is to query 18 of the *Notes on the State of Virginia*. The actual passage is: "And can the liberties of a nation be thought secure when we have removed their only firm basis, a conviction in the minds of the people that these liberties are a gift of God? That they are not to be violated but with his wrath? Indeed I tremble for my country when I reflect that God is just: that his justice cannot sleep for ever: that considering numbers, nature and natural means only, a revolution of the wheel of fortune, an exchange of situation is among possible events: that it may become probable through supernatural interference! The Almighty has no attribute which can take side with us in such a contest" (Jefferson, *Writings*, 289).

36. My focus on Jefferson is also indebted to Walker, who in his *Appeal* critically examines Jefferson more than any other figure, as we will see later in this chapter. He does not, however, discuss Jefferson's procolonization writings in detail—not surprisingly, as most of these writings are in the form of personal correspondence.

37. Again, recent exceptions are Castiglia, "Abolition's Racial Interiors" and "Pedagogical Discipline and the Creation of White Citizenship" and Onuf, "'To Declare Them a Free and Independent People.'"

38. In the words of John Chester Miller, "He signally failed to live up to his own precepts" (*Wolf by the Ears*, 277). See also Noble E. Cunningham, *In Pursuit Of Reason*, 61–62; Mayer, *Constitutional Thought of Thomas Jefferson*, 83; Miller, *The Wolf by the Ears*, 264–66.

39. In the words of Finkelman, "Scrutinizing the contradictions between Jefferson's professions and his actions . . . [suggests that] the test of Jefferson's position on slavery is . . . whether he was able to transcend his economic interests and his sectional background to implement the ideals he articulated. Jefferson fails the test" ("Jefferson and Slavery," 181). See also Berlin, "Slaves Who Were Free," 176–77.

40. In the words of Malone, "If his judgment on the Negroes was unfavorable, that of his local contemporaries generally was probably far more so. His observations were less notable in themselves, however, than in the spirit in which he made them. His comments on the race were those of a scientific mind, softened by humanitarianism. Or, to put it more precisely, they represented the tentative judgment of a kindly and scientifically minded man who deplored the absence of sufficient data and adequate criteria" (*Jefferson and His Time*, 267).

41. Jefferson, *Writings*, 44. I want to thank Peter Onuf for his challenging comments on an early version of my interpretation of Jefferson's correspondence.

42. Jefferson, *Writings*, 264.

43. According to Wilson, Jefferson's enormous correspondence is estimated at approximately 19,000 letters (Onuf, *Jeffersonian Legacies*, 67), and thus constitutes his most important body of literature.

44. Jefferson, *Writings*, 291. On the old world/new world problem in Jefferson, see, for example, Ceaser, *Reconstructing America*.

45. Subsequent parenthetical citations refer to line numbers of the letter.

46. Jefferson did, in fact, publish the first edition of *Notes on the State of Virginia* in England, in 1787.

47. Fliegelman, *Declaring Independence*, 120–40.

48. Jean Baptiste Donatien de Vimeur, or Count Rochambeau, was a French soldier who served under Washington in the Revolutionary War. Sent to the United States in 1780, he got through the British blockade in 1781 and eventually commanded French troops in the battle that led to the surrender of Lord Cornwallis. Made a Marshal of France in 1791, he was then imprisoned and almost guillotined during the Terror, but Napoleon later restored his rank and estates.

49. In recognition of Lafayette's many activities in support of revolutionaries in the United States and France, and his troubles in France after the Terror, the U.S. Congress gave him a large land grant in Louisiana in 1803, as well as $200,000 and a township in Florida in 1824.

50. Again, parenthetical citations refer to line numbers.

51. See Austin, *How to Do Things with Words*.

52. On this theme, see Onuf, "Thomas Jefferson, Missouri, and the 'Empire for Liberty.'"

53. For instance, the Declaration of Independence refers to "Laws of Nature and of Nature's God," qualities "endowed by their Creator," and the "protection of Divine Providence."

54. Both Miller (*Search for a Black Nationality*, 231–32) and Peterson (*Jefferson Image in the American Mind*, 191–93) represent Jefferson's support of Missouri's entrance into the union as a slave state as, in Miller's words, "mark[ing] the strange death of Jeffersonian liberalism" (232). As I have been arguing, a close reading of Jefferson's correspondence suggests that we place such a moment firmly within the life of such liberalism.

55. Frängsmyr et al., *The Quantifying Spirit in the 18th Century*, 2. For an overview of their research, see Heilbron, "Introductory Essay." For chapters relevant to the Jeffersonian context

considered here, see Heilbron, "Measure of Enlightenment"; Johannisson, "Society in Numbers"; Rider, "Measure of Ideas, Ruler of Language."

56. Frängsmyr et al., *The Quantifying Spirit*, 1, 2–3. Heilbron cites de Fontenelle, *Histoire du renouvellement de l'Académie royale des sciences en mdcxcix et les éloges historiques*, 1, 14.

57. Theodore M. Porter, *Rise of Statistical Thinking*, 4–5. See also Krüger et al., *Probabalistic Revolution*, vol. 1 and vol. 2; Hacking, *Taming of Chance* and "Biopower and the Avalanche of Numbers." For an intriguing, mathematical account of the rise of numeracy, see Stigler, *History of Statistics*. On the cultural politics of the rise of statistical thinking, see Alonso and Starr, *Politics of Numbers*; Desrosières, *Politics of Large Numbers*; Poovey, *History of the Modern Fact*. On the importance of the quantifying spirit to the rise of capitalism, see Hadden, *On the Shoulders of Merchants*.

58. Patricia Cline Cohen, *A Calculating People*, ix, 4. Regarding the phrase "a calculating people," Cohen refers to James Hall's *Statistics of the West, at the Close of the Year 1836*, 213, and Thomas Hamilton, *Men and Manners in America*, 222.

59. Cohen, *A Calculating People*, 12.

60. Ibid., ix, 205–26. I examine the power and limits of calculable thinking in the racialized context of the 1840 Census in a work-in-progress entitled "Racial (In)calculability."

61. Cohen, *A Calculating People*, 86, 109, 112–15, 130, 151. On Jefferson's faith in statistics and mathematics in general, see also Appleby, "Jefferson and His Complex Legacy," 7–8, and Stanton, "'Those Who Labor For My Happiness,'" 152–53. On the census, see Margo J. Anderson, *American Census*. For the context in which calculating knowledge emerged, see Richard D. Brown, *Knowledge Is Power*. For an excellent interpretation of the *Census of the Philippine Islands*, conducted by U.S. colonial officials between 1903–5, as an imperial tactic of discipline and surveillance, see Rafael, *White Love*. The "benevolent assimilation" that, according to Rafael, animated the Philippine census harkens back to the colonization discourse I am considering here, suggesting that the connections between these two articulations of U.S. imperialism need to be traced.

62. Mayr has used the term "population thinking" in his account of the rise of biology, but for him it "stress[es] the uniqueness of everything in the organic world . . . there is no 'typical' individual, and mean values are abstractions," and it is set against the "essentialism" characteristic of "racist literature," which "attempt[s] to arrive at true values in order to overcome the confusing effects of variation." See *Growth of Biological Thought*, 45–47.

63. Foucault, *Discipline and Punish*, 194. Subsequent citations will be given parenthetically. Castiglia's fascinating study of Robert Finley's work as a founder of the ACS also looks to Foucault to understand the "white citizenship" colonization pursued. He argues that Finley, who was once a teacher, was greatly influenced by the regulatory pedagogy of his own teacher, John Witherspoon, who was himself a contemporary of Bentham and who replicated Bentham's panoptic mode of power in the spheres of education and childrearing. Castiglia is extremely astute in his account of the relational, benevolent, disciplinary mode of the pedagogy that Finley learned from Witherspoon and that he applied to the ACS: "Citizenship, arising in the moment of pedagogical address, is always relational, locking citizens (teachers and students, parents and children, masters and servants), into hierarchical and regulated positions, none of which is 'free,' although some are more powerful than others" ("Pedagogical Discipline and the Creation of White Citizenship," 197).

64. Citations will be given parenthetically. As Ann Laura Stoler reminds us, Foucault finished *Discipline and Punish* the same day he began the last chapter of *The History of Sexuality*, vol. 1 (*Race and the Education of Desire*, xi). Stoler cites James Miller on this biographical information, and Miller quotes David Defert as his source (Miller, *Passion of Michel Foucault*, 240–41).

It should be noted that before Foucault's analysis of the panopticon, Polanyi exposed the transportable character of panopticism, suggesting that its deployment of power was not limited to the sphere of criminality and the institution of the prison. Polanyi argues that we examine this panopticism across a range of governmental discourses and practices, as does Foucault implicitly when he writes of a general "panoptic modality of power" and explicitly when he develops this argument in his subsequent work, as we will see below (Polanyi, *Great Transformation,* 140). Of course, for Foucault, unlike Polanyi, in principle no warden or minister is necessary for "control" to be "effective."

65. Burchell et al., *Foucault Effect,* 4.

66. Ibid., 4–5; Stoler, *Race and the Education of Desire,* 4.

67. Burchell, *Foucault Effect,* 98–100.

68. Ibid., 93.

69. Ibid., 93–94.

70. Ibid., 95.

71. Ibid., 4.

72. Foucault, *History of Sexuality,* vol. 1, 144.

73. While *The Colonizing Trick* was being prepared for publication, Foucault's 1975–76 lectures at Collège de France, in which he examines race extensively, were translated and published; they deserve careful consideration. See Foucault, *"Society Must Be Defended."* For a general discussion of Foucault's analysis of race in these lectures at the Collège de France, see Stoler, *Race and the Education of Desire,* 55–94.

74. Jefferson, *Writings,* 43–44.

75. Many of Jefferson's letters on colonization mark this scene of comparison with, and surveillance and judgment by, a generalized "Europe." For example, see a letter to St. George Tucker (Aug. 28, 1797, vol. 7. 168).

76. Derrida, "Declarations of Independence."

77. Jefferson, *Writings,* 288–89.

78. See also an 1820 letter to John Holms (April 22, vol. 10, 157–58).

79. Derrida, "Declarations of Independence," 9–10.

80. Derrida argues that in the process of retroactively bestowing upon itself its own legitimacy, the founding act of a constitution cuts or violates the existing law and thus commits the consummately ethical and incalculable act, an act conditioned upon a strictly impossible judgment to reject the law; see Derrida, "Force of Law." On incalculability in general, see Derrida, *Limited Inc,* 114–18. A crucial touchstone for this critique of calculable knowledge is Heidegger's work on calculable thinking. See, for example, *Basic Writings,* 117–41, 243–317, 374–92.

81. The Sparks letter is not unique in its representation of colonization as the governmental disposal of a calculable population. See, for example, a letter to Monroe (June 2, 1802, vol. 8, 152–53).

82. See also letters to Dr. Edward Bancroft (Jan. 26, 1789, vol. 5, 66–68); Rufus King (July 13, 1802, vol. 8, 162–63); and J. P. Reibelt (Dec. 21, 1805, vol. 8, 402–3).

83. See also an 1815 letter to David Barrow (vol. 9, 515–16).

84. On Hopkins's project and Thornton's connection to it, see Jordan, *White Over Black,* 549–50.

85. A fuller examination of this struggle, on which I am currently at work, needs to consider the debates on colonization in the black press, the colonizationist press, and the abolitionist press of the period; the archives of the ACS and its local chapters; letters to and from black colonists in Liberia and Sierra Leone; and Liberian, Sierra Leonian, U.S., and British archives. On the

press debates, see papers such as *Freedom's Journal, The Colored American, Palladium of Liberty, The Colonizationist and Journal of Freedom, The African Repository and Colonial Journal, The African Intelligencer, The Genius of Universal Emancipation,* and *The Liberator*; see also Foner and Walker, *Proceedings*; and Hutton, *Early Black Press*. For the letters, see Fyfe, *Our Children*; Wiley, *Slaves No More*; and a useful website at the University of Virginia, http://etext.lib.virginia.edu/subjects/liberia/ (I thank Jim Groom for directing me to this resource). For a nineteenth-century narrative about Sierra Leone's colonists, see Cuffe, *A brief account*. For the ACS archives, see *American Colonization Society*.

86. Silverman, "Four New Letters," 260.

87. See ibid., 260–62.

88. Quoted in ibid., 261.

89. Wheatley, *Collected Works*, 183; see also Silverman, "Four New Letters," 262.

90. Wheatley, *Collected Works*, 175.

91. Ibid., 176–77.

92. Ibid., 181–82.

93. For a thorough interpretation of Wheatley that carefully brings out her performance of "a *potential* community of black women readers (and writers)," see Bassard, *Spiritual Interrogations*, 10–86.

94. For a sketch of Walker and Stewart's Boston, see Hinks, *To Awake My Afflicted Brethren*, 63–90. See also Horton and Horton, *Black Bostonians*.

95. I quote from Walker, *David Walker's Appeal*, and Stewart, *Maria W. Stewart*, giving page numbers in parentheses.

96. Hartman, *Scenes of Subjection*, 6.

97. See Stewart, *Maria W. Stewart*, 30, 40, 57.

98. Romero, *Home Fronts*, 38–39.

99. Moten, unpublished manuscript.

100. Ibid.

101. Marx, *Capital*, vol. 1, 139.

3. Biloquial Nation

1. Brown, *Wieland and Memoirs of Carwin, the Biloquist*, 284. In the quotation from *Memoirs*, the last ellipsis is Brown's. Further references to *Memoirs of Carwin* and *Wieland* will be to this edition and will be cited parenthetically in the text.

2. On when Brown wrote *Memoirs of Carwin*, see his letter of September 5, 1798, to William Dunlap, in Pattee's introduction to *Wieland, or the Transformation, together with Memoirs of Carwin, the Biloquist*, xlii–xliii.

3. Pattee, introduction, xlii–xliv.

4. See Forbes, *Africans and Native Americans*.

5. See Davidson, *Revolution and the Word*, 83–109, 238.

6. Ibid., 238. The status of "first" of course depends on the criteria for "firstness," and such criteria are themselves socially and historically changeable; see ibid., 83–109. As Davidson notes, "by a convergence of various criteria—written in America, by an author born in America, published first in America, set in America, concerned with issues that are specifically grounded in the new country and not simply transplanted from Europe," the "first" U.S. novel is now commonly thought of as William Hill Brown's *The Power of Sympathy* (1789) (ibid., 85). The most that can be said about Brown is, perhaps, that he was one of the first "professional" writers, or

writers who tried to support themselves by writing alone (Fliegelman, introduction, vii). Others question whether Brown was the first such writer: Davidson, *Revolution and the Word*, 84; Elliott, introduction, xiii; Rosenthal, *Critical Essays*.

7. Brown, *Edgar Huntly*, 3.

8. Brown, prospectus for *Sky-Walk*, quoted in Pattee, xx. The prospectus originally appeared as "Notice of a New Work," in the *Weekly Magazine of Original Essays* (March 17, 1798), 202.

9. This self-conscious and institutional effort to found an organic national literature, and national culture more generally, was a trademark of European and U.S. nation formation in the eighteenth and nineteenth centuries. Just as Noah Webster sought to give the English language a distinct and organic American form after the American Revolution, so too did Brown and his institutional supporters set out simultaneously to construct and to naturalize the emergence of a national literature. On the effort to formulate a distinctly "American" English, see Haberly, "Search for a National Language."

10. See numerous articles in *The Monthly Magazine, The Literary Magazine*, and *The North American Review and Miscellaneous Journal*, which became *The North American Review* after 1821.

11. See Gilmore, "Literature of the Revolutionary and Early National Periods," 548.

12. On these racial theories, see Bieder, *Science Encounters the Indian*; Gossett, *Race*; Horsman, *Race and Manifest Destiny*; Stanton, *Leopard's Spots*; Vaughan, *Roots of American Racism*, 3–102.

13. Jefferson, *Writings*, 264–65.

14. Tooker, "United States Constitution and the Iroquois League," 39.

15. Hauptman, *Formulating American Indian Policy in New York State*, 4–5; Prucha, *American Indian Policy in the Formative Years*; Salisbury, "History of Native Americans," in Engerman and Gallman, *Cambridge Economic History of the United States*, 39.

It should be understood that Iroquois communities had, by 1800, experienced extensive contact with European colonists, so while this shift from conquered-people policy to forced-assimilation policy was significant, the shift itself is just part of a much more complex history of colonial interactions. Representations of either policy that depict a homogeneous, pure, or hermetic Iroquoian culture suddenly falling victim to U.S. colonization do more to continue the legacy of assimilation policy than they do to critique it. That is, assimilation policy itself repre-sented Indians as culturally homogeneous and hermetic in the past, and as past in the present, so as to idealize them for their past and assimilate them in the present. One would be hard pressed to find a moment when Iroquois—itself a hybrid name for hybrid peoples—were not culturally hybrid. For an indication of such hybridity under shifting colonialisms, see Forbes, *Africans and Native Americans*.

16. Pattee, introduction, x. See also Charvat, "Beginnings of Professionalism," 24; Chase, *American Novel and Its Tradition*; Fielder, *Love and Death in the American Novel*; Lewis, *American Adam*; Matthiessen, *American Renaissance*.

17. Davidson, *Revolution and the Word*, 246.

18. Rosenthal, introduction, 1–2.

19. Hart, *Concise Oxford Companion to American Literature*, 60.

20. See Hagenbüchle, "American Literature," 123; Kafer, "Charles Brockden Brown and Revolutionary Philadelphia," 467; Litton, "Failure of Rhetoric in Charles Brockden Brown's *Wieland*," 23; Ringe, *American Gothic*.

21. See Davidson, 246–48; Gilmore, "Literature of the Revolutionary and Early National Periods," 539–693; Grabo, *Coincidental Art of Charles Brockden Brown*; Hinds, "Frontiers of

Discourse," 109; Litton, "Failure of Rhetoric," 24; Scheiber, "'The Arm Lifted Against Me,'" 174; and Woodward, "Female Captivity," 134–36.

22. Kafer, "Charles Brockden Brown and Revolutionary Philadelphia," 498.

23. See Clemit, *The Godwinian Novel*, 134–35; Elliott, *Revolutionary Writers*, 218–70; Fliegelman, introduction, xiii; Hinds, "Frontiers of Discourse," 109; Hinds, "Charles Brockden Brown's Revenge Tragedy"; Ringe, *American Gothic*, 36–57; Shirley Samuels, *"Wieland"*; Allan Gardner Smith, "Analysis of Motives," 17, 25–26; and Tompkins, *Sensational Designs*, 39–93.

24. Davidson, *Revolution and the Word*, 251–52; Elliott, introduction to *Revolutionary Writers*; Hagenbüchle, "American Literature," 138–39, 142–44; Litton, "Failure of Rhetoric"; Voloshin, *"Edgar Huntly* and the Coherence of the Self," 276.

25. For notable recent criticism, see Burgett, *Sentimental Bodies*; Cahill, "An Adventurous and Lawless Fancy"; Hsu, "Democratic Expansionism"; Kamrath, "Charles Brockden Brown"; Kutchen, "The 'Vulgar Thread of the Canvas'"; Luciano, "'Perverse Nature'"; Mackenthun, "Captives and Sleepwalkers"; Rowe, *Literary Culture*, 25–51; Ruttenburg, *Democratic Personality*; Stern, *Plight of Feeling*.

26. For critical dismissals of *Memoirs of Carwin*, see, for example, Hart, *Concise Oxford Companion to American Literature*, which describes it as "hackwork" (60); Ringe, *American Gothic*, 39–41; Elliott, *Revolutionary Writers*, 232–34; and Clemit, *Godwinian Novel*, 134–35. For thoughtful discussions of *Memoirs of Carwin*, see Cahill, "An Adventurous and Lawless Fancy"; Hsu, "Democratic Expansionism"; Kutchen, "The 'Vulgar Thread of the Canvas'"; and Ruttenburg, *Democratic Personality*.

27. My search for what frames the "tradition versus modernity" frame draws implicitly from Derrida's reading of the "parergon," or the frame-ornament as supplement in Kant; see Derrida, *Truth in Painting*, 34–147, especially 54–55.

28. Pattee offers the following evidence for this conclusion: Brown admits as much in a letter to Dunlap written on September 5, 1798; in *Wieland* Carwin announces his intention to write his version of the story's events, but this version never appears fully in *Wieland*; and sentences with epistolary forms of address appear in *Memoirs of Carwin* but make no sense apart from *Wieland* since only *Wieland* explicitly takes an epistolary form (Pattee, introduction, xlii–xliv).

29. For recent work in literary studies that elaborates this cultural formation of the citizen-subject, see Nelson, *Word in Black and White* and *National Manhood*; Newfield, "Politics of Male Suffering" and *The Emerson Effect*; Romero, *Home Fronts*; Wald, *Constituting Americans*.

30. An anonymous review of *Memoirs of Carwin* from 1824 approvingly offers just this interpretation of Carwin. Discussing the characters in Brown's unfinished texts, the reviewer writes: "The fact is, that so far from having any thing peculiar in them, arising either from the peculiarity of disposition, or peculiarity of national manners, they are such characters as might be placed in any age and in any clime, because they are actually such as are met with at all times, and in all countries. Brown is no describer of *manners*, and, indeed, he never attempts it. His power lies in describing the passions and secret workings of the heart, and as these passions can never be grafted on national manners, founded as they are in the very nature of man, they are the same in all ages and countries. The character of 'Carwin the Biloquist' is not formed when his history concludes: we only know he had a thirst for knowledge, and a restless ambition. These are not new traits in the human character . . . It does not follow from this, that they are uninteresting characters: on the contrary, the most interesting characters are those where human nature is alone depicted" (from *European Magazine* 85 (January 1824): 55–69; reprinted in Rosenthal, *Critical Essays*, 41–42). That this reviewer takes America's "peculiarity" more for granted than Brown

did in the 1790s, and already understands Carwin's Americanness as universal, is a measure of the dubious success of Brown's foundational efforts.

31. Evans, "Origins of American Academic Psychology," 127, 16–26. Elliott (introduction, xix) and Fliegelman (introduction, xiv–xxii, xxviii–xxix) echo Smith's account of Brown's critique of rationalist-sensationalist psychologies. Edward Cahill has also recently examined Brown's "aesthetic state" in this context. See his "An Adventurous and Lawless Fancy."

32. Smith, "Analysis of Motives," 2–3. On this early period in U.S. "psychology," see Blight, "Jonathan Edward's Theory of the Mind"; Evans, "Origins of American Academic Psychology"; Fay, *American Psychology before William James*; Pfister and Schnog, *Inventing the Psychological*; Roback, *History of American Psychology*. On the relationship between such "psychology" and Brown, see Smith, "Analysis of Motives," 1–26, 125–34.

33. It is worth recalling here that in Kant the adverb "a priori" does not mean "prior," "assumed," or "taken for granted" in some general sense, but rather means "known prior to and independently of experience."

34. Writes Kant in his introduction to *The Critique of Judgement*: "Our entire cognitive faculty is, therefore, presented with an unbounded, but, also, inaccessible field—the field of the supersensible—in which we seek in vain for a territory, and on which, therefore, we can have no realm for theoretical cognition, be it for concepts of understanding or of reason. This field we must indeed occupy with ideas in the interest as well of the theoretical as the practical employment of reason, but in connection with the laws arising from the concept of freedom we cannot procure for these ideas any but practical reality, which, accordingly, fails to advance our theoretical cognition one step towards the supersensible.

"Albeit, then, between the realm of the natural concept, as the sensible, and the realm of the concept of freedom, as the supersensible, there is a great gulf fixed, so that it is not possible to pass from the former to the latter (by means of the theoretical employment of reason) just as if they were so many separate worlds, the first of which is powerless to exercise influence on the second: still the latter is *meant* to influence the former . . . There must, therefore, be a ground of the *unity* of the surpersensible *[sic]* that lies at the basis of nature" (Kant, *Critique of Judgement*, 13–14). Subsequent citations will give page numbers in parentheses. For the German, see Kant, *Kritik der Urteilskraft*.

35. Kant makes clear the provisional and artificial character of this tripartite division: "The principles of the faculty of judgement cannot, in a system of pure philosophy, form a separate constituent part intermediate between the theoretical and practical divisions, but may when needful be annexed to one or other as occasion requires. For if such a system is some day worked out under the general name of Metaphysic . . . the critical examination of the ground for this edifice must have been previously carried down to the very depths of the foundations of the faculty of principles independent of experience, lest in some quarter it might give way, and, sinking, inevitably bring with it the ruin of all" (4–5).

36. In his influential readings of *The Critique of Judgement* as one of the first texts to found a political role for and function of culture in the very process of theorizing an apolitical, disinterested, and universal faculty of aesthetic judgment, David Lloyd emphasizes that this subject's relation to judgment takes the form of "free conformity to law" (Kant, 86). That is, the subject judges neither according to fixed principles of "good taste" nor by following particular examples of "good judgement." Rather, its judgments all have a purely formal and universal character necessarily independent of any particular judgment. See Lloyd, "Kant's Examples," 34–37, and "Race under Representation," 64–65. For a related essay, see Lloyd, "Analogies of the Aesthetic."

For a related account of the way theories of the state and theories of culture interact to produce citizens in late eighteenth- and early nineteenth-century Europe, see Lloyd and Thomas, *Culture and the State*.

37. The "you" in *Memoirs of Carwin* has been taken by Pattee to address *Wieland's* Clara, and thus to be evidence of Brown's original intention to include *Memoirs of Carwin* in *Wieland* as Carwin's version of events (Pattee, xlii–xliv). I would add that this "you" doubles as an address to the reader.

38. I have attempted to limn a similar paradox in Freud's work on narcissism and paranoia, and to show how Lacan's notion of "paranoid knowledge" opens up a related critique of formal and abstract universality (see Kazanjian, "Notarizing Knowledge").

39. Although the term "strain" intensifies the resonance with the "shrill tones" of Brown's figure, the translation is liberal here; the German simply reads: *"Wenn mich jemand fragt, ob ich den Palast, den ich vor mir sehe, schön finde, so mag ich zwar sagen: ich liebe dergleichen Dinge nicht, die bloß für das Angaffen gemacht sind, oder, wie jener irokesische Sachem: ihm gefalle in Paris nichts besser als die Garküchen"* (Kant, *Kritik*, 40–41).

40. Kant, *Kritik*, 41. I would like to thank Judith Butler and Katrin Pahl for discussing this passage with me. I take responsibility for the translation.

41. This passage is also quoted and discussed in Lloyd "Race under Representation," 67–68, and in Lloyd "Analogies of the Aesthetic," 116–17.

42. The German distinguishes between society in the general sense *[Gesellschaft]* and civilization *[Zivilisierung]* (Kant, *Kritik*, 148–49).

43. I would like to thank Carolina Gonzalez and Timothy Shannon for discussing this question with me. The literature on Iroquois and Mohawks is fraught with the legacy of colonialism and so must be read carefully and critically; see Dennis, *Cultivating a Landscape of Peace*; Jennings, *The Ambiguous Iroquois Empire*; Jennings et al., *History and Culture of Iroquois Diplomacy*; Richter, *Ordeal of the Long-House*; Richter and Merrell, *Beyond the Covenant Chain*; Snow, *Iroquois*; and Tooker, *Iroquois Source Book*. For a foundational account of reading such material critically, see Deloria, *Custer Died for Your Sins*.

44. For an account of this myth of an Iroquois empire, see Jennings, *Ambiguous Iroquois Empire*, and "'Pennsylvania Indians' and the Iroquois."

45. Lewis H. Morgan, *League of the Ho-dé-no-sau-nee*. For the debate over the contribution of the Iroquois to the U.S. Constitution, see Hauptman, *Formulating American Indian Policy*; Landsman and Ciborski, "Representation and Politics"; and Tooker, "United States Constitution and the Iroquois League," 305–36.

46. Richter argues that the Great League of Peace "as a cultural and ritual institution" can be distinguished from the Confederacy "as a political and diplomatic entity" (*Ordeal of the Long-House*, 11), although the very distinction between culture-ritual and politics-diplomacy is not unaffected by colonialism.

Strictly speaking, even the more accepted transliteration "Mohawks" ought to be in quotation marks, as it is no less a mark of the epistemic violence of colonialism than is "Mohock." As Richter explains, until the nineteenth century, the people known in English as "Mohocks" or "Mohawks" were called "Ganienkeh" by fellow Iroquois, "Agniers" by the French, and "Maquas" by the Dutch (*Ordeal of the Long-House*, 1, 282). Richter also argues that "the name Mohawk is derived from a New England Algonquian word meaning 'eater of human flesh,'" and thus reflects the Mohawks' "long-standing reputation among their neighbors" as fierce warriors (*Ordeal of the Long-House*, 31). However, as Richter remarks, none of these words can be called authentic;

we know them all largely from colonial texts, and thus all are irreducibly, if not exclusively, the result of the violent translations of colonialist historiography and anthropology (*Ordeal of the Long-House*, 4–7, 281–82).

47. *Compact Edition of the Oxford English Dictionary*, s.v. "Mohawk" and "Mohock."

48. In "Kant's Examples," 38–42, Lloyd traces the emergence in *Critique of Judgement* of a pedagogical practice that would conduct this "tutoring" of the "Savoyard peasant."

49. The "differed-deferral" of the other within the same refers to Derrida's *différance*; see Derrida, "Différance."

50. This is one of the direct addresses to which Pattee refers when he argues, as I mentioned above, that *Memoirs of Carwin* was to be included in *Wieland* as Carwin's account of his life to Clara. The "you" thus presumably refers to Clara.

51. Kant, *Critique of Judgement*, 4.

52. Fliegelman, introduction, x–xi, xv–xvi.

53. *Compact Edition of the Oxford English Dictionary*, vol. 1, "Biloquial" and "Biloquist," 864; vol. 2, "Ventriloquism" and "Ventriloquist," 3607–8.

54. Fernández Retamar, *Caliban*, 6; Jane, *Four Voyages of Columbus*.

55. Fernández Retamar, *Caliban*, 6.

56. Ibid., 6, 8–9.

57. Ibid., 14.

58. Subsequent interventions into Fernández Retamar's project underline the importance of reading the intricate ways the text of colonialism is crosshatched by the discourses of racism and masculinism. See, for example, Athey and Alarcon, "*Oroonoko's* Gendered Economies of Honor/ Horror"; Loomba, *Gender, Race, Renaissance Drama*.

It is crucial to know that Fernández Retamar's own project can be critiqued for reading Caliban as an always already *mestizo* figure, thereby erasing the continuing histories and politics of Indians in Latin America. For a brilliant account of the implications of such an erasure, see Saldaña-Portillo, "Who's the Indian in Aztlán?" For a critique of the foundationalism that persists in Fernández Retamar's anti-imperialist nationalism, see Cooppan's "Mourning Becomes Kitch."

59. It should be noted that Prospero has *not* actually set Ariel free yet: perhaps Brown's odd combination of "Ariel *is made to sing*" and "finally absolved" is an indication of his only partially accurate representation of the scene from Shakespeare. Prospero still orders Ariel to do several more tasks, all under the promise of freedom. Ariel is not actually freed until the last line of the play: "Be free, and fare thou well!—Please you draw near."

60. Fliegelman describes this interpretation of Brown: "In *Wieland*, Brown dramatizes and investigates the idea—propounded also by Rousseau and Jonathan Edwards—that the manipulation of human motivation (as by, to take a contemporary example, advertising) is not a violation of human freedom, that individuals do as they please but do not determine their pleasure, that the 'willing' slave is, in fact, free. In illuminating the realm between pure freedom and compulsion, Brown is ultimately offering one of the earliest analyses of the workings of 'ideology' . . . The mystery of what [eighteenth-century rhetorician James] Burgh called 'the creation of desire' by language, 'that internal act which by influencing the will makes us proceed to action,' is, Brown suggests, the essential subject of fiction and its ideal if sometimes problematic effect . . . Silent, heartfelt listening became a new model of political submission, a submission that represented not rational assent but a new mixture of voluntarism and involuntarism. Such a mixture, which dominated the rhetoric of the entire period, was characteristically captured by Brown in

the opening line of *Wieland*, that most oratorical of novels: 'I feel,' declares Clara, 'little reluctance in complying with your request.' Such was the new *affective* version of the 'consent of the governed'" (Fliegelman, introduction, xxxv–xxxvi).

61. For a brilliant reading for echoes, see Spivak, "Echo."

62. While *The Colonizing Trick* was being prepared for publication, I came across Larry Kutchen's extensive discussion of Brown and the picaresque. It deserves careful consideration.

63. Nelson, *National Manhood*.

64. Spivak, *A Critique of Postcolonial Reason*, 13.

65. On the distinction between disavowal and foreclosure, see Laplanche and Pontalis, *Language of Psychoanalysis*, 118–21, 161–69.

66. See Brown, *Alcuin*, in *The Novels and Related Works of Charles Brockden Brown*. For a fantastic interpretation of *Alcuin* as part of a "prehistory of the history of sexuality," and as an ambivalent counterpoint to Malthus's *An Essay on the Principle of Population*, see Burgett, "Between Speculation and Population." My concluding suggestions about *Memoirs of Carwin* are in some productive tension with Burgett's suggestion, at the end of his essay, that *Alcuin* might "open our critical gaze onto queer taxonomies within which 'differences' marginalized by 'sex' may be equally important."

67. For a foundational reading of this problematic, see de Man, *Allegories of Reading*, 246–77, and "Rhetoric of Temporality," in *Blindness and Insight*, 187–228. See also Derrida's reading of de Man's discussion of this problematic in *Memoirs for Paul de Man*; the quote is from page 145. For an exemplary reading of the relationship between reading and politics, see Spivak, "Echo."

4. Ambivalent Alliance

1. *Executive Documents*, no. 43, p. 26. Rogin, *Subversive Genealogy*, 102–3, and *Ronald Reagan*, 134–68.

2. Horsman, *Race and Manifest Destiny*, 190. On his account of this shift, see 189–207.

3. On the Black Legend, see Gibson, *The Black Legend*; Mariscal, "Role of Spain in Contemporary Race Theory"; Fernández Retamar, *Caliban*, 56–73.

4. For a careful analysis of such blending of racial ideologies in the eighteenth-century British context, see Wheeler, *Complexion of Race*, 2–48.

5. For this timeline, see Griswold del Castillo, *Treaty of Guadalupe Hidalgo*, 30–61.

6. See Acuña, *Occupied America*; Chávez, *The Lost Land*; Gutiérrez, "Significant to Whom?"; Gutiérrez-Jones, *Rethinking the Borderlands*; Horsman, *Race and Manifest Destiny*; Padilla, *My History, Not Yours*; Cecil Robinson, introduction, in *View from Chapultepec*; Rogin, *Subversive Genealogy*; José David Saldívar, *Border Matters*; Rosaura Sánchez, *Telling Identities*; Streeby, "American Sensations" and "Joaquín Murrieta and the American 1848." While *The Colonizing Trick* was being prepared for publication, Shelley Streeby's important "American Sensations" was published. Streeby examines some of the texts I consider in this chapter, and briefly examines the Caste War as a crucial context for U.S.–Mexico War novelettes. Her work deserves careful consideration.

7. This account is culled primarily from Bricker, *Indian Christ*; Gilbert M. Joseph, "United States," "From Caste War," and *Rediscovering*, ch. 3; Reed, *Caste War*; Mary W. Williams, "Secessionist Diplomacy."

8. Gilbert M. Joseph, "United States," 32.

9. See Bricker, *Indian Christ*, 93–95.

10. Marx, "On the Jewish Question," in *Early Writings*, 211–41.

11. I hedge here—"seem to have," "not necessarily," "could be"—because of the difficulties that attend any attempt to cull subaltern histories. Most of these letters are written in Spanish by

Maya leaders, some of whom had been caciques who at times functioned as agents for the very Creole leaders they rose up against in 1847. To what extent do these letters represent popular Maya sentiment? What does it mean to rely on the figure "popular Maya sentiment" in this context in the first place? If such questions are hotly debated among contemporary scholars of the recent Zapatista uprising, the difficulties attending the subaltern history of the Caste War are that much more impressive. I have been researching this subaltern history and hope to add to my analysis here at a future date. For now, I want to emphasize that we must not idealize this Maya struggle, and yet we also must not homogenize it otherwise: as, for instance, a class struggle, or a race war, or a bit of *Lumpen* anarchy.

12. Nelson Reed and Gilbert Joseph have suggested that the Maya withdrew to attend to planting season, and imply that occupation of coastal urban centers was not a strategic goal of their uprising. See Reed, *Caste War of Yucatan*; Joseph, "United States."

13. *Executive Documents*, no. 43, p. 9. Some of the letters written by Yucatecan officials have been marked "translation," while others have not, though these too may have been translated from Spanish originals. I have as yet not been able to locate the original letters in U.S. or Mexican government archives, and so must treat only the English translations here. It appears that President Polk, his cabinet, the Congress, and perhaps the military officers in Mexico had no concern for this language difference, and only handled translations of these letters, making interpretations of the translations relevant to the U.S. side of this correspondence.

14. *Executive Documents*, no. 43, p. 10.

15. On *mestizaje*, see Díaz Polanco, *Indigenous Peoples in Latin America*; Knight, "Racism, Revolution, and *Indigenismo*"; Saldaña-Portillo, "Reading a Silence." I would also like to thank Christopher Conway for discussing *mestizaje* and *indigenismo* with me. As he points out, Domingo Faustino Sarmiento's *Facundo: Civilizacion y Barbarie* (1845), though probably not accessible to Yucatecos in 1848, is nonetheless a crucial touchstone for Latin American ideologies of progress in the nineteenth century.

16. *Executive Documents*, no. 43, p. 4.

17. Ibid., p. 23.

18. Ibid., p. 12.

19. Ibid., pp. 13–15.

20. Ibid., p. 16.

21. Ibid., p. 18.

22. Manning, *Diplomatic Correspondence: Inter-American Affairs*, vol. 8, 1071–72. Because it was forwarded to Congress by Polk, this letter can also be found, with some apparently typographical differences, in *Executive Documents*, no. 40, pp. 11–12. In the latter text only, the letter is described as "An official translation by John Baldwin."

23. In Manning, this word is not capitalized, but in *Executive Documents* it is. Manning appends a footnote to this word that reads "*Sic.* The note appears to have reached the Department both in the original Spanish and in translation." Since I have yet to find the original copy of this letter, Manning's note remains opaque. The "*Sic.*" might simply refer to the lack of a capital "A" or to the distinctly Spanish use of the article "the" in the phrase "the american policy." However, it might also suggest that Sierra erred in using the adjective "american" to refer to U.S. and Yucatecan policy as if they were common. This latter use is, of course, precisely the meaning I am attributing to Sierra's formulation.

24. Manning, *Diplomatic Correspondence: Inter-American Affairs*, vol. 8, 1076.

25. Ibid.

26. Ibid., 1062.

27. Ibid.

28. On November 16, U.S. Peace Commissioner Nicholas Trist had been recalled from Mexico to pressure the prowar or *Puro* faction of the Mexican government to accept U.S. terms. The day before Polk's State of the Union Address, Trist would disobey the recall order in the belief that he was on the verge of an agreement (and in the suspicion that Polk did not want peace in the first place), writing a sixty-five page letter of explanation to Secretary of State James Buchanan that Polk, in his diary, called "arrogant, imprudent, and very insulting to his government, and even personally offensive to the President." Griswold del Castillo, *Treaty of Guadalupe Hidalgo*, 36–42.

29. *Congressional Globe*, appendix, Dec. 7, 1847, 1.

30. Ibid.

31. Ibid., 2.

32. Ibid., 3.

33. In "Can the Subaltern Speak?" Spivak shows how the abolition of *sati* "by the British has been generally understood as a case of 'White men saving brown women from brown men.'" Arguing that "White women—from the nineteenth-century British Missionary Registers to Mary Daly—have not produced an alternative understanding," Spivak deconstructs the opposition between the British interpretation and "the Indian nativist argument . . . 'The women actually wanted to die'" (297).

34. *Congressional Globe*, appendix, Dec. 7, 1847, 4.

35. Ibid., 1.

36. Manning, *Diplomatic Correspondence: Inter-American Affairs*, vol. 8, 977.

37. Polk's April 29 message is referred to and debated in *Congressional Globe*, 708–13, 728–30, 738, and, in more detail, *Congressional Globe*, appendix, 590–643. The full text of Polk's April 29 message, as well as the documents he forwarded to Congress, can be found in *Executive Documents*, no. 40, pp. 1–3. Letters between U.S. and Yucatán officials about the Caste War, some of which are not included in *Executive Documents*, can be found in Manning, *Diplomatic Correspondence: Inter-American Affairs*, vol. 8.

38. Manning, *Diplomatic Correspondence: Inter-American Affairs*, vol. 8, 219. Also included in *Executive Documents*, no. 40, pp. 9–10.

39. *Congressional Globe*, April 29, 1848, 709.

40. Ibid., 710–11.

41. Ibid., 711.

42. Ibid., 712.

43. Ibid., 727.

44. *Congressional Globe*, appendix, May 4, 1848, 592; see also 596. For Crittenden's request for more information, see May 5, 1848, 601.

45. Ibid., May 5, 1848, 598.

46. Ibid., May 9, 1848, 608.

47. Ibid., May 10, 1848, 613.

48. Ibid., May 15, 1848, 632.

49. Ibid., 633.

50. Ibid.

51. Ibid., May 5, 1848, 601.

52. Ibid., May 9, 1848, 611.

53. Ibid., 612.

54. Ibid., May 17, 1848, 640.

55. See Gilbert Joseph, "United States" and *Revolution from Without*.

56. *Congressional Globe*, appendix, Dec. 7, 1947, 599–600.

57. I discuss the term *antipode*, which literally means "having the feet opposite," in more detail in the epilogue.

58. This reading public was made up of, as Denning writes, "craftworkers, factory operatives, domestic servants, and domestic workers": what the cultural elite of the era called "the Unknown Public" or "the Million" (*Mechanic Accents*, 27, 29). The high circulation rates and the working class audience are not surprising, because of fairly high, minimal literacy rates in the United States—for instance, probably 89 percent of northern artisans and 76 percent of northern farmers and laborers were literate between 1830 and 1895 (ibid., 31). On advances in print technology, see Bold, "The Voice"; Denning, *Mechanic Accents*, 1–26; Johanssen, *To the Halls*; Saxton, "Problems" and *Rise and Fall*; Sellers, *The Market Revolution*; Zboray, *A Fictive People* and "Antebellum Reading." On literacy, see Denning, *Mechanic Accents*, 27–61; Soltow and Stevens, *Rise of Literacy*.

59. Streeby, "American Sensations," 4.

60. For other U.S.–Mexico War novelettes I do not discuss below, see, for example, Averill, *Mexican Ranchero* and *Secret Service Ship*; Buntline, *Magdalena, the Beautiful Mexican Maid* and *Volunteer; or The Maid of Monterey*; Croome, *Golden Sands of Mexico*; Dallam, *Lone Star* and *Deaf Spy*; Ganilh, *Mexico versus Texas* and *Ambrosio de Letinez*; Halyard, *Chieftain of Churubusco*, *Ocean Monarch*, and *Warrior Queen*; Hazel, *Flying Artillerist*, *Rival Chieftains*, and *Light Dragoon*; Ingraham, *Montezuma, Silver Ship of Mexico*, and *Texan Ranger*; Lippard, *Legends of Mexico* and *'Bel of Prairie Eden*; St. Clair, *Senora Ines*. For historical and literary accounts of U.S.–Mexico War fiction see, for example, Bill Brown, *Reading the West*; Bold, "The Voice"; Cox, *The Dime Novel Companion*; Flanagan and Grismer, "Mexico in American Fiction"; Johanssen, *To the Halls*; Nichols, "Indian in the Dime Novel"; Simmons, "Nationalism and the Dime Novel"; Slotkin, *Regeneration*; Norman O. Smith, "Mexican Stereotypes"; Henry Nash Smith, *Virgin Land*; Streeby, "American Sensations."

61. Halyard, *Heroine of Tampico*. Citations will be given parenthetically. On the "Flag of Our Union," see Madeline Hall, *Publishers*; Noel, *Villians Galore*; Henry Nash Smith, *Virgin Land*.

62. Halyard, *Mexican Spy*. Citations will be given parenthetically.

63. Though Annabel is initially introduced as the daughter of Don Jose's brother (9), she suddenly becomes the daughter of Don Jose's sister (10), and remains so for the rest of the novel, suggesting that initial description was an editing error.

64. Says Gonzardo to Annabel: "I am a strong and hardy, though fierce and grief-stricken man; you are a slight and fragile maiden. As far as character and personal appearance go, we are the exact opposites of each other. But by a strange concurrence of circumstances, we have been brought together—an outlaw and robber and a pure and guileless maiden, to work out for each other the most grateful and benevolent purpose" (18).

65. Averill, *Secret Service Ship*. Citations will be given parenthetically.

66. Hazel, *Inez, The Beautiful*. Citations will be given parenthetically.

67. Griswold del Castillo, *Treaty of Guadalupe Hidalgo*, 190.

68. For work that invokes and, at times, complicates the internal colonization framework, see Acuña, *Occupied America*; Almaguer, *Racial Fault Lines* and "Ideological Distortions"; Barrera, *Race and Class*; Barrera et al., "The Barrio"; Gutiérrez, "Significant to Whom?" and *Walls and Mirrors*; Gutiérrez-Jones, *Rethinking the Borderlands*; Montejano, *Anglos and Mexicans*; Rosaura Sánchez, *Telling Identities*; José Saldívar, *Border Matters*; Ramón Saldívar, *Chicano Narrative*.

69. For a sampling of this scholarship, see Keller and Candelaria, *Legacy of the Mexican and Spanish-American Wars*.

70. Griswold del Castillo, *Treaty of Guadalupe Hidalgo*, 189–90.

71. The full text of article 8 reads as follows: "Mexicans now established in territories previously belonging to Mexico, and which remain for the future within the limits of the United States, as defined by the present Treaty, shall be free to continue where they now reside, or to remove at any time to the Mexican Republic, retaining the property which they possess in the said territories, or disposing thereof and removing the proceeds wherever they please; without their being subjected, on this account, to any contribution, tax, or charge whatever.

"Those who shall prefer to remain in the said territories, may either retain the title and rights of Mexican citizens, or acquire those of citizens of the United States. But, they shall be under the obligation to make their election within one year from the date of the exchange of ratifications of this treaty: and those who shall remain in the said territories, after the expiration of that year, without having declared their intention to retain the character of Mexicans, shall be considered to have elected to become citizens of the United States.

"In the said territories, property of every kind, now belonging to Mexicans not established there, shall be inviolably respected. The present owners, the heirs of these, and all Mexicans who may hereafter acquire said property by contract, shall enjoy with respect to it, guaranties equally ample as if the same belonged to citizens of the United States." Griswold del Castillo, *Treaty of Guadalupe Hidalgo*, 189–90.

72. Edward H. Thompson, "Page of American History," 240.

73. Ibid., 245. As Robert Aguirre has pointed out to me, U.S. involvement in Mexican archeology during the nineteenth century forms an important part of this page of U.S. imperialism. John L. Stephens's *Incidents of Travel in Yucatan* (1843), an archeological travelogue, was a bestseller in the United States. *Incidents* first put Yucatán on the map for most mid-century U.S. readers, and helped to spark numerous expeditions to Mayan sites in Mexico. I thank Robert for discussing this history with me, and refer the reader to his important essay "Annihilating the Distance."

74. Edward H. Thompson, "Page of American History," 246.

75. Ibid., 247.

76. Ibid., 248.

77. Ibid., 249.

78. Ibid.

79. I again thank Robert Aguirre for pointing this out to me. See Castañeda, *In the Museum*, and among Thompson's many accounts, see *Chultunes, Archeological Researches, Home*, and *People*.

80. Cockcroft, *Mexico's Hope*, 85.

81. Joseph, "United States," 177–78.

Epilogue

1. Marx, *Capital*, vol. 1, 152–53.

2. For instance, consider the dissemination of the term "antipodes" as traced by the *Oxford English Dictionary*. In 1398, John Trevisa wrote, "Yonde in Ethiopia ben the Antipodes, men that haue theyr fete ayenst our fete" (*Bartholomeus de Proprietatibus Rerum*); in 1642, Thomas Fuller wrote, "Christians were forced to be Antipodes to other men, so that when it was night with others, it was day with them" (*The Holy State and the Profane State*); also in 1642, James Howell wrote, "From the remostest parts of the Earth, yea from the very Antipods" (*Instructions for Forreine Travell*); in 1688, Daniel Defoe wrote "Antipodes to all Mankind, Enemies to Government"

(Memoirs of the Church of Scotland); in 1837, William Whewell wrote, "The existence of Antipodes, or persons inhabiting the opposite side of the globe" *(History of the Inductive Sciences)*; and in 1879, Alfred R. Wallace wrote, "New Zealand, almost the antipodes of Britain" *(Australasia).* Compact Edition of the Oxford English Dictionary, vol. 1, 93–4.

3. Marx, *Capital,* vol. 1, and *Grundrisse,* 884. Carey himself noticed his influence on Bastiat, to the point of accusing Bastiat of plagiarism (Dorfman, *Economic Mind,* 804).

4. Carey embraced mercantilism in the name of strengthening the nation and countering what he saw as the harmful, external influences of Europe, particularly Britain. This anti-British nationalism was not simply rooted in the "spirit of '76"; significant withdrawals of British capital from the United States in the 1830s, decreases in U.S. tariffs between 1832 and 1842 accompanied by the panic of 1837, and the downturn in Britain following the repeal of the corn laws in the 1840s combined to give free trade a bad name in the United States.

5. As Arnold Green points out, Carey argued to northern abolitionists that tariff increases would help to kill slavery, and to proslavery forces that tariff increases would protect slavery *(Henry Charles Carey,* 37). Despite his high profile, however, Carey has proven a troublesome figure for U.S. historians and economists, who usually dismiss him as a confused or contradictory thinker, placing particular emphasis on his supposedly momentous transformation from free trade to protectionism. As Carey himself explained, one day in 1847 "I jumped out of bed, and dressing myself, was a protectionist from that hour" (quoted in Dorfman, *Economic Mind,* 799); ninety days later, he had written *The Past, the Present, and the Future.* By contrast, I want to consider the ways in which Carey's work defies the supposedly stark distinction between free trade and mercantilism by taking seriously his antipodal combination of antistatism and mercantilism. The most textually specific analysis of Carey's work is a monograph by Rodney J. Morrison, *Henry C. Carey and American Economic Development.* For other discussions of Carey, see Conkin, *Prophets of Prosperity;* Howe, *Political Culture of the American Whigs;* Normano, *Spirit of American Economics;* Teilhac, *Pioneers of American Economic Thought.* I have offered a more detailed reading of *The Past, the Present, and the Future* in my "'Yankee Universality.'"

6. Marx, *Grundrisse,* 883–84, 885. Occasionally, Marx does seem to see a certain antipodal logic interior to Carey's text—that is, to see in Carey a paradoxical combination of both Bastiat's free tradism and the mercantilism of such French economists as F. L. A. Ferrier and Charles Ganilh *(Grundrisse,* 886; *Capital,* vol. 1, 705–6).

7. Marx, *Grundrisse,* 884.

8. Ibid.

9. Ibid., 886, 887.

10. Marx, *On America and the Civil War.*

11. Marx, *Grundrisse,* 888.

12. Ibid.

13. Marx does appear to have rewritten this section of the *Grundrisse* in chapter 22 of the first volume of *Capital,* entitled "National Wages." Here, though he no longer seems seduced by Carey's claims about the United States, he also does not offer a critique of "Yankee" claims to "universality." Rather, he leaves those claims behind, representing Carey as just another misguided bourgeois economist rather than the "original" if "abstract" representative of "the contemporary historic principle of North America" with whom he was so taken in the *Grundrisse.*

14. Carey, *The Past, the Present, and the Future,* 290. Subsequent citations will be given parenthetically.

Bibliography

Acholonu, Catherine Obianuju. "The Home of Olaudah Equiano: A Linguistic and Anthropological Search." *The Journal of Commonwealth Literature* 22.1 (1987): 5–16.

———. *The Igbo Roots of Olaudah Equiano: An Anthropological Research.* Owerri, Nigeria: AFA, 1989.

Acuña, Rodolfo. *Occupied America: A History of Chicanos.* New York: Harper, 1988.

African Repository and Colonial Journal. Volumes 1–8. Washington: Way and Gideon, Printers, 1826–32.

Aguirre, Robert D. "Annihilating the Distance: Panoramas and the Conquest of Mexico, 1822–1848." *Genre: Forms of Discourse* 35.1 (2002): 25–54.

Allen, Theodore W. *The Invention of the White Race: Racial Oppression and Social Control.* New York: Verso, 1994.

Almaguer, Tomás. "Ideological Distortions and Recent Chicano Historiography: The Internal Colonialism Model and Chicano Historical Interpretation." *Aztlan* 18.1 (Spring 1987): 7–28.

———. *Racial Fault Lines: The Historical Origins of White Supremacy in California.* Berkeley: University of California Press, 1994.

Alonso, William, and Paul Starr, eds. *The Politics of Numbers.* New York: Russell Sage Foundation, 1986.

Althusser, Louis. *Lenin and Philosophy, and Other Essays.* New York: Monthly Review Press, 1971.

———. "Contradiction and Overdetermination." *For Marx.* New York: Verso, 1990, 89–116.

Althusser, Louis, and Étienne Balibar. *Reading Capital.* Trans. Ben Brewster. London: NLB, 1970.

American Colonization Society. *Memorial of the American Society, for Colonizing the Free People of Color of the United States.* Washington, D.C.: Gales and Seaton, 1828.

———. *Condition of the American Colored Population and of the Colony at Liberia.* Boston: Peirce and Parker, 1833.

American Colonization Society: A Register of Its Records in the Library of Congress Manuscript Division. Washington, D.C.: Library of Congress, 1979.

American Social History Project. *Who Built America? Working People and the Nation's Economy, Politics, and Society.* Vol. 1: *From Conquest and Colonization through Reconstruction and the Great Uprising of 1877.* New York: Pantheon Books, 1989.

Anderson, Benedict. *Imagined Communities: Reflections on the Origin and Spread of Nationalism.* Rev. ed. New York: Verso, 1991.

Anderson, Margo J. *The American Census: A Social History.* New Haven: Yale University Press, 1988.

Anderson, Perry. *Considerations on Western Marxism.* London: Verso, 1979.

Andrews, William L. "The First Fifty Years of the Slave Narrative, 1760–1810." *The Art of the Slave Narrative: Original Essays in Criticism and Theory.* Ed. John Sekora and Darwin T. Turner. Macomb: Western Illinois Press, 1982, 6–24.

———. *To Tell a Free Story: The First Century of Afro-American Autobiography, 1760–1865.* Urbana: University of Illinois Press, 1986.

Appleby, Joyce. *Liberalism and Republicanism in the Historical Imagination.* Cambridge: Harvard University Press, 1992.

———. "Introduction: Jefferson and His Complex Legacy." *Jeffersonian Legacies.* Ed. Peter S. Onuf. Charlottesville: University of Virginia Press, 1993, 1–16.

Aptheker, Herbert. *"One Continual Cry": David Walker's Appeal to the Colored Citizens of the World (1829–1830), Its Setting and Its Meaning*. New York: Humanities Press, 1965.

———. *A Documentary History of the Negro People in the United States: Volume 1, From the Colonial Times through the Civil War*. New York: Citadel Press, 1990.

Apuntes para la Historia de la Guerra entre México y los Estados Unidos. 1848. Ed. Ramón Alcaraz, et al. Reprint, México, D. F.: Fundación Miguel Alemán, A. C., 1997. Translated as *The Other Side: Or Notes for the History of the War between Mexico and the United States*. Trans. Albert C. Ramsey. New York: Burt Franklin, 1850.

Aravamudan, Srinivas. *Tropicopolitans: Colonialism and Agency, 1688–1804*. Durham: Duke University Press, 1999.

Aristotle. *The Rhetoric and the Poetics of Aristotle*. Trans. W. Rhys Roberts and Ingram Bywater. New York: McGraw-Hill, 1984.

Armstrong, John A. *Nations before Nationalism*. Chapel Hill: University of North Carolina Press, 1982.

Arrighi, Giovanni. *The Long Twentieth Century*. New York: Verso, 1994.

Asiegbu, Johnson U. J. *Slavery and the Politics of Liberation, 1787–1861: A Study of Liberated African Emigration and British Anti-slavery Policy*. London: Longmans, Green and Co., 1969.

Athey, Stephanie, and Daniel Cooper Alarcon. "*Oroonoko*'s Gendered Economies of Honor/Horror: Reframing Colonial Discourse Studies in the Americas." *American Literature* 65.3 (September 1993): 415–43.

Austin, J. L. *How to Do Things with Words*. Cambridge: Harvard University Press, 1975.

Averill, Charles E. *The Mexican Ranchero: Or, The Maid of the Chapparal. A Romance of the Mexican War*. Boston: F. Gleason, 1847.

———. *The Secret Service Ship, or, The Fall of San Juan D'Ulloa*. Boston: F. Gleason, 1848.

Axelrod, Alan. *Charles Brockden Brown: An American Tale*. Austin: University of Texas Press, 1983.

Bailyn, Bernard. *The New England Merchants of the Seventeenth Century*. Cambridge: Harvard University Press, 1955.

———. *Voyagers to the West: A Passage in the Peopling of America on the Eve of the Revolution*. New York: Vintage, 1986.

Baker, Houston A., Jr. *Blues, Ideology, and Afro-American Literature: A Vernacular Theory*. Chicago: University of Chicago Press, 1984.

Baker, Houston A., Jr., and Patricia Redmond, eds. *Afro-American Literary Study in the 1990s*. Chicago: University of Chicago Press, 1989.

Balibar, Étienne. *Masses, Classes, Ideas: Studies on Politics and Philosophy before and after Marx*. New York: Routledge, 1994.

———. "Ambiguous Universality." *Differences: A Journal of Feminist Cultural Studies* 7.1 (1995): 48–74.

Balibar, Étienne, and Immanuel Wallerstein. *Race, Nation, Class: Ambiguous Identities*. London: Verso, 1991.

Bancroft, Frederic. "The Colonization of American Negroes." *Frederic Bancroft, Historian*. Ed. Jacob E. Cooke. Norman: University Press of Oklahoma, 1957, 145–269.

Banton, Michael. *Racial Theories*. Cambridge: Cambridge University Press, 1987.

Barbalet, J. M. *Citizenship: Rights, Struggle, and Class Inequality*. Minneapolis: University of Minnesota Press, 1988.

Barclay, James. *A Complete and Universal Dictionary of the English Language*. Bungay: Brightly and Childs, 1812.

Barrera, Mario. *Race and Class in the Southwest: A Theory of Racial Inequality.* Notre Dame: University of Notre Dame Press, 1979.

Barrera, Mario, Carlos Muñoz, and Charlie Ornelas. "The Barrio as Internal Colony." *People and Politics in Urban Society.* Ed. Harlan Hahn. Beverly Hills, Calif.: Sage, 1972, 465–98.

Barry, Andrew, Thomas Osborne, and Nikolas Rose, eds. Introduction to *Foucault and Political Reason: Liberalism, Neo-Liberalism, and Rationalities of Government.* Chicago: University of Chicago Press, 1996, 1–17.

Bassard, Katherine Clay. *Spiritual Interrogations: Culture, Gender, and Commuinity in Early African American Women's Writing.* Princeton: Princeton University Press, 1999.

Baucom, Ian. "Introduction: Atlantic Genealogies." *The South Atlantic Quarterly* 100.1 (Winter 2001): 1–13.

Beatie, J. M. *Crime and the Courts in England, 1660–1800.* Princeton: Princeton University Press, 1986.

Bendix, Reinhard. *Nation-Building and Citizenship.* Berkeley: University of California Press, 1977.

Benjamin, Walter. "Theses on the Philosphy of History." *Illuminations.* Ed. Hannah Arendt. Trans. Harry Zohn. New York: Schocken Books, 1968, 253–64.

———. *Gesammelte Schriften.* Vol. 1.2. Ed. Rolf Tiedemann and Hermann Schweppenhäuser. Frankfurt: Suhrkamp Verlag, 1974.

Bercovitch, Sacvan, ed. *The Cambridge History of American Literature.* Vols. 1 and 2. Cambridge: Cambridge University Press, 1994–1999.

Bergquist, Charles. *Labor and the Course of American Democracy: U.S. History in Latin American Perspective.* New York: Verso, 1996.

Berlant, Lauren. *The Anatomy of National Fantasy: Hawthorne, Utopia, and Everyday Life.* Chicago: University of Chicago Press, 1991.

Berlin, Ira. "Slaves Who Were Free: The Free Negro in the Upper South, 1776–1861." Ph.D. diss., University of Wisconsin, 1970.

Bewes, Timothy. *Reification, or the Anxiety of Late Capitalism.* London: Verso, 2002.

Beyan, Amos J. *The American Colonization Society and the Creation of the Liberian State.* New York: University Press of America, 1991.

Bianchi, Emanuela, ed. *Is Feminist Philosophy Philosophy?* Evanston, Ill.: Northwestern University Press, 1999.

Bieder, Robert E. *Science Encounters the Indian, 1820–1880: The Early Years of American Ethnology.* Norman: University of Oklahoma Press, 1986.

Blackburn, Robin. *The Overthrow of Colonial Slavery: 1776–1848.* London: Verso, 1988.

———. *The Making of New World Slavery: From the Baroque to the Modern, 1492–1800.* London: Verso, 1997.

Blight, James G. "Jonathan Edward's Theory of the Mind: Its Applications and Implications." *Explorations in the History of Psychology in the United States.* Ed. Josef Brozek. London: Associated University Presses, 1984, 61–120.

Bojórquez Urzaiz, Carlos. "Estructura agraria y maíz a partir de la 'guerra de castas.'" *Revista de la Universidad de Yucatán* 20 (November–December, 1978): 15–35.

Bold, Christine. "The Voice of the Fiction Factory in Dime and Pulp Westerns." *Journal of American Studies* 17 (1983): 29–46.

Bolster, W. Jeffrey. "'To Feel Like a Man': Black Seamen in Northern States, 1800–1860." *The Journal of American History* 76.4 (March 1990): 1173–99.

———. "'Every Inch a Man:' Gender in the Lives of African American Seamen, 1800–1860."

Iron Men, Wooden Women: Gender and Seafaring in the Atlantic World, 1700–1920. Ed. Margaret S. Creighton and Lisa Norling. Baltimore: Johns Hopkins University Press, 1996, 138–68.

———. *Black Jacks: African American Seamen in the Age of Sail.* Cambridge: Harvard University Press, 1997.

———. "An Inner Diaspora: Black Sailors Making Selves." *Through a Glass Darkly: Reflections on Personal Identity in Early America.* Ed. Ronald Hoffman, Mechal Sobel, and Fredrika J. Teute. Chapel Hill: University of North Carolina Press, 1997, 419–48.

Bontatibus, Donna R. *The Seduction of the Early Nation: A Call for Socio-Political Reform.* East Lansing: Michigan State University Press, 1999.

Bontemps, Arna, ed. *Great Slave Narratives.* Boston: Beacon Press, 1969.

———, ed. *Five Black Lives: The Autobiographies of Venture Smith, James Mars, William Grimes, The Rev. G. W. Offley, James L. Smith.* Middletown, Conn.: Weslyan University Press, 1971.

Boorstin, Daniel J. *The Lost World of Thomas Jefferson.* Boston: Beacon Press, 1960.

Boskin, Joseph. *Into Slavery: Racial Decisions in the Virginia Colony.* Philadelphia: Lippincott, 1976.

Bower, William W. *America's Virgin Islands: A History of Human Rights and Wrongs.* Durham, N.C.: Carolina Academic Press, 1983.

Bracey, John H., August Meier, and Elliott Rudwick. *Free Blacks in America, 1800–1860.* Belmont, Calif.: Wadsworth Publishing Co., 1971.

Brack, Gene M. *Mexico Views Manifest Destiny, 1821–1846. An Essay on the Origins of the Mexican War.* Albuquerque: University of New Mexico Press, 1975.

Braudel, Fernand. *Civilization and Capitalism, 15th–18th Century.* Vol. 1: *The Structures of Everyday Life.* Berkeley: University of California Press, 1981.

———. *Civilization and Capitalism, 15th–18th Century.* Vol. 2: *The Wheels of Commerce.* Berkeley: University of California Press, 1982.

———. *Civilization and Capitalism, 15th–18th Century.* Vol. 3: *The Perspective of the World.* Berkeley: University of California Press, 1982.

Breitwieser, Mitchell. "Jefferson's Prospect." *Prospects* 10 (1985): 315–52.

Brenner, Robert. "The Origins of Capitalist Development: A Critique of Neo-Smithian Marxism." *The Brenner Debate.* Ed. T. H. Aston and C. H. E. Philpin. New York: Cambridge University Press, 1985.

Breuilly, John. *Nationalism and the State.* 2nd ed. Chicago: University of Chicago Press, 1993.

Bricker, Victoria Reifler. *The Indian Christ, the Indian King: The Historical Substrate of Maya Myth and Ritual.* Austin: University of Texas, 1981.

Bridenbaugh, Carl. *Cities in the Wilderness: The First Century of Urban Life in America, 1625–1742.* New York: Knopf, 1955.

British Museum Catalogue of Printed Books to 1955, Compact Edition. Vol. 4. New York: Readex Microprint Corporation, 1967.

Brown, Bill. *Reading the West: An Anthology of Dime Westerns.* Boston: Bedford Books, 1997.

Brown, Charles. *Agents of Manifest Destiny: The Life and Times of the Filibusters.* Chapel Hill: University of North Carolina Press, 1980.

Brown, Charles Brockden. *Wieland, or The Transformation, together with Memoirs of Carwin, the Biloquist.* Ed. Fred Lewis Pattee. New York: Harcourt Brace Jovanovich, 1926.

———. *Edgar Huntly, or Memoirs of a Sleep-Walker.* Kent, Ohio: Kent State University Press, 1984.

———. *The Novels and Related Works of Charles Brockden Brown.* Vol. 4. Kent, Ohio: Kent State University Press, 1984.

———. *Wieland and Memoirs of Carwin, the Biloquist.* New York: Penguin Classics, 1991.

Brown, Gillian. *Domestic Individualism: Imagining Self in Nineteenth-Century America*. Berkeley: University of California Press, 1990.

Brown, Richard D. *Knowledge Is Power: The Diffusion of Information in Early America, 1700–1850*. New York: Oxford University Press, 1989.

Brown, Wendy. *States of Injury: Power and Freedom in Late Modernity*. Princeton: Princeton University Press, 1995.

Buell, Lawrence. "American Literary Emergence as a Postcolonial Phenomenon." *American Literary History* 4.3 (Fall 1992): 411–42.

Buntline, Ned [Edward Zane Carroll Judson]. *Magdalena, the Beautiful Mexican Maid. A Story of Buena Vista*. New York: Williams Brothers, 1846.

———. *The Volunteer; or The Maid of Monterey. A Tale of the Mexican War*. Boston: F. Gleason, 1847.

———. *Crusings, Afloat and Ashore, from the Private Log of Ned Buntline*. New York: Robert Craighead, 1848.

Burchell, Graham. "Liberal Government and Techniques of the Self." *Foucault and Political Reason: Liberalism, Neo-Liberalism, and Rationalities of Government*. Ed. Andrew Barry, Thomas Osborne, and Nikolas Rose. Chicago: University of Chicago Press, 1996, 19–36.

Burchell, Graham, Colin Gordon, and Peter Miller, eds. *The Foucault Effect: Studies in Governmentality*. Chicago: University of Chicago Press, 1991.

Burgett, Bruce. *Sentimental Bodies: Sex, Gender, and Citizenship in the Early Republic*. Princeton: Princeton University Press, 1998.

———. "Between Speculation and Population: The Problem of 'Sex' in Our Long Eighteenth Century." *Early American Literature* 37.1 (2002): 119–53.

Burstein, Andrew. "Jefferson and the Familiar Letter." *Journal of the Early Republic* 14.2 (Summer 1994): 195–220.

Bushman, Richard L. *From Puritan to Yankee: Character and the Social Order in Connecticut 1690–1765*. Cambridge: Harvard University Press, 1967.

Butler, Judith. *Bodies That Matter: On the Discursive Limits of "Sex."* New York: Routledge, 1993.

———. *The Psychic Life of Power: Theories in Subjection*. Stanford: Stanford University Press, 1997.

Butler, Judith, Ernesto Laclau, and Slavoj Zizek. *Contingency, Hegemony, Universality: Contemporary Dialogues on the Left*. New York: Verso, 2000.

Cadava, Eduardo. *Emerson and the Climates of History*. Stanford, Calif.: Stanford University Press, 1997.

Cahill, Edward. "An Adventurous and Lawless Fancy: Charles Brockden Brown's Aesthetic State." *Early American Literature* 36.1 (2001): 31–70.

Caldwell, Tanya. "'Talking Too Much English': Languages of Economy and Politics in Equano's *Interesting Narrative*." *Early American Literature* 34.3 (1999): 263–82.

Callinicos, Alex. *Althusser's Marxism*. London: Pluto Press, 1976.

Carretta, Vincent. "Olaudah Equiano or Gustavus Vassa? New Light on an Eighteenth-Century Question of Identity." *Slavery and Abolition* 20.3 (December 1999): 96–105.

———. "Defining a Gentleman: The Status of Olaudah Equiano or Gustavus Vassa." *Language Sciences* 22 (2000): 385–99.

Carey, Henry Charles. *Essay on the Rate of Wages: with an examination of the causes of the differences in the condition of the labouring population throughout the world*. Philadelphia: Carey, Lea and Blanchard, 1835.

———. "Commercial Associations of France and England." *Merchants' Magazine and Commercial Review* 12.5-6 (May–June 1845): [401]–420, [499]–520.

———. *The Past, the Present, and the Future.* 1847. Reprint, New York: Augustus M. Kelley, 1967.

———. *The Slave Trade: Foreign and Domestic.* Philadelphia: Henry Carey Baird, 1853.

Carey, Henry Charles, and J. Lea. *The Geography, History, and Statistics of America, and the West Indies; Exhibiting a Correct Account of the Discovery, Settlement , and Progress of the Various Kingdoms, States, and Provinces of the Western Hemisphere, to the Year 1822.* London: Sherwood, Jones and Co., Paternoster-Row, 1823.

Carey, M. *Letters on the Colonization Society; and on its Probable Results; Under the Following Heads.* Philadelphia: L. Johnson, 1833.

Castañeda, Quetzil E. *In the Museum of Maya Culture: Touring Chichén Itzá.* Minneapolis: University of Minnesota Press, 1996.

Castiglia, Christopher. *Bound and Determined: Captivity, Culture-Crossing, and White Womanhood from Mary Rowlandson to Patty Hearst.* Chicago: University of Chicago Press, 1996.

———. "Pedagogical Discipline and the Creation of White Citizenship: John Witherspoon, Robert Finley, and the Colonization Society." *Early American Literature* 33.2 (1998): 192–214.

———. "Abolition's Racial Interiors and the Making of White Civic Depth." *American Literary History* 14.1 (Spring 2002): 32–59.

Castree, Noel. "Invisible Leviathan: Speculations on Marx, Spivak, and the Question of Value." *Rethinking Marxism* 9.2 (1996–97): 45–78.

Castronovo, Russ. *Fathering the Nation: American Genealogies of Slavery and Freedom.* Berkeley: University of California Press, 1995.

———. *Necro Citizenship: Death, Eroticism, and the Public Sphere in the Nineteenth-Century United States.* Durham: Duke University Press, 2001.

Ceaser, James W. *Reconstructing America: The Symbol of America in Modern Thought.* New Haven: Yale University Press, 1997.

Cecelski, David S. *The Waterman's Song: Slavery and Freedom in Maritime North Carolina.* Chapel Hill: University of North Carolina Press, 2001.

Chakrabarty, Dipesh. *Provincializing Europe: Postcolonial Thought and Historical Difference.* Princeton: Princeton University Press, 2000.

Charvat, William. "The Beginnings of Professionalism." *The Profession of Authorship in America, 1800–1870.* Ed. Matthew J. Bruccoli. Columbus: Ohio State University Press, 1968, 5–28.

Chase, Richard. *The American Novel and its Tradition.* Baltimore: The Johns Hopkins University Press, 1980.

Chasin, Alexandra. *Selling Out: The Gay and Lesbian Movement Goes to Market.* New York: St. Martin's Press, 2000.

Chávez, John R. *The Lost Land: The Chicano Image of the Southwest.* Albuquerque: University of New Mexico Press, 1984.

Cherniavsky, Eva. "Subaltern Studies in a U.S. Frame." *boundary 2* 23.2 (1996): 85–110.

Chinosole. "Tryin' To Get Over: Narrative Posture in Equiano's Autobiography." *The Art of the Slave Narrative: Original Essays in Criticism and Theory.* Ed. John Sekora and Darwin T. Turner. Macomb: Western Illinois Press, 1982, 45–54.

Chrisman, Laura. "Journeying to Death: Gilroy's *Black Atlantic*." *Race and Class* 39.2 (1997): 51–64.

Claims of the Africans: or The History of the American Colonization Society. Boston: Massachusetts Sabbath School Union, 1832.

Clemit, Pamela. *The Godwinian Novel: The Rational Fictions of Godwin, Brockden Brown, Mary Shelley.* Oxford: Clarendon Press, 1993.

Cline, Howard F. *Regionalism and Society in Yucatán, 1825–1847. Related Studies in Early Nineteenth Century Yucatecan Social History.* Chicago: University of Chicago Press, 1958.

Cockburn, Cynthia. *Machinery of Dominance: Women, Men, and Technical Know-How.* Boston: Northeastern University Press, 1988.

Cockcroft, James D. *Mexico's Hope: An Encounter with Politics and History.* New York: Monthly Review Press, 1998.

Cohen, Morris L. "Thomas Jefferson Recommends a Course of Law Study." *University of Pennsylvania Law Review* 119 (1971): 823–44.

Cohen, Patricia Cline. *A Calculating People: The Spread of Numeracy in Early America.* New York: Routledge, 1999.

Coleman, D. C. "Eli Heckscher and the Idea of Mercantilism." *Scandinavian Economic History Review* 8 (April 1957): 280–95.

———. *Revisions in Mercantilism.* London: Methuen, 1969.

———. "Mercantilism Revisited." *Historical Journal* 23. 4 (1980): 773–91.

Compact Edition of the Dictionary of National Biography. Vol. 2. London: Oxford University Press, 1975.

Compact Edition of the Oxford English Dictionary. Glasgow: Oxford University Press, 1971.

Congressional Globe. 30th Cong., 1st sess., new series. Washington, D.C., 1847–48.

Congressional Globe, appendix. 30th Cong., 1st sess., new series. Washington, D.C., 1847–48.

Conkin, Paul K. *Prophets of Prosperity: America's First Political Economists.* Bloomington: Indiana University Press, 1980.

Cooppan, Vilashini. "Mourning Becomes Kitsch: The Aesthetics of Loss in Severo Sarduy's *Cobra.*" *Loss: The Politics of Mourning.* Ed. David L. Eng and David Kazanjian. Berkeley: University of California Press, 2003, 251-77.

Costanzo, Angelo. *Surprising Narrative: Olaudah Equiano and the Beginnings of Black Autobiography.* Westport, Conn.: Greenwood Press, 1987.

Countryman, Edward, and Susan Deans. "Independence and Revolution in the Americas: A Project for Comparative Study." *Radical History Review* 27 (1983): 144–71.

Cox, J. Randolph. *The Dime Novel Companion: A Source Book.* Westport, Conn.: Greenwood Press, 2000.

Creighton, Margaret S., and Lisa Norling, eds. *Iron Men, Wooden Women: Gender and Seafaring in the Atlantic World, 1700–1920.* Baltimore: The Johns Hopkins University Press, 1996.

Creque, Darwin D. *The U.S. Virgins and the Eastern Caribbean.* Philadelphia: Whitmore Publishing, 1968.

Croome, W. *The Golden Sands of Mexico. A Moral and Religious Tale.* Philadelphia: Lindsay and Blakiston, 1850.

Cuffe, Paul [Jr.]. *Narrative of the life and adventures of Paul Cuffee, a Pequot Indian: during thirty years spent at sea, and in travelling in foreign lands.* Vernon, Conn.: Horace N. Bill, 1839.

Cuffe, Paul [Sr.]. *A brief account of the settlement and present situation of the colony of Sierra Leone, in Africa; as communicated by Paul Cuffee (a man of colour) to his friend in New York; also an explanation of the object of his visit, and some advice to the people of colour in the United States. To which is subjoined, an address to the people of colour, from the Confention of Delegates from the Abolition Societies in the United States.* New York: Samuel Wood, 1812.

———. The Paul Cuffe Papers. New Bedford Free Public Library: New Bedford, Mass.

Cugoano, Quobna Ottobah. *Thoughts and Sentiments on the Evil of Slavery.* 1787. Reprint, New York: Penguin Classics, 1999.

Cunningham, Noble E. *In Pursuit of Reason: The Life of Thomas Jefferson*. Baton Rouge: Louisiana State University Press, 1987.

Cunningham, William. *The Growth of English Industry and Commerce*. Cambridge, U.K.: The University Press, 1922.

Dallam, James Wilmer. *The Lone Star: A Tale of Texas*. Baltimore: W. Taylor, 1848.

———. *The Deaf Spy: A Tale Founded upon Incidents in the History of Texas*. Baltimore: W. Taylor, 1848.

Daniels, Bruce C. "Economic Development in Colonial and Revolutionary Connecticut: An Overview." *William and Mary Quarterly*, 3rd series, 37 (1980): 429–50.

Darwin, Erasmus. *Zoonomia, or, The Laws of Organic Life*. 1796. Reprint, Philadelphia: Edward Earle, 1818.

Davidson, Cathy N. *Revolution and the Word: The Rise of the Novel in America*. New York: Oxford University Press, 1986.

Davis, Angela. *Women, Race and Class*. New York: Vintage Books, 1983.

Davis, David Brion. "Some Themes of Counter-Subversion: An Analysis of Anti-Masonic, Anti-Catholic, and Anti-Mormon Literature." *Mississippi Valley Historical Review* 47. 2 (September 1960): 205–24.

———, ed. *The Fear of Conspiracy: Images of Un-American Subversion from the Revolution to the Present*. Ithaca: Cornell University Press, 1971.

Davis, Hugh. "At the Crossroads: Leonard Bacon, Antislavery Colonization, and the Abolitionists in the 1830s." *The Moment of Decision: Bibliographical Essays on American Character and Regional Identity*. Ed. Randall M. Miller and John R. McKivigan. Westport, Conn.: Greenwood Press, 1994, 134–54.

———. "Northern Colonizationists and Free Blacks, 1823–1837: A Case Study of Leonard Bacon." *Journal of the Early Republic* 17.4 (Winter 1997): 651–75.

Davis, R. C. "American Psychology 1800–1885." *The Psychological Review* 43.6 (November 1936): 471–93.

Davis, Ralph. *The Rise of the Atlantic Economies*. London: Weidenfeld and Nicolson, 1973.

Defoe, Daniel. *Memoirs of the Church of Scotland*. 1688. Reprint, London: E. Matthews and T. Warner, 1969.

del Castillo, Adelaida, ed. *Between Borders: Essays on Mexicana/Chicana History*. Encino, Calif.: Floricanto Press, 1990.

Deleuze, Gilles. *Nietzsche and Philosophy*. Trans. Hugh Tomlinson. New York: Columbia University Press, 1983.

Deloria, Vine, Jr. *Custer Died for Your Sins: An Indian Manifesto*. Norman: University of Oklahoma Press, 1988.

de Man, Paul. *Allegories of Reading: Figural Language in Rousseau, Nietzsche, Rilke, and Proust*. New Haven: Yale University Press, 1979.

———. "The Rhetoric of Temporality." *Blindness and Insight: Essays in the Rhetoric of Contemporary Criticism*. Minneapolis: University of Minnesota Press, 1983, 187–228.

Denning, Michael. "'The Special American Conditions': Marxism and American Studies." *American Quarterly* 38 (1986): 356–80.

———. *Mechanic Accents: Dime Novels and Working-Class Culture in America*. New York: Verso, 1987. Revised ed., 1998.

Dennis, Matthew. *Cultivating a Landscape of Peace: Iroquois-European Encounters in Seventeenth-Century America*. Ithaca: Cornell University Press, 1993.

Derrida, Jacques. "Différance." *Speech and Phenomena, and Other Essays on Husserl's Theory of Signs.* Trans. David B. Allison. Evanston, Ill.: Northwestern University Press, 1973, 129–60.

———. *Margins of Philosophy.* Sussex: Harvester Press, 1982.

———. "The Principle of Reason: The University in the Eyes of Its Pupils." *Diacritics* (Fall 1983): 3–20.

———. "My Chances/*Mes Chances*: A Rendezvous with Some Epicurean Stereophonies." *Taking Chances: Derrida, Psychoanalysis, and Literature.* Ed. Joseph H. Smith and William Kerrigan. Baltimore: The Johns Hopkins University Press, 1984, 1–32.

———. "Declarations of Independence." *New Political Science* 15 (Summer 1986): 7–15.

———. *Memoires: For Paul de Man.* Trans. Cecile Lindsey, Jonathan Culler, and Eduardo Cadava. New York: Columbia University Press, 1986.

———. *Truth in Painting.* Trans. Geoff Bennington and Ian McLeod. Chicago: University of Chicago Press, 1987.

———. *Limited Inc.* Evanston, Ill.: Northwestern University Press, 1988.

———. "The Force of Law: The 'Mystical Foundation of Authority'". Trans. Mary Quaintance. *Cardozo Law Review* 11 (1990): 920–1045.

———. "Mochlos; or, The Conflict of the Faculties." *Logomachia: The Conflict of the Faculties.* Ed. Richard Rand. Lincoln: University of Nebraska Press, 1992.

———. *Specters of Marx: The State of Debt, the Work of Mourning, and the New International.* Trans. Peggy Kamuf. New York: Routledge, 1994.

de Ruggiero, Guido. *The History of European Liberalism.* Trans. R. G. Collingwood. Boston: Beacon Press, 1959.

Desrochers, Robert E., Jr. "'Not Fade Away': The Narrative of Venture Smith, an African American in the Early Republic." *The Journal of American History* 84 (June 1997): 40–66.

Desrosières, Alain. *The Politics of Large Numbers: A History of Statistical Reasoning.* Cambridge: Harvard University Press, 1998.

Dewey, Frank L. *Thomas Jefferson, Lawyer.* Charlottesville: University Press of Virginia, 1986.

Díaz Polanco, Héctor. *Indigenous Peoples in Latin America: The Quest for Self-Determination.* Boulder, Colo.: Westview Press, 1997.

Dippie, Brian. *The Vanishing American: White Attitudes and U.S. Indian Policy.* Middletown, Conn.: Wesleyan University Press, 1982.

Donker, Margorie, and George M. Muldrow. *Dictionary of Literary-Rhetorical Conventions of the English Renaissance.* Westport, Conn.: Greenwood Press, 1982.

Dorfman, Joseph. *The Economic Mind in American Civilization, 1606–1865,* Vol. 2. New York: Viking Press, 1946.

Earle, Carville V. *The Evolution of a Tidewater Settlement System: All Hallow's Parish, Maryland, 1650–1783.* Chicago: University of Chicago Press, 1975.

Earle, Carville V., and Ronald Hoffman. "Staple Crops and Urban Development in the Eighteenth-Century South." *Perspectives in American History* 10 (1976): 7–78.

Eaton, Clement. "A Dangerous Pamphlet in the Old South." *The Journal of Southern History* 2.3 (August 1936): 323–34.

Edwards, Brent Hayes. "Black Globality: The International Shape of Black Intellectual Culture." Ph.D. diss., Columbia University, 1998.

———. "The Uses of 'Diaspora.'" *Social Text* 19.1 (2001): 45–73.

Elliott, Emory. *Revolutionary Writers: Literature and Authority in the New Republic, 1725–1810.* New York: Oxford University Press, 1982.

————. Introduction to *Wieland and Memoirs of Carwin, the Biloquist*, by Charles Brockden Brown. Oxford: Oxford University Press, 1994, vii–xxx.

Elmer, Jonathan. "The Archive, the Native American, and Jefferson's Convulsions." *Diacritics* 28.4 (Winter 1998): 5–24.

Elrod, Eileen Razzari. "Moses and the Egyptian: Religious Authority in Olaudah Equiano's *Interesting Narrative*." *African American Review* 35.3 (2001): 409–25.

Emmanuel, Arghiri. "White-Settler Colonialism and the Myth of Investment Imperialism." *New Left Review* 73 (May–June 1972).

Engerman, Stanley L., and Robert E. Gallman, eds. *The Cambridge Economic History of the United States*. Vol. 1: *The Colonial Era*. New York: Cambridge University Press, 1996.

Equiano, Olaudah (Gustavus Vassa). "The Interesting Narrative of the Life of Olaudah Equiano." 1814. Reprint. *The Classic Slave Narratives*. Ed. Henry Louis Gates Jr. New York: Penguin Books, 1987, 1–182.

————. *The Interesting Narrative and Other Writings*. 1789. Reprint. Ed. Vincent Carretta. New York: Penguin Books, 1995.

————. *The Interesting Narrative of the Life of Olaudah Equiano, Written by Himself*. 1791. Reprint. Ed. Robert J. Allison. Boston: Bedford Books of St. Martin's Press, 1995.

"An Essay on the Late Institution of the American Society for Colonizing the Free People of Colour, of the United States." Washington, D.C.: Davis and Force, 1820.

Essed, Philomena, and David Theo Goldberg, eds. *Race Critical Theories: Text and Context*. Oxford: Blackwell, 2002.

Evans, Rand B. "The Origins of American Academic Psychology." *Explorations in the History of Psychology in the United States*. Ed. Josef Brozek. London: Associated University Presses, 1984, 17–60.

Executive Documents. 30th Cong., 1st sess., nos. 40, 42, 43, 45, 46, 49.

Faulkner, Harold U. "The Development of the American System." *Annals of the American Academy of Political and Social Science* 141 (January 1929): 11–17.

Fay, J. W. *American Psychology before William James*. 1939. Reprint, New York: Octagon Books, 1966.

Ferguson, Robert A. "'We Hold These Truths': Strategies of Control in the Literature of the Founders." *Reconstructing American Literary History*. Ed. Sacvan Bercovitch. Cambridge: Harvard University Press, 1986, 1–28.

Fernández Retamar, Roberto. *Caliban and Other Essays*. Minneapolis: University of Minnesota Press, 1989.

Fichtelberg, Joseph. "Word between Worlds: The Economy of Equiano's *Narrative*." *American Literary History* 5 (1993): 459–80.

Fielder, Leslie. *Love and Death in the American Novel*. New York: Criterion Books, 1960.

Finkelman, Paul, ed. *Slavery, Revolutionary America, and the New Nation*. New York: Garland Publishing, 1989.

————. "Jefferson and Slavery: 'Treason Against the Hopes of the World.'" Ed. Peter S. Onuf. *Jeffersonian Legacies*. Charlottesville: University of Virginia Press, 1993, 181–221.

Flanagan, John T., and Raymond L. Grismer. "Mexico in American Fiction Prior to 1850." *Hispania* 23.4 (December 1940): 307–18.

Fliegelman, Jay. Introduction to *Wieland and Memoirs of Carwin, the Biloquist*, by Charles Brockden Brown. New York: Penguin Books, 1991, vii–xlii.

————. *Declaring Independence: Jefferson, Natural Language, and the Culture of Performance.* Stanford: Stanford University Press, 1993.

Fogel, Robert William. *Without Consent or Contract: The Rise and Fall of American Slavery.* Vols. 1–3. New York: Norton, 1989.

Fogel, Robert William, and Stanley Engerman. *Time on the Cross: The Economics of American Negro Slavery.* Vols. 1 and 2. Boston: Little, Brown, 1974.

Foley, Neil. *The White Scourge: Mexicans, Blacks, and Poor Whites in Texas Cotton Culture.* Berkeley: University of California Press, 1997.

Foner, Philip S. *History of Black Americans: From Africa to the Emergence of the Cotton Kingdom.* Westport, Conn.: Greenwood Press, 1975.

————. *History of Black Americans: From the Emergence of the Cotton Kingdom to the Eve of the Compromise of 1850.* Westport, Conn.: Greenwood Press, 1983.

Foner, Philip S., and Ronald L. Lewis, eds. *The Black Worker: A Documentary History from Colonial Times to the Present.* Vol. 1: *The Black Worker to 1869.* Philadelphia: Temple University Press, 1978.

Foner, Philip S., and George E. Walker, eds. *Proceedings of the Black National and State Conventions, 1865–1900.* Philadelphia: Temple University Press, 1986.

de Fontenelle, Bernard le Bovier. *Histoire du renouvellement de l'Académie royale des sciences en mdcxcix et les éloges historiques.* 2 vols. Amsterdam: Pierre du Coup, 1719–20.

Forbes, Jack D. *Africans and Native Americans: The Language of Race and the Evolution of Red-Black Peoples.* 2nd ed. Urbana: University of Illinois Press, 1993.

Ford, Paul Leicester. *The Writings of Thomas Jefferson, in 10 Volumes.* New York: G. P. Putnam's Sons, 1899.

Foster, Charles I. "The Colonization of Free Negroes in Liberia, 1816–1835." *Journal of Negro History* 38.1 (1953): 41–66.

Foster, Frances Smith. *Witnessing Slavery: The Development of the Ante-bellum Slave Narratives.* Madison: University of Wisconsin Press, 1979.

Foster-Carter, Aidan. "The Modes of Production Debate." *New Left Review* 107 (1978).

Foucault, Michel. *The Archaeology of Knowledge.* New York: Pantheon Books, 1972.

————. "Nietzsche, Genealogy, History." *Language, Counter-Memory, Practice: Selected Essays and Interviews.* Ithaca: Cornell University Press, 1977, 139–64.

————. *Discipline and Punish: The Birth of the Prison.* New York: Vintage Books, 1979.

————. *The History of Sexuality.* Vol. 1: *An Introduction.* New York: Vintage Books, 1980.

————. *"Society Must Be Defended." Lectures at the Collège de France.* Trans. David Macey. New York: Picador, 2003.

Fox, Early L. *The American Colonization Society, 1816–1840.* Baltimore: The Johns Hopkins University Press, 1919.

Fox-Genovese, Elizabeth, and Eugene Genovese. *The Fruits of Merchant Capital: Slavery and Bourgeois Property in the Rise and Expansion of Capital.* New York: Oxford University Press, 1983.

Frängsmyr, Tore, J. L. Heilbron, and Robin E. Rider. *The Quantifying Spirit in the 18th Century.* Berkeley: University of California Press, 1990.

Frank, André Gunder. "The Development of Underdevelopment." *Monthly Review* (September 1966): 17–31.

————. *Capitalism and Underdevelopment in Latin America: Historical Studies of Chile and Brazil.* New York: Monthly Review Press, 1969.

———. *World Accumulation, 1492–1789*. New York: Monthly Review Press, 1978.

Frederickson, George M. *The Black Image in the White Mind*. New York: Harper and Row, 1971.

Freeman, Joanne B. "Slander, Poison, Whispers, and Fame: Jefferson's 'Ana' and Political Gossip in the Early Republic." *Journal of the Early Republic* 15.1 (Spring 1995): 25–58.

Fukuyama, Francis. *The End of History and the Last Man*. New York: Avon Books, 1992.

Fuller, John. *The Movement for the Acquisiton of All Mexico, 1846–1848*. Baltimore: The Johns Hopkins University Press, 1936.

Fuller, Thomas. *The Holy State and the Profane State*. 1642. Reprint. Ed. Maximilian Graff Walten. New York: Columbia University Press, 1938.

Furtwangler, Albert. *American Silhouettes: The Rhetorical Identities of the Founders*. New Haven: Yale University Press, 1987.

Fyfe, Christopher, ed. *"Our Children Free and Happy:" Letters from Black Settlers in Africa in the 1790s*. With a contribution by Charles Jones. Edinburgh: Edinburgh University Press, 1991.

Gales, Joseph, Sr. *Annals of Congress, 1st Congress, 1789–90, Part 1*. Washington, D.C.: Gales and Seaton, 1834.

Ganilh, Anthony. *Mexico versus Texas: A Descriptive Novel*. Philadelphia: N. Siegfried, 1838.

———. *Ambrosio de Letinez, or The First Texian Novel*. New York: Charles Francis, 1838.

Gardner, Jared. *Master Plots: Race and the Founding of an American Literature, 1787–1845*. Baltimore: The Johns Hopkins University Press, 1998.

Garrison, William Lloyd. *An Address Delivered Before the Free People of Color in Philadelphia, New-York, and Other Cities, During the Month of June, 1831*. Boston: Steven Foster, 1831.

———. *Selections from the Writings and Speeches of William Lloyd Garrison*. Boston: R. F. Wallcut, 1852.

———. *Thoughts on African Colonization*. 1832. Reprint, New York: Arno Press and the *New York Times*, 1968.

Gates, Henry Louis, Jr. *Figures in Black: Words, Signs, and the "Racial" Self*. New York: Oxford University Press, 1987.

———. *The Signifying Monkey: A Theory of African-American Literary Criticism*. New York: Oxford University Press, 1988.

Gautier, Gary. "Slavery and the Fashioning of Race in *Oroonoko, Robinson Crusoe*, and Equiano's *Life*." *Eighteenth Century: Theory and Interpretation* 42.2 (Summer 2001): 161–79.

Gellner, Ernest. *Nations and Nationalism*. Ithaca: Cornell University Press, 1983.

Genovese, Eugene D. *Roll, Jordan, Roll: The World the Slaves Made*. New York: Vintage Books, 1976.

———. *The Political Economy of Slavery: Studies in the Economy and Society of the Slave South*. 2nd ed. Middletown, Conn.: Wesleyan University Press, 1989.

Gerzina, Gretchen Holbrook. "Mobility in Chains: Freedom of Movement in the Early Black Atlantic." *South Atlantic Quarterly* 100.1 (Winter 2001): 41–59.

Gibson, Charles. *The Black Legend: Anti-Spanish Attitudes in the Old World and New*. New York: Knopf, 1971.

Gilman, Sander L. *The Jew's Body*. New York: Routledge, 1991.

Gilmore, Michael T. *American Romanticism and the Marketplace*. Chicago: University of Chicago Press, 1985.

———. "The Literature of the Revolutionary and Early National Periods." *The Cambridge History of American Literature. Volume 1: 1590–1820*. Ed. Sacvan Bercovitch. Cambridge: Cambridge University Press, 1997, 541–693.

Gilroy, Paul. *There Ain't No Black in the Union Jack*. London: Hutchinson, 1987.

————. *The Black Atlantic: Modernity and Double Consciousness.* Cambridge: Harvard University Press, 1993.

Gipson, Lawrence Henry. "The Great Debate." *Pennsylvania Magazine of History and Biography* 86 (1962): 10–41.

Glaude, Eddie S., Jr. *Exodus! Religion, Race, and Nation in Early Nineteenth-Century Black America.* Chicago: University of Chicago Press, 2000.

Glendon, Mary Ann. *Rights Talk: The Impoverishment of Political Discourse.* New York: Free Press, 1991.

Goddu, Teresa A. *Gothic America: Narrative, History, and Nation.* New York: Columbia University Press, 1997.

Gold, Alex, Jr. "It's Only Love: The Politics of Passion in Godwin's *Caleb Williams.*" *Texas Studies in Literature and Language* 19.2 (Summer 1977): 135–60.

Goldberg, David Theo, ed. *Anatomy of Racism.* Minneapolis: Minnesota University Press, 1990.

————. *Racist Culture: Philosophy and the Politics of Meaning.* Oxford: Blackwell, 1993.

Gomes, Leonard. *Foreign Trade and the National Economy: Mercantilist and Classical Perspectives.* London: Macmillan, 1987.

González Navarro, Moisés. *Raxo y tierra: La guerra de castas y el henequén.* Mexico City: El Colegio de México, 1969.

Gossett, Thomas F. *Race: The History of an Idea in America.* Dallas: Southern Methodist University Press, 1963.

Gould, Clarence P. *Money and Transportation in Maryland, 1720–1765.* Baltimore: The Johns Hopkins University Press, 1915.

Gould, Philip. "Race, Commerce, and the Literature of Yellow Fever in Early National Philadelphia." *Early American Literature* 35.2 (2000): 157–86.

————. "Free Carpenter, Venture Capitalist: Reading the Lives of the Early Black Atlantic." *American Literary History* 35.4 (Winter 2000): 659–84.

Gould, Stephen Jay. *The Mismeasure of Man.* New York: Norton, 1981.

Gove, Philip Babcock. *The Imaginary Voyage in Prose Fiction: A History of Its Criticism and a Guide for Its Study, with an Annotated Check List of 215 Imaginary Voyages from 1700 to 1800.* London: Holland Press, 1961.

Grabo, Norman S. *The Coincidental Art of Charles Brockden Brown.* Chapel Hill: University of North Carolina Press, 1981.

Graymont, Barbara. *The Iroquois in the American Revolution.* Syracuse: Syracuse University Press, 1972.

Green, Arnold W. *Henry Charles Carey: Nineteenth-Century Sociologist.* Philadelphia: University of Pennsylvania Press, 1951.

Green, James. "The Publishing History of Olaudah Equiano's Interesting Narrative." *Slavery and Abolition* 16.3 (1995): 362–75.

Greene, Jack P. *Pursuits of Happiness: The Social Development of Early Modern British Colonies and the Formation of American Culture.* Chapel Hill: University of North Carolina Press, 1988.

————. *Imperatives, Behaviors, and Identities: Essays in Early American Cultural History.* Charlottesville: University of Virginia Press, 1992.

Griswold del Castillo, Richard. *The Treaty of Guadalupe Hidalgo: A Legacy of Conflict.* Norman: University of Oklahoma Press, 1990.

Guillaumin, Colette. "The Specific Character of Racist Ideology." *Racism, Sexism, Power, and Ideology.* New York: Routledge, 1995, 29–60.

Gunn, Grewey Wayne. *American and British Writers in Mexico, 1556–1973.* Austin: University of Texas Press, 1969.

Gutiérrez, David G. *Walls and Mirrors: Mexican Americans, Mexican Immigrants, and the Politics of Ethnicity.* Berkeley: University of California Press, 1995.

———. "Significant to Whom? Mexican Americans and the History of the American West." *A New Significance: Re-Envisioning the History of the American West.* Ed. Clyde A. Milner. New York: Oxford University Press, 1996, 67–89.

Gutiérrez-Jones, Carl. *Rethinking the Borderlands: Between Chicano Culture and Legal Discourse.* Berkeley: University of California Press, 1995.

Haakonssen, Knud. *Natural Law and Moral Philosophy: From Grotius to the Scottish Enlightenment.* Cambridge: Cambridge University Press, 1996.

Haberly, David. "The Search for a National Language." *Comparative Literature Studies* 2 (1974): 85–97.

Hacking, Ian. "Biopower and the Avalanche of Numbers." *Humanities in Society* 5 (1982): 279–95.

———. *The Taming of Chance.* Cambridge: Cambridge University Press, 1990.

Hadden, Richard W. *On the Shoulders of Merchants: Exchange and the Mathematical Conception of Nature in Early Modern Europe.* Albany: SUNY Press, 1994.

Haferkorn, Henry E. *The War with Mexico, 1846–1848. A Select Bibliography on the Causes, Conduct, and the Political Aspect of the War, together with a Select List of Books and other printed Material on the Resources, Economic Conditions, Politics and Government of the Republic of Mexico and the Characteristics of the Mexican People.* 1914. Reprint, New York: Burt Franklin, 1970.

Hagenbüchle, Roland. "American Literature and the Nineteenth-Century Crisis in Epistemology: The Example of Charles Brockden Brown." *Early American Literature* 23.2 (1988): 121–51.

Hall, Benjamin F., ed. *Official Opinions of the Attorneys General of the United States, Advising the President and Heads of Departments, In Relation to Their Official Duties.* Vol. 1. Washington, D.C.: GPO, 1852.

Hall, James. *Statistics of the West, at the Close of the Year 1836.* Cincinnati: J. A. James, 1836.

Hall, Madeleine, ed. *Publishers for Mass Entertainment in Nineteenth-Century America.* Boston: Hall and Co., 1980.

Hall, N. A. T. *Slave Society and the Danish West Indies: St. Thomas, St. John, and St. Croix.* Ed. B. W. Higaman. Baltimore: The Johns Hopkins University Press, 1992.

Hall, Stuart. "Pluralism, Race and Class in Caribbean Society." *Race and Class in Post-colonial Society.* Paris: UNESCO, 1977.

———. "Race, Articulation, and Societies Structured in Dominance." *Sociological Theories: Race and Colonialism.* Paris: UNESCO, 1980. Reprinted in Philomena Essed and David Theo Goldberg, eds. *Race Critical Theories: Text and Context.* Oxford: Blackwell, 2002, 38–68.

———. "On Postmodernism and Articulation: An Interview with Stuart Hall." Ed. Lawrence Grossberg. *Stuart Hall: Critical Dialogues in Cultural Studies.* Ed. David Morley and Kuan-Hsing Chen. London: Routledge, 1996, 131–50.

———. "Reflections on 'Race, Articulation, and Societies Structured in Dominance' (S. Hall)." *Race Critical Theories: Text and Context.* Ed. Philomena Essed and David Theo Goldberg. Oxford: Blackwell, 2002, 449–54.

Hall, Stuart et al. *Policing the Crisis.* London: Macmillan, 1978.

Halyard, Harry. *The Heroine of Tampico: or, Wildfire the Wanderer. A Tale of the Mexican War.* Boston: F. Gleason, 1847.

———. *The Chieftain of Churubusco, or, The Spectre of the Cathedral. A Romance of the Mexican War.* Boston: F. Gleason, 1848.

———. *The Mexican Spy: or, The Bride of Buena Vista. A Tale of the Mexican War.* Boston: F. Gleason, 1848.

———. *The Ocean Monarch: Or, The Ranger of the Gulf. A Mexican Romance.* Boston: F. Gleason, 1848.

———. *The Warrior Queen; or, The Buccaneer of the Brazos! A Romance of Mexico.* Boston: F. Gleason, 1848.

Hamer, Philip M. "Great Britain, the United States, and the Negro Seamen Acts, 1822–1848." *Journal of Southern History* 1 (February 1935): 3–28.

———. "British Consuls and the Negro Seamen Acts, 1850–1860." *Journal of Southern History* 1 (May 1935): 138–68.

Hamilton, Alexander. "Report on the Subject of Manufactures." 1791. Reprint, *State Papers and Speeches on the Tariff.* Ed. F. W. Taussig. Cambridge: Harvard University Press, 1892.

Hamilton, Stanislaus Murry, ed. *The Writings of James Monroe, in 7 volumes.* New York: G. P. Putnam's Sons, 1898–1903.

Hamilton, Thomas. *Men and Manners in America.* 1833. Reprint, New York: A. M. Kelley, 1968.

Hammon, Briton. *A NARRATIVE of the UNCOMMON SUFFERINGS, AND Surprizing DELIVERANCE of Briton Hammon, A Negro Man,—Servant to GENERAL WINSLOW, of Marshfield, in New-England; Who returned to Boston, after having been absent almost Thirteen Years.* 1760. Reprint, New York: Garland Publishing, 1978.

Handlin, Oscar, and Mary F. Handlin. "Origins of the Southern Labor System." *William and Mary Quarterly,* 3rd series, 7 (1950): 199–222.

Harding, Sandra, ed. *The "Racial" Economy of Science: Toward a Democratic Future.* Bloomington: Indiana University Press, 1993.

Harding, Vincent. *There Is a River: The Black Struggle for Freedom in America.* New York: Harcourt Brace Jovanovich, 1981.

Harris, Sharon M. "Feminist Theories and Early American Studies." *Early American Literature* 34.1 (1999): 86–93.

Harris, Sheldon H. *Paul Cuffe: Black America and the African Return.* New York: Simon and Schuster, 1972.

Hart, James D., ed. *The Concise Oxford Companion to American Literature.* New York: Oxford University Press, 1986.

Hartman, Saidiya. *Scenes of Subjection: Terror, Slavery, and Self-Making in Nineteenth-Century America.* New York: Oxford University Press, 1997.

Hastings, Adrian. *The Construction of Nationhood: Ethnicity, Religion, and Nationalism.* Cambridge: Cambridge University Press, 1997.

Hauptman, Laurence M. *Formulating American Indian Policy in New York State, 1970–1986.* Albany: SUNY Press, 1988.

Hay, Philip C. *Our Duty to Our Coloured Population: A Sermon for the Benefit of the American Colonization Society, Delivered in the Second Presbyterian Church, Newark; July 23, 1826.* Newark: W. Tuttle and Co., 1826.

Hazel, Harry [Justin Jones]. *The Flying Artillerist. A Tale of Mexican Treachery.* New York: H. Long and Brother, n.d.

———. *The Flying Artillerist, or The Child of the Battle-field. A Tale of Mexican Treachery.* Philadelphia: T. B. Peterson and Brothers, n.d.

————. *The Rival Chieftains: or, The Brigands of Mexico. A Romance of Santa Anna and His Times.* Boston: F. Gleason, 1845.

————. *Inez, The Beautiful: or, Love on the Rio Grande.* Boston: Harry Hazel, 1846.

————. *The Light Dragoon; or, The Rancheros of the Poisoned Lance. A Tale of the Battle Fields of Mexico.* Boston: Star Spangled Banner Office, 1848.

Hebel, Udo J., ed. *The Construction and Contestation of American Cultures and Identities in the Early National Period.* Heidelberg: Winter, 1999.

Heckscher, Eli F. *Mercantilism.* London: George Allen and Unwin, 1934.

Heidegger, Martin. *Basic Writings.* New York: Harper and Row, 1977.

Heilbron, J. L. "Introductory Essay." *The Quantifying Spirit in the 18th Century.* Ed. Tore Frängsmyr, J. L. Heilbron, and Robin E. Rider. Berkeley: University of California Press, 1990, 1–23.

————. "The Measure of Enlightenment." *The Quantifying Spirit in the 18th Century.* Ed. Tore Frängsmyr, J. L. Heilbron, and Robin E. Rider. Berkeley: University of California Press, 1990, 207–42.

Hellenbrand, Harold. *The Unfinished Revolution: Education and Politics in the Thought of Thomas Jefferson.* Newark: University of Delaware Press, 1990.

Henretta, James A., and Gregory H. Nobles. *Evolution and Revolution: American Society, 1600–1820.* Lexington, Mass.: D. C. Heath, 1987.

Henry, George. *Life of George Henry, together with a Brief History of the Colored People in America.* 1894. Reprint, Freeport, N.Y.: Books for Libraries Press, 1971.

High Court of Admiralty (HCA) and Vice-Admiralty Court (VAC) Records. Public Record Office. Kew, Richmond, Surrey, England.

Hill, William. "The First Stages of the Tariff Policy of the United States." *Publications of the American Economic Association* 8.6 (1893): 455–614.

Hindess, Barry. "Liberalism, Socialism and Democracy: Variations on a Governmental Theme." *Foucault and Political Reason: Liberalism, Neo-Liberalism, and Rationalities of Government.* Ed. Andrew Barry, Thomas Osborne, and Nikolas Rose. Chicago: University of Chicago Press, 1996, 65–80.

Hinds, Elizabeth Jane Wall. "Charles Brockden Brown and the Frontiers of Discourse." *Frontier Gothic: Terror and Wonder at the Frontier in American Literature.* Ed. David Mogen, Scott P. Sanders, and Joanne B. Karpinski. London: Associated University Presses, 1993, 109–25.

————. "Charles Brockden Brown's Revenge Tragedy: *Edgar Huntly* and the Uses of Property." *Early American Literature* 30.1 (1995): 51–70.

————. "The Spirit of Trade: Olaudah Equiano's Conversion, Legalism, and the Merchant's Life." *African American Review* 32.4 (1998): 635–47.

Hinks, Peter P. "'There Is a Great Work for You to Do': The Evangelical Strategy of David Walker's *Appeal* and His Early Years in the Carolina Low Country." *The Moment of Decision: Bibliographical Essays on American Character and Regional Identity.* Ed. Randall M. Miller and John R. McKivigan. Westport, Conn.: Greenwood Press, 1994, 134–54.

————. *To Awaken My Afflicted Brethren: David Walker and the Problem of Antebellum Slave Resistance.* University Park: Pennsylvania State University, 1997.

Hirschman, Albert O. *The Strategy of Economic Development.* New Haven: Yale University Press, 1958.

————. *The Passions and the Interests: Political Arguments for Capitalism before its Triumph.* Princeton: Princeton University Press, 1977.

Hobsbawm, Eric. *Nations and Nationalism Since 1780: Programme, Myth, Reality.* Cambridge: Cambridge University Press, 1990.

Hobsbawm, Eric, and Terence Ranger. *The Invention of Tradition.* Cambridge: Cambridge University Press, 1992.

Hodges, Graham Russell, ed. *Black Itinerants of the Gospel: The Narratives of John Jea and George White.* Madison: Madison House, 1993.

Hogan, Michael. *The Irish Soldiers of Mexico.* Guadalajara: Fondo Editorial Universitario, 1998.

Horsman, Reginald. *Race and Manifest Destiny: The Origins of American Racial Anglo-Saxonism.* Cambridge: Harvard University Press, 1981.

Horton, James Oliver. *Free People of Color: Inside the African American Community.* Washington, D.C.: Smithsonian Institution Press, 1993.

Horton, James, and Louis Horton. *Black Bostonians: Family Life and Community Struggle in the Antebellum North.* New York: Holmes and Meier, 1979.

Howe, Daniel Walker. *The Political Culture of the American Whigs.* Chicago: University of Chicago Press, 1979.

Howell, James. *Instructions for Forreine Travell.* 1642. Reprint. Ed. Edward Arber. Westminster: A. Constable, 1903.

Hsu, Hsuan L. "Democratic Expansionism in 'Memoirs of Carwin.'" *Early American Literature* 35.2 (2000): 137–56.

Hubbard, Dolan. "David Walker's *Appeal* and the American Puritan Jeremiadic Tradition." *Centennial Review* 30.3 (Summer 1986): 331–46.

Hutcheson, Francis. *An Inquiry into the Original of our Ideas of Beauty and Virtue.* London: J. Darby, 1726.

———. *Essay on the Nature and Conduct of the Passions and Affections.* 1728. Reprint, Gainesville, Fla.: Scholar's Facsimiles and Reprints, 1969.

Hutton, Frankie. *The Early Black Press in America, 1827 to 1860.* Westport, Conn.: Greenwood Press, 1993.

Ikenberry, John G. "Rethinking the Origins of American Hegemony." *Political Science Quarterly* 104.3 (1989): 375–400.

Ileto, Reynaldo. *Pasyon and Revolution: Popular Movements in the Philippines, 1840–1910.* Quezon City: Ateneo de Manila University Press, 1979.

Imbarrato, Susan Clair. *Declarations of Independency in Eighteenth-Century American Autobiography.* Knoxville: University of Tennessee Press, 1998.

Ingraham, Joseph Holt. *Montezuma, the Serf; or, The Revolt of the Mexitili. A Tale of the Last Days of the Aztec Dynasty.* Boston: H. L. Williams, 1845.

———. *The Silver Ship of Mexico: A Tale of the Spanish Main.* New York: H. L. Williams, 1846.

———. *The Texan Ranger; or, The Maid of Matamoras. A Tale of the Mexican War.* New York: Williams Brothers, 1847.

Isenberg, Nancy. *Sex and Citizenship in Antebellum America.* Chapel Hill: University of North Carolina Press, 1998.

Issac, Rhys. *The Transformation of Virginia, 1740–1790.* Chapel Hill: University of North Carolina Press, 1982.

Ito, Akiyo. "Olaudah Equiano and the New York Artisans: The First American Edition of the *Interesting Narrative of the Life of Olaudah Equiano, or Gustavus Vassa, the African.*" *Early American Literature* 32.1 (1997): 82–101.

Jane, Cecil, ed. *The Four Voyages of Columbus: A History in Eight Documents, Including Five by Christopher Columbus, in the Original Spanish, with English Translations*. New York: Dover, 1988.

JanMohamed, Abdul R. "Sexuality on/of the Racial Border: Foucault, Wright, and the Articulation of 'Racialized Sexuality.'" *Discourses of Sexuality: From Aristotle to AIDS*. Ed. Domna C. Stanton. Ann Arbor: University of Michigan Press, 1992, 94–116.

Jea, John. *The Life, History, and Unparalleled Sufferings of John Jea, the African Preacher*. Portsea: J. Jea [1815].

———. *Hymns*. Portsea: J. Williams, 1816.

Jefferson, Thomas. *Writings*. New York: Library of America, 1984.

Jennings, Francis. *The Ambiguous Iroquois Empire: The Covenant Chain Confederation of Indian Tribes with English Colonies from Its Beginnings to the Lancaster Treaty of 1744*. New York: Norton, 1984.

———. "'Pennsylvania Indians' and the Iroquois." *Beyond the Covenant Chain: The Iroquois and Their Neighbors in Indian North America, 1600–1800*. Ed. Daniel K. Richter and James H. Merrell. Syracuse: Syracuse University Press, 1987, 75–91.

Jennings, Francis, William N. Fenton, Mary A. Druke, and David R. Miller, eds. *The History and Culture of Iroquois Diplomacy: An Interdisciplinary Guide to the Treaties of the Six Nations and Their League*. Syracuse: Syracuse University Press, 1985.

Jessop, Bob. *The Capitalist State: Marxist Theories and Methods*. Oxford: Martin Robertson, 1982.

———. *State Theory: Putting Capitalist States in their Place*. University Park: Pennsylvania State University Press, 1990.

Johannisson, Karin. "Society in Numbers: The Debate over Quantification in 18th Century Political Economy." *The Quantifying Spirit in the 18th Century*. Ed. Tore Frängsmyr, J. L. Heilbron, and Robin E. Rider. Berkeley: University of California Press, 1990, 343–61.

Johanssen, Robert W. *To the Halls of the Montezumas: The Mexican War in the American Imagination*. New York: Oxford University Press, 1985.

Johnson, Walter. "Possible Pasts: Some Speculations on Time, Temporality, and the History of Atlantic Slavery." *Amerikastudien/American Studies* 45.4 (2000): 485–99.

Johnson, Whittington B. *The Promising Years, 1750–1830: The Emergence of Black Labor and Business*. New York: Garland Publishing, 1993.

Jonas, Peter M. "William Parrott, American Claims, and the Mexican War." *Journal of the Early Republic* 12.2 (Summer 1992): 213–40.

Jones, Daryl. *The Dime Novel Western*. Bowling Green: Bowling Green University Popular Press, 1978.

Jones, Richard. "Primitive Political Economy of England." *Literary Remains Consisting of Lectures and Tracts on Political Economy*. New York: Augustus M. Kelley, 1964.

Jordan, Winthrop D. *White Over Black: American Attitudes Toward the Negro, 1550–1812*. New York: Norton, 1977.

Joseph, Gilbert M. "From Caste War to Class War: The Historiography of Modern Yucatán (c. 1750–1940)." *Hispanic American Historical Review* 65.1 (1985): 111–34.

———. *Rediscovering the Past at Mexico's Periphery: Essays on the History of Modern Yucatán*. Birmingham: University of Alabama Press, 1986.

———. *Revolution from Without: Yucatán, Mexico, and the United States, 1880–1924*. Durham: Duke University Press, 1988.

———. "The United States, Feuding Elites, and Rural Revolt in Yucatán, 1836–1915." *Rural Revolt in Mexico: U.S. Intervention and the Domain of Subaltern Politics*. Ed. Daniel Nugent. Durham: Duke University Press, 1998, 173–206.

Joseph, Miranda. "The Performance of Production and Consumption." *Social Text* 54 (Spring 1998): 25–61.

———. *Against the Romance of Community.* Minneapolis: University of Minnesota Press, 2002.

Judges, A. V. "The Idea of a Mercantile State." *Revisions in Mercantilism.* Ed. D. C. Coleman. London: Methuen, 1969, 35–60.

Kafer, Peter. "Charles Brockden Brown and Revolutionary Philadelphia: An Imagination in Context." *Pennsylvania Magazine of History and Biography* 116.4 (October 1992): 467–98.

Kamrath, Mark L. "Charles Brockden Brown and the 'Art of the Historian': An Essay Concerning (Post)Modern Historical Understanding." *Journal of the Early Republic* 21 (Summer 2001): 231–60.

Kant, Immanuel. *Critique of Judgement.* 1790. Reprint. Trans. James Creed Meredith. Oxford: Clarendon Press, 1952.

———. *Kritik der Urteilskraft.* Hamburg: Felix Meiner Verlag, 1990.

Kaplan, Amy. *The Social Construction of American Realism.* Chicago: University of Chicago Press, 1988.

———. "Romancing the Empire: The Embodiment of American Masculinity in the Popular Historical Novels of the 1890s." *American Literary History* 2.4 (Winter 1990): 659–90.

———. "Manifest Domesticity." *American Literature* 70.3 (September 1998): 581–606.

Kaplan, Amy, and Donald E. Pease. *Cultures of United States Imperialism.* Durham: Duke University Press, 1993.

Kazanjian, David. "Notarizing Knowledge: Paranoia and Civility in Freud and Lacan." *Qui Parle* 7.1 (Fall/Winter 1993): 102–39.

———. "Racial Governmentality: Thomas Jefferson and the African Colonization Movement in the United States." *Alternation: Journal of the Centre for the Study of Southern African Literature and Languages* 5.1 (1998): 39–84.

———. "Race, Nation, Equality: Olaudah Equiano's *Interesting Narrative* and a Genealogy of U.S. Mercantilism." *Post-Nationalist American Studies.* Ed. John Carlos Rowe. Berkeley: University of California Press, 2000, 129–63.

———. "Charles Brockden Brown's Biloquial Nation: National Culture and White Settler Colonialism in *Memoirs of Carwin, The Biloquist.*" *American Literature* 73.3 (September 2001): 459–96.

———. "'Yankee Universality': Race, Nation, and Empire in H. C. Carey's *The Past, the Present, and the Future.*" *New Formations* 47 (2002): 87–110.

———. "Mercantile Exchanges, Mercantilist Enclosures: Racial Capitalism in the Black Mariner Narratives of Venture Smith and John Jea." *New Centennial Review* 3.1 (Spring 2003): 147–78.

———. "'To ship as cook': Notes on the Gendering of Black Atlantic Maritime Labor." Forthcoming in *Radical Philosophy Review.*

Keane, John. *Democracy and Civil Society: On the Predicaments of European Socialism, the Prospects for Democracy, and the Problem of Controlling Social and Political Power.* New York: Verso, 1988.

———. *Civil Society.* Stanford, Calif.: Stanford University Press, 1998.

Keenan, Thomas. "The Point Is to [Ex]Change It: Reading Capital, Rhetorically." *Fetishism as Cultural Discourse.* Ed. Emily Apter and William Pietz. Ithaca: Cornell University Press, 1993, 152–85.

Keller, Gary D., and Cordelia Candelaria, eds. *The Legacy of the Mexican and Spanish-American Wars: Legal, Literary, and Historical Perspectives.* Tempe: Bilingual Press, 2000.

Kennedy, Paul. *The Rise and Fall of the Great Powers.* New York: Random House, 1987.

Keohane, Robert. "The World Political Economy and the Crisis of Political Liberalism." *Order and Conflict in Contemporary Capitalism.* Ed. J. H. Goldthorpe. New York: Oxford University Press, 1984, 15–38.

Kerber, Linda K. *Toward an Intellectual History of Women.* Chapel Hill: University of North Carolina Press, 1997.

Kettner, James. *The Development of American Citizenship (1660–1870).* Chapel Hill: University of North Carolina Press, 1984.

King, Boston. "Memoirs of the Life of Boston King, a Black Preacher." *The Methodist Magazine* (March 1798): 105–10; (April 1798): 157–61; (May 1798): 209–13; (June 1798): 261–65.

Kinshasa, Kwando M. *Emigration vs. Assimilation: The Debate in the African American Press, 1827–1861.* Jefferson, N.C.: McFarland and Company, 1988.

Knight, Alan. "Racism, Revolution, and *Indigenismo*: Mexico, 1910–1940." *The Idea of Race in Latin America, 1870–1940.* Ed. Richard Graham. Austin: University of Texas Press, 1990, 71–113.

Kovel, Joel. *White Racism: A Psychohistory.* London: Free Association Books, 1988.

Kowalewski, Michael. *Reading the West: New Essays on the Literature of the American West.* Cambridge: Cambridge University Press, 1996.

Krüger, Lorenz, Lorraine Daston, and Michael Heidelberger, eds. *The Probabalistic Revolution.* Vol. 1: *Ideas in History.* Cambridge: MIT Press, 1987.

Krüger, Lorenz, Gerd Gigerenzer, and Mary S. Morgan, eds. *The Probabalistic Revolution.* Vol. 2: *Ideas in the Sciences.* Cambridge: MIT Press, 1987.

Krupat, Arnold. "Postcoloniality and Native American Literature." *Yale Journal of Criticism* 7.1 (1994): 163–80.

Kulikoff, Allan. *The Agrarian Origins of American Capitalism.* Charlottesville: University Press of Virginia, 1992.

Kutchen, Larry. "The 'Vulgar Thread of the Canvas': Revolution and the Picturesque in Ann Eliza Bleecker, Crèvecoeur, and Charles Brockden Brown." *Early American Literature* 36.3 (2001): 395–426.

Laclau, Ernesto. "Feudalism and Capitalism in Latin America." *New Left Review* 67 (May–June 1971): 19–38.

———. *Politics and Ideology in Marxist Theory: Capitalism, Fascism, Populism.* London: NLB, 1977.

———. *Emancipation(s).* London: Verso, 1996.

Laclau, Ernesto, and Chantal Mouffe. *Hegemony and Socialist Strategy: Towards a Radical Democratic Politics.* London: Verso, 1985.

Landsman, Gail, and Sara Ciborski. "Representation and Politics: Contesting Histories of the Iroquois." *Cultural Anthropology* 7.4 (1992): 425–47.

Laplanche, Jean, and J.-B. Pontalis. *The Language of Psychoanalysis.* New York: Norton, 1973.

Larrain, Jorge. *Theories of Development: Capitalism, Colonialism and Dependency.* Cambridge, U.K.: Polity Press, 1989.

Lazarus, Neil, Steven Evans, Anthony Arnove, and Anne Menke. "The Necessity of Universalism." *Differences: A Journal of Feminist Cultural Studies* 7.1 (1995): 75–145.

Lee, A. Robert, and W. M. Verhoeven. *Making America/Making American Literature: Franklin to Cooper.* Amsterdam: Editions Rodopi B. V., 1996.

Leibiger, Stuart. "Thomas Jefferson and the Missouri Crisis: An Alternative Interpretation." *Journal of the Early Republic* 17.1 (Spring 1997): 121–30.

Lemisch, Jesse. *Jack Tar vs. John Bull.* New York: Garland Press, 1997.

Lemon, James T. *The Best Poor Man's Country: A Geographical Study of Early Southeastern Pennsylvania.* Baltimore: The Johns Hopkins University Press, 1972.

Levernier, James A. "Phillis Wheatley and the New England Clergy." *Early American Literature* 26 (1991): 21–38.

Levine, Robert S. *Conspiracy and Romance: Studies in Brockden Brown, Cooper, Hawthorne, and Melville.* Cambridge: Cambridge University Press, 1989.

Lewis, R. W. B. *The American Adam.* Chicago: University of Chicago Press, 1955.

Liddell, Henry George, Robert Scott, Sir Henry Stuart Jones, and Roderick McKenzie. *A Greek-English Lexicon.* New York: Oxford University Press, 1996.

Lindström, Therese. "The History of the 'Article': A Study of a Part of Speech from Its First Appearance in Ancient Greek Philosophy to Its Use in Traditional English Grammar." Ph.D. diss., University of Uppsala (Sweden), 2000.

Linebaugh, Peter. "All the Atlantic Mountains Shook." *Labour/Le Travailleur* 10 (Autumn 1982): 87–121.

———. *The London Hanged: Crime and Civil Society in the Eighteenth Century.* Cambridge: Cambridge University Press, 1992.

Linebaugh, Peter, and Marcus Rediker. "The Many-Headed Hydra: Sailors, Slaves, and the Atlantic Working Class in the Eighteenth Century." *Journal of Historical Sociology* 3.3 (September 1990): 225–52.

———. *The Many-Headed Hydra: Sailors, Commoners, and the Hidden History of the Revolutionary Atlantic.* Boston: Beacon, 2000.

Lippard, George. *Legends of Mexico.* Philadelphia: T. B. Peterson and Brothers, 1847.

———. *'Bel of Prairie Eden: A Romance of Mexico.* Boston: Hotchkiss and Co., 1848.

Lipson, Charles. "The Transformation of Trade." *International Organization* 36.2 (1982): 417–55.

List, Friedrich. *The National System of Political Economy.* Trans. Sampson S. Lloyd. London: Longmans, 1885.

Literary Magazine and American Register. Philadelphia: J. Conrad and Co., 1804–8.

Litton, Alfred G. "The Failure of Rhetoric in Charles Brockden Brown's *Wieland.*" *Lamar Journal of the Humanities* 16.2 (Fall 1990): 23–40.

Lloyd, David. "Arnold, Ferguson, Schiller: Aesthetic Culture and the Politics of Aesthetics." *Cultural Critique* 2 (Winter 1985–86): 137–69.

———. "Kant's Examples." *Representations* 28 (Fall 1989): 34–54.

———. "Analogies of the Aesthetic: The Politics of Culture and the Limits of Materialist Aesthetics." *New Formations* 19 (Spring 1990): 109–26.

———. "Race under Representation." *Oxford Literary Review* 13.1–2 (1991): 62–93.

Lloyd, David, and Paul Thomas. *Culture and the State.* New York: Routledge, 1998.

Locke, John. *An Essay Concerning Human Understanding.* 1690. Reprint, Oxford: Clarendon Press, 1947.

Looby, Christopher. *Voicing America: Language, Literary Form, and the Origins of the United States.* Chicago: University of Chicago Press, 1996.

Loomba, Ania. *Gender, Race, Renaissance Drama.* Manchester: Manchester University Press, 1989.

Lowe, Lisa. *Immigrant Acts: On Asian American Cultural Politics.* Durham: Duke University Press, 1996.

Luciano, Dana. "'Perverse Nature': Edgar Huntly and the Novel's Reproductive Disorders." *American Literature* 70.1 (March 1998): 1–27.

Lukács, Georg. *History and Class Consciousness*. Trans. Rodney Livingstone. Cambridge: MIT Press, 1988.

Mackenthun, Gesa. "Captives and Sleepwalkers: The Ideological Revolutions of Post-Revolutionary Colonial Discourse." *European Review of Native American Studies* 11.1 (1997): 19–26.

Macpherson, C. B. *The Political Theory of Possessive Individualism: Hobbes to Locke*. Oxford: Oxford University Press, 1989.

Maddox, Lucy. *Removals: Nineteenth-Century American Literature and the Politics of Indian Affairs*. New York: Oxford University Press, 1991.

Magnusson, Lars, ed. *Mercantilist Economics*. Boston: Kluwer Academic Publishers, 1993.

———. *Mercantilism: The Shaping of an Economic Language*. London: Routledge, 1994.

Malone, Dumas. *Jefferson and His Time*. Vol. 1: *Jefferson the Virginian*. 1948. Reprint, Boston: Little, Brown, 1993.

Mamdani, Mahmood. *Beyond Rights Talk and Culture Talk: Comparative Essays on the Politics of Rights and Culture*. New York: St. Martin's Press, 2000.

Manning, William R., ed. *Diplomatic Correspondence of the United States Concerning Independence of the Latin-American Nations*. Vol. 3, parts 8–14. New York: Oxford University Press, 1925.

———. *Diplomatic Correspondence of the United States: Inter-American Affairs, 1831–1860*. Vols. 3, 8, 9, and 12. Washington: Carnegie Endowment for International Peace, 1937.

Manno, Francis Joseph. "Yucatán en la guerra entre México y Estados Unidos." *Revista de la Universidad de Yucatán* 5 (1963): 51–72.

Mannoni, O. *Prospero and Caliban: The Psychology of Colonization*. Trans. Pamela Powesland. New York: Praeger, 1964.

Mapp, Alf J. *Thomas Jefferson: A Strange Case of Mistaken Identity*. New York: Madison, 1987.

Marietta, Patrick. "Charles Brockden Brown's *Ormond*: A Psychological Portrait of Constantia Dudley." *Journal of Evolutionary Psychology* 5.1-2 (1984): 112–28.

———. "The Transformation Myth in *Edgar Huntly*." *Journal of Evolutionary Psychology* 10.3-4 (1989): 360–71.

Mariscal, George. "The Role of Spain in Contemporary Race Theory." *Arizona Journal of Hispanic Cultural Studies* 2 (1998): 7–22.

Marren, Susan M. "Between Slavery and Freedom: The Transgressive Self in Olaudah Equiano's Autobiography." *Publications of the Modern Language Association* 108.1 (January 1993): 94–105.

Marshall, T. H. *Class, Citizenship and Social Development*. New York: Anchor Books, 1965.

Martínez-Fernández, Luis. *Torn between Empires: Economy, Society, and Patterns of Political Thought in the Hispanic Caribbean, 1840–1878*. Athens: University of Georgia Press, 1994.

Marx, Karl. *Werke*, Band 26.2. Berlin: Dietz Verlan, 1967.

———. *On America and the Civil War*. Trans. Saul K. Padover. New York: McGraw-Hill, 1972.

———. *Grundrisse: Foundations of the Critique of Political Economy*. Trans. Martin Nicolaus. New York: Vintage Books, 1973.

———. *Political Writings Volume One: The Revolutions of 1848*. Ed. David Fernbach. New York: Vintage Books, 1974.

———. *Political Writings Volume Two: Surveys from Exile*. Ed. David Fernbach. New York: Vintage Books, 1974.

———. *Early Writings*. New York: Vintage Books, 1975.

———. *Capital: A Critique of Political Economy*. Vol. 1. Trans. Ben Fowkes. New York: Vintage Books, 1977.

———. *Collected Works*. Vol. 31: *Karl Marx, 1861–63*. New York: International Publishers, 1989.

Marx, Karl, and Frederick Engels. *Ireland and the Irish Question*. Moscow: Progress Publishers, 1971.

Matthiessen, F. O. *American Renaissance: Art and Expression in the Age of Emerson and Whitman*. London: Oxford University Press, 1941.

May, Henry F. *The Enlightenment in America*. Oxford: Oxford University Press, 1976.

May, Robert E. "Young American Males and Filibustering in the Age of Manifest Destiny: The United States Army as a Cultural Mirror." *Journal of American History* 78.3 (December 1991): 857–86.

Mayer, David N. *The Constitutional Thought of Thomas Jefferson*. Charlottesville: University Press of Virginia, 1994.

Mayr, Ernst. *The Growth of Biological Thought: Diversity, Evolution, and Inheritance*. Cambridge: Harvard University Press, 1982.

McCartney, John T. *Black Power Ideologies: An Essay in African-American Political Thought*. Philadelphia: Temple University Press, 1992.

McCloskey, Donald N. *The Rhetoric of Economics*. Madison: University of Wisconsin Press, 1985.

McCulloch, J. R. Introduction to *The Wealth of Nations*, by Adam Smith. Edinburgh: Adam Black and William Tait, 1928.

McPherson, James M., Laurence B. Holland, James M. Banner Jr., Nancy J. Weiss, and Michael D. Bell, eds. *Blacks in America: Bibliographical Essays*. Garden City, N.Y.: Doubleday, 1971.

Mehlinger, Louis. "The Attitude of the Free Negro Toward African Colonization." *Journal of Negro History* 1 (July 1916): 271–301. Reprinted in Okon Edet Uya, ed. *Black Brotherhood: Afro-Americans and Africa*. Lexington, Mass.: D. C. Heath, 1971.

Merrens, Harry Roy. *Colonial North Carolina in the Eighteenth Century: A Study in Historical Geography*. Chapel Hill: University of North Carolina Press, 1964.

Miller, Floyd. *The Search for a Black Nationality: Black Colonization and Emigration, 1787–1863*. Urbana: University of Illinois Press, 1975.

Miller, James. *The Passion of Michel Foucault*. New York: Simon and Schuster, 1993.

Miller, John Chester. *The Wolf by the Ears: Thomas Jefferson and Slavery*. New York: Free Press, 1977.

Miller, Perry. *Errand into the Wilderness*. Cambridge: Harvard University Press, 1956.

Mirabueau, Victor de Riquetti, Marquis de. *Philosophie rurale, ou économie generale et politique de l'agriculture, reduite a l'ordre immuable des loix physiques & morales, qui affurent la prospérité des empires*. Amsterdam: Les Libraires Associés, 1764.

Mitchell, Isabel S. *Roads and Road-Making in Colonial Connecticut*. New Haven: Yale University Press, 1933.

Mitchell, Robert D. *Commercialism and Frontier: Perspectives on the Early Shenandoah Valley*. Charlottesville: University Press of Virginia, 1977.

Mitchell, Trent A. "The Politics of Experiment in the Eighteenth Century: The Pursuit of Audience and the Manipulation of Consensus in the Debate over Lightning Rods." *Eighteenth-Century Studies* 31.3 (1998): 307–31.

Mjoset, Lars. "The Turn of Two Centuries: A Comparison of British and U.S. Hegemonies." *World Leadership and Hegemony*. Ed. D. P. Rapkin. Boulder, Colo.: Lynne Reiner, 1990, 21–47.

Monaghan, Jay. *The Great Rascal: The Life and Adventures of Ned Buntline*. Boston: Little, Brown, 1952.

Montejano, David. *Anglos and Mexicans in the Making of Texas, 1836–1986*. Austin: University of Texas Press, 1987.

Montgomery, David. *Citizen Worker*. Cambridge: Cambridge University Press, 1993.

Monthly Magazine, and American Review. New York: T. and J. Swords, 1799–1800.

Morgan, Edmund S., ed. *The Stamp Act Crisis: Sources and Documents*. Providence, 1952. Reproduced from typewritten copy.

———. *Inventing the People: The Rise of Sovereignty in England and America*. New York: Norton, 1989.

Morgan, Edmund S., and Helen M. Morgan. *The Stamp Act Crisis: Prologue to Revolution*. Chapel Hill: University of North Carolina Press, 1995.

Morgan, Lewis H. *League of the Ho-dé-no-sau-nee, or Iroquois*. Rochester, N.Y.: Sage and Brother, 1851.

Morley, David, and Kuan-Hsing Chen, eds. *Stuart Hall: Critical Dialogues in Cultural Studies*. London: Routledge, 1996.

Morris, Richard B. *Government and Labor in Early America*. New York: Octagon Books, 1965.

Morrison, Rodney J. *Henry C. Carey and American Economic Development*. Philadelphia: American Philosophical Society, 1986.

Moses, Wilson Jeremiah, ed. *The Golden Age of Black Nationalism, 1850–1925*. Hamden, Conn.: Archon Press, 1978.

———. *Black Messiahs and Uncle Toms: Social and Literary Manipulations of a Religious Myth*. University Park: Pennsylvania State University Press, 1982.

———. *Classical Black Nationalism: From the American Revolution to Marcus Garvey*. New York: New York University Press, 1996.

Mosse, George L. *Nationalism and Sexuality: Middle-Class Morality and Sexual Norms in Modern Europe*. Madison: University of Wisconsin Press, 1985.

Mossman, Philip L. *Money of the American Colonies and Confederation: A Numismatic, Economic, and Historical Correlation*. New York: American Numismatic Society, 1993.

Mott, Frank Luther. *A History of American Magazines, 1850–1865*. Cambridge: Harvard University Press, 1938.

Moyano Pahissa, Ángela. *La Resistencia de las California a la Invasión Norteamericana (1846–1848)*. México, D. F.: Consejo Nacional para la Cultura y las Artes, 1992.

Mtumbani, Victor C. D. "The Black Voice in Eighteenth-Century Britain: African Writers against Slavery and the Slave Trade." *Phylon* 45.2 (1984): 85–97.

Mulcaire, Terry. "Public Credit; or, The Feminization of Virtue in the Marketplace." *PMLA* 114 (October 1999): 1029–42.

Murphy, Geraldine. "Olaudah Equiano, Accidental Tourist." *Eighteenth-Century Studies* 27 (Summer 1994): 551–68.

Narin, Tom. *The Break-Up of Britain*. London: New Left Books, 1977.

———. *Faces of Nationalism: Janus Revisited*. London: Verso, 1997.

Nash, Gary B. *The Urban Crucible: Social Change, Political Consciousness, and the Origins of the American Revolution*. Cambridge: Harvard University Press, 1979.

———. *Race, Class, and Politics: Essays on American Colonial and Revolutionary Society*. Urbana: University of Illinois Press, 1986.

———. *Forging Freedom: The Formation of Philadelphia's Black Community, 1720–1840*. Cambridge: Harvard University Press, 1988.

———. *Race and Revolution*. Madison: Madison House, 1990.

Negri, Antonio. *Marx Beyond Marx: Lessons on the Grundrisse*. Brooklyn: Autonomedia, 1991.

Nelson, Dana D. *National Manhood: Capitalist Citizenship and the Imagined Fraternity of White Men.* Durham: Duke University Press, 1998.

———. *The Word in Black and White: Reading "Race" in American Literature, 1638–1867.* New York: Oxford University Press, 1992.

Nettels, Curtis P. "British Mercantilism and the Economic Development of the Thirteen Colonies." *Journal of Economic History* 12 (1952): 105–14.

Newfield, Christopher. "The Politics of Male Suffering: Masochism and Hegemony in the American Renaissance." *Differences* 1.3 (Fall 1989): 55–87.

———. *The Emerson Effect: Individualism and Submission in America.* Chicago: University of Chicago Press, 1996.

Nichols, Charles. *Many Thousand Gone: The Ex-Slaves' Account of their Bondage and Freedom.* Bloomington: Indiana University Press, 1969.

Nichols, Roger L. "The Indian in the Dime Novel." *Journal of American Culture* 5 (1982): 49–55.

Noel, Mary. *Villains Galore: The Heyday of the Popular Story Weekly.* New York: Macmillan, 1954.

Normano, J. F. *The Spirit of American Economics: A Study in the History of Economic Ideas in the United States Prior to the Great Depression.* New York: John Day Co., 1943.

North, Douglass C. *The Economic Growth of the United States, 1790–1860.* Englewood Cliffs, N.J.: Prentice-Hall, 1961.

North American Review and Miscellaneous Journal. Boston: O. Everett, 1815–21.

Nourie, Alan, and Barbara Nourie, eds. *American Mass-Market Magazines.* Westport, Conn.: Greenwood Press, 1990.

Ogude, S. E. "Facts into Fiction: Equiano's Narrative Revisited." *Okike: An African Journal of New Writing* 22 (September 1982): 57–66.

Olguín, G. V. "Angre Mexicana/Corazón Americano: Identity, Ambiguity, and Critique in Mexican American War Narratives." *American Literary History* 14.1 (Spring 2002): 83–114.

Omi, Michael, and Howard Winant. *Racial Formation in the United States: From the 1960s to the 1990s.* New York: Routledge, 1994.

Onuf, Peter S., ed. *Jeffersonian Legacies.* Charlottesville: University of Virginia Press, 1993.

———. "Thomas Jefferson, Missouri, and the 'Empire for Liberty.'" *Thomas Jefferson and the Changing West.* Ed. James P. Ronda. Albuquerque: University of New Mexico Press, 1997, 111–53.

———. "'To Declare Them a Free and Independent People': Race, Slavery, and National Identity in Jefferson's Thought." *Journal of the Early Republic* 18 (Spring 1998): 1–46.

Opper, Kent P. "The Mind of White Participants in the African Colonization Movement, 1816–1840." Ph.D. diss., University of North Carolina, 1972.

Orban, Katalin. "Dominant and Submerged Discourses in the Life of Olaudah Equiano (or Gustavus Vassa?)." *African American Review* 27.4 (1993): 655–64.

Osborne, Peter. *The Politics of Time: Modernity and the Avant-Garde.* London: Verso, 1995.

Padilla, Genaro. *My History, Not Yours: The Formation of Mexican American Autobiography.* Madison: University of Wisconsin Press, 1993.

Palgrave, Robert Harry Inglis. *Dictionary of Political Economy.* London: Macmillan, 1917.

Palumbo-Liu, David. "The Minority Self as Other: Problematics of Representation in Asian-American Literature." *Cultural Critique* 27 (Fall 1994): 75–102.

———. "Universalisms and Minority Culture." *Differences: A Journal of Feminist Cultural Studies* 7.1 (1995): 188–208.

Paravisini-Gebert, Lizabeth, and Ivette Romero-Cesareo, eds. *Women at Sea: Travel Writing and the Margins of Caribbean Discourse.* New York: Palgrave, 2001.

Pateman, Carole. *The Disorder of Women: Democracy, Feminism and Political Theory.* Stanford: Stanford University Press, 1989.

Pattee, Fred Lewis. Introduction to *Wieland, or The Transformation, together with Memoirs of Carwin, the Biloquist,* by Charles Brockden Brown. New York: Harcourt Brace Jovanovich, 1926, ix–xlvi.

Patterson, Mark R. *Authority, Autonomy, and Representation in American Literature, 1776–1865.* Princeton: Princeton University Press, 1988.

Peace, William H., and Jane H. Peace. *They Who Would Be Free: Blacks' Search for Freedom, 1830–1861.* New York: Atheneum, 1974.

———. "Walker's *Appeal* Comes to Charleston: A Note and Documents." *Journal of Negro History* 59.3 (July 1974): 287–92.

Pedersen, Svend E. Green. "The Scope and Structure of the Danish Negro Slave Trade." *Scandinavian Economic History Review* 19 (1971): 149–97.

Peskin, Lawrence. "From Protection to Encouragement: Manufacturing and Mercantilism in New York City's Political Discourse, 1783–1795." *Journal of the Early Republic* 18 (Winter 1998): 589–615.

Peterson, Carla. *Doers of the Word: African American Women Speakers and Writers in the North, 1830–1880.* New York: Oxford University Press, 1995.

Peterson, Merril D. *The Jefferson Image in the American Mind.* New York: Oxford University Press, 1960.

Pfister, Joel, and Nancy Schnog, eds. *Inventing the Psychological: Towards a Cultural History of Emotional Life in America.* New Haven: Yale University Press, 1997.

Piggott, Sir Francis. *Nationality, Including Naturalization and English Law on the High Seas and Beyond the Realm.* London: W. Clowes and Sons, 1906.

Pita, Beatrice, and Rosaura Sánchez. Introduction to *The Squatter and the Don.* Houston: Arte Público Press, 1992, 5–51.

Plato. *The Collected Dialogues of Plato, Including the Letters.* Trans. Lane Cooper et al. Princeton: Princeton University Press, 1978.

Polanyi, Karl. *The Great Transformation.* Boston: Beacon Press, 1957.

Poovey, Mary. *A History of the Modern Fact: Problems of Knowledge in the Sciences of Wealth and Society.* Chicago: University of Chicago Press, 1998.

Porter, Carolyn. *Seeing and Being: The Plight of the Participant Observer in Emerson, James, Adams, and Faulkner.* Middletown, Conn.: Wesleyan University Press, 1981.

———. "What We Know That We Don't Know: Remapping American Literary Studies." *American Literary History* 6.3 (Fall 1994): 467–526.

Porter, Dorothy, ed. *Early Negro Writing, 1760–1837.* Boston: Beacon Press, 1971.

Porter, Theodore M. *The Rise of Statistical Thinking, 1820–1900.* Princeton: Princeton University Press, 1986.

Postone, Moishe. "Anti-Semitism and National Socialism." *Germans and Jews Since the Holocaust: The Changing Situation in West Germany.* Ed. Anson Rabinbach and Jack Zipes. New York: Holmes and Meier, 1986, 302–14.

———. *Time, Labor, and Social Domination: A Reinterpretation of Marx's Critical Theory.* Cambridge: Cambridge University Press, 1993.

Potkay, Adam. "Olaudah Equiano and the Art of Spiritual Autobiography." *Eighteenth-Century Studies* 27 (Summer 1994): 677–92.

Potkay, Adam, Srinivas Aravamudan, and Roxann Wheeler. "Forum: Teaching Equiano's *Interesting Narrative*." *Eighteenth-Century Studies* 34.4 (2001): 601–24.

Pribram, Karl. *A History of Economic Reasoning*. Baltimore: The Johns Hopkins University Press, 1983.

Prince, Nancy. "A Narrative of the Life and Travels of Mrs. Nancy Prince." *Collected Black Women's Narratives*. Ed. Henry Louis Gates Jr. New York: Oxford University Press, 1988, 1–89.

Pringle, Rosemary, and Ann Game. *Gender at Work*. Boston: Allen and Unwin, 1983.

Prucha, Francis Paul. *American Indian Policy in the Formative Years: The Indian Trade and Intercourse Acts, 1780–1834*. Cambridge: Harvard University Press, 1962.

Putney, Martha S. *Black Sailors: Afro-American Merchant Seamen and Whalemen Prior to the Civil War*. New York: Greenwood Press, 1987.

Quintilian. *Institutiones Oratoriae*. 4 vols. Trans. H. E. Butler. Loeb Classical Library. Cambridge: Harvard University Press, 1979–86.

Rafael, Vicente L. *White Love and Other Events in Filipino History*. Durham, N.C.: Duke University Press, 2000.

Rawick, George P. *From Sundown to Sunup: The Making of the Black Community*. Westport, Conn.: Greenwood, 1973.

Rediker, Marcus. *Between the Devil and the Deep Blue Sea: Merchant Seamen, Pirates and the Anglo-American Maritime World, 1700–1750*. Cambridge: Cambridge University Press, 1987.

Reed, Nelson. *The Caste War of Yucatan*. Stanford, Calif.: Stanford University Press, 1964. Revised edition, 2001.

Reid-Pharr, Robert. *Conjugal Union: The Body, the House, and the Black American*. New York: Oxford University Press, 1999.

Reina, Leticia. *Las rebeliones campesinas en México*. Mexico City: Siglo XXI, 1980.

Remini, Robert Vincent. *The Legacy of Andrew Jackson: Essays on Democracy, Indian Removal, and Slavery*. Baton Rouge: Louisiana State University Press, 1988.

Remmers, Lawrence J. "Henequen, the Caste War, and the Economy of Yucatán, 1846–1883: The Roots of Dependence in a Mexican Region." Ph.D. diss., University of California, Los Angeles, 1981.

Report Adopted by the Legislature of Georgia on African Colonization. Washington, D.C.: Gales and Seaton, Feb. 8, 1828.

Richter, Daniel K. *The Ordeal of the Long-House: Peoples of the Iroquois League in the Era of European Colonization*. Chapel Hill: University of North Carolina Press, 1992.

Richter, Daniel K., and James H. Merrell. *Beyond the Covenant Chain: The Iroquois and Their Neighbors in Indian North America, 1600–1800*. Syracuse: Syracuse University Press, 1987.

Rider, Robin E. "Measure of Ideas, Ruler of Language: Mathematics and Language in the 18th Century." *The Quantifying Spirit in the 18th Century*. Ed. Tore Frängsmyr, J. L. Heilbron, and Robin E. Rider. Berkeley: University of California Press, 1990, 113–40.

Ringe, Donald A. *American Gothic: Imagination and Reason in Nineteenth-Century Fiction*. Lexington: University Press of Kentucky, 1982.

Roback, Aaron A. *History of American Psychology*. New York: Library Publishers, 1952.

Roberts, Edward G. "The Roads of Virginia, 1607–1840." Ph.D. diss., University of Virginia, 1950.

Roberts, J. M. *The Mythology of the Secret Societies*. New York: Charles Scribner's Sons, 1972.

Robinson, Cecil, ed. *The View from Chapultepec: Mexican Writers on the Mexican-American War.* Tucson: University of Arizona Press, 1989.

Robinson, Cedric J. *Black Marxism: The Making of the Black Radical Tradition.* London: Zed Books, 1983.

Robinson, William H. *Phillis Wheatley: A Bio-Bibliography.* Boston: G. K. Hall, 1981.

Rodgers, N. A. M. *The Wooden World: An Anatomy of the Georgian Navy.* Annapolis: Naval Institute Press, 1986.

Rodríguez Piña, Javier. "Guerra de castas y azúcar: el comercio de indígenas mayas con Cuba (1848–1861)." *Anales del Caribe: Centro de Estudios del Caribe. Casa de las Americas* 7–8 (1987–88): 28–93.

Roediger, David R. *The Wages of Whiteness: Race and the Making of the American Working Class.* New York: Verso, 1991.

Rogin, Michael. *Subversive Genealogy: The Politics and Art of Herman Melville.* New York: Alfred A. Knopf. 1983.

———. *Ronald Reagan, The Movie, and Other Episodes in Political Demonology.* Berkeley: University of California Press, 1987.

Romero, Lora. *Home Fronts: Domesticity and Its Critics in the Antebellum United States.* Durham: Duke University Press, 1997.

Rosdolsky, Roman. *The Making of Marx's Capital.* Trans. Pete Burgess. London: Pluto Press, 1977.

Rose, Gillian. *The Melancholy Science: An Introduction to the Thought of Theodor W. Adorno.* London: Macmillan, 1978.

Rose, Nikolas. "Governing 'Advanced' Liberal Democracies." *Foucault and Political Reason: Liberalism, Neo-Liberalism, and Rationalities of Government.* Ed. Andrew Barry, Thomas Osborne, and Nikolas Rose. Chicago: University of Chicago Press, 1996, 37–64.

Rose, Sonya. *Limited Livelihoods: Gender and Class in Nineteenth-Century England.* London: Routledge, 1992.

Rosenthal, Bernard. *Critical Essays on Charles Brockden Brown.* Boston: G. K. Hall, 1981.

Ross, Dorthy. *The Origins of American Social Science.* Cambridge: Cambridge University Press, 1991.

Rostow, W. W. *The Stages of Economic Growth: A Non-Communist Manifesto.* Cambridge: Cambridge University Press, 1960.

Rothbard, Muray N. *Economic Thought before Adam Smith: An Austrian Perspective on the History of Economic Thought.* Vol. 1. Hants, U.K.: Edward Elgar Publishing, 1995.

Round, Phillip H. *By Nature and by Custom Cursed: Transatlantic Civil Discourse and New England Cultural Production, 1620–1660.* Hanover: University Press of New England, 1999.

Rousseau, Jean-Jacques, and Johann Gottfried Herder. *On the Origin of Language.* Trans. John H. Moran. Chicago: University of Chicago Press, 1986.

Rowe, John Carlos. *Through the Custom-House: Nineteenth-Century American Fiction and Modern Theory.* Baltimore: The Johns Hopkins University Press, 1982.

———. *At Emerson's Tomb: The Politics of Classic American Literature.* New York: Columbia University Press, 1997.

———. *Literary Culture and U.S. Imperialism: From the Revolution to World War II.* Oxford: Oxford University Press, 2000.

———. *The New American Studies.* Minneapolis: University of Minnesota Press, 2002.

Ruggie, John G. "International Regimes, Transactions, and Change: Embedded Liberalism in the Postwar Economic Order." *International Organization* 36.2 (1982): 379–415.

Rush, Benjamin. *Sixteen Introductory Lectures.* Philadelphia: Bradford and Inskeep, 1811.

Ruttenburg, Nancy. *Democratic Personality: Popular Voice and the Trial of American Authorship.* Stanford: Stanford University Press, 1998.

Sabin, Joseph. *Bibliotheca Americana: A Dictionary of Books Relating to America, from Its Discovery to the Present Time.* 29 vols. Amsterdam: N. Israel, 1961.

Sabino, Robin, and Jennifer Hall. "The Path Not Taken: Cultural Identity in the Interesting Life of Olaudah Equiano." *MELUS* 24.1 (Spring 1999): 5–19.

Saillant, John. "Lemuel Haynes's Black Republicanism and the American Republican Tradition, 1775–1820." *Journal of the Early Republic* 14.3 (Fall 1994): 292–324.

———. "The American Enlightenment in Africa: Jefferson's Colonizationism and Black Virginians' Migration to Liberia, 1776–1840." *Eighteenth-Century Studies* 31.3 (Spring 1998): 261–82.

St. Clair, A. S. *Senora Ines; or, The American Volunteers. A Tale of the Mexican War.* Boston: F. Gleason, 1848.

Sakai, Naoki. "Modernity and Its Critique: The Problem of Universalism and Particularism." *South Atlantic Quarterly* 87 (Summer 1988): 475–504.

Saldaña-Portillo, María Josefina. "Who's the Indian in Aztlán? Rewriting *Mestizaje,* Indianism, and Chicanismo from the Lacandon." *Latin American Subaltern Studies Reader.* Ed. Ileana Rodríguez. Durham: Duke University Press, 2001, 402–23.

———. "Reading a Silence: The 'Indian' in the Era of Zapatismo." *Nepantla: Views from South* 3.2 (2002).

Saldívar, José David. *Border Matters: Remapping American Cultural Studies.* Berkeley: University of California Press, 1997.

Saldívar, Ramón. *Chicano Narrative: The Dialectics of Difference.* Madison: University of Wisconsin Press, 1990.

Salisbury, Neal. "The History of Native Americans." *The Cambridge Economic History of the United States.* Vol. 1, *The Colonial Era.* Ed. Stanley L. Engerman and Robert E. Gallman. New York: Cambridge University Press, 1996, 1–52.

Samuels, Shirley. "Infidelity and Contagion: The Rhetoric of Revolution." *Early American Literature* 22.2 (1987): 183–91.

———. "*Wieland*: Alien and Infidel." *Early American Literature* 25.1 (1990): 46–66.

———, ed. *The Culture of Sentiment: Race, Gender, and Sentimentality in Nineteenth-Century America.* New York: Oxford University Press, 1992.

Samuels, Warren, ed. *Economics as Discourse: An Analysis of the Language of Economics.* Boston: Kluwer Academic Publishers, 1990.

Samuels, Wilfred D. "Disguised Voice in *The Interesting Narrative of Olaudah Equiano, or Gustavus Vassa, The African.*" *Black American Literature Forum* 19.2 (Summer 1985): 64–69.

Samuelson, Paul A. *Economics.* New York: McGraw Hill, 1980.

Sánchez, George J. *Becoming Mexican American: Ethnicity, Culture and Identity in Chicano Los Angeles, 1900–1945.* New York: Oxford University Press, 1993.

Sánchez, Rosaura. *Telling Identities: The Californio Testimonios.* Minneapolis: University of Minnesota Press, 1995.

Sánchez-Eppler, Karen. *Touching Liberty: Abolition, Feminism, and the Politics of the Body.* Berkeley: University of California Press, 1993.

Sarmiento, Domingo Faustino. *Facundo: Civilizacion y Barbarie.* 1845. Edicion de Roberto Yahni, 3rd. ed. Reprint, Madrid: Catedra, 1997.

Sartre, Jean-Paul. *Anti-Semite and Jew: An Exploration of the Etiology of Hate.* New York: Schocken Books, 1976.

Saxton, Alexander. "Problems of Class and Race in the Origins of the Mass Circulation Press." *Amercan Quarterly* 36.2 (1984): 211–34.

———. *The Rise and Fall of the White Republic.* New York: Verso, 1990.

Sayre, Gordon M. "The Mound Builders and the Imagination of American Antiquity in Jefferson, Bartram, and Chateaubriand." *Early American Literature* 33.3 (1998): 225–49.

Scheiber, Andrew J. "'The Arm Lifted Against Me': Love, Terror, and the Construction of Gender in *Wieland.*" *Early American Literature* 26.2 (1991): 173–94.

Scheingold, Stuart A. *The Politics of Rights.* New Haven: Yale University Press, 1974.

Schick, Frank L. *The Paperbound Book in America.* New York: Bowker, 1958.

Schmoller, Gustav. *The Mercantile System and Its Historical Significance.* New York: Macmillan, 1896.

Schroeder, John H. *Mr. Polk's War: American Opposition and Dissent, 1846–1848.* Madison: University of Wisconsin Press, 1973.

Schweitzer, Mary McKinney. "Economic Regulation and the Colonial Economy: The Maryland Tobacco Inspection Act of 1747." *Journal of Economic History* 40 (1980): 551–69.

Scott, Joan W. *"Only Paradoxes to Offer": French Feminists and the Rights of "Man," 1789–1994.* Cambridge: Harvard University Press, 1995.

———. "Universalism and the History of Feminism." *Differences: A Journal of Feminist Cultural Studies* 7.1 (1995): 1–14.

Sedgwick, Eve Kosofsky. *Between Men: English Literature and Homosocial Desire.* New York: Columbia University Press, 1985.

Sekora, John. "Black Message/ White Envelope: Genre, Authenticity, and Authority in the Antebellum Slave Narrative." *Callaloo* 10 (1987): 482–515.

Sekora, John, and Darwin T. Turner, eds. *The Art of the Slave Narrative: Original Essays in Criticism and Theory.* Macomb: Western Illinois Press, 1982.

Sellers, Charles Grier. *The Market Revoluton: Jacksonian America, 1815–1846.* New York: Oxford University Press, 1991.

Shakespeare, William. *The Tempest.* New York: Washington Square Press, 1961.

Shapiro, Stephen. "Mass African Suicide and the Rise of Euro-American Sentimentalism: Equiano's and Stevenson's Tales of the Semi-Periphery." *Revolutions and Watersheds: Transatlantic Dialogues, 1775–1815.* Ed. W. M. Verhoeven and Beth Dolan Kautz. Amsterdam: Rodopi, 1999.

Sharpe, Jenny. "Is the United States Postcolonial? Transnationalism, Immigration, and Race." *Diaspora* 4.2 (1995): 181–99.

Sheridan, Richard. "The Domestic Economy." *Colonial British America: Essays in the New History of the Early Modern Era.* Ed. Jack P. Greene and J. R. Pole. Baltimore: The Johns Hopkins University Press, 1984, 43–85.

Sherwood, Henry Noble. "The Formation of the American Colonization Society." *Journal of Negro History* 2.2 (1915): 333–53.

———. "Early Negro Deportation Projects." *Mississippi Valley Historical Review* 2.4 (1916): 484–508.

———. "Paul Cuffe." *Journal of Negro History* 2.8 (1923): 153–229.

Shick, Tom W. *Behold the Promised Land: A History of Afro-American Settler Society in Nineteenth Century Liberia.* Baltimore: The Johns Hopkins University Press, 1980.

Shuffelton, Frank. "Power, Desire, and American Cultural Studies." *Early American Literature* 34.1 (1999): 94–102.

Sigler, Phil. "The Attitude of Free Blacks Toward Emigration to Liberia." Ph.D. diss., Boston University, 1969.

Silverman, Kenneth. "Four New Letters by Phillis Wheatley." *Early American Literature* 8.3 (Winter 1974): 257–71.

Simmons, Michael. "Nationalism and the Dime Novel." *Studies in the Humanities* 9.1 (1981): 39–44.

Slack, Jennifer Daryl. "The Theory and Method of Articulation in Cultural Studies." *Stuart Hall: Critical Dialogues in Cultural Studies.* Ed. David Morley and Kuan-Hsing Chen. London: Routledge, 1996, 112–27.

Slotkin, Richard. *Regeneration through Violence: The Mythology of the American Frontier, 1600–1860.* Middletown, Conn.: Wesleyan University Press, 1973.

———. *The Fatal Environment: The Myth of the Frontier in the Age of Industrialization, 1800–1890.* New York: Atheneum, 1985.

Smith, Abbot Emerson. *Colonists in Bondage: White Servitude and Convict Labor in America, 1607–1776.* 1947. Reprint, Gloucester, Mass.: Peter Smith, 1965.

Smith, Adam. *An Inquiry into the Nature and Causes of the Wealth of Nations.* 1776. Reprint, Chicago: University of Chicago Press, 1976.

———. *The Theory of Moral Sentiments.* 1759. Reprint, Indianapolis: Liberty Fund, 1982.

Smith, Allan Gardner. "The Analysis of Motives: Early American Psychology and Fiction." *Costerus: Essays in English and American Language and Literature* 27, new series (1980): i–195.

Smith, Anthony D. *The Ethnic Origins of Nations.* Oxford: Blackwell, 1986.

Smith, Gladdis. "Black Seamen and the Federal Courts, 1789–1860." *Ships, Seafaring, and Society: Essays in Maritime History.* Ed. Timothy J. Runyan. Detroit: Wayne State University Press, 1987, 321–38.

Smith, Henry Nash. *Virgin Land: The American West as Symbol and Myth.* New York: Vintage, 1950.

Smith, John David, ed. *Emigration and Migration Proposals.* New York: Garland, 1993.

Smith, Norman O. "Mexican Stereotypes on Fictional Battlefields: Or Novel Romances of the Mexican War." *Journal of Popular Culture* 13.3 (1980): 526–40.

Smith, Valerie. *Self-Discovery and Authority in Afro-American Narrative.* Cambridge: Harvard University Press, 1987.

Smith, Venture. *A Narrative of the Life and Adventures of Venture, a Native of Africa: But Resident above Sixty Years in the United States of America.* New-London [Conn.]: A Descendant of Venture, 1835.

Snelling, Thomas. *A View of the Copper Coin and Coinage of England . . .* London: G. T. Snelling, 1766.

Snow, Dean R. *The Iroquois.* Oxford: Blackwell, 1994.

Solow, Barbara, ed. *Slavery and the Rise of the Atlantic System.* Cambridge, Mass.: W. E. B. DuBois Institute for Afro-American Research, Harvard University; New York: Cambridge University Press, 1991.

Solow, Barbara, and Stanley Engerman, eds. *British Capitalism and Caribbean Slavery: The Legacy of Eric Williams.* New York: Cambridge University Press, 1987.

Soltow, Lee, and Edward Stevens. *The Rise of Literacy and the Common School in the United States: A Socioeconomic Analysis to 1870.* Chicago: University of Chicago Press, 1981.

Sotomayor, Arturo. *La Pérdida de Tejas: De Poinsett al TLC*. Xalapa: Universidad Veracruzana, 1994.

Speck, W. A. "The International and Imperial Context." *Colonial British America: Essays in the New History of the Early Modern Era*. Ed. Jack P. Greene and J. R. Pole. Baltimore: The Johns Hopkins University Press, 1984, 384–407.

Spiegel, Henry William. *The Rise of American Economic Thought*. Philadelphia: Chilton Company, 1960.

Spiller, Robert E., et al. *A Literary History of the United States*. 4th ed. New York: Macmillan, 1974.

Spillers, Hortense J. "Mama's Baby, Papa's Maybe: An American Grammar Book." *Diacritics* 17.1 (Summer 1987): 65–81.

Spivak, Gayatri Chakravorty. "Scattered Speculations on the Question of Value." *In Other Worlds: Essays in Cultural Politics*. New York: Routledge, 1985, 154–75.

———. "Speculations on Reading Marx: After Reading Derrida." *Post-Structuralism and the Question of History*. Ed. Derek Attridge, Geoff Bennington, and Robert Young. Cambridge: Cambridge University Press, 1987, 30–62.

———. "Can the Subaltern Speak?" *Marxism and the Interpretation of Culture*. Ed. Cary Nelson and Lawrence Grossberg. Urbana: University of Illinois Press, 1988, 271–313.

———. *The Post-Colonial Critic: Interviews, Strategies, Dialogues*. Ed. Sarah Harasym. New York: Routledge, 1990.

———. "Poststructuralism, Marginality, Post-coloniality and Value." *Literary Theory Today*. Ed. Peter Collier and Helga Geyer-Ryan. Ithaca: Cornell University Press, 1990, 219–44.

———. "Remembering the Limits: Difference, Identity and Practice." *Socialism and the Limits of Liberalism*. Ed. Peter Osborne. London: Verso, 1991, 227–39.

———. "Acting Bits/Identity Talk." *Critical Inquiry* 18.4 (Summer 1992): 770–803.

———. "Echo." *New Literary History* 24 (1993): 17–43.

———. "Limits and Openings of Marx in Derrida." *Outside in the Teaching Machine*. New York: Routledge, 1993, 97–119.

———. "Ghostwriting." *Diacritcs* 25.2 (Summer 1995): 65–84. ·

———. *A Critique of Postcolonial Reason: Toward a History of the Vanishing Present*. Cambridge: Harvard University Press, 1999.

Sprinker, Michael, ed. *Ghostly Demarcations: A Symposium on Jacques Derrida's Specters of Marx*. New York: Verso, 1999.

Stanton, Lucia C. "'Those Who Labor For My Happiness': Thomas Jefferson and His Slaves." *Jeffersonian Legacies*. Ed. Peter S. Onuf. Charlottesville: University of Virginia Press, 1993, 147–80.

Stanton, William. *The Leopard's Spots: Scientific Attitudes toward Race in America, 1815–1859*. Chicago: University of Chicago Press, 1960.

Staudenraus, Peter J. *The African Colonization Movement, 1816–1865*. New York: Octagon Books, 1980.

Stephens, John L. *Incidents of Travel in Yucatan*. Vols. 1 and 2. New York: Dover Publications, 1963.

Stern, Julia. *The Plight of Feeling: Sympathy and Dissent in the Early American Novel*. Chicago: University of Chicago Press, 1997.

Stewart, Maria W. *Maria W. Stewart, America's First Black Woman Political Writer*. Ed. Marilyn Richardson. Bloomington: Indiana University Press, 1987.

Stigler, Stephen M. *The History of Statistics: The Measurement of Uncertainty before 1900*. Cambridge: Harvard University Press, 1986.

Stirn, James. "Urgent Gradualism: The Case of the American Union for the Relief and Improvement of the Colored Race." *Civil War History* 25.4 (1979): 309–28.

Stoler, Ann Laura. *Race and the Education of Desire: Foucault's History of Sexuality and the Colonial Order of Things.* Durham: Duke University Press, 1995.

Streeby, Shelley. "Joaquín Murrieta and the American 1848." *Post-Nationalist American Studies.* Ed. John Carlos Rowe. Berkeley: University of California Press, 2000, 166–96.

———. "American Sensations: Empire, Amnesia, and the US-Mexican War." *American Literary History* (2001): 2–40.

Strictures on Dr. Hodgkin's Pamphlet on Negro Emancipation and American Colonization (from "The Imperial Magazine" for July, 1833). London: H. Fisher, R. Fisher, and P. Jackson, 1833.

Stuckey, Sterling. *The Ideological Origins of Black Nationalism.* Boston: Beacon Press, 1972.

Tabili, Laura. "'A Maritime Race': Masculinity and the Racial Division of Labor in British Merchant Ships, 1900–1939." *Iron Men, Wooden Women: Gender and Seafaring in the Atlantic World, 1700–1920.* Ed. Margaret S. Creighton and Lisa Norling. Baltimore: The Johns Hopkins University Press, 1996, 169–88.

Tate, Claudia. *Domestic Allegories of Political Desire: The Black Heroine's Text at the Turn of the Century.* New York: Oxford University Press, 1992.

Taussig, F. W. *The Tariff History of the United States.* New York: G. P. Putnam's Sons, 1931.

Teja, Jesús de la. "Discovering the Tejano Community in 'Early' Texas." *Journal of the Early Republic* 18.1 (Spring 1998): 73–98.

Teilhac, Ernest. *Pioneers of American Economic Thought in the Nineteenth Century.* Trans. E. A. J. Johnson. New York: Macmillan, 1936.

Thomas, Brook. *Cross-Examinations of Law and Literature: Cooper, Hawthorne, Stowe, and Melville.* Cambridge: Cambridge University Press, 1987.

Thomas, Lamont D. *Rise to Be a People: A Biography of Paul Cuffe.* Urbana: University of Illinois Press, 1986.

Thomas, P. D. G. *British Politics and the Stamp Act Crisis.* Oxford: Clarendon Press, 1975.

Thompson, Edward H. *The Chultunes of Labna, Yucatan: Report of Explorations by the Museum, 1888–89 and 1890–91.* Cambridge, Mass.: The Museum, 1897.

———. *Archaelogical Researches in Yucatan: Reports of Explorations for the Museum.* Cambridge, Mass.: The Museum, 1904.

———. "A Page of American History." *American Antiquarian Society Proceedings* (October 1905): 239–52.

———. *The Home of a Forgotten Race: Mysterious Chichen Itza, in Yucatan, Mexico.* Washington, D.C.: National Geographic Magazine, 1914.

———. *People of the Serpent.* New York: Capricorn Books, 1965.

Thompson, Edward Palmer. *The Poverty of Theory and Other Essays.* New York: Monthly Review Press, 1978.

Tinkler-Villani, Valeria, and Peter Davidson, eds. *Exhibited by Candlelight: Sources and Developments in the Gothic Tradition.* Amsterdam: Editions Rodopi B.V., 1995.

Tompkins, Jane. *Sensational Designs: The Cultural Work of American Fiction 1790–1860.* New York: Oxford University Press, 1985.

Tooker, Elisabeth, ed. *An Iroquois Source Book.* 3 vols. New York: Garland Publishing, 1984.

———. "The United States Constitution and the Iroquois League." *Ethnohistory* 34.4 (1988): 305–36.

———. *Lewis H. Morgan on Iroquois Material Culture.* Tucson: University of Arizona Press, 1994.

Towle, Dorothy S., ed. *Records of the Vice-Admiralty Court of Rhode Island, 1716–1752*. Washington, D.C.: American Historical Association, 1936.

Trevisa, John. *Bartholomeus de Proprietatibus Rerum*. 1398. Reprint, Westminster: Wynkyn de Worde, 1983.

Tutino, John. *From Insurrection to Revolution in Mexico: Social Bases of Agrarian Violence, 1750–1940*. Princeton: Princeton University Press, 1986.

Ubbelohde, Carl. *The Vice-Admiralty Courts and the American Revolution*. Chapel Hill: University of North Carolina Press, 1960.

U.S. National Archives and Records Administration, Naval Records Collection of the Office of Naval Records and Library, National Archives, Washington, D.C. *Correspondence of the United States Department of State, Miscellaneous Letters, July 1–Dec. 20, 1846*.

———. *Confidential Letters Sent*. Vol. 1. Record group 45.

———. *Letters from Officers Commanding Squadrons, 1841–86, Home Squadron , Voyages of Commodore Matthew C. Perry and Commodore David Connor*.

———. *The Letters of President Polk*.

Vatalaro, Paul. "*Edgar Huntly*: Charles Brockden Brown's Early American Fairy Tale." *Journal of Evolutionary Psychology* 15.3–4 (1994): 259–68.

Vaughan, Alden T. "The Origins Debate: Slavery and Racism in Seventeenth-Century Virginia." *Virginia Magazine of History and Biography* 97 (July 1989): 311–54.

———. *The Roots of American Racism: Essays on the Colonial Experience*. New York: Oxford University Press, 1995.

Viner, Jacob. "Early English Theories of Trade." *Studies in the Theory of International Trade*. London: Allen and Unwin, 1937, 1–118.

Virgin Islands of the United States: A General Report by the Governor. Washington, D.C.: GPO, 1928.

Voloshin, Beverly R. "*Edgar Huntly* and the Coherence of the Self." *Early American Literature* 23.3 (1988): 262–80.

Wald, Priscilla. *Constituting Americans: Cultural Anxiety and Narrative Form*. Durham: Duke University Press, 1995.

Walker, David. *David Walker's Appeal, In Four Articles, Together With A Preamble, To The Coloured Citizens Of The World, But In Particular, And Very Expressly, To Those Of The United States of America*. 1829. Reprint, New York: Hill and Wang, 1995.

Walker, Juliet E. K. "Racism, Slavery, and Free Enterprise: Black Entrepreneurship in the United States before the Civil War." *Business History Review* 60 (1986): 343–482.

Wall, Cheryl A., ed. *Changing Your Own Words: Essays on Criticism, Theory, and Writing by Black Women*. New Brunswick, N.J.: Rutgers University Press, 1989.

Wallace, Alfred R., ed. *Australasia*. London: Edward Stanford, 1879.

Wallace, Anthony F. C. *The Long Bitter Trail: Andrew Jackson and the Indians*. New York: Hill and Wang, 1993.

Wallerstein, Immanuel. *The Modern World-System I: Capitalist Agriculture and the Origins of the European World-Economy in the Sixteenth Century*. New York: Academic Press, 1974.

———. "The Rise and Future Demise of the World Capitalist System: Concepts for Comparative Analysis." *The Capitalist World-Economy*. Cambridge: Cambridge University Press, 1979, 1–36.

———. *The Modern World-System II: Mercantilism and the Consolidation of the European World-Economy, 1600–1750*. New York: Academic Press, 1980.

———. *The Modern World-System III: The Second Era of Great Expansion of the Capitalist World-Economy, 1730s–1840s*. New York: Academic Press, 1989.

————. "American Slavery and the Capitalist World-Economy." *The Capitalist World-Economy.* Cambridge: Cambridge University Press, 1993, 202–21.

Walton, Gary M., and James F. Shepherd. *The Economic Rise of Early America.* Cambridge: Cambridge University Press, 1979.

Walzer, John Flexer. "Transportation in the Philadelphia Trading Area, 1740–1755." Ph.D. diss., University of Wisconsin, 1968.

Warfel, Harry R. *Charles Brockden Brown: American Gothic Novelist.* Gainesville: University of Florida Press, 1949.

Warner, Michael. *The Letters of the Republic: Publication and the Public Sphere in Eighteenth-Century America.* Cambridge: Harvard University Press, 1990.

Warren, Kenneth. *Black and White Strangers.* Chicago: University of Chicago Press, 1993.

Webb, Stephen S. *The Governors-General: The English Army and the Definition of Empire, 1569–1681.* Chapel Hill: University of North Carolina Press, 1979.

Weber, Max. *General Economic History.* New York: Collier, 1961.

Webster, Noah. *Dissertations on the English Language.* 1789. Reprint, London: Routledge/Thoemmes, 1997.

————. *An American Dictionary of the English Language.* Vol. 1. New York: S. Converse, 1828.

————. *A Dictionary of the English Language: Abridged from the American Dictionary.* New York: N. and J. White, 1835.

————. *An American Dictionary of the English Language.* New York: White and Sheffield, 1839.

Wedderburn, Robert. *The Horrors of Slavery and Other Writtings.* Ed. Ian McCalman. Princeton: Markus Wiener Publishers, 1991.

Weeks, William Earl. "American Nationalism, American Imperialism: An Interpretation of United States Political Economy, 1789–1861." *Journal of the Early Republic* 14 (Winter 1994): 485–95.

Weinbaum, Alys Eve. "Marx, Irigaray, and the Politics of Reproduction." *Differences: A Journal of Feminist Cultural Studies* 6.1 (1994): 98–129.

Weinbaum, Alys Eve, and Brent Edwards. "On Critical Globality." *ARIEL: A Review of International English Literature* 31.1–2 (January–April 2000): 255–74.

Wheatley, Phillis. *The Collected Works of Phillis Wheatley.* Ed. John C. Shields. New York: Oxford University Press, 1988.

Wheeler, Roxann. *The Complexion of Race: Categories of Difference in Eighteenth-Century British Culture.* Philadephia: University of Pennsylvania Press, 2000.

Whewell, William. *History of the Inductive Sciences, from the Earliest to the Present Times.* Parts 1–3. 1837. Reprint, London: Frank Cass, 1967.

Wickstron, Werner. "The American Colonization Society and Liberia: An Historical Study in Religious Motivation and Achievment." Ph.D. diss., Hartford Seminary. 1949.

Wilentz, Charles M. Introduction to *David Walker's Appeal* by David Walker. New York: Hill and Wang, 1992, vii–xii.

Wiley, Bell I. *Slaves No More: Letters from Liberia 1833–1869.* Lexington: University Press of Kentucky, 1980.

Williams, Eric. *Capitalism and Slavery.* 1944. Reprint, Chapel Hill: University of North Carolina Press, 1994.

Williams, Mary W. "The Secessionist Diplomacy of Yucatán." *Hispanic American Historical Review* 9 (1929): 132–43.

Willock, John. *Voyages to various parts of the world, and remarks on different countries in Europe,*

Africa and America, with the customs and manners of the Inhabitants. By John Willock, Mariner. Penrith: Printed by Ann Bell, [1789].

————. *The Voyages and Adventures of John Willock, Mariner. Interspersed with remarks on different countries in Europe, Africa, and America; with the customs and manners of the inhabitants; and a number of original antecdotes.* Hogan and McElroy: Philadelphia, 1798.

Wills, Gary. *Inventing America: Jefferson's Declaration of Independence.* New York: Doubleday, 1978.

Winch, Donald. *Classical Political Economy and the Colonies.* Cambridge: Harvard University Press, 1965.

Witmore, Michael. "Culture of Accidents: Unexpected Knowledges in Early Modern England." Ph.D. diss., University of California, Berkeley, 1997.

Wolfson, Michelle. "The Narrative Terrains of Indian Removal: The Impact of Jacksonian American Class Relations on the Representation and Treatment of Native Americans." Ph.D. diss. Manuscript, University of California, Berkeley, 1997.

Wood, Gordon S. *The Creation of the American Republic, 1776–1787.* New York: Norton, 1969.

Woodward, Mareen L. "Female Captivity and the Development of Race in Three Early American Texts." *Papers on Language and Literature* 32.2 (Spring 1996): 115–46.

Yáñez, Aaron P. Mahr. *Proceedings of the First Annual Palo Alto Conference.* Washington, D.C.: U.S. Department of the Interior, 1994.

Yuval-Davis, Nira, and Floya Anthias, eds. *Woman, Nation, State.* Hampshire: Macmillan, 1989.

Zafar, Rafia. *We Wear the Mask: African Americans Write American Literature, 1760–1870.* New York: Columbia University Press, 1997.

Zboray, Ronald. "Antebellum Reading and the Ironies of Technological Innovation." *Reading in America: Literature and Social History.* Ed. Cathy N. Davidson. Baltimore: The Johns Hopkins University Press, 1989, 182–92.

————. *A Fictive People: Antebellum Economic Development and the American Reading Public.* New York: Oxford Unversity Press, 1993.

Index

Abolitionism, 137, 215, 222, 235n56; colonization and, 91, 94, 95, 96, 126, 240n18; racial-national separation and, 98; tariffs and, 257n5

Aborigines, 11, 120, 121, 122, 144, 173, 174

ACS. *See* American Colonization Society

Aesthetics, 85, 152, 195, 249n32; articulation of, 32, 172; assimilation, 145, 147; Kantian, 153; politics and, 140, 172; rationalist-sensationalist psychology and, 150, 151

Afric-American Female Intelligence Society, 134, 137

African Intelligencer, The, 246n85

African Masonic Hall, 134, 135, 138

African Repository and Colonial Journal, The, 246n85

Agriculture: diversification of, 41

Aguirre, Robert, 256nn73, 79

Alcuin: A Dialogue, 171, 252n67

Alexandria, 68, 69, 82

Allen, Richard: colonization and, 91, 130

Allerton, Avaline, 196, 197

Allerton, George, 196

Almagro, Doctor, 196

Almonte, Don Vincensio de, 196

Althusser, Louis, 25; Hegelianism and, 16; overdetermined substantiality and, 20; structuralism and, 14–15, 17

American Antiquarium Society (journal): Thompson in, 209

American Colonization Society (ACS), 126, 240n18, 241n27; colonization and, 92, 94; critique of, 138; history of, 96, 98; members of, 97

American Dictionary (Webster), 8; on articulation, 25

American Revolution, 67; emancipation and, 123; Iroquois and, 145; universal equality and, 91

Ames, Fisher, 57, 58; citizenship and, 36; on duties, 76; mercantilism and, 37; tariff bill and, 35

Ampudia, General, 201, 202

Anamaboe, 60, 89, 93, 124

Annabel, 198, 199, 255n63; assimilation of, 200; Gonzardo and, 255n64

Annals of Congress (Madison), 35, 40

Annexation: Creoles and, 193, 194; Mexico and, 184, 185, 187, 188, 192; rejection of, 194; Yucatán and, 175, 187, 212

Anticolonization, 96, 124–38

Antipode, 213, 215, 218, 255n57, 256–57n2; abstract meaning of, 214

Antislavery forces, 37; colonization and, 96, 241n21

Antislavery literature, restrictions on, 26

Apostles' Creed, 8

Appeal (Walker), v, 9, 95, 127, 128, 132, 136, 138; articles of, 1, 10; circulation of, 25–26, 229n68; colonization and, 29; publication of, 1–2, 96

Apposition, 32, 136–38

Archeology, 5, 12, 256n73

Ariamento, 199, 200

Ariel: as allegory, 163; Caliban and, 162, 163, 166; Mohock and, 164, 165; Prospero and, 251n60

Arrighi, Giovanni, 41, 213

Arthur Mervyn (Brown), reading, 146–47

Articles, 9; etymological progression of, 7–8; meanings of, 8

Articles of Confederation, 39

Articulation, 7–17, 26, 56, 74, 226n14; definitions of, 9, 25; discursive significance of, 17; figure of, 12, 13; forced, 22; genealogy of, 17; historical, 84–85; interpretation of, 227n26; linkage/separation and, 27; as Marxian theoretical category, 14; normative meaning of, 16; race and, 227n26; structuralist understanding of, 15

Articulus, 7, 8, 136

Artificial manufacturing, 85–86

Assimilation, 5, 163, 168, 174, 178, 200, 208, 210; aesthetics of, 145, 147; blackness and, 144; civilization and, 197; cultural,

Mercantilism, 36, 49, 53–54, 70, 72–73, 222; antistatist, 215; artificial manufacturing of, 85–86; black mariners and, 76, 84, 85; capitalism and, 30, 40–41, 235n55; colonization and, 40; context of, 8; Declaration of Independence and, 40; discursive practices of, 59; economic nationalism and, 40; encounters with, 48; equality and, 52, 57, 83; free trade and, 213, 214, 215, 216, 218; gender and, 77; imperialism and, 40; mechanics of, 50; protectionism and, 43, 232n14; race and, 39–43, 77, 84, 143; repudiation of, 64; slavery and, 37, 39, 50, 55, 235n55; social relations and, 87–88; Spanish, 66; state-sponsored, 214; territorialism and, 41. *See also* Capitalism

Merchant marine, 56, 194, 238n86; black men in, 30; condemnation of, 59; freedom in, 91. *See also* Black mariners

Merchants, 77; gendered critique of, 238n92

Mérida, 177, 192, 194

Mestizaje, 33, 178, 180, 253n15

Methodist Magazine, The: King narrative in, 73

Mexican Americans: assimilation of, 33–34, 177; discrimination against, 12, 206, 207; subjectivity of, 209

Mexican Chamber of Deputies: Guadalupe Hidalgo and, 174

Mexican Revolution, 175, 178, 212

Mexicans, 175, 192; appropriations from, 185–86; assimilation of, 201, 206; character of, 207, 208; foreign investors and, 211; indianization of, 185, 186, 201; removal of, 187; subjectivity of, 209; U.S. citizens and, 186

Mexican Senate: Guadalupe Hidalgo and, 174

Mexican Spy: or, The Bride of Buena Vista, The (Halyard), 198, 201, 205; civilization and, 200; identities/interests in, 199

Middle Passage, 49, 60, 61, 62, 126

Mill, John Stuart: Carey and, 215

Miller, James, 244n64

Mirabeau, Marquis de: *système mercantile* and, 231n14

Miscegenation, 141, 199–200, 203, 204; as-

similation through, 142; Mexican women and, 206

Missionaries: colonization and, 122, 126

Missouri Crisis, 106–7, 108–9, 243n54

Mitchell, A. Trent, 29

Mixed bloods, 181, 191

Modernity, 32, 50, 140, 147, 164, 166, 168; Brownian, 165, 173; criticism of, 141; enlightened, 148; tradition versus, 248n28; white settler, 17

Moglen, Seth, 230n75, 239n12

Mohawks, 140, 156; assimilation of, 157; literature on, 250nn44, 47; representation of, 157

Mohocks, 156–57

Mohock savage, 32, 140, 149, 151; Ariel and, 165; assimilation of, 165, 166; Caliban and, 163–64; Carwin and, 162; foundational figure of, 147; reading of, 171–72; shrill tones of, 139, 141, 143, 150, 157, 161, 162, 163, 164, 170, 171, 174

Monroe, James, 101, 122, 242n34; Jefferson and, 117, 118, 119

Monroe Doctrine, 187, 190, 239n7

Monuments, cultural, 10–11

Moors, 116, 121

Moral questions, 109–10

Morellet, Abbé, 104

Morgan, Lewis H., 156

Moses, Ruth, 239n4

Moten, Fred, 7, 93, 136, 137, 138

Mulcaire, Terry, 77

Mumford, Thomas, 60

Napoleon: Rochambeau and, 243n48

Narrative of the Life and Adventures of Venture, a Native of Africa, A (Smith), 28, 60, 69

Narrative of the Uncommon Sufferings and Surprizing Deliverance of Britton Hammon, A Negro Man, Servant to General Winslow, of Marshfield, in New-England, A (Hammon), 45

Nash, Gary, 74

Nation: articulation of, 27, 32, 59, 71, 88, 116, 138; concept of, 7, 14, 15; hierarchies of, 2, 92; race and, 48, 134, 225n6

Perry, Matthew C., 173, 179, 180
Phantasmagoria, 20, 228nn52, 53
Philanthropists: colonization and, 126
Philosophe Rurale (Mirabeau), 231n14
Picaresque, 167, 168
Pinkus, Edward, 210, 211, 212
Plantations: Marx on, 21
Plymouth, 100
Polanyi, Karl: panopticon and, 245n64
Poles: as feeble people, 137
Politics, 113, 114, 168, 216; action and, 172;
  aesthetics and, 140, 172; articulation of,
  172; cultural, 48, 227n32, 244n57
Polk, James K., 192; annexation and, 184, 185;
  Caste War and, 33, 193, 195; citizenship
  and, 187; Creoles and, 189, 191; Home
  Squadron and, 194; intervention and, 190;
  on Mexican Government, 184–85; Mon-
  roe Doctrine and, 187; racial alliance and,
  189; on savages, 185, 186; Sierra and, 184,
  190; State of the Union Address by, 184,
  185, 254n28; Yucatán and, 174, 178–79,
  186–87, 188, 212
Poot, Leandro, 210, 211, 212
Population, 111, 244n62; calculable, 245n81;
  colonization and, 121; problem of, 119
Porter, Theodore M., 110
Positivism, 30
Power, 7, 115; increase in, 220; panoptic
  modality of, 245n64
Power of Sympathy, The (Brown), 140, 246n6
Prejudices, 53, 54
Primitive accumulation, 86, 217
Prince, Nancy: narrative of, 231n11
Principles of Natural Philosophy (Newton), 159
PRO. *See* Public Record Office
Procolonizationists, 131
Production, 229n62; capitalist mode of, 23;
  economic, 31; slavery and, 21; trade
  and, 24
Projection: psychological theories of, 15
Property rights, 207, 208
Proslavery groups: colonization and, 94, 95, 96
Prospero, 162, 163, 164
Protectionism, 39, 41, 43, 122; blacks and,
  43; concentration and, 222–23; free trade

and, 257n5; mercantilism and, 232n14;
  Stamp Act and, 57
Proudhon, 24
Psychic Life of Power, The (Butler): quote
  from, 6
Psychologie de la Colonisation (Mannoni), 163
Psychology, 150, 151, 249n33
Public Record Office (PRO), 231n10

Quamine, John, 89, 124, 125
Quantifying spirit, 110, 111, 133
Quaque, Philip, 125
Querétaro, 174
"Query XI—Aborigines" (Jefferson), 10–11

Race, 14, 15, 88; articulation of, 27, 32, 59,
  71, 116, 136, 138; binary models of, 28;
  hierarchies of, 2, 92; institutionalization
  of, 42; labor and, 45; maritime labor and,
  42–43; nation and, 48, 134, 225n6; psy-
  chologizing, 44; slavery and, 21, 225n4
"Race, Articulation, and Societies in Structured Dominance" (Hall), 14
Racial codification, 7, 10, 24, 30, 38, 55–60,
  88, 92, 99, 101, 116, 123, 124, 131, 133,
  176, 177, 206, 209, 215, 222, 223; equality
  and, 5, 39
Racial conflict: response to, 121
Racial difference, 100, 180, 198; national
  difference and, 51
Racial discourse: scientific turn of, 242n32
Racial formations, 3, 4, 34, 42, 48, 142, 157,
  178, 182, 187, 189; black/white, 176;
  Chicano, 176; defining, 5, 28–29
Racial hierarchies, 51, 93
Racial identities, 4, 30, 39, 88, 120, 179, 223;
  ambiguous, 141; blood and, 130; discursive practices of, 68
Racialization, 16, 22
Racial nation, 98, 134; mercantilism and,
  39–43
Racism, 2, 55, 62, 63, 78, 80, 88; drive
  against, 81, 83; egalitarianism and, 44;
  extralegal, 38; general history and, 15; individual psychology and, 15; liberal, 121;
  nationalism and, 5, 52, 53, 56, 84, 85,

121; economics of, 42, 47; emancipation and, 130; end of, 52, 111; England and, 221–22; Enlightenment and, 106, 115; freedom and, 29, 74; mercantilism and, 37, 39, 50, 55; moral problem of, 109–10; race and, 21, 37, 225n4; sexual, 167, 168; wage labor and, 21, 23, 24

Slaves, 223; deporting, 102; narratives of, 45; smuggling, 52; strangers and, 51

Smith, Adam, 218, 231n14, 249n32; on gendered terms, 76–77; mercantilism and, 232n14, 238nn92, 95; on nonnational merchants, 77

Smith, Allan Gardner, 150, 151

Smith, Col., 62, 63

Smith, James L., 231n11

Smith, Meg, 62

Smith, Venture, 28, 30, 78, 83; capital and, 62; citizenship and, 65; equality and, 65; freedom for, 61, 62; narrative of, 60–65, 69; punishment of, 64–65; resistance by, 61; vagabondage and, 88

Smith, William Loughton, 241n21

Social conflict: in U.S./Mexico, 176

Social formations, 14, 24, 25, 40; *differentiae specificae* of, 16; elements of, 15

Sociality, 18, 153

Social relations, 18, 19, 161, 228n40; black men/women and, 75; capitalism and, 20, 22; mercantilism and, 87–88; premodern, 24; value for, 17

Sons of Africa, v, 2, 10, 95

Spain: conflicts with, 111

Spaniards, 175, 189; Creoles and, 192; deportation by, 121

Sparks, Jared, 119, 120, 121, 245n81

Speech, 27; black, 10, 17; disembodied, 17; embodied, 10, 17; inhuman, 17

Spirit of the Sea, The (ship), 201

"Spirit of Trade" (Hinds), 235n56

Spivak, Gayatri Chakravorty, 185; on Kant, 170, 171; on reading for echoes, 252n62; on *sati*, 254n33; on value theory, 227–28n39

Stages of Economic Growth: A Non-Communist Manifesto (Rostow), 216

Stamp Act, 56–57, 84, 236nn63, 66

Stamp Act Congress (1765), 56

Starkweather, Jedediah, 196, 197–98, 201, 209

State of the Union Address (Polk), 184, 185, 186–87, 254n28

Stephens, Alexander H., 188, 189

Stephens, John L., 256n73

Stewart, Maria W., 31, 129, 141; on ACS, 138; anticolonial discourse of, 137; colonization and, 91, 93, 126; on equality, 135; Farewell Address of, 132; race/equality and, 136; racial characteristics and, 133; reinterpretation of, 127; scientific mantle and, 134; on spiritual education, 127; subject formation and, 133, 135

Stoic grammarians: articulation and, 7

Stoler, Ann Laura, 113, 244n63

Strangers, 60–69; codified population of, 66; slaves and, 51

Streeby, Shelley, 196, 252n6

Strother's Point, 82, 79

Structuralism, 14–15, 16, 17

Subjectivity, 6–7, 50, 115, 129, 133; black, 70; circumscribed humanity and, 6; economic, 77, 82; national, 66; producing, 88, 154; universal/abstract, 154, 157

Subjugation, 6, 192, 238n111

Sugar industry, 178, 194

Sumner, Charles, 79

Susan Ellen (ship), 82, 83

Sycorax, 162

Système mercantile, 231n14

Tabili, Laura, 74, 75, 238n86

Tampico, 177, 196, 199

Tariffs, 39, 40, 42, 57, 233n17, 257n4; abolitionists and, 257n5; debate on, 36–37, 50, 58; first, 35–36

Taylor, Zachary, 185

Tempest, The (Shakespeare), 162–63, 163, 164, 165

Terceiro, Don Jose, 205–6, 255n63; darkness of, 204, 206

Territorialism, 41, 130

Theoretical texts, 14, 29

Theories of Surplus Value (Marx), 21

David Kazanjian is associate professor of English at Queens College, City University of New York. He is coeditor (with David L. Eng) of *Loss: The Politics of Mourning.*